DEMANDS
& DECISIONS

BUSINESS INFORMATION TECHNOLOGY SERIES

DEMANDS & DECISIONS

BRIEFINGS ON ISSUES IN INFORMATION TECHNOLOGY STRATEGY

BART O'BRIEN

PRENTICE HALL

NEW YORK LONDON TORONTO SYDNEY TOKYO SINGAPORE

First published 1992 by
Prentice Hall International (UK) Ltd
Campus 400, Hemel Hempstead
Hertfordshire HP2 7EZ
A division of
Simon & Schuster International Group

Printed and bound in Great Britain by
Dotesios Ltd, Trowbridge, Wiltshire.

Library of Congress Cataloguing-in-Publication Data

O'Brien, Bart.
  Demands and decisions: Briefings on issues in information
technology strategy/Bart O'Brien.
    p.   cm.-(Business information technology)
  Includes bibliographical references and index.
  ISBN O-13-502691-1
  1. System design.   2. Information technology.   I. Title.
II. Series.
QA76.9.S88O27 1992
658.4 038-dc20
                                              91-42723
                                                  CIP

British Library Cataloguing in Publication Data

O'Brien, Bart.
  Demands and decisions: Briefings on issues in
  information technology strategy.
  I. Title
  003

  ISBN 0-13-502691-1

1 2 3 4 5 96 95 94 93 92

ABOUT THE SERIES

The existing literature about information technology (IT) places heavy emphasis on the *how?* and less on the *why?* and the *what?* Meanwhile the rapid and apparently never-ending improvements in the cost/performance of IT is steadily creating new opportunities for its use. Senior managers already know that IT may be the key to their future ability to compete or to operate effectively, while all departmental managers need to appreciate how IT may affect the way they run their part of the business operation.

The **Prentice Hall Business Information Technology Series** aims to fulfil two related tasks:

* to help specialists and non-specialists to understand *what* they should be doing with IT and *why* various problems arise
* to help specialists to adjust to the changes made necessary by the advances in information technology and by the closer involvement of non-specialists in the process of technology management.

Explaining in realistic and practical terms what IT can (and cannot) contribute in a business context, what problems it is likely to raise and how it should be planned for and managed, the **Business Information Technology Series** embraces the three resources on which systems based on IT draw:

* the **information** that is handled – what can IT do for a particular business in its particular circumstances today
* the **technology** used – controlling and maximising the potential of this complex and dynamic technology
* the **people** who build, operate and manage systems – what can be realistically achieved through the available human resources.

Different books concentrate on different aspects of the overall task, but all of them approach it from a similarly broad perspective, making the series both accessible and of wide-reaching significance.

Structure

IT Strategy Decisions:
Typical Cases and Unifying Model

Reference Cases

Reference Model

Exploring Problems and Approaches
with the help of Cases and Model

I Problems of Supply and Demand

II Option-based Approaches

III Problems of Commitment and Flexibility

IV Level-based Approaches

V Special Approaches

Contents

    1. Supply and Demand **29**
    If technology is supply and the features of working computer
    systems are demand, then decisions about IT strategy are con-
    cerned with resolving the interaction between supply and demand.
    Can these plausible concepts be given a sharper edge?

    2. The Trend to Demand-driven Planning **38**
    Most organisations used to allow IT supply factors to drive their
    decision-making. Lately the trend has been towards demand-
    driving. What are the pros and cons?

    3. Supply–Demand Interactions **47**
    Why not set up a genuine interaction between supply and demand
    factors? What does this entail? What advantages and complica-
    tions does it lead to?

    4. Problems with Demand-then-supply **55**
    People define their needs for a new system, and change their minds
    once it is built. Or their definition is too strongly influenced by
    their previous experience. Or the choice of a certain technology
    solution changes the definition of the problem. How does such
    awkward feedback affect decision-making?

PART III: PROBLEMS OF COMMITMENT AND FLEXIBILITY

The economics of IT investment encourage you to plan far into the future, but the advantages of flexibility encourage you to commit yourself as little as possible. So how do you strike a balance?

If you are committed to certain IT plans, that must surely mean that you will suffer penalties, if you ever alter the plans. How should this logic affect IT plans and decisions?

You often have to decide about database and telecommunications infrastructure before considering individual system developments in detail. But where should you draw the line between infrastructure and project decision-making?

A database of information is often shared by a number of systems. It seems plausible to distinguish between common, infrastructure-like information and information that is application-specific. What difficulties does this idea lead to?

Why not have a master framework to coordinate an organisation's developments of systems and databases over the years ahead? This sounds sensible, but doesn't it entail making bold forecasts and accepting long-term commitments?

Modern database technology can store information so flexibly that it can be used in many ways not originally envisaged. Or can it? How does this topic affect IT decision-making?

PART IV: LEVEL-BASED APPROACHES

Any technique for modelling a business is bound to stress some features, while leaving out or misrepresenting others. What are the possibilities and why do they matter?

Acknowledgements

Grateful acknowledgement is made to the following publishers for permission to quote excerpts from the following material: Frederick P. Brooks Jr, *The Mythical Man-Month*, © 1975 by Addison-Wesley Publishing Co., Inc; reprinted by permission of Addison-Wesley Publishing Co., Inc. Reading, MA; Ted Nelson, *Computer Lib / Dream Machines*, Tempus Books of Microsoft Press.

Introduction

Should you define the non-technical requirements of your information systems first, and then go on to determine the technology to be used? This turns out to be a harder question than at first appears. The more clearly you recognise the *obstacles* in the way of a straightforward and confident answer, the better equipped you are to make rational decisions about the use of information technology (IT) in an organisation.

Plainly the relevance of the opening question is not restricted to any particular industry or business situation or type of computer application or technology. Here are some more questions of the same sort:

How far ahead should you plan investments in IT? What does it really mean to say that you are committed to a certain five-year strategy? Is it like an intention to redecorate all the rooms of the Palace of Versailles — something you could break off half way through, without wasting your whole investment? Or is it an all-or-nothing investment like a tunnel under the English Channel?

Should a data model for an organisation describe the way things objectively are, or should it describe requirements for new computer systems? Should the model help in determining strategy for the use of IT, or should the strategy determine the scope of the model?

Is it essential to evaluate radically different options before taking any IT strategy decision? How should IT planning take account of the possibilities of technology change? What should you do if the benefits of an attractive IT investment can't be quantified?

The Purpose of This Book

Most of these issues could be relevant to the long-term IT strategy of mighty Corkwood Bank, to the feasibility study for one project using advanced technology in the legal department of Angophora Mining , to the rescue plan for Snowgum Supplies, a medium-sized manufacturing company whose system developments have all misfired, and to any number of other situations calling for decisions. Recognising such issues of principle beneath the surface detail is often the key to making astute decisions about the use of IT in an organisation. Ignoring them often results in decisions based on faulty reasoning, arbitrary choices and unstated assumptions.

Issues of principle, common to many individual cases, arise in any number of fields: ecology, health care provision, aerospace policy, evolutionary biology and so on. In some of these it is a feasible project to summarise the main concepts usually applied to the issues, noting important opposing viewpoints where necessary. But the discipline of IT management is still too immature for such treatment. Very few people have yet had time to develop a set of reliable concepts about the logic of IT decision-making.

Some advocate the use of a standardised step-by-step methodology for IT planning. But these methodologies tend to force the problem into a predefined layout without exposing many aspects of the most demanding issues.

Management gurus enthusiastically describe the case histories of companies that prospered through adventurous use of IT, and urge their audience to go on and do even better. But exemplary case histories and general exhortations to be innovative don't really help you to cope with many of the snags you encounter.

This book is not concerned with summarising current practice, because the field is too immature; neither does it present a step-by-step methodology or depict shining examples of the use of IT. It provides an essentially personal analysis of issues that affect rational decision-making about IT. This involves posing dilemmas, identifying tradeoffs, recognising pitfalls, unravelling confusions and demystifying hype.

'Strategy'

Phrases such as 'strategic decision' and 'IT strategy' creep into the discussion very naturally, but what do these abstract terms really mean? How could you show that a certain decision was strategic while some other decision was not? Given two documents, how could you recognise that one was an authentic IT strategy document and the other was not? Answering such questions in a rigorous fashion, that avoided tautology, platitude and arbitrariness, and was also useful, would be an onerous undertaking. Fortunately, it can be bypassed.

Plainly, some decisions and some aspects of decisions are more important, are more basic, have wider implications or have more impact on the shape of the problem than others. When an IT plan looks convincing on paper and also succeeds in practice, the reason is usually that the planners have maintained a clear perspective on what is fundamental and what is less so; they have correctly seen the relative importance of different parts of the problem. When IT decisions go wrong, retrospective analysis frequently shows that people have given undue attention to some matters and allowed other important matters to go virtually unconsidered.

This book is largely concerned with unravelling and discriminating between factors relevant to important IT decisions. 'Strategic' is simply a convenient term to describe those matters that possess the qualities of being important, being basic, having wide implications, having an impact on the shape of the problem and so on. The 'strategy' of an organisation or of a project can be regarded as simply an aggregation of strategic decisions — not as an entity that needs to be given a separate definition of its own.

Yes, but *what kind of things* actually do count as strategic (important, basic, etc.) in practice? That is the subject of the whole book, but the following paragraphs provide an indication.

A Unifying View of IT Decision-making

The book contains thirty-one independent 'briefings' on a variety of issues, but they are unified by a certain general view of the characteristics of IT decision-making.

In order to think clearly about decisions, much material may have to be swept aside: *platitudes* ('Data processing should be managed for the effective support of business goals'), *exhortations* ('Increase executive confidence in major information systems') and *unfounded assumptions* ('Information should be planned on a corporate-wide basis').[1] Once this is done, it becomes apparent that IT decision-making possesses certain characteristic *sources of tension*..

For example, one source of tension is the *interaction between supply and demand*. In its simple form, this interaction may generate the following dilemma. There are many possible *demands* for the use of IT to help the organisation become more successful. On the other hand, the more ambitious the scope of the demands you plan to *supply* through the use of technology, then the greater the financial investment, elapsed time, organisational upheaval, vulnerability to uncertainties and risk of failure. In many cases, a wise decision is equivalent to a decision that provides the most sensible resolution of that particular dilemma.

The interaction between supply and demand can generate problems in more complex formats too; also, it is not the only source of tension characteristic of IT decision-making. In general, IT decisions that turn out well do justice — whether explicitly or implicitly — to these characteristic tensions. Bad decisions can often be diagnosed as resulting from misjudgement or lack of awareness of the tensions: crucial interactions are not examined, relevant tradeoffs are overlooked and so on.

Insight into a basic source of tension such as the interaction between supply and demand can play a prominent part in resolving many issues of principle. For example, in considering the relevance of the data model to decision-making, it may well be helpful to realise that some, though not all, data models constitute a definition of *demand untouched by interaction with supply factors*.

The characteristic sources of tension can be found in varying forms in case after case of IT decision-making. Once you are used to sweeping away platitudes, exhortations and unfounded assumptions, you are well placed to recognise the underlying tensions and issues of principle in any specific case. The more cases you encounter, the keener your awareness of tensions and issues becomes, and the more easily you grasp the essentials of any new case you experience. This book aims to assist that process.

How the Book is Structured

First comes a brief account of a body of *Reference Cases*, that will be discussed throughout the book. This body of cases is a kind of definition of the book's scope: the book contains the concepts needed to handle real-life situations that are similar to any of the reference cases. Following the body of cases, a *Reference Model* presents the main sources of tension characteristic of IT decision-making. The rest of the book uses this reference *model* as a framework for locating discussions of particular concepts; the reference *cases* are introduced whenever concrete examples are needed.

The main body of the book consists of *briefings* on issues of principle in IT decision-making. For example, there are briefings on the question of how far ahead to make investment plans, on the relation between data modelling and strategy, on dealing with investments that have unquantifiable benefits, and so on. In each briefing, the purpose is to explore the main points that can affect decisions in real-life cases. Very often, the key is to see why there is no straightforward answer available, and why different cases need to be handled in different ways.

Each briefing is organised in three standard divisions: to set out the main *issues* that make the briefing necessary; then to provide an *analysis* of the main points that come up for discussion; and finally to offer some brief *practical advice*. Unlike the rest of the text, the advice at the end of the briefing is written in the imperative mode; it provides a simplified summary of the practical implications of the briefing's analysis.

Each of the main *parts* of the book contains a group of related briefings. The introduction to each part explains how the briefings are related, and locates the issues they cover within the framework of the Reference Model.

Some of the book's briefings are *problem-driven*; they investigate certain problem issues that may be relevant to a decision — although, of course, better understanding of the nature of a problem often suggests ways of dealing with it. *Approach-driven* briefings, on the other hand, examine certain important approaches to tackling problems — although this often casts light, too, on the true nature of the problems concerned. Problem-driven and approach-driven briefings are grouped together in separate parts of the book.

How to Use This Book

This book is for non-IT managers, IT managers, consultants and analysts who are involved in strategic decisions about the use of IT, whether at organisation or at project level. If you find the questions contained in the *Contents* list relevant to your role, or if any of the *Reference Cases* resemble those you have been involved in, then you should find the book valuable.

There are two different ways of using the book. One way is start from the beginning and see how the ideas discussed gradually build up a whole picture of the relations between the fundamental issues in IT decision-making.

Alternatively, take advantage of the independence of the briefings: pick from the *Contents* list any briefing that seems relevant to your current concerns, or that simply sounds interesting — and go straight to it.

Reference Cases

This is an extended *Dramatis Personae*, listing the organisations that are used as representative examples from time to time in the body of the book. The test of any idea discussed in the briefings is whether it can help in tackling the issues of any of these reference cases.

Like the characters in a novel, the cases are based on the author's experiences of real life, reworked by selection, exaggeration and combination. The names are imaginary; no connection is intended with any organisation that really is called after a species of tree found in Australia.

Angophora Mining. An international mining company. A project to automate the storage of textual information in the legal department at head office is under discussion. Though small in the whole scheme of things, this project raises interesting issues: there is a variety of possible approaches, differing widely in scope, technology and cost. The more elaborate the technology, the greater the scope of the system's functions and the higher the costs. What is the best buy? How do you identify and choose between the available options in this kind of case? And how do you evaluate the benefits of this kind of system?

Antarctic Beech Corporation (ABC). A conglomerate with a range of interests in entertainment, travel, employment agencies and communications. The company's management is faced with a wide range of opportunities for using IT to develop innovative products and services. It would be rash to make a huge investment in a new family of integrated systems — nobody knows how the market for all the new products and services will develop. On the other hand, if ABC doesn't innovate, perhaps its competitors will. How should ABC form an IT strategy that contains a heterogeneous range of risky innovations, while avoiding any substantial commitment?

Black Ash Bank. A large bank in a country in Asia. Its telex arrangements are about a decade behind the times by international standards. The bank's management wonders whether to invest in something more up to date. Many different technological options are available, but any rational choice between them must surely be based on their effects on the bank's business. How can business-oriented management choose between the different technological possibilities?

Blue Gum Machines. Manufacturers of machines for making cigars. The business has been unprofitable and is now in serious trouble. A recovery plan has been devised by the company's management. As well as reducing the workforce in the factory by one-third, this plan assumes, unfortunately without any documented justification, that increased use of computers will work wonders. On the day after the factory-workers are made redundant, a committee is set up to define the new IT strategy. How can you make a sensible strategy, if you have to start out from such a chaotic situation?

Buloke. A distributor of commodities such as sunflower oil, olive oil, seed, grain and so on. Its management is rightly ashamed of the poor quality of the present systems for controlling distribution, but there is very little capital available for new investment. For the moment, the main task must be to introduce straightforward new systems that at least reach acceptable minimum standards of efficiency, within the constraints of the shortage of investment funds. How do you make an IT strategy for a large company, to improve systems as much as possible, while at the same time spending as little as possible?

Cabbage Palm Project. A four-year construction project to build a sports stadium in a very distant and undeveloped country. IT systems are required to support the administration and management of the project. The interesting feature of the strategy case is that all the project's IT hardware and software must be treated as written off at the end of the project. This is a neat little classic of a self-contained, 'green field' case.

Candlebark Insurance. A multi-national insurance company. A working group of people with varied backgrounds is set up to brainstorm through many of the generic problems of IT strategy, and thereby, everyone hopes, to improve the quality of the decisions taken throughout the whole company.

Casuarina. An agency for temporary office staff; part of the Antarctic Beech group, but a household name in its own right. Casuarina has a strong network of branches and there are now big plans to move upmarket to place senior clerical and professional staff. There are two main components in this strategy. One is a tremendous marketing campaign to change the company's image; the other is the introduction of lavish computerised facilities, to support activities in the new and more demanding market. But Casuarina can't realistically expect to have a complete, ideal system right from the very first day. So what should the initial system contain and what should it leave out? In fact, is it even sensible for Casuarina managers to firm up the requirements of a complete system, before they have developed more practical experience?

Cedar Wattle City. A go-ahead city wanting to make a name as the place for stylish modern businesses to be located. The mayor is very keen to invest in a special, hi-tech, high-speed, high-capacity telecommunications network that will link buildings in the science park and the prestige offices of the downtown business centre. Though this project may add glamour to the city's image, there is no obvious way of cost–justifying it. How do you make rational decisions in such a case?

Corkwood Bank. A large and profitable retail bank, with very moderate computer systems. The board decides to take a completely fresh look at all aspects of the bank's operations, but particularly its use of IT. Funds for investment are not a problem; at least, that is the initial assumption. This case seems an ideal candidate for using a large-scale, top-down, strategic planning methodology, in order to arrive at a framework for a whole new generation of integrated systems. What issues of principle are likely to arise?

Eucalyptus City. A huge construction project is under way to build a substantial new city in the jungle. As part of the city's infrastructure, there will be first-rate computer systems, using the latest database technology, to support civic administration. Some information in the database will be stored as a common infrastructure for many systems, while other information will be system-specific. But how do you decide which information should count as infrastructure and which information should be system-specific? Why does it have major implications for the whole IT strategy?

Forest Oak Energy. A utility company, responsible for the supply of gas, electricity and a variety of other things (e.g. water and cable television) to buildings in the Forest Oak region. For years work has been going on to design and implement a massive, all-encompassing set of database systems. Somehow there is always one more problem to be solved before anything gets agreed and implemented. One day somebody expresses the view that, if they set up a database, then even if it is only more or less adequate, they can always modify it later. How far can the flexibility of relational database technology really mitigate Forest Oak's plight?

Hill Banksia. A large firm of accountants, offering a wide range of complementary professional services, such as management consultancy, executive search, relocation planning, market research and so on. Hill Banksia intends to set up a personnel modelling system, to help maintain the right mix of people and skills in the organisation. Since the shape of this system is so hard to define, Hill Banksia opts for an iterative, prototyping approach to development. But if you don't start out with a clear idea of what you want to build, if the scope of the system is highly flexible, if the appropriate technology is still uncertain, how can you ever have a well controlled project?

Ironbark Insurance. A subsidiary of Candlebark Insurance. Ironbark is a small company but it underwrites all the main classes of insurance. Its managers decide to replace all their administrative systems completely, in order to make better use of the opportunities of modern IT. But should they do everything all at once or be more selective? How do you structure that kind of decision? Can modelling techniques be useful?

LP Library. The LP Library (as it is usually known) hires out recorded music, on vinyl records, cassettes and compact discs (CDs) to residents of the town of Lilli-Pilli (named after the Australian tree). The director of the library has a large budget for computer systems. The library is a real adventure playground for people who enjoy data modelling. But where is the strategy behind the modelling?

Mulga Group. A famous 'high street' retailer of electrical goods. Mulga has just taken over the country's largest distributor of video-cassettes, CDs and similar consumer products. As a result, it now has two data centres with totally incompatible systems. One data centre is to close and its systems are to be converted to run at the other. But for each of the many systems there is a choice: should it merely be converted or enhanced at the same time or completely redeveloped? How can Mulga form a coherent overall policy to guide all these decisions?

Murray Pine Organisation (MPO). One of the biggest names in the publishing industry. MPO has seven large operating units; one is a national newspaper, one a leading publisher of academic textbooks, and so on. There is also a substantial head office, organised as eight special departments (legal, PR, etc.). Some of the most interesting IT strategy issues concern the relationships between the different parts of the organisation. Should these units interact and collaborate on IT matters as much as possible, for the good of the whole organisation? Or should they not?

Pink Gum Products. A medium-sized manufacturer of kitchen equipment, which currently relies for its main computer systems on a bureau service operated by an associated company. Its management team decide to make a fresh start with new systems on PGP's own computer installation. With this stimulus, they identify many attractive opportunities for using IT. Strategic problems arise less in finding the opportunities, than in deciding which opportunities to exploit, without being too ambitious and taking too many risks. How do you handle that kind of problem?

Red Box Data Services (RBDS). Originally an ordinary computer services bureau, RBDS has formed a whole new business strategy. With substantial capital backing from its multi-national parent company, RBDS intends to become an electronic publisher, by providing on-line database information that customers can access through terminals. The key thing is to offer more original ways of accessing more imaginative collections of information than any competitors already in this market. The policy is attractive, but it raises an important generic question: How do you make an IT strategy that fosters experiments in imaginative, wayout, risky ideas, without degenerating into turmoil and confusion?

Red Cedar Service. RBDS's first big commitment to an on-line database information service. Red Cedar is targeted at a special group of customers: defence industry experts and strategic analysts. The project requires database software that can handle both text and graphics, as well as highly structured information. This difficult technological issue could influence the main strategic decisions about the nature of the information stored and the way it is accessed. But should technology be allowed to influence strategy in this way?

Red Mahogany and **Red Pine Projects**. Two of RBDS's experimental projects. Both are concerned with providing on-line 'current awareness' information. The database of the Red Mahogany service provides up to date information about the latest learned articles in anthropology and related disciplines such as linguistics and archaeology. The Red Pine service alerts its users to all the latest publications in the humanities that originate from a group of collaborating universities. The strategy for these projects is very different from that for RBDS's Red Cedar Service. The Red Mahogany and Red Pine projects each set up a temporary experimental service, for the exclusive purpose of gaining experience and market feedback. Only after that, will RBDS be in a position to decide whether and how to set up a real profit-making service. In other words, investment in Red Mahogany or Red Pine is not like a commitment to building an operational system that is expected to be financially viable. But, if that constraint is absent, how do you devise a rational strategy for investment in such experimental systems?

Red Rivergum and **Red Sallee Projects**. Two more experimental projects at RBDS. Both are concerned with providing access to an on-line database that customers can access through terminals. Red Rivergum's database stores a great variety of information concerned with ecology; some of the information is the latest news, some information has more of a reference character. Red Sallee's database is essentially the content of one large reference book, a cultural guide to Italy. Like Red Mahogany and Red Pine, these two projects are pure experiments, so many of the principles of managing projects to develop normal, operational systems simply don't apply. What rules do apply to an experiment-driven IT strategy?

Rosewood Bank. A small retail bank. Rosewood already has an image as an upmarket bank for stylish people. The bank's managers are keen to invest in IT in order to strengthen this image and continue offering superior services to their rich clientele. How do they set about translating these hazy aspirations into genuine strategy?

Sassafras Magazines. A publisher of magazines about medical equipment, agricultural machinery and various other areas of technology. A cost–benefit analysis shows beyond any reasonable doubt that a large investment in extensive new computer systems will be well justified by the resulting savings in administration costs. This makes Sassafras a rare and classic strategy case.

Smoothbark Assurance. A subsidiary of Candlebark Insurance, exclusively concerned with reinsurance. Defying the warnings of the parent company, Smoothbark sign a contract for an ideal system to automate virtually all the complexities of their fiendishly complicated business. After three years the project has already cost twice as much and taken twice as long as originally planned — and is only one-third complete. Smoothbark provides a splendid example of how not to make an IT strategy.

Snowgum Supplies. A medium-sized manufacturer of medical supplies, whose new minicomputer-based systems have turned out to be a fiasco. The combination of bad implementation management and bugs in the database software mean that the accounts receivable system is out of control. That is only one of the many problems that could drive the company into bankruptcy. What are Snowgum's options?

Stringybark Assurance. Arch-rival of Candlebark Insurance. When they are brainstorming together, the strategists at Candlebark often say: 'Now suppose Stringybark were to. . .'

Sycamore Supplies. A wholesaler of stationery and office equipment products with a network of depots around the country. Sycamore clearly needs to set up new administrative systems at the depots. Many big questions are tangled up together, though two main themes are dominant: How much communication is needed between depots and head office? How sophisticated and ambitious should the new systems be? So how should Sycamore managers go about unravelling their whole collection of strategic issues?

Turpentine Tours (TT). Another subsidiary of Antarctic Beech Corporation (ABC), this time in the travel business. ABC have selected TT as a good place to experiment with a new idea: a system to provide travel information and display high-quality maps that are relevant to holidays in Greece. This is meant to be a breakthrough in service to the discerning client who is deciding which places to visit. This case is a classic example of the way awareness of possibilities offered by technology (in this case geographical information system technology) can feed back to influence people's view of what is required from a system. Or shouldn't you allow that to happen?

White Cypress, White Gum, White Mallee and **White Wattle**. Four manufacturing companies that are all faced by the same management problem. A company needs a comprehensive range of new systems to control inventory, production and related functions. Should it buy a standard software package? That is the cheapest, quickest solution, but the package may not do precisely what is required. Or should it commission development of its own software to do exactly what is needed? But that will be very expensive. Or should it arrange for a standard package to be modified? But deciding what to modify and at what cost can be very tricky. How do you navigate around this whole set of possibilities?

Woody Pear Homes. A company that runs a number of nursing-homes. Woody Pear has entered a joint-venture project, together with a software house and a firm of health care consultants. The joint-venture has two objectives: to produce packaged software that can be sold profitably to other nursing-homes and hospitals; and to produce the systems Woody Pear needs to run its own business. But the project has fallen way behind schedule. What are Woody Pear's options now?

Yellow Carbeen. Manufacturers of vending machines. A project is planned to introduce new JIT (just-in-time) inventory systems. There is a long chain of responsibilities starting with the inventory controller and ending with the software house writing the programs. Who is responsible for what?

Yellow Mallee Transport (YMT). The public transport authority of the Yellow Mallee urban area. The director of the authority wants to invest in new passenger information systems. Computer-controlled indicator boards at key points in the network, will show which trams are coming, which trams are late, when to change from tram to metro, and so on. But how sophisticated should this system be? What is the 'best buy' strategy for this situation — the strategy that provides the best balance between useful system features and the required investment?

Reference Model

> I can call spirits from the vasty deep.
> Why so can I, or so can any man;
> But will they come when you do call for them?[1]

Frederick P. Brooks Jr quotes this passage from Shakespeare in *The Mythical Man-Month*, his classic work on the management of software development projects.[2] Brooks remarks:

> The modern magic, like the old, has its boastful practitioners: 'I can write programs that control air traffic, intercept ballistic missiles, reconcile bank accounts, control production lines'. To which the answer comes, 'So can I, and so can any man, but do they work when you do write them?'

That was published in 1975. Since then the boastful magicians have moved on to: 'I can make strategies to transform your business, turn information into a management asset, incorporate IT into end-products and services, and bring competitive advantage in the Information Age'. To which the response is, 'Why so can I, and so can any man; but will they work when you do make them?'

IT strategies that seem fine in concept are very often disappointing in practice. An organisation undertakes a large-scale planning exercise, intended to impose order on its IT activities for years ahead, and yet after six months, serious new policy questions are emerging unexpectedly, while some of the commitments just made are already beginning to look misguided. Or a business designs and develops a major new system in a way that seems perfectly natural and sensible, and yet before very long, people sense that if things had been considered from a different angle, the system could have been simpler, better and cheaper. Or a company invests in extensive new systems that will create competitive advantage, strengthen the focus on customers and total quality, assimilate IT into the culture of the business and so on — and yet when the systems are finally operational at the price of tremendous effort, nothing very momentous seems to have been achieved at all.

Why do IT strategy decisions so often turn out to be inadequate? Sometimes the reason is lack of awareness of the opportunities: perhaps the decision-makers don't realise that portable computers would be useful for certain applications, or that certain business procedures could be well handled by expert system technology, or that certain departments could benefit by being linked into a network. But the causes of unrealistic, fragile decisions often go much deeper than a failure to spot certain possibilities. The really hard part of IT decision-making seems to be recognising the shape of the problem as a whole — determining which issues are important, understanding the way different factors interact with each other, identifying crucial tradeoffs and so on.

If that is a valid assessment, then the idea arises of trying to identify some of the *typical characteristics* of IT decision-making. Any generalisations that are forthcoming should be useful tools for understanding how the issues fit together in individual cases. This in turn should lead to more realistic decisions.

Characteristic Shapes

In many fields the most important decisions take a characteristic shape. For example, the manager controlling the inventory in a factory is responsible for regulating *one dominant tradeoff*. The fewer spare items of all the thousands of parts that are held in stock the better, because then the lower are the costs of financing the stock. But stopping the production line for lack of one vital item has a cost too; from that point of view, the more stock held as a safety margin for unpredictable problems or for changes in requirements, the better. The shape of the challenge facing the inventory controller is the tradeoff between these conflicting considerations. Of course, there are second- and third-order dilemmas and difficulties too, but a high proportion of the issues arising in the management of inventory for almost any type of factory can be traced back to the characteristic tradeoff between the two factors of financing and flexibility.

In other fields the typical shape for decisions may not be the resolution of one dominant tradeoff. Decisions of military logistics usually take a different shape: drawing up the Schlieffen plan to invade France and Belgium is essentially a question of devising schedules within certain *fixed constraints* on moving armies — the capacities of roads and railways and their junctions and bottlenecks. Planning the construction of a new shopping mall is a task with a rather different shape; there are has fewer fixed constraints, and there is more stress on *combining activities* in a critical path network. Managing a chicken farm (if done with ruthless efficiency) involves decision-making in a different shape again: *many variables have to be optimised* — to decide on different proportions of many possible animal feeds, with different properties, leading to different characteristics in the animals.

The Supply–Demand Interaction

IT decision-making also has its characteristic shape, though of the four examples the inventory controller's is the closest. One of the main sources of tension inherent in many IT strategy decisions is an *interaction between two main factors*.

On the one hand, there may be a variety of different opportunities available for using IT to benefit the organisation; these can be called *demand factors*. If the organisation chooses to meet some of the demands, then it must invest in *supply factors*, the technology that supports the systems that benefit the organisation. Supply and demand factors are usually related in a tradeoff. The more *demands* you decide to meet, then, all being well, the more benefits IT will bring to the organisation. On the other hand, the more ambitious the plans for investing in technology and building the systems to *supply* the demands, then the greater the financial investment, elapsed time, organisational upheaval, vulnerability to uncertainties and risk of failure.

The essence of many important decisions about IT strategy is to find the right mixture of supply and demand. The tradeoff factors are often related in quite a delicate interaction. Deciding how plausible and relevant a certain demand is may involve assessing how readily it can be supplied; assessment of supply may lead to new insight into the demands that could benefit the organisation. To define demand first and work out supply afterwards may be like ordering from a menu without any prices, but to put supply before demand may be like running a hospital for the benefit of the doctors.

Some IT decisions and plans are less obviously affected by the Supply–Demand Interaction, but they are usually concerned with working out the detail of some logically prior decision. For example, planning a software development project may seem analogous to planning the construction of a shopping mall. But the project planning only makes sense if the decision has already been taken to undertake a certain project with a certain scope — that is, if the main supply and demand factors have already been settled, in outline at any rate. Planning an organisation's telecommunications network, while taking account of capacity requirements and possible bottlenecks, may be rather like drawing up the Schlieffen plan. But it only makes sense to begin this planning after some decisions have already been taken about the demand that a network should supply. Finding the best technical design for a database may involve discovering the optimum combination of many variables, affecting the performance of the database in many subtle ways. But this work is dependent on the prior decision to set up a certain database possessing a certain scope.

The Commitment–Flexibility Tradeoff

Very often an IT decision is complicated by a second source of tension — the tradeoff between commitment and flexibility. If you are prepared to define exactly what you want now and far into the future, you can invest in hardware and systems far more efficiently than if you refuse to look more than a few months ahead. IT is like many other fields, in this respect: building a five-bedroom house is normally cheaper in the long run than building a one-bedroom house and extending it with new rooms one at a time; ordering wine by the bottle in a restaurant is normally better value for money than ordering by the glass. In other words up-front *commitment* is generally more cost-efficient than investment spread over many small steps.

On the other hand, it is no use investing cost-efficiently in something that turns out afterwards to be not what you want at all. Whatever the longer-term possibilities for expansion, it can still be a sensible idea to start with a one-bedroom house or one glass of wine. For example, powerful uncertainty factors may exist, that are likely to invalidate any forecast of future requirements, however carefully made. In a fast-moving field like IT, with many unpredictable developments and shifts of perspective, there is a lot to be said for retaining the *flexibility* to change your assessment of what are the most important demands and the most appropriate supply factors.

Commit yourself to IT plans too heavily, in too much detail, too far ahead and you sacrifice flexibility. But minimise commitment for the sake of flexibility and you waste time and money in the long run. Very often the best way of clarifying the essential problems in an IT strategy decision is to show how this Commitment–Flexibility Tradeoff is intertwined with the Supply–Demand Interaction.

Shortcomings of a Level-based Approach

This analysis suggests that good IT strategy decisions do justice to two main sources of tension — Supply–Demand and Commitment–Flexibility — that are at the heart of many problems. But what generalisations can be made about effective approaches to such problems?

Characteristics of Level-based Approaches

	Extreme	Opposite
standardisation of level breakdown	generalised	case-specific
rigidity of level breakdown	fixed at start	open to amendment during work
profile of level breakdown	tidy	jagged
means of progress within each level	translation and expansion	options and brainstorming
relations between levels	ratchet	feedback
pros & cons	clear outline, easy to organise; but awkward at handling interactions and tradeoffs	more intricate more agile

A good start is to examine one plausible but incomplete general approach. One popular way of developing IT strategy is to start out from very general business factors, which are not specifically related to IT (e.g. 'Candlebark Insurance aims to become the most profitable European insurance company'). Then IT plans and decisions are developed at a succession of clearly demarcated levels: e.g. 'information should be held mainly at the branch offices' and, perhaps a level below, 'all the main IT systems must be redeveloped' and, at a lower level, 'all systems will use the DB2 database software product'. In this approach to decision-making, the progression through planning levels is a movement from the general to the specific and from the non-technical to the technical — that is, from demand factors to supply factors.

The approach can be summarised in just a paragraph, but its basic principles are the justification for the immense, cathedral-like piles of strategies, models, blueprints and plans that are built up within some large organisations. Many standard methodologies for developing IT strategy rest on the validity of this approach.

Can a pure level-based approach do justice to most real-life cases where important decisions have to be taken? The body of Reference Cases, for example? Often it is not at all easy to arrange the issues of such cases into a set of levels. Angophora Mining, Antarctic Beech Corporation, Black Ash Bank, Blue Gum Machines . . . Their problems just don't seem to fit into the required format.

If a level-based approach seems inadequate in practice, what is wrong with it in theory? To articulate the shortcomings, consider the main characteristics of an *extreme level-based approach*. The breakdown into levels is standardised, as opposed to being decided from case to case. It is fixed at the start, rather than open to amendment during the decision-making process. The levels form a tidy pyramid where the later levels tend to have more detailed products; or at the least, the profile of the levels is not noticeably jagged. Progress is made within each level largely by translation into different terms or expansion into more detail of decisions already reached at the previous level — rather than, say, by searching out and comparing a variety of options. After each level a 'ratchet' closes to prevent any feedback from subsequent levels.

The question whether such an extreme approach can really do justice to the Supply–Demand Interaction and the Commitment–Flexibility Tradeoff inherent in typical cases comes close to being purely rhetorical. Though a rigid separation of demand from supply into discrete levels may seem very logical at first sight, it actually prevents you from examining the *interactions* between supply and demand. In the first reference case, for example, Angophora Mining needs to choose between a variety of possibilities, differing widely in scope, technology and cost. There are several options open to Angophora, each a certain *combination of demand and supply choices*. An extreme level-based approach makes it very hard to identify and compare such options.

What about the Commitment–Flexibility Tradeoff? There is no particular place in an extreme level-based approach where this matter belongs. The Antarctic Beech Corporation (ABC), second in the list of reference cases, can easily identify a vast range of possible ways of investing in IT, and it definitely doesn't want to commit to all of them. The essential strategic problem here is to decide how the company can minimise its commitments in risky innovation, but still position itself with the flexibility to respond effectively to moves by competitors. An extreme level-based approach simply doesn't address problems of that kind.

The Option–Level Blend

Scepticism about extreme level-based approaches is certainly in order, but not outright dismissal of the whole notion of organising decisions in levels so that more general matters come before more specific.

Any approach to decision-making and planning must arrange matters in levels *to some degree*; otherwise it is impossible to separate the essential from the incidental. But — this book argues — any approach also needs to do justice to the Supply–Demand Interaction and the Commitment–Flexibility Tradeoff. Interactions and tradeoffs tend to straddle the boundaries of apparently natural levels; therefore the traits of an extreme level-based approach need to be tempered to do justice to the issues of the particular case. For example, progress through the translation or expansion of decisions already reached at a previous level may have to be combined with progress through searching out and comparing a variety of mutually exclusive options.

Seen in this light, each decision-making case needs its own approach, blending different styles of work together. Any assumption that a certain predefined standard approach will be always or nearly always appropriate is unwarranted. It isn't necessarily possible to predefine the moments when important options will present themselves, to know in advance at what point in a case feedback to question conclusions reached at earlier levels ought to be stimulated, or to lay down how intensively two alternatives ought to be investigated in parallel before one is finally chosen.

All this prompts recognition of a third source of tension underlying IT decision-making. Good decisions require an approach that moderates level-based discipline (at its most extreme: generalised, fixed, tidy, translation and ratchet) with the appropriate measure of freedom (case-specific, amendable, jagged, options and feedback). The *Option–Level Blend* is a convenient, impressionistic name for this whole complex of factors.

The Reference Model

The analysis so far can be summarised in the form of a general Reference Model. The model contains the three sources of tension that are characteristic of IT decision-making.

In IT strategy decisions, the essence of the problem is usually to find the best resolution of the *Supply–Demand Interaction*. This is often associated with the *Commitment–Flexibility Tradeoff*.

To tackle the problem effectively you need to find the right approach

Reference Model of IT Decision-making

an Interaction, a Tradeoff and a Blend

To arrive at *Rational Decisions*:

➤ Expose the essence of the Problem:
   its *Supply–Demand Interaction*
   and *Commitment–Flexibility Tradeoff*

➤ Approach this by finding the right
   Option–Level Blend

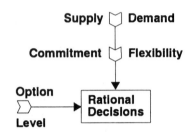

to investigate and understand them. Finding the right approach is tantamount to finding the right *Option–Level Blend*.

In other words, the model rests on the claim that good IT decision-making generally results from following an approach that has the right Option–Level Blend to do justice to the problems of the Supply–Demand Interaction and the Commitment–Flexibility Tradeoff — in the particular case.

The model can be helpful in several ways. Firstly, it provides the tools for cutting through the surface detail of a case. For example, having learnt a little of the affairs of Angophora Mining, ABC or Black Ash Bank, you can focus investigations by considering questions such as: What are the awkward interactions between supply and demand? Are there major Commitment–Flexibility issues at stake here? Does the situation call for more free-ranging discussions of options or for more disciplined level-based work? Conversely, if you are already sated with detail about Blue Gum,Buloke or Cabbage Palm, similar questions can be used to expose what is really important in the case.

Secondly, recognising the three basic sources of tension in IT decision-making makes it easier to handle other issues of principle that are more specific. Finding a rational justification for projects whose benefits are hard to quantify is a tough problem; it becomes more tractable if the question is redefined as one of choosing between a range of options. Some authorities put forward techniques of 'Strategic Information Systems Planning' where large matrices relate an organisation's main functions and data; it is good to be aware that unspoken assumptions about commitment can easily creep in here. Prototyping is a useful technique for system development, but it can become an expensive luxury, that is difficult to control; be clear whether your prototype is intended to test demand possibilities or test supply possibilities or test the interaction of supply and demand. And so on.

The Rest of the Book

So far, the importance of the elements of the Reference Model has been asserted rather than comprehensively demonstrated. In the rest of the book, the Reference Model is the chart for the exploration of the issues of principle in IT decision-making. Whenever specific issues and example cases are discussed, they can be related to the elements of the model. Equally, as more and more details are shown to fit in neatly, the validity of the model itself is strengthened.

You may feel that, however plausible all this may be, the Reference Model doesn't touch on certain other important matters, such as the need for personal qualities in an IT decision-maker: being able to win people's confidence or to tell when they are lying, for example. This is perfectly true, but such things come under the heading of the *skills* that are needed to operate effectively; they don't raise important issues in the discussion of rational decision-making, which is the main territory covered by this book. The book also devotes little attention to *sociological* themes, such as the need to have a clear 'project champion' for an innovative project, or the challenge of curbing the power of an organisation's MIS department without totally demoralising its members. Though important in themselves, such concepts aren't crucial to a discussion of the principles involved in making rational decisions. Equally, the book can conduct its arguments without commenting on *technological* questions, such as the choices available in setting up a local area network or the possible importance of hand-written input.

The Reference Model serves to focus the issues of IT decision-making more exactly: 'I can make demands to be supplied by information technology.' To which the response is, 'Why so can I, or so can any man; but will they be the best resolution of Supply–Demand Interaction when you do make them?'

Part I:

Problems of Supply and Demand

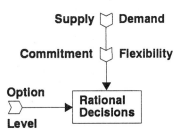

BRIEFINGS AND MODEL

This book starts out with a body of summarised cases, helping to define the practical concerns in IT decision-making. After that, a more general discussion of problems and approaches leads to the definition of a Reference Model. This first group of briefings now examines the nature of the problems raised by certain cases in much more detail. The briefings explore the implications of the interactions between supply and demand that are fundamental to very many IT decisions.

Introducing Supply and Demand

The Reference Model stresses the distinction between supply and demand factors. Technology is a supply factor; the functions and benefits of working computer systems are demand factors. But this is only an outline view of the matter; it needs to be elaborated in far more detail for the implications to become clear.

The first of a trio of briefings presents the basic supply and demand model, illustrated by some relatively simple examples in a variety of circumstances. (**1. Supply and Demand**)

To say that supply and demand factors can interact in complex ways is to suggest that one set of factors should not be fixed before the other is considered. If dealing with either in isolation were an adequate approach, then it would be misleading to characterise their relationship as interaction. So the question needs to be tackled: What happens if you do deny the interaction? Suppose you let either supply or demand dominate the other in driving decision-making? (**2. The Trend to Demand-driven Planning**)

The Supply–Demand Interaction is one of the three main elements in the Reference Model of IT decision-making. It is the most complex. With Commitment–Flexibility, for example, there is usually a tradeoff of the approximate form: as x is increased, then y is correspondingly reduced. Regulating supply and demand certainly includes the evaluation of such tradeoffs; the right balance between advantageous demand factors and expensive, risky supply factors has to be struck. But the relations between factors can often be more complex than this: sometimes several different demand factors interact with several different supply factors; and sometimes a small change in demand results in a large change in supply. That is why 'Interaction' rather than the more limited term 'Tradeoff' is used to describe this source of tension in decision-making. The third briefing examines the implications of the interaction between the factors of supply and demand. (**3. Supply–Demand Interactions**)

Undermining the Methodical Outlook

The other four briefings in this part of the book explore more aspects of the interaction between supply and demand. A natural, methodical outlook on IT decision-making is to decide what to do first and after that to plan how to do it. But that is to fix demand first and supply afterwards, which, in effect, denies the interaction between the two. A good way of studying the intricacies of the Supply–Demand Interaction is to see how this 'methodical' outlook on decision-making is undermined by a number of specific practical difficulties.

The first briefing in this category identifies certain classic situations where feedback may go awkwardly against the downward flow of the arrows from the definition of demand to the determination of supply. For example, it is a fact of life that people often change their view of what they really need from a computer system once they have gained experience from using the system. Also, they sometimes allow their view of what they need to be unduly influenced by what they already have. Then again, the choice of a specific technical solution to meet a need sometimes generates new insight into what is really needed. All these phenomena create difficulties for the 'methodical' demand-driven outlook; to take them into account, a more subtle approach to structuring IT decisions is required. (**4. Problems with Demand-then-supply**)

It would be easier to apply the 'methodical' outlook on IT decision-making if there were just one category of users, who presented their demands to the technical people, whose job was to arrange supply. At one time things were approximately like that, but now the situation is far more complex. However you classify the different types of role-players, whose demands and supply capabilities may affect the way the use of IT develops in an organisation, you are unlikely to find that the simple division between demanders and suppliers is adequate. That, in turn, undermines the strict 'methodical' separation of decisions about demand and decisions about supply. (**5. Classifying IT Role-players**)

The next briefing points out another complication. Since technology is changing all the time, the appropriate supply solution to a formulated demand may often be subject to considerable uncertainty. You shouldn't just translate defined demand into appropriate supply, by looking up the specifications and prices in the latest catalogue of goods in the IT emporium; you may also need to judge how the catalogue itself is likely to change. This juggling with uncertainty factors creates further complications for the 'methodical' demand-driven outlook. (**6. Coping with Technology Uncertainty**)

The last briefing looks critically at the epitome of the 'methodical' outlook: the development of an organisation's IT strategy by progressing through levels of planning, from the summary to the detail and from the non-technical to the technical. This idea of treating decisions as links in a kind of demand–supply chain is vulnerable to a number of awkward snags. For example, there are often factors making it impossible to define a suitable general business strategy as a starting point; or strong external uncertainties may weaken the effect of any long-term planning; or it may simply not be realistic to expect to reach your desired endpoint, starting out from the situation you are actually in. (**7. Supply–Demand: Links and Snags**)

Back to the Reference Model

These briefings highlight a variety of problems that can disturb the natural, methodical outlook on IT decision-making. This analysis of problems has several uses. First, since most of these problems are related to the underlying tension between supply and demand, they help to build up a more detailed view of the intricacies of that interaction. Second, they describe a range of generic issues that may be relevant to any case — potential factors the decision-maker needs to be aware of. Third, the more clearly such problems are defined, the more readily solutions come to mind.

The Reference Model suggests that there is a much greater chance of arriving at rational decisions about IT, if the Supply–Demand Interaction is recognised as central to the problem and decision-making is approached accordingly. It may be messy, frustrating and awkward to arrange, but it may also be essential to unravelling the real issues of the case.

This doesn't remove the need for work in expanding detail and translating implications from one planning level to another. The essential thing in approaching any IT strategy case is to identify the important supply and demand factors and understand where the tricky interactions occur. Then you can see how to approach decision-making so that fruitful, relevant interactions are dealt with effectively, and constructive level-based work is free from unjustified assumptions.

1.   Supply and Demand

ISSUES

Candlebark Insurance has a family of information systems that carry out certain tasks useful to the business. They produce the customers' policy documents; they compare premium income against the money paid out in claims for each type of insurance policy; they ensure Candlebark staff are paid correctly; and so on. All these things are clearly good and necessary. Even if computers didn't exist, they would still be needed. There is a *demand* for them from the business itself.

The technological resources found at Candlebark, such as computer hardware, telecommunications networks, software, technical experts and so on, are only good in so far as they support the information systems that carry out the tasks demanded. From a purely rational point of view, any of these technology components could be replaced at a moment's notice, if some other component became available to do the same job cheaper or more reliably. They are the *supply* that meets the demand.

An organisation's planning for the use of IT will always possess demand-side and supply-side components. One *minimum* condition of competent management is that the demand-side and the supply-side plans be consistent with each other. If, for example, the technology chosen is just not adequate for the application systems envisaged, or if technological investments are made that have no benefit for the business, then something must be wrong.

But this consistency is not a *sufficient* condition for sound decisions about IT. Even if the chosen technology is quite appropriate for the chosen systems, the organisation's plans may still not be sensible. For example, the plans might require investment of an absurdly high proportion of the organisation's whole turnover; or the main efforts might be directed at relatively trivial new projects, while other attractive opportunities for applying IT are missed. There may be many consistent mixes of supply and demand factors available; the real trick is to find *the most appropriate mix of supply and demand* for the organisation.

Looking at problems in terms of supply and demand is a useful working-tool for unravelling the factors in decisions about the way an organisation should use IT. This briefing explores some of the ways the tool can be applied.

ANALYSIS

There is nothing specifically IT-related about the distinction between supply and demand. Decisions and plans in many other fields can be expressed in this format. A power station is justified by its ability to supply a certain demand for electricity. If it breaks down under the demand or produces expensive electricity that isn't needed or is less cost-effective than some other type of generator, then (unless other issues such as safety are involved) no amount of pleading about the subtlety of the power station's design or the inherent interest of its technology can be considered relevant.

In the world outside IT supply and demand factors are often linked together: the mine supplies coal to the power station, which supplies electricity to the sugar refinery, which supplies sugar to the sweets factory, which supplies sweets (via several other stages) to the child. Whether you regard sugar as a supply-side factor or a demand-side factor depends on whether you are managing a sugar refinery or a sweets factory.

Supply–Demand in Project and Technology Areas

On an IT project, the difference between supply and demand factors depends on your point of view. For the inventory controller at Yellow Carbeen, the vending machine manufacturers, the demand is a new system embodying some JIT (just-in-time) principles he has sketched out; from his point of view, everything else is supply. The clever logistics consultant he has engaged formulates his own demand, a detailed functional description of a new system; to him, every detail of the implementation of that system is supply. The MIS department at Yellow Carbeen meets this demand by arranging two supply factors: they order a certain hardware configuration and they engage a certain software house to develop the system at a fixed price. From the point of view of the software house, the demand to be met is software for the defined functions that must run on the defined hardware; its supply factors will be its own staff writing the programs.

Forgetting that the same factor can be supply from one point of view and demand from another point of view is a common source of confusion or, in some cases, bitter recriminations — for example between inventory controller and MIS department or between software house and logistics consultant.

Analysis into supply and demand factors is often an effective way of maintaining a sense of direction deep in technology country. Coaxial cables are very supply-oriented items. They can be important elements in the construction of a telecommunications network, but are of no use at all unless there is a demand for some worthwhile information to go along the cable. By comparison with coaxial cables, an electronic mail service is much closer to being something that people might demand; and is itself dependent on supply-side items such as coaxial cables.

But to say that every item of telecommunications technology belonged to one of two categories — a supply or a demand factor — would be to over-simplify. There can be gradations. A coaxial cable supplies a demand of a local area network (LAN) for a transmission medium. A LAN is itself a supply factor with respect to the demand for a communications infrastructure, that is made by an electronic mail service. Non-technical people using an electronic mail service may see this as the supply-side technical solution to their demands for improved communications with colleagues. Therefore somebody who claims that the way to achieve improved communications within a company is to introduce coaxial cabling may actually be correct, but only if the claim can be supported by a chain of reasoning in supply–demand terms.

Supply–Demand Banishing Confusion

Analysis into supply and demand factors can be used as a general-purpose tool for making sense of confusing and complex areas.

Anton, the Innovation Director of the Antarctic Beech Corporation, is having a discussion with Bernard and Colin about the innovative possibilities of *hypermedia* technology. He is already aware that hypermedia is a somewhat general term for the concept of using a computer to present cleverly arranged mixtures of information in different forms — animated graphics, sound, colour photos and so on. The discussion ranges over many topics that seem to be associated with hypermedia — hypertext, multimedia, HyperCard, interactive learning, picture databases, knowledge-based systems, to name only a few. Anton doesn't necessarily want to know very much about any of these things, but he is concerned to establish some sense of direction for a useful discussion.

After a while he realises that Bernard is primarily concerned with the technological challenges of integrating text and sound and various types of images, all together in one affordable computer system. This explains his interest in such matters as the amount of disk storage needed for digitised music and the problems of reproducing moving images on a computer screen to an acceptable standard of quality. Colin, on the other hand, is stimulated by the challenge of organising information in new ways to create new types of product for industrial training use. He is concerned with issues like: How do you allow the user of such a system to keep a sense of direction amid the welter of information? Is it a good thing to show different information in four different segments of the screen or is it confusing? Can music convey information or is it just a gimmick?

In short, Bernard is more supply-oriented and Colin is more demand-oriented. If Bernard and Colin are talking at cross purposes, this may be the result of confusing supply issues and demand issues. With this insight, Anton can chair the meeting effectively. He avoids fruitless arguments about issues that are too demand-oriented for Bernard's contribution to be useful or too supply-oriented for Colin's. He tries to ensure that if hypertext or any other technology comes up, at least one of two criteria is met. Bernard's contribution should give Colin a better awareness of the opportunities and the constraints inherent in the supply-side technology, and therefore help him formulate sensible demands. Colin's contribution should give Bernard a better awareness of the demand-side desiderata, and therefore direct him towards those supply-side matters where investment in expertise should be made.

These supply–demand assessments are relative. Another meeting might be attended by David, who is more supply-oriented still than Bernard, because he is an expert in the fine detail of techniques for the compression of colour images. Edward, on the other hand, is more demand-oriented than Colin; he is a marketing manager, interested in all aspects of the industrial training market, rather than in the details of individual products.

Supply–Demand Interactions Affect Project Planning

Demand is not usually a fixed independent factor. If generating costs rise at a power station and price increases are passed on to consumers, then (at least in economic theory) this may cause demand to fall. Or if new technology allows electricity to be generated more efficiently, the costs of supply can fall, and the lower consumer prices that result may well stimulate demand.

But power stations require huge investments; for this and various other reasons there are not many entrepreneurs continually engaged in electricity supply price wars. More spectacular examples showing that demand is not just a fixed quantity independent of supply, are provided by the rise of the car, television or practically any consumer product. In each case increases in demand and economies of scale in supply feed on each other. This *interaction* between supply and demand is of course a characteristic feature of a market economy.

At Candlebark Insurance there are some good examples of interactions between IT supply factors and IT demand factors.

For example, Candlebark's main data centre already possesses a certain database infrastructure — *a supply factor*. A new Business Statistics system — *a demand factor* — is proposed. If the new system is supplied within the context of the present infrastructure, its cost will be low, but its functions can't be precisely what have been demanded by the management. On the other hand, the possibilities of undertaking this system outside the existing infrastructure or of modifying the infrastructure itself, are very unattractive, because of all the associated costs and complications. Therefore the supply-side constraints may well cause the initial demand-side aspirations for this system to be modified.

Another proposed new system, Life Assurance Valuation, values the investments of the life assurance funds and compares them to the company's liabilities towards policy-holders. A ready-made software package — a supply factor — can certainly be acquired, but it doesn't have all the features that the people in the life department ideally want — the demand factors. However, developing a completely new system instead would cost roughly five times as much. There are also intermediate options: for example, buy the package and extend it to do half the extra things wanted by the department. Whatever the final decision may be, it seems useful to regard the problem essentially as a matter of finding the right tradeoff between the supply-side and the demand-side factors.

There is nothing special about the insurance industry in this respect. Examples of interaction between supply and demand factors can easily be found at Angophora Mining, Forest Oak Energy, Pink Gum Products, Snowgum Supplies or practically any other organisation that uses IT.

Supply–Demand Interactions Affect Overall Planning

Supply and demand factors interact in more complex ways at Corkwood Bank. At the top level of planning, the board defines a certain very general *demand* factor: to become the most profitable bank in the country. To meet that demand, at the next level of detail, the policy chosen is to open new branches and to offer new services, both of which should attract profitable business from new customers. To meet the demand contained in that approach, the answer is to develop extensive new computer systems of an innovative character. In this sequence, the policy to open new branches and offer new services is supply in relation to the demand of the level above it; but this policy itself defines the demand that must be supplied at the next level down.

This seems very straightforward: becoming the most profitable bank entails new branches and services, which entail new computer systems.

But if it were that easy, every bank would have such a strategy. The reason IT decision-making is so challenging is that there are usually awkward *interactions* between the supply and demand factors in this kind of case.

For example, the more new branches and services the bank starts up, the more it will need to invest in new computer facilities to support them, and so the less profitable it may be, in the short or even medium term. Possibly information about the costs, risks and timescales of these new facilities should be fed back to the board, to arrive at a modified policy on new branches and services that optimises profitability. Again, certain ideas for advanced new services may prove on investigation to require such sophisticated and costly computer systems that their effect on the bank's profitability will be negative. On the other hand, some other bank might attract away customers by offering similar advanced new services as loss-leaders. Perhaps the surest way to optimise profitability — at least for the next few years — is to avoid investment in any new branches and services and costly, risky new computer systems and to refurbish existing systems carefully.

If any of these are real rather than just theoretical factors, it would be prudent to go back to the board and explain that investigation of supply factors has called some of the demand factors into question.

Clarifying Concepts and Terminology

This briefing starts with the idea that an organisation's overall IT policy can be summarised by dividing everything into two parts, supply and demand. The relativism of some of the examples may seem to contradict this concept, but this isn't really so. Some factors change from being supply to demand as the standpoint from which they are observed changes. Nevertheless, from any given standpoint, it is generally possible to decide which factors should count as supply and which as demand. Thus from the macro standpoint, surveying the whole of an organisation's plans to use IT, one set of things can be regarded as supply factors and others as demand factors, without further qualification.

Sometimes people use terms other than 'supply' and 'demand' to express rather similar concepts. For example, 'functionality' may be contrasted with 'technology' (or with 'implementation'). There is a lot to be said for sticking to the terms 'supply' and 'demand'; they form a clear, easily remembered pair.

Moreover, by association with the sphere of economics, the pair 'supply and demand' conveys the impression of *interacting* factors; this makes it more appropriate than other pairs such as 'ends and means'.

The term 'requirement' is sometimes used rather than 'demand' (paired with 'solution', perhaps). 'Requirement' is an unsatisfactory word because it often suggests 'something we simply must have, without any question'. Since there are very few wants so great that they must literally be satisfied at all costs, this can cause confusion.

Supply, Demand and Strategy

Occasionally people argue to the effect that *strategic* IT decisions are those determining the *demand-side* of an organisation's use of IT, while supply-side matters are non-strategic. Is that valid, in any useful sense of the word 'strategic'?

As formulated, this suggestion is ambiguous. If it means that 'strategic' is demand-side and supply-side is non-strategic *by definition*, then it merely amounts to a suggestion that the pairs of words strategic and demand, and non-strategic and supply, should be assigned overlapping meanings like elated and exhilarated, or dejected and despondent. This is not justified by the use of the words in normal English: it may easily confuse people and it forces the use of other terms such as 'very important' to describe any supply-side factors that may in fact have far-reaching significance.

If the argument is that *in practice* demand-side matters usually turn out to be strategic (i.e. important, basic, etc.), whereas supply-side matters do not, then this is an argument from experience. It may be your own experience that nearly all the important complexities to be unravelled and the issues of principle that really make a difference to organisations' effective use of IT are on the demand-side, but the examples given in most of the briefings of this book don't show that at all. They indicate very strongly that the crucial strategic issues arise neither on the demand-side nor on the supply-side. Time and again, it is the *interaction* between supply and demand factors, the fact that you can't safely resolve one side in isolation from the other, that generates the real strategic issues. So 'strategic' is definitely a quite separate concept from 'demand-side'.

Why Look at Things This Way?

Analysis in supply–demand terms is a valuable tool. Working out which factors of a situation get their importance from supplying demands raised by other factors is a good way of thinking clearly about what is at stake. Once this kind of order is imposed on the problem, there is a better chance of finding the issues that really count, that make the difference between unrealistic plans to fulfil idealised aspirations and decisions based on a real understanding of the possibilities and constraints of the situation.

This way of looking at things is not exactly a *method* for developing

IT strategy — if a method is regarded as something with its own paraphernalia of standard diagrams and steps to follow. Moreover nobody can demonstrate that understanding the interaction between supply and demand factors is the only possible way to make good strategy decisions about IT, in quite the sense that a bishop has to be moved diagonally across a chessboard or that an authentic moussaka has to be made with aubergines.

Anyone is free to say that the supply–demand view seems less appropriate than some other way of looking at IT strategy. For example, a claim that the analogy of Darwinian evolution provided far more insight into IT decisions than any ideas of supply and demand couldn't really be *proved* to be false.

But there are tests that help in deciding whether the supply–demand view is *more useful* than some other candidate way of looking at things. Which view seems to have greater power in explaining success and failure in actual cases? Which view makes it easier to get to grips with the matters that reason and common-sense suggest are important? In other words, you can judge the usefulness of analysis into supply and demand factors by seeing whether or not the briefings in this book ring true.

PRACTICAL ADVICE

➤ Develop the habit of analysing any IT situation in terms of supply and demand factors; distinguish between things that are good in themselves (demand) and things that are good because they meet the demand (supply).

➤ Think of IT strategy decisions as problems of finding the right combination of supply and demand factors for the situation.

➤ Remember that supply and demand are not absolute terms. The factor that supplies one demand very often itself generates a demand that is met by another supply factor.

➤ Use supply and demand analysis as a multi-purpose tool: to clarify responsibilities within a project; to show up the logical relations between different technology factors; to cut through the complications of any thoroughly confused area; to summarise the essential choices in planning a certain project; and to examine the chain of reasoning on plans for the use of IT within a business strategy.

➤ Bear in mind that the influences between supply and demand factors are not all one way with demand always defining supply. Often the availability or otherwise of supply resources can modify the definition of the demand factors. Therefore don't regard 'requirements' for computer systems as written on stone tablets, that can be finalised independently of the means of achieving them.

2. The Trend to Demand-driven Planning

ISSUES

If good decisions about the use of IT result from finding the right mix of demand factors (such as the functions of the systems that serve the organisation) and supply factors (such as the technology to provide the systems), then the question arises: How do you find the right mix?

The most basic problem is to ensure that the chosen supply and demand factors are *coherent*. There is no point willing the demand in the form of systems with marvellous functions, if you don't also will the appropriate technology to supply the systems. Equally, there is no point acquiring sophisticated new technology unless it can be used to supply systems that are beneficial to the organisation.

One way of keeping things consistent is to begin by fixing demand, the functional requirements of desired systems, and then carefully fill in the hardware and software technology that are needed as supply factors; that is a *demand-driven* approach to planning. A *supply-driven* approach, by contrast, begins with a number of technical decisions, that set up a certain environment of resources, and only then goes on to define the systems that take advantage of these resources.

Either approach can lead to a coherent choice of supply and demand factors, but whether the result is the *best available* coherent choice is another matter. This briefing discusses the pros and cons of demand-driven and supply-driven approaches and their influence among people who take IT strategy decisions.

ANALYSIS

When computers first began to be used in business, much of the planning was supply-driven, since those in charge of supplying technology were the only ones who understood it, and those who might have expressed the demands were as yet inarticulate. Over the last three decades there has been an interesting change from supply-driven to demand-driven approaches to IT strategy. Some people think this is self-evidently a good thing; others are not so sure.

Supply-drive and Objections

In the most simple form of supply-driven planning, top management sets an annual budget for IT and allows the IT management to acquire whatever hardware, software and technical personnel they think sensible within this budget. As time goes by, ideas for new application systems come up and, as far as possible, they are handled within the constraints of the available resources.

Summarised like this, such an approach seems hard to justify. There are obvious objections: How can top management decide what a sensible budget should be? How can IT management decide the right technology to invest in, if those decisions precede decisions about the systems to be implemented? A university might as well build and equip a laboratory and then debate what branch of science it might be used for. A company might purchase some mining equipment before deciding what substance to mine for, or buy a fleet of aircraft before deciding what routes to travel. These examples all make the same point. If you race ahead investing too enthusiastically in supply resources, you inevitably close off many demand options without even noticing them, and you implicitly make unjustified choices of those demands that you should meet.

Nevertheless, during the 'sixties and 'seventies, many organisations, such as the huge Candlebark Insurance and Buloke, the large commodities distributors, did operate in the supply-driven way. How did they get away with it? Were they all too blind to notice the illogicality of what they were doing?

Supply-driven Company Strategy

Under certain specific conditions, a supply-driven approach can be arguably the least bad way of doing things; consider the following scenario: Candlebark already has a massive commitment in data centre hardware, software, expert staff, data preparation staff, premises and so on. At any given moment, a lot of this investment has already been written off, but even more of it still has years of depreciation ahead. This state of affairs has an inhibiting effect on any radical decision-making.

Much of the new programming work done and the hardware upgrades made in any given year arise from compulsory maintenance or expansion of existing systems. The decisions to do most of this work are not very taxing. Immutable, external, regulatory pressures or unavoidable business developments generate demands that simply have to be met as quickly as possible. This seriously diminishes the available capacity for doing any really new things.

Moreover very little understanding of computers is to be found anywhere outside the data centre. There is no alternative but to rely on the judgements of the specialists. Every year the Candlebark board increases the MIS budget by some reasonable, though not spectacular, percentage.

In this scenario, the people who have the real power are MIS managers and, because of their massive responsibilities, they act more like risk avoiders than change agents. Change does come of course; new ways of making the supply-side more efficient are introduced and some people even get bright new demand-side ideas — albeit often in a rather indirect way.

For example, over a certain period during the 'seventies, MIS at Candlebark moves cautiously towards database instead of file-based applications, because the concept of storing information in one coherently organised, central database should (in theory, at least) allow the existing hardware resources to be used more efficiently. A side effect of this supply-side move is that database technology permits certain application systems to be developed, that were previously unrealistic; so the demand-side is stimulated too.

During the 'eighties, relational database technology replaces first-generation database technology, because it helps to use scarce programmer resources more efficiently. At least in theory, it eliminates the problem that tiny pieces of software maintenance require enormous effort because the linkages between items in the database are so incredibly complicated. This supply-side progress affects the demand-side; relational database technology allows the development of some new systems with new types of functions, that were scarcely feasible with first-generation database technology.

So a supply-driven approach to the organisation's overall IT strategy can have a certain ongoing momentum to it, that, under the right conditions, can prevail for quite a long period without displaying too many scandalous weaknesses or generating too many spectacular blunders.

Supply-driven Project Strategy

A supply-driven approach to the strategy for a given project can also prevail quite easily. For example, Buloke, the large commodities distributor, needs a new system to ensure that all the inventory figures at the various depots can be reconciled every night; this system is bound to entail writing new software and acquiring new hardware.

From a theoretical point of view, Buloke's approach to strategy leaves a great deal to be desired. The board simply approaches its customary mainframe hardware supplier, who, on the basis of a very superficial study, proposes selling Buloke a collection of minicomputers to be located around the country, together with some operating system, telecommunications and data management software. This proposal is accepted immediately; Buloke staff are told to train themselves in using the hardware and software and to build the best system that is possible with that technology within a time-limit of eighteen months.

This is shocking of course; there are so many different ways of choosing the functions of the system and so many different technical approaches that should have been considered and were not even noticed. The probability that the strategy chosen is anywhere near the optimal strategy notionally available seems very slight. These criticisms are valid in theory, but it all happened some years ago. Options you might toy with today (dialling in with stock figures from laptop PCs in delivery vans, providing customers with a videotex service, using optical character recognition to read documents, etc.) weren't very relevant then, so the scope for being radical and creative was that much less. A supply-driven project strategy wasn't the best way of doing things even at that time, but it didn't necessarily lead to a catastrophe either.

Demand-driven Reaction

Nevertheless, the inherent illogicality of allowing means to have more weight than ends was bound to become obvious sooner or later. Once computing power spread over the desktop and the departmental mini-computer as well as the mainframe, and as more and more people outside the data centre became knowledgeable about IT's possibilities, supply-driven planning became an untenable approach. It may still be widely *practised* in fact today, but hardly anybody *advocates* it as an excellent concept that should be applied more widely. It is normally only mentioned in seminars or articles as an example of how not to do things.

The opposite of supply-driving is demand-driving. The demand-driven enthusiast sees the IT management as a dangerous producer lobby — like teachers who run schools for their own benefit rather than to educate children, or doctors and hospital workers concerned with their own interests rather than the patients'.

The argument that you should decide what you want to do before you decide how to do it sounds pretty sensible. If you are forming an overall IT strategy for an organisation, the reasoning goes, you should define its business goals in detail until they lead naturally into demands for certain systems; only then should you determine how to supply the demands through technology. Similarly, if you are looking at just one new system, define the system's non-technical requirements first; only after that, should you consider the technological solution that meets them.

Demand-side extremists begin by identifying all non-technical issues associated in any way, however indirect, with an organisation's use of IT: organisational structure, corporate culture, product development possibilities, competition in the market and so on. Then they develop detailed but technology-independent plans of the organisation's 'requirements', that are to be met by the application of information technology.

The plans are technology-independent because of the view that IT can nowadays do more or less anything you are likely to need. This leads to the attitude that the really important thing is to decide what you need, because working out how it should be achieved is a secondary, overwhelmingly technical issue. Once established, the technology-independent plan can be handed over to well-paid, helot technicians, charged with doing whatever it takes to arrange the details of supplying the demands.

There are certainly some advantages to the general approach. The separation of means from ends has a neat, satisfying logic to it. If your IT planning activities involve a wide range of people in the organisation, with various skills and interests, this tidy arrangement makes it easier for them all to grasp their roles in the whole process. Moreover the fairly strict dividing line between technical and non-technical work may well suit the profiles of the people available within the organisation. For example, there may be good technologists and good business analysts available, but nobody who is very good at combining both areas of expertise.

By-products of Demand-driving

There are two clear by-products of the rise of demand-driven sentiments. One is the avowed know-nothing business analyst or consultant. In the past, an analyst often had to manoeuvre discreetly to avoid admitting ignorance of some technology relevant to a user's problems. As the number of potentially relevant technologies increased during the 'eighties, so did the scope for ignorance. But now the demand-drive doctrine enables technological ignorance to be proclaimed as a matter of principle. The analyst can maintain that immunity from interest in technology is an advantage, and even take the offensive, feistily dismissing anybody who does want to discuss technology as too interested in electronic toys, too lazy to study the issues that really count and so on. In the face of the deluge of technology developments, some people adopt an aggressive justification for abandoning the struggle to keep their knowledge up to date.

The other important phenomenon is the rise of demand-driven methodologies. Most of the step-by-step methodologies offered as solutions to the problems of IT strategy are strongly imbued with demand-driven ideas. Why? Suppose such a methodology is not driven primarily by either the demand-side or the supply-side. Then it will have to handle complex *interactions*, that can be quite delicate even in any one individual case. Devising a standard, generally applicable structure that does justice to such interactions, is very hard. Allowing a standard approach to be driven by one side or the other, demand or supply, is a welcome simplification. Since the supply-driven approach is discredited, the natural result is demand-driven step-by-step methodologies.

Practical Problems with Demand-driving

Thirty years ago, a good programmer was one who could program to optimise memory, execution speed and so on, in order to use the computer hardware as efficiently as possible. But in the 'seventies, computing power became much cheaper and it was no longer so important to squeeze the last drop of performance out of the hardware. So the emphasis changed; the good programmer was now someone who eschewed clever tricks, and was good at structuring program code logically and documenting it neatly. A sort of *de-technologising* of the work of the average programmer took place.

Here is a possible parallel. Formerly, a good analyst had a good understanding of the main characteristics of the available technologies, and could therefore design systems that helped people as much as possible, while remaining within the bounds of what was technically feasible. But nowadays, the argument runs, computers can do practically everything the user is likely to need, and technology is no great constraint. Therefore the good analyst gives most of his attention now to defining the non-technical needs and integrating them within the non-technical planning of the whole organisation as well as possible. This job too has been *de-technologised*.

If you think that this parallel is broadly valid then you are of the demand-driven tendency. But what about the suggestion that, nowadays, computers can do practically everything? As well as still finding certain things impossible, computers can also do certain tasks very much more easily than certain other tasks. Even among those tasks that are well within the capabilities of established technology, some things are still much more expensive and time-consuming to achieve than others. If you believe that these are important considerations, then you may begin to suspect that pure demand-driving can be almost as irrational as pure supply-driving.

Fundamental Problems with Demand-driving

The ethologist Richard Dawkins remarks in one of his books that, if you asked an expert on aeronautics to design the wing that would allow a certain bird to fly as effectively as possible, you would have to specify the problem rather carefully; otherwise, the designer might come back with a design based on the use of titanium.[1] This may sound a trivial point, that could be simply resolved by adding the constraint that the material used must be of a type normally found in the bird's body. But in fact, there are other much less obvious constraints too. For example, a wing whose efficiency is achieved at the price of impairing the bird's ability to feed itself, protect itself, care for its young and so on, is of little value. Demands for perfect wings have to be traded off against other constraints on the design of the whole bird. In summary, demands posed in the abstract, without a very clear understanding of supply constraints and without the awareness that meeting one demand fully may mean failing to meet other demands, can lead to absurd or at least sub-optimal results.

There is one glaringly obvious problem with demand-driving in IT. The supply-side factors — technology and people — determine the price to be paid for the demanded systems — and the price is measured not only financially, but in timescale and risk as well. Firming up demand first without reference to supply is like choosing your meal from a menu without any prices.

Taken too far, demand-driven planning often leads to plans for ideal systems or ideal architectures for families of systems, without much regard to any practical reality. Smoothbark Assurance fell into this trap when they defined the requirements for an ideal system to automate virtually all the complexities of the fiendishly complicated reinsurance business. After two years the project has already cost twice as much as originally budgeted and taken twice as long — and is only one-third complete.

A project to develop an ideal system or a family of projects within an ideal strategy is extremely hard to control. Apart from this practical problem, there is another fundamental objection to demand-driving. Often, there is a possible shape for a system to be found, that could meet (say) 90% of the ideal demands, and be supplied at (say) 60% of their cost. But how can you ever know that this possibility exists if you insist on fixing demand first, before you even consider supply? Smoothbark would certainly have been far better off if they had considered a strategy based on this kind of tradeoff.

Summing up

Suppose somebody enunciates the following policy: 'After detailed investigation of all the current technology offerings, we've decided that the Unix operating system and Oracle database software are second to none. Our primary objective over the coming two years will be to convert all our systems to run in this environment. This is self-evidently a good thing to do.' Such an attitude seems dangerously *supply-dominated*. After all, even though a certain technology might be judged the best available in some abstract sense, it doesn't follow that any specific organisation will gain sufficient tangible benefits to justify the expense of converting to it.

But what of the following policy? 'Within two years we must have an integrated database holding information about all our customers in such a way that any combination of data about their business with the company can be called up on the screen at any time. That's the policy. The rest is detail for the technical boys to sort out.' This sounds dangerously *demand-dominated*; it seems unlikely that all the right factors have been considered in order to reach the most appropriate decisions for the organisation. What about humdrum matters such as cost, availability of appropriate technical staff, risk of doing a project of that magnitude in two years, and so on?

Letting the supply-side of the equation dominate policy may be as odd as scheduling the rail services to suit the engine-drivers, but preoccupation with the demand-side can be as ruinous as letting the children loose in the toyshop.

PRACTICAL ADVICE

➤ Get used to looking at any IT strategy case and judging whether either the supply or the demand side is in fact driving the strategy.

➤ If supply is driving demand, then judge whether this is because the management are still in the dark ages, or whether there is some good reason for it in this particular case.

➤ Be on your guard: the trend of the last few years has been towards demand-side driving. Many standard methodologies, many books, many consultants work on the implicit assumption that demand-side driving is the right way of doing things.

➤ Be sceptical about demand-driving; in fact, use this scepticism as one of the main tools to demystify the hype surrounding IT strategy matters.

➤ Judge each case on its merits. There can be occasions where it is sensible to allow demand a relatively dominant influence over supply.

➤ Both demand-side and supply-side extremism are potentially harmful, but demand-side driving is the more insidious, because it is superficially sensible. Be on the lookout for the snares it presents: choosing from a menu without prices, ignoring the relevance of awkward constraints and lapsing into unrealistic, idealised systems and architectures.

3. Supply–Demand Interactions

ISSUES

Who could quarrel with the idea that strategic decisions about IT should take full account of demand factors — opportunities for advantageous facilities and services — and full account of supply factors — the range of possibilities made available by current technology? But how is this to be achieved in practice?

One approach to IT decision-making is to allow either supply or demand to dominate the other, thereby simplifying the relation between them. Nowadays, hardly anyone suggests that an organisation should determine the supply of technology first and only then consider what kind of demand for systems should be met; but many do concentrate on demand and treat the practicalities of supply as something to be worked out afterwards. Either way, firming up one side of the supply–demand interaction first makes it impossible to take full account of the relevant possibilities on both sides.

To consider these possibilities effectively you need to set up an interaction between them; interaction between two things means that each influences the other, not that the influence is all one way. True, an iterative process, generating interaction between demand aspirations and supply potential, may be messy and awkward to structure. But as a general rule you can't have a neat, clear, methodical demand-driven strategy and also be sure of finding the 'best buy' choice out of all the available supply–demand combinations; the two things tend to be contradictory.

So far the idea of interaction between supply and demand factors has only been vaguely suggested; this briefing contains some of the concepts needed to render it more precise.

ANALYSIS

A novelist usually has a dominant status in relation to a translator. The novelist is free to exercise considerable creativity, but the translator's task is bounded by the content of the novel that is to be translated. The translator of a best-selling novel into Hungarian is in a rather passive situation with respect to the author. A translator doesn't normally add new characters, rewrite scenes, express judgements about what will sell in the Hungarian market and so on.

In a pure demand-driven approach to IT decisions, those responsible for defining the functions of systems in non-technical terms are analogous to authors, while those who design the technical aspects of systems are like translators. This really permits no genuine interaction at all. True interaction between supply and demand would be like turning the translator into someone entitled to tell the author: 'Well, for the Hungarian market, I think we ought to change the setting of the book from Al Capone's Chicago to 19th century Vienna; we'll have to take out that sub-plot about the oil millionnaire. . . and so on.' Or even: 'You know, I don't really think there's room in the Hungarian market for this book especially with the other three I already have on my desk for translation. . .'

The technologist may well have a challenging task — but its scope isn't normally considered to include complaining that the defined information requirements are misguided, or that the organisational implications have been underestimated, or that it would be preferable to leave out certain requirements and reduce the cost, or that the analyst has ignored many other benefits the technology could provide.

The model of the technologist as translator is a useful fixed point from which to start considering interaction. Seeing why the model is inadequate is a necessary exercise.

Cases of Dangerous Demand-driving

Interaction may be better than demand-driving in theory but how often does it really matter in practice? Very frequently. In fact, many of the most demanding decisions arise from an awkward interaction between supply and demand factors. Candlebark Insurance, for instance, have two cases where it would be dangerous to allow decision-making to be demand-driven.

There is already a certain database infrastructure at Candlebark's main data centre. If a new Business Statistics system is developed within this context, its cost will be fairly low, but it will only be a mediocre system because the functions can't be precisely what managers have said they would like to have. They want to use a graphical interface and a mouse in order to make certain on-demand enquiries, and the database infrastructure just wasn't set up with that kind of thing in mind. Moreover some of the enquiries would call for so much clever interpretation by the computer that they move into the realm of artificial intelligence. The costs of doing this system with all the ideal functions outside the established infrastructure, or the costs of modifying the infrastructure in order to accommodate an ideal system, would be very high indeed; much higher than the costs of the mediocre system.

Nonetheless, in a pure demand-driven approach, Candlebark would just go ahead and define an ideal Business Statistics system and accept the consequences, whatever they might be. On principle, they wouldn't even consider a mediocre system.

As another example, the proposed new Life Assurance Valuation system values the investments of the life assurance funds and compares them to the company's liabilities towards policy-holders. A ready-made software package can be acquired for this system, but, though it provides the most essential processing required, it doesn't do quite everything the company's managers ideally want. The result of taking the package will be just a mediocre system. But to develop an ideal system instead would cost five times as much. In a demand-driven approach, there is no dilemma; Candlebark simply develops the ideal system; a package that doesn't fully meet all demands is considered to be *ipso facto* unacceptable.

In both these cases, reduced as they are to skeletal form, it seems obvious that the rational approach would be to compare the *marginal functions* of the ideal system over the mediocre system, with the *marginal costs* (taking account also of matters like timescale, risk and so on). But that means making a careful study of the *interaction* between supply and demand factors, especially since the ultimate 'best buy' may well combine gradations of function and technology that lie somewhere above the mediocre and below the ideal.

Optional Projects and Complex Implications

Here is a last example that the planners at Candlebark sketch out just to show their senior management how easily the interaction between supply and demand can become very complex. The proposed new Global Clients system is a system for servicing clients who have Candlebark policies in many countries. It is not an absolutely vital system; if it costs too much, it shouldn't be done. To decide whether to include Global Clients in Candlebark's *applications plan*, some estimates of its hardware and telecommunications costs are needed. But that entails making *hardware and telecommunications infrastructure plans*. But these plans have to take account of the *software infrastructure plan*, otherwise no estimates of throughput and performance can be made.

But making the software infrastructure plan entails taking decisions on the operating system and database and telecommunications software, and these decisions are connected with the decision on whether or not to implement the proposed Expert Agent system — which would allow insurance brokers to use a laptop computer to dial in to a system that uses artificial intelligence to assess risks. The Expert Agent system is another system that the company could do without for a couple of years, if it were too expensive. This system also has requirements for certain scarce staff resources, which the *personnel plan* has to take account of; and so on.

If they were lazy, the planners at Candlebark would just write the Expert Agent and Global Clients systems straight into their plans, on the grounds that these systems have been demanded, and no further argument is relevant. Then decisions on supply-side features such as the new hardware to be bought and the specialist staff to be recruited and so on would all follow automatically. This would make everything much easier — but at the price of abandoning any attempt to control the company's investment in IT effectively.

To do justice to the decisions about Expert Agent and Global Clients, it would probably be necessary to set up some complex procedure that considers those systems together with any other luxury (or at least not mandatory) systems and work out which are the best buys in terms of the resources they call for. This can only be done by setting up real interaction between supply and demand.

Feedback

What about feedback? Why not take the natural demand-driving approach, but with the safeguard that, if investigation of the supply possibilities makes it necessary, there may be feedback that redefines the demand? Unless the role of the feedback is specified more exactly, this formulation may be no better than the politician's compromise wording that solves nothing.

Even the purest demand-side extremist has to allow the technologist *some right* to come back to the author of the non-technical requirements; for example, it may be that certain details are ambiguous or certain requirements are just technically impossible. But if that is as far as it goes, then there is no real feedback or interaction to speak of. It means that a non-technical demand, whatever its wisdom, its cost or its other implications, will never be questioned by the technical supply people, provided the demand is a, clear and b, not impossible.

If on the other hand, this kind of feedback is regarded as far more than just a fallback procedure to avoid confusion and disaster, if a significant amount of effort is budgeted in advance for the evaluation of feedback passing in the direction of supply to demand, if a shortage of feedback is considered a mark of failure in the decision-making process — then these arrangements are no longer based on demand-driving at all; they are arrangements for fostering supply–demand interaction.

Interactions in the World Outside IT

The great advantage of one-way influences such as that between novelist and translator is simplicity. Once a genuine dialogue is allowed, things can easily get out of control. But if the thought of anarchic interaction between IT supply and demand appals you, look outside to see what a gross over-simplification demand-driven planning usually is.

For decades, planners in Soviet Russia made detailed demand-side plans of what the economy needed and left it to factory managers to meet the supply-side. All very logical, but it didn't work, because the interaction between demand and supply factors is just too complex. Planning demand in isolation from supply results in a sub-optimal national economy, to put it mildly.

Everyday life frequently calls for decision-making that is a compromise between the ideally methodical and the practical. Suppose you say to a travel agent: 'We've decided to go to Antarctica for our vacation. Please arrange it.'

'Well, it can be done, with enough time and effort and money — but it would be far easier and cheaper to go to the Canadian Arctic, and the scenery there is not very different.'

'No, we've already chosen Antarctica; it's less crowded than the Arctic. That stage in the decision-making process is complete. Your job as travel agent is merely to take care of the technical details. Please don't waste my time with quibbles over things like costs and timescales.'

This is absurd, because practically nobody behaves in such an over-structured way. When decisions have to be taken and plans made, allowing factors to interact with each other is normal and sensible.

IT strategy is like many other types of problem where different elements are interrelated. You need to compare options, tradeoffs and best buys in order to arrive at the most appropriate *balance* of supply and demand factors for the situation. Fixing demand factors first and then translating them into supply factors isn't usually adequate, because the definition of demand is just not sufficiently influenced by awareness of potential supply factors.

Practical Problems

About now you may want to protest that all this seems to imply that a structured approach to planning IT is a bad thing; that can't be right, can it? When 'structured' is used in this context it can have two different senses. If it simply means the opposite of 'irrational, arbitrary, chaotic' then of course nobody can be against a structured approach; examining interactions need not lead to irrational, arbitrary or chaotic decision-making. But if what you mean by a structured approach is a standard arrangement of problem-solving steps, that are fixed in advance before the real issues of the case are even identified, then this seems quite a good thing to be against. Surely the most rational aim is to find the *right structure for the specific case*, that exposes the most relevant interactions most efficiently.

You may concede all this, but still point to genuine practical difficulties. Once you get away from the simplicity of demand-driving, and start exploring interactions thoroughly, there is a danger of endless trails around a maze of inter-related supply and demand possibilities. This is a valid point; it means that the job of coordinating decision-making with a strong interactive character is quite demanding, though not impossible, of course.

Even if the interactive process is efficiently structured in a decision-making sense, there may be another practical difficulty. Some of the people involved may find it hard to understand and accept their role in the process. With a pure demand-driven approach, the analyst can say to the manager of the Fire department of Ironbark Insurance: 'We have now firmed up your department's detailed requirements for recalculating premiums when the details of an insurance policy change'. With a more interactive approach, it may be necessary to say cautiously: 'We have now defined the requirements for recalculating premiums. But please remember, we haven't yet decided how much of this the computer will actually be doing fully automatically. That can only be decided when we've investigated a whole lot of other things.' This is just one more organisational challenge that may have to be accepted as part of the price of examining the interactions that are essential in finding the most sensible strategy.

Typical Cases and Approaches

Compelling though the arguments for interaction between supply and demand may be, plainly some balance is required between interactive brain-storming and methodical division of labour. There is surely something to be said for encouraging each manager, analyst and technologist to stick to playing a certain role, with as clear a boundary as possible between them. Surely there are grave dangers of indecision and confusion once the neat distinction between supply and demand is undermined by interaction.

Why not accept that demand-side driving is a bad thing when taken to extremes, but still develop a pragmatic view, based on the features of the case? For example, in a certain case, you might spot a few key aspects of the situation, where interaction between supply and demand was absolutely necessary, otherwise the problem would be disgracefully over-simplified. But having resolved this interaction in broad terms, you could be as demand-driven as possible, even at the expense of making a few unjustified assumptions. In another case, an enlightened supply-driven approach might be appropriate. After an initial survey of the main supply and demand factors, you might give priority to setting up infrastructure — telecommunications networks, database systems, technology enabling new systems to be developed more quickly, for example. This would be investment in supply factors that were not closely linked to any specific demands. You might intend that, with the infrastructure in place, the demands would be articulated more clearly and met relatively easily within the infrastructure.

This is all very reasonable, in principle, but everything depends on the situation. There are certain generic types of situation where complex interaction is really at the heart of the problem.

At Pink Gum Products the sheer quantity of demand in the organisation for new systems, enhancements and so on is far too great for the supply resources that can realistically be made available. The company needs to select the most compelling demand-side possibilities, without being too ambitious in the supply-side obligations it takes on. The only way to search for this 'best buy' combination is by thoroughly examining the way the supply and demand factors interact.

That excess of demand is characteristic of one common generic case. Here are three more: the case where the availability of new technology suggests the idea of developing innovative new systems to gain competitive advantage, as at the Antarctic Beech Corporation; the case of application systems that have an experimental character, or are very dependent on unpredictable outside factors, such as market feedback on new products at Red Rivergum; the case where inept management in the past has produced a situation requiring an extremely pragmatic approach, as at Snowgum Supplies. The trouble is that these generic cases cover a fair proportion of all the situations that arise in practice.

Methods

Many approaches offered as standard methods for developing IT strategy simplify matters by taking a strong demand-driven approach — though, of course, their advocates may not put it quite that way. If you are evaluating any proposed method, one useful ploy is to see where it stands on this interaction issue. Consider the four generic cases that have just been briefly mentioned and try to judge whether it could handle them effectively. Consider the Candlebark Insurance examples described earlier and think how the proposed method might help you tackle those cases.

If a standard method isn't the answer, how do you structure the process of decision-making to expose the really important interactions, without becoming enmeshed in endlessly complicated iterations? To generate maximum insight as efficiently as possible requires application of experience and judgement and familiarity with the nature of IT strategy decisions. Apart from that, there is no standard answer.

PRACTICAL ADVICE

➤ Get practised in seeing how supply and demand factors *interact* in any strategy case. That is usually the single most powerful way of seeing the real issues and their implications.

➤ Watch out for the dangers of demand-driving that lead to idealised plans without regard for constraints.

➤ Distinguish between the weak interaction of mere translation and the more complex, iterative, awkward to structure interaction that is often required to find the best mix of supply and demand factors in an IT strategy case.

➤ Don't confuse feedback from supply to demand that clarifies ambiguities and removes absurdities with the feedback that produces a real interchange of ideas.

➤ To handle an IT strategy case effectively, find the structure for decision-making which produces the best tradeoff. Order and control and logic and efficiency of effort are important. But they shouldn't be absolutes; you also need to expose, explore and evaluate those key issues where supply and demand factors need to interact.

➤ Be aware of certain generic cases where complex interaction between supply and demand possibilities is at the heart of the problem: where there is an over-abundance of demand possibilities; where there are demands for particularly innovative systems; where plans are vulnerable to external uncertainties; and where the situation is so serious that a very pragmatic approach is required.

4. Problems with Demand-then-supply

ISSUES

Is the most sensible way to develop a new information system to get the potential users of the system to think very carefully about what the system should be like and then, once this is agreed, to go ahead and build the system? Most people tend to think so. It seems natural first to firm up the demands of the system and then go on to work out the details of supplying them. Many standard methods for developing systems are implicitly based on the simple logic of what may be called the demand-then-supply model.

Of course, the work of defining a system's demands needs to be supported by analysts who are good at ensuring that no key points are left out, checking that the full implications are grasped and so on. Even so, in very many cases, the resulting systems are far from being perfect or even acceptable. Once the system is ready its users point out short-comings and start asking for awkward modifications, or outsiders find it easy to spot opportunities missed, things that could have been done more effectively or more imaginatively. Often the technical people can point out that they have competently done everything the users originally asked for. The blame, it seems, must lie with the users or the analysts; they can't have worked hard enough to ensure that the requirements document was watertight before signing it off. So, everyone agrees to try harder next time; but next time it happens all over again.

A similar demand-then-supply approach is often followed with an organisation's overall IT strategy. The desired characteristics of the main systems are discussed and firmed up, through the collaboration of board directors and MIS management and business analysts and perhaps consultants. With the demand factors agreed, the technical measures needed to supply the body of demands are worked out. And yet very often, it becomes clear within a few months that all kinds of influences were ignored and misjudged and underestimated, and the main features of the strategy are soon pulled out of shape. So, everyone agrees to do a more thorough job next time; but next time things turn out just as badly.

Since it so often misfires, there is a strong incentive to search for weaknesses in this basic model of first carefully deciding what you want to build and then building it. On the other hand, it seems rather strange to argue against such a sensible approach. How could there be anything wrong with it?

This briefing describes how the demand-then-supply model often fails for reasons that are more fundamental and less avoidable than careless-ness, incompetence and the like. These findings suggest that the model itself should never be accepted uncritically.

ANALYSIS

One important reason that the demand-then-supply model is often inade-quate is the fact that it chooses from a menu without any prices. The costs of supplying the defined demand only become clear after the demand has been fixed and so there is no chance of finding the best tradeoff of benefits and costs. Problems can also arise from the rapid changes in technology costs and possibilities. But these and some other relevant themes are covered in other briefings. This briefing concentrates on three particular phenomena, that awkwardly complicate the demand-then-supply model, by generating feedback in an awkward direction contrary to the natural flow of the model.

Word Processing at Murray Pine

The Murray Pine Organisation is a publishing conglomerate, whose component parts have always enjoyed considerable autonomy. It has long been debated whether there should be some form of organisation-wide IT strategy, and if so, what it should cover, and how it should be achieved. It so happens that most parts of the organisation decide at about the same time to stop using old-fashioned word processing equipment and switch over to PC-based technology for preparing documents. It seems a safe gesture in the direction of coordination to appoint an analyst to carry out a survey of user needs as the basis for selecting a word processing software package that will become the standard throughout the organisa-tion.

The survey results show a consensus that any new system must be as good as the existing facilities in every way, but it must offer really big improvements in some areas, particularly in printing with different founts, point sizes and line spacing; also it must make it easier to 'cut-and-paste' pieces of text from one part of a document to another. In his discussions with people in different parts of Murray Pine, the analyst raises a number of other possible features of a word processing system. For example, he explains how some of the more advanced packages on the market allow you to split the screen into several 'windows', which can each contain different documents or different parts of the same document. Nobody has a requirement for such a facility and all agree that superfluous complications are best avoided.

On the basis of the defined requirements a word processing software package is selected and installed on several thousand PCs throughout the Murray Pine Organisation. After nine months a meeting is held to evaluate progress. The office managers are all quite happy with the printing of founts, line spacing and so on, and one of the pleasant surprises with the new system is how very much easier the 'cutting-and-pasting' of text is. This means that far more cutting-and-pasting goes on now than before; pieces of texts are often reused with minor modifications in several documents, where previously a new text would have been composed and retyped; sometimes extracts from several documents are merged together in quite complex ways and then edited to make a new document.

But for some of the managers the big problem with the chosen word processing software is that it can't split the screen into windows. They have heard of an alternative package, supposedly just as good at printing founts etc., that also offers this 'windowing'. If you could actually see parts of (say) four different documents in different windows on the screen together, it would be much easier and less error-prone to cut-and-paste between them. They find it very unfortunate that the whole organisation has now fully committed itself to the other window-less package.

The 'Moving Abroad' Problem

That is a simple example of a very important phenomenon. No matter how confident analysts and users may be that their agreed set of requirements is correct, as soon as the system starts up everything may look very different. Simply to criticise the analysts or the users for incompetence is too facile. The analyst in the example is competent; not only does he faithfully record the requirements, he even poses the right questions about other possible requirements. The users don't do badly; in defining their requirements they correctly spot opportunities for possible improvements and they are right; the only fault of these people, people who don't even claim to be knowledgeable about IT, is that they fail to see two steps ahead, rather than only one.

Ted Nelson's book *Computer Lib / Dream Machines* contains a large number of aphorisms. Of those relating to this particular problem, the most telling is probably this:

> Choosing software is like moving to another country — what you want to know beforehand can't be found out until you get there.[1]

This *Moving Abroad* problem is a fact of life in IT. It is just not realistic to discount it as something that only happens to people who are lazy or incompetent. Who is to blame then at Murray Pine, if the users and the analyst are innocent? Surely the guilt should be attached to the person who made the assumption that it was sensible to define demands in that area at that time with that degree of detail, and expect to arrive at results that were reliable enough to form the basis for the massive company-wide commitment.

A more wily decision-maker would have been aware that the Moving Abroad factor is potentially relevant to some degree in practically every situation, and that in this particular case, it might be a dominant factor, shaping the whole problem. Then a more subtle approach could have been taken to discovering the best match of demand and supply; for example, one department might have tried out a provisional choice first and generated feedback that could have changed perceptions of the set of demands that should be made.

The Moving Abroad factor is not unique to IT; it can apply whenever any new technology is used to do a certain job. But the phenomenon does seem to be more pronounced in IT than in many other fields.

The 'Familiar Hammer' Phenomenon

Almost the reverse of the Moving Abroad problem is the *Familiar Hammer* phenomenon: 'If all you have is a hammer, every problem looks like a nail'.

The Greek astronomers explained the movement of the planets by inventing the concept of epicycles. It was obvious that the planets didn't move in perfect cycles round the earth; but if you assumed that each planet moved at a constant speed in a circle around a point in space, while that point itself was moving in a circle at a constant speed around the earth, then that model could make sense of most astronomical observations. Thus, planets were thought to move in circles-on-circles called epicycles. As more and more detailed observations mounted up, the concept of circles-on-circles-on-circles had to be introduced. By the sixteenth century the model of the universe based on epicycles had became impossibly intricate and awkward; Copernicus complained that it was a monster. Even so, he couldn't escape from using epicycles within his own system. Eventually Kepler and Newton introduced a completely new way of making sense of the heavens and everyone wondered why it had taken so long.

A typical spreadsheet software product such as Lotus 1-2-3 or Excel has some fairly weak facilities for database-like storage and searching of data, provided as a kind of supplement to the package's main calculation functions. With practice and patience you can find ways of using these possibilities for quite complex database functions, just as with practice and patience, you can even use the epicycles model to represent an orbit of one body around another in the shape of a square.

The financial director of Pink Gum Products, a medium-sized manufacturing company, is a spreadsheet *aficionado*. Whenever he is asked to define his company's database requirements, he does so in terms of what could be done within the confines of the Lotus 1-2-3 spreadsheet — even if the proposed system will actually be using real database software. He doesn't know, doesn't want to know, about all his extra 'needs' that could be met so conveniently if his company took full advantage of the opportunities provided by one of the genuine, upmarket database software products.

His model of what a database can and can't do is bounded by his experience of spreadsheets, just as a medieval astronomer's view of what counts as a suitable explanation of astronomical observations was bounded by the epicycles model. One day, somehow or other, he may discover the advantage of generating intricate *ad hoc* queries, by using the mouse to click icons and drag lines between linked files on popup menus with, say, the 4th Dimension software product on the Macintosh. Then he will probably complain because all the database applications already installed throughout the company seem to be so old-fashioned.

Who is at fault here? Not necessarily anybody, since no great disaster has taken place. On the other hand, such cases don't provide grounds for confidence in the classic demand-then-supply model. Superficially, the financial director of Pink Gum may be defining demands that are then supplied. In reality, his experience of the constraints and the possibilities of one particular supply factor, spreadsheet, is feeding back to affect, and in fact distort, his perceptions of appropriate demands to be met by a different supply factor, database.

Familiar Hammer Variants

The Familiar Hammer phenomenon can exist in several variants. For example, there is the problem of the technology specialist who sees any new problem in terms of a certain technical speciality. For example, in another case similar to Murray Pine, where the strategic issue is also policy on word processing, the person leading the study is a telecommunications expert. He regards the matter of keying in and modifying documents as trivial. In his view of the problem, the real challenge is the optimum way of transmitting documents from one location to another. He selects the word processing software that scores highest on this particular issue. In this case, the Familiar Hammer factor has a very bad effect, because it distorts perceptions of demand quite dangerously.

Another variant is the case where everything looks like a nail for the newly acquired hammer. People in an organisation have just discovered hypertext or electronic data interchange or object-oriented database. Now any new demands that arise are defined as far as possible in terms that can be supplied by using the hammer of the new technology.

Ideally of course, people who define new systems should take advantage of their own knowledge and experience, but at the same time avoid being unduly influenced by them. But urging this is rather like giving the advice: if suddenly attacked by a tiger, try to get your knife in about 3cm below its right shoulder-blade.

The Familiar Hammer factor is *potentially* relevant to many situations; the challenge is to assess its force in *particular* cases. Often it may be relatively benign, but on occasions it can lead to grossly inadequate decisions. Those are the cases where users or experts may have to be told that, although they think they have defined the shape of the systems they need or the technology to apply, perhaps they should think again.

The 'Available Jeep' Stimulus

Suppose you plan a holiday on the island of Java. First you summarise the main things you want to see (these are your demand factors). Then you evaluate the different modes of transport (possible supply factors). On balance, the best approach might be to hire a jeep; perhaps a jeep is the only way of visiting a couple of spectacular volcanoes.

But now that the jeep has been adopted as the means of transport (the supply factor), wouldn't it be sensible to go back and perhaps revise the list of things you want to see (the demand factors)? For example, there may be certain mahogany plantations and fishing villages that are only accessible by jeep. Perhaps they were not important enough to be on the original list of demand factors, but are well worth seeing if you are in the area with a jeep. Now that you have examined more carefully the possibilities accessible by jeep, you might even trade off one sultan's palace that was on the original list, in order to find time for several of the extra things.

What is suggested here is a feedback from supply to demand, stimulated by awareness of the supply factor. Surely it would be rather odd to reject such feedback on principle, regarding the original list as inviolable and refusing to even consider any revision. You would run the risk of finding out after the holiday that you'd missed all kinds of interesting things that you could in fact have seen, with very little extra trouble.

Here is an example of what might be called the *Available Jeep* stimulus in an IT setting. The managers of the Red Cedar project have outlined the details of an on-line database service they want to offer their customers. But there is some question whether the desired features can be properly supported by mainstream relational database technology; if not, there are several alternative but more esoteric technical options to be considered. After much discussion, the decision is taken that the demands posed by this system will have to be supplied by a special database software product that includes some unusual features for the handling of both texts and images, in addition to mainstream structured information.

Should Red Cedar now just go ahead and implement the system? Why shouldn't they go back and look at the defined demand features over again, starting from the assumption that the facilities of this special DBMS are going to be available anyway and determining to make good use of them? Awareness of this supply factor may well stimulate some new ideas: ideas about the information to be stored, the access possibilities to be provided, the user interface to be offered, and so on. Some of the ideas may be over-ambitious, but others could be just the thing to make the new on-line service a winner. Also, awareness of this supply factor may show that certain parts of the original demands are undesirably complicated and that similar results can be achieved much less awkwardly.

This Available Jeep factor differs from the interaction between supply and demand that is discussed in several other briefings. More often than not this interaction suggests constraints on ambitious demands and indicates that the 'best buy' strategy might be one that meets (say) 95% of the demand at only 60% of the cost. With the Available Jeep stimulus it may (though not necessarily) be the other way round. The supply-side arrangements may suggest opportunities of meeting (say) 140% of the originally envisaged demand at only 110% of the original cost.

Applying Judgement to Awkward Feedback

All three phenomena — Moving Abroad, Familiar Hammer, Available Jeep — can undermine the demand-then-supply model of system development and strategy-making. They are all *potentially* relevant to a very high percentage of cases. That doesn't mean that the structure of every case ought to be twisted to fit them all. On the other hand they shouldn't be ignored either.

To say that autumn follows summer is to point out a phenomenon; it is not to advocate tearing the leaves off all the trees in August, nor sticking them back again in October. Here the important thing is to recognise that the phenomena discussed in this briefing are real and to a large degree inescapable. They shouldn't just be shrugged aside as inconvenient complications that can be avoided if everyone is very careful. To point these phenomena out is not to say that they are good things that should be applauded — or the reverse. They are just relevant factors that invariably have to enter into the decision-maker's calculations.

Sometimes the *Moving Abroad* factor may be dominant. This could lead to the view that making a five-year strategy for the organisation would be futile, because so much would probably be learned through practical experience during the first two years, that the original strategy for the remaining three would almost certainly be overturned anyway. One obvious counter to the Moving Abroad factor is the prototyping of small-scale versions of systems, to get a firmer view of what is required. That is not a complete answer, but is often worth considering. Also, in some situations the soundest judgement may be that, although the Moving Abroad factor does have some force, it is outweighed by other factors. Then it may be worth accepting the risk inherent in commitment to extensive, detailed demands.

When the *Familiar Hammer* factor is spotted in one of its forms, the right judgement may be that, although people believe that they know what they want, they shouldn't be believed because they have been too influenced by habit and need to be stimulated to broaden their horizons. On other occasions though, the Familiar Hammer may be quite welcome. It may mean that the details of reasonably sensible systems are defined fairly efficiently, within the limits of well understood technology. This can be all to the good — provided that there is at least one person involved who is competent to be sure that other angles for looking at the problem that have been disregarded, or other technologies that are being ignored, would not offer significantly better opportunities.

The stimulus of the *Available Jeep* needs to be approached warily. Sometimes spotting early on that some very different technological approaches need to be considered may be the key to the problem. It may be best to avoid defining demand factors in great detail until these questions of technical supply have been settled, and only then to go back and work on the system demands again. Or that may not be a good idea at all; perhaps allowing this kind of feedback from supply to demand would cause chaos and indecision — in the particular case concerned. On the other hand, if you don't risk that chaos and indecision, you may find that the regrets over missed opportunities start as soon as the system is ready. There can be no standard answer. As with all these phenomena of awkward feedback, you have to be aware that the Available Jeep stimulus exists and to judge those cases where it should be encouraged and those where it can be ignored.

PRACTICAL ADVICE

➤ It is natural to define what you want to build before you plan how to build it, but don't take this logic too far. Temper the demand-then-supply pattern by allowing for awkward feedback.

➤ Be familiar with three main forms of awkward feedback that frequently undermine the simple demand-then-supply pattern. They are: Moving Abroad, Familiar Hammer, Available Jeep.

➤ Do your best to minimise the damage from these factors, whenever they arise from sloppy thinking, reluctance to finalise decisions, illogical fixation with means rather than ends, and so on.

➤ On the other hand, don't always insist on wiping them out entirely, because that may simply store up trouble for the future.

➤ Acknowledge that one or several of these forms of awkward feedback may be unavoidable in certain cases. In fact, they may well be desirable as a way of exposing the true issues of the case and the interactions between them.

➤ Recognise that in a case where awkward feedback actually needs to be encouraged, then a pure demand-then-supply approach to IT decision-making will be seriously inadequate.

➤ If potential awkward feedback is a major feature, be open-minded about the structure of decision-making. Recognise that uncertainties exist which are themselves important factors in the strategy problem. Avoid making substantial commitments that are vulnerable to the awkward feedback.

5.   Classifying IT Role-players

In the 'sixties 'users' were the non-technical people who needed the support of IT systems to do their work; technical people were a separate class who provided the systems that users needed. Because the two classes were so distinct, there were also intermediaries (systems analysts, business analysts, consultants, etc.), to help the users articulate their demands for IT systems, in such a way that the technical people could supply them. In the 'seventies the rise of the minicomputer began to undermine that class system and in the 'eighties the personal computer completed the job. Nevertheless many ideas and methods in IT management still rest implicitly on the old model.

An actuary at Candlebark Insurance uses the Excel spreadsheet software product to model certain life assurance scenarios with varying probabilities. He uses Excel a great deal and really exploits its finer points; people throughout the company know that if you want advice on advanced use of Excel, that actuary is the person to contact. But if you ask him what he does for a living he will reply without hesitation that he is an actuary — not an IT specialist, nor a business analyst or a consultant or anything of that sort. Plainly a case like this can't really be fitted into the simple model of demanders and suppliers.

But if that is so, there must be some impact on any concepts of IT management that are implicitly based on the idea of a very simple relation between systems that are demanded and technology that supplies them.

This briefing looks at some of the dimensions that may be useful in getting a more accurate view of the different types of *IT role-players* (a neutral term, to avoid begging questions about users and specialists and intermediaries). It doesn't define a complete, generalised model, to map out all possible roles from managing director to assembly language programmer. The purpose is to suggest the issues that are worth raising in order to gain insight into any specific IT strategy case.

ANALYSIS

There are three main questions worth discussing. First, how can IT role-players be classified? Second, assuming credible ways of classification can been found, how can such knowledge be relevant to tackling actual cases? Third, assuming some relevance to actual cases can been shown, what insight does this provide on the logic of IT decision-making in general?

Recipient/Provider and Development Role

As with many tasks of imposing order on a whole range of complex phenomena, a good approach is to distinguish several different dimensions, that can be used in classification.

One obvious dimension relates the *recipient* and the *provider* roles of a player. Typical recipients receive the information they need with little more effort than choosing an option from a screen menu or having a printed report delivered. Providers perform certain tasks that are necessary to ensure that there is information to receive; data input, say, or taking regular backups of all the information in the system. A secretary using a computer system to compile information for the benefit of a manager stands midway along the dimension.

This dimension is not quite like a one-dimensional ruler. A player can be both a heavy recipient and a moderate provider of the same system. Indeed, in the case of a purely private system on a PC, there is only one recipient and one provider.

The recipient/provider dimension applies to systems that are up and running. A different dimension is needed to classify players' *development roles* when a new system is needed. Different points on this dimension can indicate just how computer-oriented a player's role in development is. Here is an incomplete outline, just to suggest the possibilities. From 'left' to 'right' along the scale: no involvement at all; then, involved in generalised discussions about the functions of a system; next, has to ensure that any non-technical definition of a system's functions is precise and complete; next, uses a query-by-forms language to specify the format of the data required from a database query; next, uses advanced features such as macros, functions and style sheets for spreadsheet or word processing software; next, writes applications in a language such as dBase; next, carries out technical design of databases.

Of course, a certain role-player may be located at different points on a dimension under different circumstances; for example, somebody might be very little involved in most development activities within a department, but heavily involved in one particular system.

More Possible Dimensions

An analysis resting on these two fundamental dimensions — *recipient/provider* for existing systems and *development* for new systems

— may seem more than adequate at first glance — especially since, these are dimensions *along which* players can be located, rather than either/or choices. In practice, there are some additional distinctions between role-players that are sometimes useful.

For example, another angle is *management*: a player may have varying degrees of decision-making power or influence about the use of IT. Along the way from 'final say on the organisation's IT policy' through to 'barred from exercising any initiative whatsoever', there could be a midway region containing players with a big role in the various monitoring and organisational functions necessary to keep a system or installation going or to keep a development project coordinated.

Another dimension possibility might be called '*formal involvement*'. At one extreme is the player whose job description entails working full-time on activities that are clearly computer-related (e.g. the manager of a large organisation's data centre); then comes the player who must formally spend some time on activities that are clearly computer-related (e.g. the controller of a small network in a department); much further along is someone who obviously must use computer systems, but only because they are necessary tools for doing the real job (e.g. a typical secretary using a PC for word processing); at the far end is somebody such as a sales manager or personnel manager, where involvement with IT systems is very much a question of taste and style.

Yet another candidate dimension can record a player's *outlook on IT* — interest in the subject, and keenness to try out new possibilities. This dimension may be the only means of differentiating two people classified identically in all other ways — even though one always tries to rely on the computer as little as possible, whereas the other's attitude is to try to exploit all the possibilities technology offers. Such differences in outlook on IT are often found between people with identical IT-related job titles, such as systems manager or information architect.

All these dimensions except the last classify players according to what they actually do, while the last one is more concerned with attitudes. None of these dimensions records *knowledge and experience* — such things as a player's knowledge of IT, years' experience of certain types of IT-related activity, ability to form realistic ideas about the way IT can be applied, talent at performing various types of function and so on.

Each of the dimensions mentioned can add something to the realism of any analysis; if you ignored any one, you might lose something in certain situations. Moreover, given the stimulus of any specific case, some new dimension to expose important distinctions more clearly often suggests itself. On the other hand, a complete theoretical model of the players in an organisation which mapped them all onto (say) a five-dimensional space would surely be overkill in most circumstances. The important thing is to be aware that these and similar possibilities exist, for slicing up the population of role-players in an organisation. Then you are well equipped to decide how to gain the most insight most economically in any specific case.

Practical Application

Why should this kind of analysis of the IT players within an organisation be relevant? And even if it may be relevant, how can the analysis be carried out? These two questions hang together.

Suppose you develop some standard generic model for classifying IT role-players; suppose you then arrange a mass mailing of a standard questionnaire to people throughout the organisation, designed to discover the roles they play, their attitudes, their knowledge, etc. Then you use the results to analyse the population in terms of your standard model; then you draw wider conclusions from the way the resulting model of players in the organisation looks. This procedure is not intrinsically absurd; there are even one or two companies in the computer services industry that will carry out a survey for you along those lines. An article in *Communications of the ACM* suggests one generalised multi-dimensional taxonomy of users.[1]

But applying a generalised approach seems a cumbersome and laborious way of generating coarse findings about a rather subtle matter. It seems more promising to address the specific issues of each situation. First form an impression of the kind of issues likely to be relevant to the case. On the basis of this, decide to what extent an analysis of IT role-players is relevant and which dimensions should be chosen for investigation. Then, do whatever is necessary to perform that analysis. From the results, generate some input that helps resolve the real issues that affect decision-making. This sounds rather abstract; here are a couple of example cases.

Pink Gum Products

Pink Gum Products (PGP) is a medium-sized manufacturer of kitchen equipment, which currently relies for its main computer systems on a bureau service operated by an associated company. It seems plausible that PGP should set up fresh systems of its own with its own computer installation. But adding detail to that very broad judgement isn't so easy.

It is easy to see that nearly everyone in the company is clustered down at the null end of almost every dimension discussed so far. They have been almost exclusively recipients rather than providers; almost nobody has played any active role (even at the specification level) in developing systems, and so on. You don't need a formal survey to establish those obvious features of the situation.

But, of the dimensions already mentioned, the *attitude* dimension turns out to be a very relevant means of insight into the PGP case. In fact, it is so important that a more refined analysis is called for. For each person within the broad body of potential IT players, from managing director through production controller and middle management to everyone in any kind of supervisory role, two questions can be asked. First, how enthusiastic or suspicious is the player towards IT as an important factor in the success of the company? Second, how keen is the player to be personally involved in IT systems? These things can't really be measured by questionnaire or by quantitative scoring; however, once the dimensions have been sketched out, impressionistic assessments can be made.

Looked at this way, PGP displays a classic but dangerous pattern: very low experience of developing systems, generally high enthusiasm for IT to introduce sweeping changes, generally strong desire for somebody else to make the management decisions and do the work and bear the responsibility for the IT systems.

This pattern of attitudes is probably the single most important factor in determining the company's policy towards IT. The last thing the company should do in this situation is to make an inventory of everybody's ideas for using IT and draw up a five-year plan for implementing it all. With the degree of naivety that is prevalent, a few minor setbacks in the early stages could change the prevailing atmosphere into deep suspicion and ruin the whole plan. The wisest is to form a modest strategy based on, say, a two-year horizon; implement systems that are modest but manifestly useful; and expect, if all goes well, to embark on a longer-term strategy, on a more secure footing, thereafter.

Whether or not you find this line of reasoning convincing doesn't really matter to this discussion. The main point is that analysing the characteristics of the people who will generate PGP's demand and supply greatly improves the quality of the debate about the company's IT decisions.

Antarctic Beech Corporation

Antarctic Beech Corporation (ABC) is a conglomerate with a range of interests in entertainment, travel, employment agencies and communications. Many varied opportunities exist for using IT to develop innovative products and services. The challenge is to find a way of managing the innovation.

As part of a general survey of ABC's situation, the following train of thought develops. There are about fifty middle managers in different ABC subsidiaries, who are in key positions for identifying serious possibilities for innovative IT-based products and services. Any one of them could become a 'champion' for a certain project, and power the idea through. In theory, that is.

But contrast alternative possibilities. Suppose this analysis is true in practice as well as in theory; suppose most of these 'Key 50' are in fact skilful enough to spot imaginative but realistic possibilities and energetic enough to carry them through. In that case, the real issues calling for decision now are probably matters related to setting up a decentralised, entrepreneurial environment for IT innovation with the appropriate minimum of coordination and control. But, on the other hand, suppose the 'Key 50' are not really like this at all. Then the strategy issues will look quite different. They probably involve setting up some kind of catalysing, driving-force, innovation-directed unit, as a separate entity.

Therefore, getting a clear view of these 'Key 50', the roles they currently play, the experience they have, their attitudes and their aspirations is vital to clarifying the issues for decision.

Taking the 'Key 50' as a group, a fairly clear profile can be discerned by informal means. Most of these people stand low as recipients and as providers and on formal involvement too. This is understandable because most of ABC's existing systems are administrative in character and most of the 'Key 50' currently play outgoing rather than internal administrative roles. But most of them do stand midway along the development dimension; they are just the kind of people who are included in committees to agree what the detailed functions of any new IT systems should be. Though homogeneous on all these counts, they vary widely on the Outlook dimension, or to be more precise, analysis of the Outlook dimension is too tricky to permit any simple generalisations.

As the next step, a list of topics is drawn up, consisting mainly of technologies that might be relevant to ABC (e.g. expert system, desktop publishing, optical disk, etc.), as well as different types of services (e.g. on-line booking, information provided on PC in a customer's home, knowledge updating service for anyone interested in a certain field, etc.). One way or another, the opinions, awareness and general views of each of the 50 on each of these topics are collected.

This fairly well structured information is a good preparation for going deeper into this area of strategy. Quite how ABC finally resolves matters is not relevant here. The point is that analysis of ABC's 'Key 50' provides the starting point for realistic discussions.

Supply and Demand Implications

What insight do the PGP and ABC cases provide on the logic of IT decision-making in general? The intermingling of roles which now makes it necessary to analyse players rather carefully is just another instance on a different plane of the rich *interaction between supply and demand* discussed in many of the other briefings.

One area affected is standardised methods for planning and decision-making. It is relatively easy to devise a standard method that implicitly assumes that 'users' define 'requirements' and technical people carry them out; but that kind of standard method is unlikely to do justice to many cases today. Once you acknowledge that different people play a whole variety of different roles and that the nature of 'requirements' may be strongly affected by the nature of the person expressing them, then you are practically forced to approach each case according to its specific features.

Treating 'demand' as simply 'whatever may be demanded' is often a dangerous over-simplification. One important input to strategic decisions is an appreciation of the degree to which 'whatever may be demanded' is likely to be based on a realistic appreciation by the players of the supply–demand possibilities. That will depend, in part, on the players' roles in using IT supply factors themselves, their attitudes towards their experiences with the technology, and so on. In other words, this is another illustration of the complexity of interaction between supply and demand.

PRACTICAL ADVICE

➤ Discard the simple, old distinction between users generating demands for systems and computer people supplying the systems demanded. Distinctions today are far more complex; also the most relevant distinctions vary from organisation to organisation.

➤ Decide for yourself the right distinctions for your specific strategy case; that can be a big help towards understanding its interactions between supply and demand.

➤ Consider plotting role-players along the dimension that runs from the providers of information through to its recipients.

➤ Use another dimension to show the relative degree of involvement in the development of new information-producing systems.

➤ Keep in mind that other dimensions for plotting role-players may be more useful; one possibility is management authority; another is formal involvement; another is outlook on IT.

➤ Make a rough, general analysis of roles and attitudes throughout the organisation, if that will lead to useful insight into the interaction between supply and demand.

➤ Home in on certain key classes of people if their roles and attitudes are seminal to the issues of the situation.

➤ Don't assume that any of these classification approaches is the most appropriate to your own strategy case. Be ready to innovate to get the clearest understanding of the essential features of the situation.

6.   Coping with Technology Uncertainty

ISSUES

Everyone knows that technology is constantly advancing, prices are falling and new possibilities becoming feasible. This characteristic of IT surely can't be ignored; it ought to affect strategy decisions. But how exactly?

If you accept that a strategy decision about IT ought to take some account of future technology change, aren't you forced into making rash forecasts about the future — even though the forecasts of even the greatest authorities in the industry frequently turn out to be wrong? And, since you are obliged to rely on technical specialists to make the forecasts, won't important decisions be taken by people who, by their avocation, are out of touch with wider non-technical issues?

In tackling these concerns, one useful distinction is a good starting point. To understand the way a certain phenomenon works and the way it affects other factors is one thing; to make forecasts about it in specific cases is something else. An economist might reasonably have little interest in forecasting inflation rates in particular economies; he might be primarily interested in, say, trade policy. But he still needs an understanding of the phenomenon of inflation; he needs to grasp how it interacts with trade tariffs and money supply and so on.

Similarly, it is important in IT decision-making to be aware of the *nature* of technology change and to understand the way this factor typically interacts with other factors in the whole problem. It is perfectly possible to achieve this degree of insight, even if you have neither the time nor the knowledge to become an authority on any particular technologies. This may seem a bold claim. The aim of this briefing is to make it good.

ANALYSIS

A good start is to recognise some of the typical features of cases where judgements about uncertain technology developments plainly must affect a strategy decision. After that, tentative steps towards a way of resolving such cases soon lead to an insight into the reasons that technology forecasting is so tough. This in turn produces a more acute awareness of the place of this factor in strategy decisions.

Three Cases Where Technology Uncertainty Matters

Not every strategy decision need be affected by uncertainty about price/performance trends. For example, if a certain project is considered to be amply justified at present price levels and the doubt is how great the future improvement in price/performance will be, there is no point in agonising further and holding the project back. However, this still leaves many cases where IT strategy decisions are unavoidably affected by the problem of technology uncertainty. Here are three representative cases.

First, plans have been made for a certain project; the technology to be used is not in doubt and its costs will be spread over a number of years; they include, say, the rental and maintenance of certain minicomputer hardware. On an optimistic but not preposterous forecast of price trends for this technology, the project is very attractive, but on a pessimistic but also not preposterous forecast, the project is quite unattractive. Plainly any decision has to be based on a forecast of the way technology prices will move.

In the second representative case, too, the technology to be used is not an issue, but the whole investment will be made over a fairly short period. The problem is *when* to make the investment. For example, the managers of a company believe they must replace all their old-fashioned word processing equipment by PCs, but there is no one deadline by which this must happen. Since PC prices seem to be constantly falling, the temptation is to keep on waiting for prices to fall ever further.

The third case is trickier because there are alternative technologies possible for a certain system. The choice is, say, between alternative ways of storing a large quantity of documents — either by *imaging*, storing the facsimiles of document pages on special high-capacity disks; or by *text retrieval*, storing the text contained in the pages on normal disks, with sophisticated search facilities. Neither is currently a mainstream technology. If you could know that one or the other would become much better established within a few years, this could be a strong argument in favour of adopting it — because of the price/performance improvements and other advantages that would very likely follow.

Clearly, in each of these three representative cases, a rational decision has to make some assumptions about future technology change. The logic of the situation makes this inescapable. Such cases provide fresh lines of argument against the crude demand-driving approach to IT decisions. Anyone who operates by first firming up detailed non-technical demands and only then going on to consider how they are best supplied technically is unlikely to do justice to the content of these cases.

Appreciating that the *interactions* between demand and supply need to be studied is a good start. It escapes from a certain handicap, but what more specific approach to the problem is feasible?

Some Figures

If you are forced to take a view of the future price movements of some commodity, one obvious move is to find some published statistics about its past price movements and published forecasts about its future trends. This might be supported by more narrowly focused personal research into price movements, and by published indexes and forecasts of more general factors. These figures need not be accepted or extrapolated blindly, but at least they are a useful starting point for developing assumptions. How feasible is this approach in IT?

An article in the December 1990 issue of *Byte*, quoting from a book by Raymond Kurzweil, states that computer performance per unit cost has been doubling every 22 months, an improvement factor of 2000 in 20 years.[1]

PC Magazine reports that the average price of 256-kilobit RAM chips fell from $12.13 in July 1988 to $1.25 in December 1990; the price of 1-megabyte 100-nanosecond SIMM packs fell from $592.50 to $51 in the same period.[2] You don't need to be well up on RAM chips and SIMM packs to see that these are spectacular price changes. Of course, the prices of such items fluctuate, but any detailed research is likely to show an overall trend in line with the dramatic progress implied by the more general figures quoted in *Byte*.

Dell is one of the largest suppliers of IBM-standard PCs. Here are some notes comparing its advertised prices, at two moments, March 1987 and March 1991.[3] Ignoring certain configurations as too primitive, in March 1987 the *main low-price PC* available from Dell cost $1795. Four years later, the cheapest system in Dell's pricelist cost $1549; as well as being cheaper, it had a more powerful processor, the 286/12, and was superior in a few other technical ways. Computers with that 286/12 processor had also been available in 1987, but Dell's cheapest cost $3095.

In 1987, Dell's *most luxurious model*, also using the 286/12 processor, with 40Mb of disk and a colour screen, cost $3695. In 1991, you could buy a machine with 40Mb of disk and a superior colour screen and a more powerful processor still, for about 40% less — $2099. If $3695 was your limit in 1991, you could buy a much better computer (much more powerful processor, more disk storage, etc.) for that price. But if you chose the most expensive model of all in the pricelist that was now $10,499.

Certainly comparison of the 1987 and 1991 Dell prices shows impressive improvements in value for money. But they don't show that computer performance per unit cost has been doubling every 22 months; Dell's PC prices have not been falling at that dramatic rate.

This apparent discrepancy is easily explained. SIMMs and the like are components, while PCs are finished products. Plainly the prices of components and finished products change at different rates: the dramatic figures quoted in *Byte* apply to raw computer performance per unit cost (in the sense of factors such as dollars per RAM-chip-kilobyte), but this in itself doesn't say anything about the changes in price of complete PCs.

Three Types of Price Changes

For most IT strategy decisions, the price of any raw technology factor is not directly relevant. It is perfectly possible to take good strategy decisions about IT without knowing what a SIMM pack even is, let alone forecasting its price movements. The most important thing to know about the dramatic statistics on raw computer performance is that you don't need to know them. They won't help you make better decisions about how to use IT effectively in an organisation.

This distinction between raw technology and finished products is often useful; published statistics often blur it confusingly. For example, the statistics quoted in *Byte* (that computer performance per unit cost has enjoyed an improvement factor of 2000 in 20 years) are accompanied by the comment that if Detroit had done as well, the typical auto would cost two dollars. But, on examination, this statement amounts to reasoning along the lines of: 'If the price movements of *finished products* in the *auto* industry had matched the price movements of *raw technology* in the *IT* industry . . .' Expressed this way, the comparison is revealed as pointless.

The Dell figures illustrate another aspect of the subtle relationship between raw technology and finished product prices. The assumption was slipped in above that the 1987 $1795 model was the minimum worthwhile personal computer available. After all, who would want to buy a cheaper PC without any hard disk storage at all? But this is actually a 1991 assumption. Back in 1987, Dell were selling many less powerful models, primitive by the standards of 1991, that were quite a lot cheaper than $1795. The $1795 model of 1987 was mid-range, whereas the $1549 model of 1990 was the cheapest on offer in a pricelist stretching up to the $10,000 mark.

Although PCs become better value for money, the price of the average PC bought from the dealer may not go down at all. Improved value for money often leads to people being prepared to pay the same or even a little more in order to get a great deal more. This factor is summed up neatly by the saying that the personal computer that you really want is always priced at $5,000 (or some other constant number, depending how naturally greedy you are). In other words, the computer you want today costs $5,000, but it may be substantially cheaper next year; however, by then, a new model, incorporating advances in screen technology or disk storage or some other factor, will be on the market at about $5,000.

There is another important distinction, albeit a less likely source of confusion. Trends in *IT hardware costs* are not the whole story. The costs of employing the specialists who design and build application systems and look after them in operation certainly don't decline by orders of magnitude. On the whole, these costs have increased over the years.

In its Christmas 1990 edition *The Economist* compared the price changes in a selection of goods and services in Britain over the twentieth century — not including any IT items.[4] These led to some plausible generalisations about price movements.

When a technology-based product or service remains essentially unchanged (e.g. getting from London to Nairobi by air or, on the above figures, providing RAM memory), there is a spectacular fall in price. When a technology product becomes much more sophisticated (e.g. a camera or a PC) prices tend to remain stable. Services based on labour rather than technology (e.g. a three-course dinner or the work of a database administrator) just rise and rise.

What Is To Be Done?

Statistics about price changes in raw technology won't help in resolving the three representative cases for decision at the beginning, because they don't provide any clear basis for assumptions about the future of finished products such as minicomputers, PCs and imaging. But why not simply ignore the raw technology figures given in books and magazines and consult statistics about IT finished products instead?

The trouble is that far fewer useful statistics about the prices of IT finished products are researched and published, and the Dell figures suggest why. Even if copious data about past prices is collated, imposing order on it and quantifying trends may be a tough job — because straightforward changes in price/performance are mixed up with qualitative improvements and changes in customer expectations. The problem is similar to quantifying the changes of prices in technology-based consumer products like cameras.

Since making sense of the past is so hard, the idea of extrapolating future price changes in any methodical way seems very unpromising. But if that is so, there seems little alternative to relying on the unsubstantiated forecasts of individual technology specialists. But, in many organisations, asking technology specialists for forecasts on the future of imaging, say, may be as hazardous as consulting a rather unhelpful oracle. It may be hard to verify the validity of the answer received, or to establish the assumptions it rests on, or to discuss the implications that follow from it, or even to be sure that the right question was asked and understood. Having to consult an oracle may be a serious handicap in rational decision-making.

But price changes in IT finished products derive from improvements in raw technology and from other factors in extremely complex ways; that is why formal extrapolation of price trends is rarely effective. There is often no alternative to relying on the oracular hunches of specialists. The principles suggested in the rest of the briefing can't eliminate the oracle problem; their purpose is to make it more manageable.

Decision-making Logic

Other things being equal, it seems better to have a plan whose logic rests on two forecasts (that may be wrong or misunderstood or unsatisfactory in some other way) than a plan dependent on five that are just as vulnerable. It seems good practice to minimise the number of occasions that an oracle needs to be consulted.

First of all, if taking a certain decision inevitably entails making a hazardous forecast about technology, check if the decision can be put off, without adverse effect; if it can, then put it off.

But very often there is something to lose by delay; in the first of the three representative cases, for example, presumably attractive financial benefits are expected to come from the new system. If there is a price to be paid for delaying a decision, the next question is: Is the price a bargain? It could be — if the time bought is likely to lead to a far better decision. For example, perhaps the technology concerned is currently in an exceptional state of flux, so that now seems the worst possible time to make long-term forecasts. That might be plausible in the case of imaging.

But with minicomputers, for example, it would probably be difficult to use that argument. Here, if delaying a decision brings adverse effects, there may be no rational alternative to grasping the nettle and making the forecast.

With this style of approach, the issues raised with the oracular technologist have become more subtle. As well as asking questions of the type: 'What is your best-guess forecast of the future of imaging technology?', you are asking questions of the type: 'Is imaging technology now in a state of extreme flux and uncertainty, compared to, say, two years ago or two years hence?' Very often it is easier to have rational, relatively non-technical discussions about this second type of question.

This approach can reduce the number of times you have to take a firm decision on the basis of an oracular judgement. A second principle can help demystify technology forecasts and make them seem less oracular.

Great uncertainty is not restricted to the supply side of a decision. Fallible assumptions of varying degrees of uncertainty are usually made about many other factors affecting a project or an overall strategy: about the attainment of the projected labour-savings or the increased market share, about inflation in the national economy, about the actions of competitors and so on. To act as if all the demand-side planning for a project is based on indubitable certainties which will then be at the mercy of oracular judgements on the supply-side is not reasonable.

Sometimes the force of this point can affect the whole structure of the problem. Suppose some people in the organisation judge by a tiny margin that, despite the many market uncertainties, now is the right time to invest in a new service to customers based on use of IT; they formulate the appropriate demands. A separate group meets to consider these demands from a supply point of view; they judge that there are many awkward technology uncertainties, though if it is inescapable, they can make some very tenuous assumptions about technology change. In these circumstances, the organisation will probably make a more rational decision if all the uncertainty factors, whether supply- or demand-side, are considered together in one decision-making process. It may be that, taken together, there are just too many uncertainties for it to be sensible to go ahead, or perhaps the effect of some of the demand uncertainties is to make some of the technology supply uncertainties irrelevant; any number of possibilities exist.

In any event, technology forecasts should not be given a special status, rendering them necessarily more mysterious than forecasts about non-technical uncertainties.

The Phenomenon of Lift-off

If you need to ask a technology oracle whether a particular IT end-product is in a state of exceptional flux and uncertainty, an awareness of the phenomenon of 'lift-off' is a valuable preparation. Then you can pose more searching questions and appraise the answers more critically.

When introduced in the mid-'eighties, the laser printer was much more expensive than established dot matrix and daisy wheel printers, and many people originally expected its use to be restricted to specialised applications. Nevertheless by 1986 the laser printer was already selling well for general office use to wide-awake organisations who saw the benefits of its speed, quietness, print quality and page formatting possibilities. By 1991, it was a dull organisation that hadn't already switched to a laser (or closely related) printer. Daisy wheel printers were already relics of the past and it was hard to find any justification for buying a new dot matrix printer.

In other words, the second half of the 'eighties saw a 'lift-off' in laser printer technology: the end-products became ever more sophisticated and better value for money; rival technologies were driven out; turnover grew explosively; numerous companies entered the market; a healthy variety of product was offered. A technology that a decision-maker could regard as esoteric at one moment had become the norm just a few years later.

In late 1986 the Ventura Publisher software product was released; it was the first commercially successful software product for page makeup to run on the IBM-standard PC. In combination with a laser printer, Ventura could produce documents that would previously have had to be typeset. During 1986 and 1987 magazine articles on page makeup software packages described an incredible miscellany of other software products, with all kinds of approaches, functions, strengths and weaknesses and a vast range of prices. At that time it was clear that some kind of lift-off was in progress, but the picture was very confused.

By 1990 things had settled down. The main page makeup software products all had sophisticated features, offering formidable competition to any potential rivals. It seemed clear that this kind of software was established quite healthily in its own niche, but that it wouldn't become a mainstream item, like database or spreadsheet or the laser printer. The lift-off had been of only moderate force. The differences in the history of the lift-offs of laser printers and page makeup software could be analysed in detail, but the main point is the fact that they were considerably different.

Lift-off tends to be a concept more relevant to finished products than to raw technology. In fact, lift-off typically occurs when progress in several different raw technologies occurs in some favourable combination that makes some new species of finished product viable. This is one of the main reasons that price movements in finished products and raw technology follow different patterns.

Imagine sending a roll of ordinary camera film to a lab which returns the images stored on compact disc, rather than (or as well as) in the form of prints. The images can then be read from the compact disc and viewed on the screen of a personal computer. Progress in various technologies, such as optical storage media, colour scanning, colour screen display and image compression, has already reached the point where the idea is at least plausible. In November 1990 Kodak announced such a service, planned to begin in 1992.

If the idea lifts off, costs will come tumbling down and an important new technology possibility will be available. There could be big implications for any publishing systems concerned with colour images, but it could also lead to the use of colour photos in many general business applications, as well as to new developments in the consumer products market. But it may not lift off. Perhaps the concept won't be a big enough hit for the price to be kept low enough to support the idea. It may just fizzle out.

There have been examples in the past of technologies where lift-off seemed to many people to be assured, and yet it didn't happen. For instance a book published in 1979 was boldly entitled *The Viewdata Revolution*.[5] On the first page viewdata (also known as videotex) was said to be a new medium of comparable significance to print, radio and television and a technology to be ranked with the steam engine and the internal combustion engine. Hardly anybody would make such claims today. Viewdata just didn't lift off.

The Significance of Lift-off

Clearly there is a close relation between 'lift-off' and the general concept of a technology being in a state of flux. Talking in terms of lift-off enables you to pose rather more specific questions to a technology oracle: Are you saying that this technology is just about to lift off? Are you saying that this technology has had a lift-off, which is almost spent? And so on.

The three representative cases at the beginning can all be discussed more clearly by using the lift-off concept. In the first, it might be judged, lift-off need not be an issue, because the minicomputer is a mature technology; therefore a sober costs projection should be possible. In the second case, a lift-off has clearly occurred in the case of PCs, and a judgement must be made on whether it will continue. The third case is the most interesting, because the question is whether either technology — imaging or text retrieval — will go into a lift-off and, if both do, which lift-off will develop more favourably.

This indicates two rather distinct strands to this problem of technology change. On the one hand, there is the general tendency of the broad mass of technology to become better value for money. On the other hand there is the phenomenon of the lift-off, that rapidly makes a whole new category of technology viable.

If the lift-off phenomenon didn't exist, many IT decisions would be much easier. You would know that the technology supply factors identified by competent professionals were likely to remain the right ones to meet the demands of the systems; any costing projections should be fairly safe from dramatic developments in the technology marketplace. The lift-off phenomenon places this in jeopardy.

The example of Murray Pine shows how the phenomenon of lift-off can affect the whole logic of the approach to a strategy decision.

A Lift-off Problem at Murray Pine

At the beginning of 1985, everyone in the Murray Pine Organisation, the large publishers, agrees that it is time to stop using old-fashioned word processing equipment and switch over to PC-based technology. An analyst surveys people's requirements, to select a word processing software product as the standard throughout the organisation. In most of the operating units, things go fairly smoothly but in one department there is a surprising reaction.

This department publishes low-circulation, high-subscription newsletters on specialised topics such as sewage engineering and Thai antiques. Its manager has the vision to argue that his people need more than the normal word processing software product. They want to prepare and format their newsletters on their own PCs. The ideal system has to handle the hyphenation and pagination of the text in various subtle ways, allow the use of very large letter sizes for titles and headings, allow a mixture of two- and three-column text on the same page, integrate diagrams and graphics into the page makeup; and so on. Such a system would be far more convenient than the present arrangements with an external typesetter.

In fact, without knowing it, the people in this department are describing the demands that are about to be met by a certain technology — page makeup software — that in 1985 is on the verge of lift-off. You might argue that the technology experts in a publishing company really ought to be well aware that this lift-off is imminent. In that case, assume it all happens in 1984 or 1983; the point of the case is to explore the issues raised by uncertainty about lift-off.

The analyst might respond to the unexpected demand in a variety of ways. *Possible Response 1*, if the analyst is a demand-side extremist, might be: 'There is no software product available performing the functions you describe. But requirements are requirements. My job is to serve you, the user. We'll make a plan to write all the necessary software. It will take a while and cost several hundred thousand pounds.'

Possible Response 2 is: 'What you suggest could only be cost-effective if there were a mass-market software product for PC, performing the functions you describe. Well, there isn't right now and there may never be, but the idea is not unthinkable. We could discuss the matter again in, say, eighteen months.'

Possible Response 3 is: 'I forecast there will be a suitable software product released in about 1986. Let's plan on that basis.'

Possible Response 4 is: 'There is no suitable software product available and there probably won't be within any reasonable timeframe. Let's try and work out some less ambitious approach, to give you part of what you want, perhaps combining a word processing software product with some software we write ourselves.

Possible Response 5 is: 'I forecast that your need will gradually be met as the established word processing software products develop organically in that direction; by about 1989, Microsoft Word will probably do about three-quarters of what you've described. Let's plan on that basis.'

Possible Response 6 is: 'We shouldn't waste our time discussing page makeup software. There is a big new technology just about to lift off; it's called hypertext. It will drive printer manufacturers out of business. You don't need to print your newsletters on paper any more; just send the information out to customers on diskette using hypertext storage techniques. That's what we should be planning now.'

The lift-off phenomenon makes it very easy for quite sensible people to take steps in completely the wrong direction. Possible Response 1 is just a caricature to show the disastrous consequences of ignoring the issue of technology change. Possible Response 2 (seen in retrospect, of course) the correct answer. Possible Response 3 produces a satisfactory outcome, but only by making outrageously bold assumptions. Possible Response 4 follows the right logic in considering the problem; unfortunately wrong assumptions are fed into the logic, producing a wrong answer (in retrospect). Possible Response 5 also arrives at the wrong answer; it probably deserves lower marks than Possible Response 4, since it doesn't even consider the possibility that a lift-off might occur — at least Response 4 considers and rejects the idea. Possible Response 6 is grotesquely wrong (in retrospect); this response is too obsessed with the lift-off concept.

Supply–Demand Implications

The analysis in this briefing of the technology uncertainty factor helps to show that the model of defining a set of demands and asking technologists to work out the details of the appropriate technology for supplying them is inadequate.

First, even though there may be one obvious, undisputed technology choice (e.g. minicomputer or word processing on PC), judgements about its future progress may still need to be made in order to make a rational decision about the viability of meeting the demands.

Second, it may not be adequate simply to make judgements of the form 'My best guess is that this technology will be 10% cheaper in two years' time'. It may be essential to make judgements one stage removed, to weigh up the costs of not deciding now against the possible benefits of waiting till things are clearer. This involves making judgements about lift-off developments. In other words, examination of the supply-side may generate the feedback that now is not the right time to commit to meeting the demands.

Third, when alternative feasible technologies exist, e.g. imaging or text retrieval, or when no established technology exists, e.g. page makeup before 1985, the decision logic becomes a good deal more complex. Lift-off judgements are unavoidable. Moreover, two alternative technologies are unlikely to be fully interchangeable ways of doing exactly the same thing; one will make certain demands easier to fulfil than others, one may redefine demands in subtle ways and so on; such factors also need to be assessed together with the uncertainties.

Once any appreciable degree of uncertainty about technology change exists, the walls between the compartments of demand-planning and supply-planning begin (or at least should begin) to crumble. Decisions should be structured to provide a broad view of both the likely demand and the likely supply factors very early on. Then you can take a view of the status of the supply factors; for example, you may judge some to be rather straightforward, established technology; others may call for technology so wayout that as to be pioneering work, unlikely to experience a real lift-off for some time yet; others may be in the middle of a lift-off with unpredictable scope; of others you may have a very strong hunch that a lift-off is coming; in other cases . . . A predefined framework of categories isn't necessary; the important thing, however achieved, is to analyse the supply factors in lift-off terms.

Having formed the necessary judgements, of course, the last thing to do is carefully to build a complicated strategy on the presumption that all the judgements will turn out perfectly correct. The task is normally to take decisions that maximise benefit, while minimising vulnerability to the possible uncertainties.

PRACTICAL ADVICE

➤ Recognise that, although technology seems to get much cheaper and more powerful every year, the nature of change is far more complex than it appears at first sight. Therefore avoid making simple assumptions about uniform progress.

➤ Be aware of a few general phenomena: hardware drops dramatically in price per unit of raw performance; but for a variety of complex reasons, this doesn't lead to corresponding reductions in the prices of finished products; labour-based costs such as technical expertise rise.

➤ Accept that you have to make some assumptions, but admit that they are vulnerable; therefore structure decision-making to minimise the need for the assumptions and to mitigate the consequences if they turn out wrong.

➤ Don't turn over your demands to a supply-side technologist, who is allowed to decide the right supply factors, by making private assumptions or oracular pronouncements about about technology trends. Get these assumptions out in the open to rank as major uncertainty factors along with any less technical uncertainties.

➤ Try to avoid making a decision that rests heavily on assumptions about the future development of a certain technology as supply factor, if it is currently in a state of flux.

➤ Concentrate on the strategy problems associated with the 'Lift-off' phenomenon, where a certain technology goes into a process of rapid development fed by exploding increase in demand. Those are the cases that can significantly impact the validity of an IT strategy.

➤ Temper the 'demand-then-supply' approach, by allowing assessments of technology uncertainty to generate feedback that influences other factors in the decision.

7.   Supply–Demand: Links and Snags

ISSUES

The natural way to develop IT strategy, it may plausibly appear, is to start out from very general business factors (e.g. 'We want to be the biggest in our industry') and pass through a succession of clearly demarcated levels, containing decisions such as 'IT spending must be doubled' and 'Information should be held mainly at the branches' and 'We will use a client–server database architecture'.

In this model of decision-making, there is a progression from the general to the specific, from the summarised to the detailed and from less technical factors to more technical factors. Each piece of work done and each decision taken forms a link in a chain: it *supplies* the demand expressed by previous work and *defines the demand* to be supplied by the work that follows.

The approach is attractive because it seems to promise long-term plans for the use of IT that will really meet the business needs of the organisation. Even the very detailed plans for new systems that emerge at the end of the process can be shown to be the logical outcome of a chain of reasoning that begins with general statements about the aims of the organisation.

Many methodologies marketed as generalised solutions to the problems of IT strategy rest on this logic of the *demand–supply chain*. Two methodologies may differ in their details: one has five main planning stages, the other seven; one says 'strategy' where the other says 'policy'; one uses diagrams with certain conventions to model the relation between data and processing, the other uses different diagrams; and so on. But such differences are trivial if both are implicitly based on the same view of the logic of IT decision-making. Similar logic is often applied in organisations with their own procedures that don't follow any proprietary methodology.

The idea of planning in levels that form a demand–supply chain seems so plausible that it can easily be taken much too far. The trouble is that the *interactions* between supply and demand and the *tradeoff* between commitment and flexibility may be more intricate than the analogy of links in a chain suggests. If interactions and tradeoffs are treated too crudely, unrealistic decisions invariably result. This briefing shows what this rather abstract criticism means in practice, by revealing some possible snags in the chain.

ANALYSIS

The members of the thinktank at Candlebark Insurance are resolved to take a fresh look at the issues of IT strategy. As part of this enterprise, they feel they ought to take note of some standardised approaches offered by consultancies and software houses.

After studying the documentation of several methodologies, the Candlebark people begin to realise what vague and insubstantial things words and concepts can be. One methodology's 'enterprise infrastructure definition' seems to be much the same as another's 'business policy framework'; and the 'strategic data architecture' in one place is probably much the same as the 'information management blueprint' somewhere else. When you look to see how any one of these terms is defined, you only come across a new set of abstract nouns. In some cases, the whole construction of the methodology seems to be a network of verbal abstractions. Of course, there are diagrams, with their boxes and arrows showing how all the abstractions fit together. But if the diagram of one methodology shows a different patterning of abstractions from the diagram of another methodology, does that really have any significance? Who can tell?

The first priority must be to find a general tool for demystifying methodologies. That is a prerequisite of judging how well any specific methodology can handle the problems of IT decision-making.

DSC — the Representative Methodology

One of the Candlebark thinktank believes he has distilled the essence of a certain representative methodology. Here is his summary of the way the eight levels of the DSC methodology might develop at Candlebark.

At *Level 1*, the top decision level, discussions with the Board result in strategic aims such as 'Be the most profitable European insurance company within five years.' This aim is reinforced with the principal means of making Candlebark the most profitable European insurance company; for example: cut administration costs, offer new types of insurance policy and become more customer-oriented.

At *Level 2* the principal strategic means are expanded in various ways relevant to the use of IT. For example, just expanding the aim to be more customer-oriented, one idea adopted may be to have a head office department of elite people, who coordinate the insurance requirements of multi-national companies with policies in many countries. Perhaps such a department is only feasible if it has sophisticated computer systems in support, and perhaps this has become technologically feasible and economically viable only recently. Thus, during the work of Level 2, the general concepts of a new IT-supported, Global Clients service and department are outlined.

At *Level 3*, together with much else, the details of the operations of the Global Clients department and its information needs are fleshed out — albeit still in technology-independent form. This work produces a model, expressed in terms non-technical managers can understand and approve, of the information and functions that the new department will need to operate the service. The material on Global Clients is, of course, only a small part of the definition of all the other information and functionality needed by the Candlebark organisation.

At *Level 4* the main characteristics of Global Clients information needs and systems (along with those of the rest of the company) are defined in much more rigorous and well disciplined terms. The documentation produced at this level is still non-technical but it provides a very clear definition of the facilities that the technology will have to support. Moreover it shows how the requirements of all the departments (including Global Clients) fit together in one common structure.

At *Level 5* the main characteristics of the information needs of Global Clients are defined from a technology point of view. This material is collated with equivalent material about other parts of the organisation in one coherent structure, and fundamental decisions are taken about the technology needed to achieve all the non-technical targets set up by Level 4. For example, it may be decided there should be one main data centre and also a minicomputer installation at head office and each of the branches. Plans for national and international telecommunications networks are outlined.

At *Level 6* the technology is worked out in more detail; individual systems and sub-systems, databases and sub-databases, and telecommunications interactions are all clearly identified. The Global Clients system, for example, may be sharing the minicomputer at head office and part of a database with certain other systems. The Level 6 product defines the final scenario that Candlebark will work towards over the next few years.

Level 7 is concerned with documenting the present state of affairs in Candlebark's systems and technology — the starting point from which the Level 6 scenario will have to be reached. Global Clients is a new system, but in the case of other systems, the status of existing systems and technology arrangements are recorded.

At *Level 8* the technology scenario described in Level 6 is compared with the details of the present situation, described in Level 7, while taking account of any wider non-technical factors from previous levels. A master plan is worked out for getting from here to there in phases and sub-phases. The plan may show, for example, that the Global Clients development project will begin in year 2 and that the system will become operational in year 3.

That is the endpoint of the DSC strategy methodology. The activities of development projects, such as Global Clients, that are contained in the masterplan, are considered project rather than strategy work.

DSC's Demystification Diagram

This description can be summarised in a diagram that helps to demystify the methodology. It shows the essential eight levels of the DSC structure, and distinguishes four aspects — four types of things that are the subject of discussion and planning: demand present and demand future and supply present and supply future.

Demand covers all the non-technical facilities and functions and characteristics required from IT systems, while *supply* covers the technological resources, such as computer hardware, telecommunications networks and software that support the information systems demanded. *Present* and *future* are shorthand for 'how things actually are at the moment' and 'how we'd like things to be eventually'. This distinction is difficult to maintain at levels 1 and 2. If you just look at the Global Clients portion of Candlebark total strategy, then these levels are all demand future — because the department and its systems don't exist yet. But other aspects may well be the same in the present and in the future; for example the network of branch offices or the procedures for no-claim-discounts on motor policies.

The two sorts of arrow in this diagram convey an important distinction. The main characteristic of the DSC structure is that you normally move from one level to another by *translation*. The product of one level is *translated* into another form to become the product of the next level down. It is characteristic of translation that one main input to the process leads to one main output. Also, the output is bounded by the input; in other words, the person working on the output is restricted by the content of the input that is provided. In the DSC methodology, that is true of the progress between the first six levels — hence the *translation* arrow.

But the process at Level 8 is rather different. Here there are *four* different inputs, not one. For contrast with translation, this type of work can be called *puzzle-solving*, though that doesn't mean that it is trivial. The task is to accept all the four inputs as given and to solve the puzzle of reconciling them as well as possible; in other words to find the best practical plan to get from the 'demand and supply present' to the 'demand and supply future'. This is analogous to a task in metallurgy where the

Demand-Supply Chain

A Common Approach to IT Planning

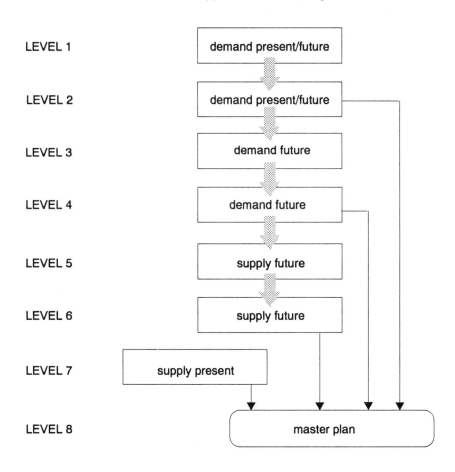

LEVEL 1	demand present/future
LEVEL 2	demand present/future
LEVEL 3	demand future
LEVEL 4	demand future
LEVEL 5	supply future
LEVEL 6	supply future
LEVEL 7	supply present
LEVEL 8	master plan

SYMBOLS USED

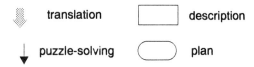

translation   description

puzzle-solving   plan

starting point is technical information about the characteristics of four different metals, plus a definition of the properties required for some alloy (in terms of strength, weight, brittleness, etc.), and the challenge is to find the best way of combining the metals to arrive at the desired alloy. Thus puzzle-solving amounts to a rather different kind of activity from translation.

The different-shaped document boxes in the diagram reinforce the distinction between translation and puzzle-solving. The document generated at Levels 1 to 7 is a *description* of a state of affairs — present or future, demand or supply. But the Level 8 document is a different thing entirely: it is a *plan* recording many different activities occurring at many different times — not a description of one state of affairs at one time.

A General Tool for Demystifying Methodologies

The DSC methodology just described doesn't literally exist. It is an artificial generic approach, intended to be representative of many actual standard methodologies.

Candlebark finds that the majority of standard methodologies for IT strategy can be *demystified* by reducing them to a diagram using these conventions — probably not with exactly eight levels, but that isn't the essential point. The concepts contained in the diagram are what count: the *four aspects* — demand present, demand future, supply present and supply future; the mode of *progress between levels* as either translation or puzzle-solving; the *two types of document* — description or plan. If any methodology's documentation is too opaque for these distinctions to be drawn, asking the salesman how the specific example of the Global Clients service would fare should do the trick.

When this tool is used to compare the different methodologies available, the differences usually lie in the relative stress given to the *present* and *future* aspects. The DSC, as described, is relatively future-driven. Some other approaches devote much less attention to the distinction between present and future demand, because they assume that most of the present, non-technical, characteristics of the organisation will prevail in the future too.

Although the emphasis may vary from case to case, most methodologies can still be represented fairly by a diagram which uses these conventions. They rarely propose anything other than translation or puzzle-solving as the mode of progress between levels.

The artificial generic approach just described is called DSC for demand–supply chain. Its whole structure is a natural development of the idea of distinguishing demand (non-technical needs) from supply (technicalities of meeting the needs). As the diagram shows, taking the body of planning as a whole, decisions about demand (Levels 1, 2, 3 and 4) can be distinguished from decisions about supply (Levels 5, 6 and 7). But looked at more closely, the work at each level can be seen as a link in a demand–supply chain. Level 3 (say) *supplies* the demand expressed by Level 2, in the sense that it works out more practical and detailed plans for achieving the objectives set at the previous level. Similarly, Level 3 sets the *demands* for Level 4 to supply.

Thus an elaborate planning exercise based on such a multi-level approach can be seen as the natural expression of the plausible concepts of distinguishing demand from supply and translating one into the other. What then can be wrong with it?

Two Types of Issues with the Approach

The people in the thinktank at Candlebark are a feisty group, who have seen decision-making in a variety of situations. They can envisage many difficulties with the idea of basing an approach entirely on the logic of a chain of demand and supply. Their leader soon has to impose some order on the discussions. He reasons that there are two broad categories of issues worth discussing.

There are what might be called *structural issues*; for example, what happens if you arrive at (say) Level 6 and suspect a foolish decision was made at (say) Level 3? The role of feedback and the definition of 'top-down' are typical issues here. Then there is a separate category of *specific issues*; for example, suppose your plans are extremely vulnerable to external factors that you can't control, or suppose it is impossible to make any credible plan at all at Level 8.

The leader of the thinktank rules that structural issues can be left for another occasion, because there are quite enough interesting specific issues to discuss; moreover they are the ones that illustrate the delicate *interaction* between supply and demand most vividly.

Good and Bad Application

The first point is not a devastating objection, more an observation: such a planning model may be applied well or applied badly, and applying it well can be quite a challenge.

For example, in the early levels, business aspirations such as 'Become one of the world's great companies' are too vague to be of any use as a basis for action. 'Be the most profitable European insurance company within five years' is better; it includes a measurable quantity (five years) and it states (or at least, implies) that profit is more important than turnover. But ideally the Candlebark board ought to define what they really mean by 'profitable'. (In absolute terms? Earnings per share? Under-writing profit? What about life assurance, where most of the profit belongs to the policy-holders?) And how should 'European' be defined? The more you examine it, the harder the objective is to pin down.

Conversely, you can also go wrong by becoming too precise. To take a classic example from a different industry, 'Improve safety in the manufacturing process' is too vague, but 'Ensure there are no accidents at all in the next ten years', though a laudable aspiration and clearly quantified, is just too naive.

There is another generic opportunity for going wrong. When Candlebark is expanding the material of one level into the detail of the next level down, there is a big temptation to choose all the toys in the shop window. For example, when discussing how to become the most profitable European insurance company, a planning committee might decide that the company needs a radical programme to cut administration costs *and* the development of many new types of insurance policy *and* a major drive to become more customer-oriented *and* a tremendous improvement in underwriting skills *and* a completely new attitude towards agents *and* a colossal new advertising campaign *and* extensive acquisitions financed by new borrowing and new equity.

As a general rule, the best way to achieve a certain objective is to identify the best route and follow it, rather than to divide up your energy among a whole miscellany of activities, any of which may possibly be of some help in getting there.

The people involved in top-level strategy formulation may well succeed in defining clear, unambiguous, concrete objectives, which are at the same time realistic and sensibly quantified. Quite possibly they will be ruthless about concentrating on what is vitally important at the expense of what is merely desirable. The point is not that these things can't be done, but that they can be very demanding.

The Measurement Confusion

One rather simple confusion sometimes smudges the logic of this kind of work. Some authorities give the impression that the main task is to define such things as quantitative business objectives, performance indicators, critical success factors and so on at the higher levels and then, at the lower levels, to design an information architecture *to ensure that the necessary measurements can be taken*, to monitor the organisation's performance, day by day and week by week.[1]

This is fine in itself, but it slides over one important distinction: measuring is not the same as achieving. A thermometer measures the temperature, but is not an instrument for altering the temperature.

Similarly a new computer system that produces daily statistics on customer complaints, may be an excellent instrument for measuring performance against the goal of improving customer service; but it does not in itself improve the service. Conversely, a system which prints out insurance policy documents in a clearer, more attractive format may be said to improve customer service, but it doesn't provide information about improved customer service. Measuring and achieving are different things.

Complications of Awkward Policy

The classic approach based on a demand–supply chain is usually illustrated by case studies where a large organisation has a good deal of freedom about its future strategy. There is no terrible crisis and ample capital is available for investment. The organisation uses its freedom to define expansionary business objectives, which in turn lead to far-reaching plans for a whole new family of computer systems. That is the kind of situation where the approach is at its most plausible.

But many cases don't fit this pattern. The Antarctic Beech Corporation (ABC) is a conglomerate with a range of interests in entertainment, travel, employment agencies and communications. ABC is large and profitable and not in crisis. The company's management is faced with a wide range of opportunities for using IT to develop innovative products and services. They fear that if they don't become innovators, their competitors will — perhaps, one day.

ABC develops the following strategy: 'We intend to continue earning good profits from our existing products and services, dull though they may be. There is no necessary virtue in trying to turn our markets upside down by making huge investments in innovation. If successful, we'd probably be no more profitable than we are now; if unsuccessful, we'd be worse off. However, we do have to be careful that competitors may use innovation to challenge our market leadership. Therefore we shall invest cautiously in a variety of innovative ventures on a limited, experimental basis. Then if we are ever challenged by innovative competitors, we shall be well-placed to strike back quickly and effectively.' This is not a self-evidently stupid strategy. If you studied the situation in detail, you might even conclude that it is the most rational of all the strategies available to ABC.

It is very hard to see how ABC could sensibly apply the straightforward demand–supply chain to their strategy development. Their business policy doesn't take the form: 'increase this factor by 10% within three years; double that factor within five. . .' They have no basis for developing a chain of demand and supply that leads inexorably to extensive new systems and integrated databases and so on. ABC have an awkward policy that can't be expanded naturally through successive levels of detail to arrive at the large-scale programme of developments that is customary in the classic model.

If the model were applied somehow to generate a coherent family of interlocking systems to be implemented in phases, it might produce entirely the wrong answer for ABC. The whole point of its strategy is to *avoid* becoming heavily committed to a vast programme of developments and to stay flexible to respond to any challenge from any quarter. Someone might perhaps argue that the ABC case is a very untypical one, and that strategies for most organisations *can* be expressed in the classic form of 'increase this factor by 10% within three years; double that factor within five . . .' Whether this argument is convincing is something everyone must judge on the basis of personal experience.

Uncertainty Complications

ABC's awkward strategy is actually a particular illustration of a very general problem — uncertainty. Plans based on an elaborate demand–supply chain often rest on the unspoken assumption that there will be no significant influence from uncontrollable, external factors. If there are some really wild and unpredictable uncertainty factors and they do blow up to produce surprises to invalidate many of the judgements made at the higher levels, then much of the detail in the lower levels will very likely turn out to be misdirected.

Since there is some degree of uncontrollable uncertainty in practically every single case, it would be wrong to take this argument too far. The essential point is that the *degree* of uncontrollable external influences varies from case to case, and therefore the degree of certainty and precision you can sensibly attach to your planning also varies from case to case.

Sometimes, allowance has to be made for uncertainties, but this is not the most important aspect of the planning problem to be solved. In other cases, though, uncertainties about competitive developments in the market, or about customer reaction to new products, or about possible government or regulatory moves, or about the volatility of developments in key technologies have to be recognised as the dominant features of the situation. In that event, long-term planning based on a detailed demand–supply chain may well be futile.

Green Field and *In Medias Res*

The Cabbage Palm Project is a four-year construction project to build a huge modern sports stadium, together with supporting infrastructure, in a distant, undeveloped country. The project's total budget is as great as the annual turnover of a medium-sized manufacturing company. The project's managers are keen to make as much use as possible of IT systems to support administration and management. This 'green field' case is a fine example of the situation best suited to the demand–supply chain model. General objectives can be made very clear. The starting point is simple to define (nothing). So is the endpoint, because after four years there must be a stadium ready and, for political reasons, all the project's IT hardware and software must then be written off. Ample funds are available for investment. The project takes place miles from anywhere, insulated from outside influences. There are no major uncertainties to confuse plans.

One characteristic of approach under discussion is that it seems to insist on starting decision-making at the very beginning and proceeding smoothly from there. That is fine for Cabbage Palm, but that is an exceptional case. In most real-life cases a complex situation often exists *already* and there is an urgent need to decide what to do next. Complaining that the organisation should never have got itself into the situation in the first place, and starting out nevertheless at Level 1 of a methodology is not acceptable.

The managing director of Blue Gum Machines calls in an expert consultant on IT strategy. He describes the situation: the business of making cigar-making machines has been unprofitable for some years; Blue Gum's parent company has just parachuted in a new management team; they have started by firing one-third of the workforce; they intend to reorganise the whole untidy administration of the stores and factory; a revolutionary product for making cigars more efficiently has just been invented; this is seen as the lifeline that will save the company; the other main strand in the rescue plan is to increase use of computers to make up for the people who have been fired and to get all the administration reorganised. That is why they now need an expert on IT strategy, he says.

The trouble is that this is scarcely an ideal time to work through many levels to develop an IT strategy for Blue Gum. The decision-makers are right in the middle of things: *in medias res*. Everywhere you look there are constraints limiting freedom of action. The main constraint is that, whatever else is done next week, something must be done to prevent the factory and its administration collapsing into even worse chaos, when one-third of the people are no longer there.

Shortage of adequate funds to invest in systems is another constraint. In any case, the company doesn't have the time for well coordinated four-year, or even two-year, system development plans. Management naivety about the wonder-working power of computers is one more constraining factor. Then there is the revolutionary cigar-manufacturing machine; how long it takes to come to market, whether it is a success and whether it saves the company, are all quite unpredictable factors. The situation just isn't appropriate for the kind of approach to strategy described at Candlebark.

Some generals are at their best planning and carrying out a spring offensive, making aggressive use of a slight superiority in men and tanks to win a decisive victory. Others excel when taking over an outnumbered army, retreating through howling snow-storms, when the only possible objective is to avoid complete annihilation. The same applies to methods for dealing with IT decisions. If a case bears any resemblance to retreat through a snow-storm, then more pragmatic methods than working down an elaborate demand–supply chain are probably needed. Almost every case, other than the exceptional Cabbage Palm, begins *in medias res* to some degree, though few are quite as bad as Blue Gum. How far this factor should influence the shape of decision-making is a matter of judgement.

Awkward Starting Point Complications

One striking characteristic of many planning approaches based on a demand–supply chain is the way the *supply factors of the present situation* — systems, technologies used, people — only come in towards the end of the process. Nearly all the effort goes into defining the ideal scenario you want to reach in the future. Working out how to get there from where you are now is treated as a secondary issue.

Sometimes it can be very hard to define a straightforward 'current situation', in the sense of one readily definable jumping-off point, for the journey towards the ideal scenario. In a large organisation, the 'current situation' usually exists at multiple levels: there are well established operational systems, there are systems just gone or soon going live, systems already seriously under development but some way off going live, projects that are being seriously discussed in workgroups and projects being talked about without any serious commitment. For 'systems' or 'projects', substitute also 'hardware upgrades', 'new network facilities', 'new software packages' and so on. Very often these levels of reality are tricky to clarify (people talk as if the system they are hoping for already existed, forget to mention that another system is going live next month and so on). With enough effort, these nuances can be sorted out, though the resulting picture may be very complex.

The second snag is more fundamental. In the really classic demand–supply chain, the nature of the final scenario you decide to strive for is influenced by many factors, but one factor that has little or no influence is the difficulty or ease of reaching it from the current situation. Only on the day after everybody has signed off the massive document describing the desired final scenario, does attention turn to the issue of how feasible it will be to get there from here, at a reasonable expenditure of effort and time and cost.

Suppose a health care consultant were to say: 'Here you are: this is the product of a year's work, 300 interviews: detailed plans for the modern 500-bed hospital you need, with all the most modern facilities. Now remind me. Did you want it built on a green-field site or do we have to convert an existing nineteenth-century hospital in the middle of a city, without evacuating any patients?' You might feel he had ignored a rather important point that could have influenced some of the earlier decisions.

Similarly, there may be certain features about the present IT situation that should be taken into account as constraints (or possibly as a stimuli) in the early levels of strategy discussions. For example, the organisation might be in the middle of some lengthy process (e.g. converting applications between operating systems) that it would be folly to interrupt; or the limited expertise of the company's IT personnel might make it irresponsible to undertake certain large-scale plans, however desirable their objectives.

Supply and Demand Analysis

The snags described above can all be traced back to one root cause. The demand–supply chain, in its pure form, as described for Candlebark, is an expression of demand-side extremism. It exemplifies the view that decisions about the supply of technology should always be left until after decisions about the demands to be supplied.

As the snags show, IT strategy is more complicated than that. Supply and demand need to interact. Obviously demand must influence supply, but the shrewd strategist needs to judge when to allow supply to interact with demand as well.

The demystification diagram and the inventory of snags in this briefing provide a powerful means of assessing any particular structure, whether standard or special-purpose, that may be proposed for developing IT strategy.

In almost any situation, most of the potential snags are likely to be present to some degree. That doesn't mean that the whole concept of a chain of supply and demand should be abandoned. The trick is to judge how significant each is likely to be to the specific case, and to design the structure of the decision-making process accordingly.

If the pure demand–supply chain is inadequate as a model to be followed religiously from, what is the right model? There is no alternative of comparable detail which is better as a generalised model. Why should there be? Reconciling supply and demand is a delicate business. Nobody expects to find a detailed level-by-level model to standardise the work of lawyers handling their cases or admirals planning naval strategy or ecologists studying ecosystems.

The sensible approach is to recognise that some portions of a case can usefully be handled in a broadly level-based way, but more subtlety of structure is needed to take those particular decisions that are *dominated* by the clash of supply and demand.

PRACTICAL ADVICE

➤ Don't assume that a strict level-by-level approach to IT strategy is always appropriate. It may seem fine on paper, but may be too vulnerable to real-life snags, because it underplays the interaction between supply and demand factors.

➤ Demystify any level-based methodology by reducing it to a diagram based on the distinctions: supply and demand; present and future; translation and puzzle-solving; description and plan.

➤ Know the main generic snags to the demand–supply chain. Appraising their relevance to your specific case is a good way of finding the right structure for decision-making.

➤ Don't confuse plans for systems that will measure the performance of the organisation with plans for systems intended to improve its performance.

➤ Gauge how 'awkward' the organisation's policy will be: that is, how far it will deviate from the idea of planning a complete new family of systems over many years ahead. The more awkward the policy, the less appropriate the idea of building layer on layer.

➤ Weigh up the main uncertainty factors. The stronger they are, the less stable the level-based construction for decision-making.

➤ Appraise the impact of the *in medias res* problem, where there are simply too many hectic things going on to permit calm, staged planning and development of new systems.

➤ Get an early view of the likely distance between the present situation and the ideal long-term goal that is likely to be sketched out. If the gap seems too great, use the factors of the present situation as constraints to temper ideas all the way through.

➤ Don't turn away completely from approaches based on multiple levels and chains of demand and supply, but make them less rigid, according to your judgement of all the above factors.

Part II:

Option-
Based
Approaches

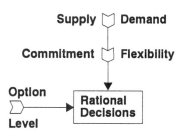

BRIEFINGS AND MODEL

The Reference Model rests on the view that the problems of IT decision-making are often shaped by an underlying interaction between supply and demand factors. It also implies that the natural, methodical, level-by-level approach to planning should be supplemented by activities that generate and compare options. The two themes are closely associated: in practice, the best way of examining the interaction of supply and demand factors is usually to compare options that offer different mixes of supply and demand.

The briefings in Part I elaborate the problems arising from the Supply–Demand Interaction; those in this part of the book look into the idea of approaching the problems through the discussion of options.

Examples of Options

The first of a trio of briefings concerned with options describes a representative sample of cases where options are fundamental to the management problem. They range from rather high-level policy on the organisation's use of IT through to decisions on the scope of a relatively minor project. In each case, supply and demand factors interact to generate a range of plausible options. (**8. Finding Strategic Options**)

If crucial options exist, it is better to be aware of them than not. But how do you choose between them? Often there is no single option that is better than all others in every relevant respect. The next briefing looks into ways of identifying the options that are most likely to provide the 'least bad' or 'best buy' combination of factors. As the cases in the briefing show, the best way to understand the tradeoffs is usually to grasp the workings of the interaction between supply and demand. **(9. Exposing Options and Interactions)**

But suppose the most perceptive analysis possible in a certain case leads to tradeoffs between options in terms of incommensurables, such as prestige and employee relations and other unquantifiable business factors. There is no comprehensive answer to resolve that kind of problem, but the cases in the next briefing show that even here there is scope for some clear reasoning. **(10. Handling Incommensurable Tradeoffs)**

Two Classic Problems

In developing a new system, there is often a choice between writing completely new software and using a software package; a middle course of taking a package and then modifying it may be available too. This is a classic illustration of the way supply and demand factors can interact to present some very tricky dilemmas. The next briefing looks at this problem in more detail. The decision-making can be structured naturally as a comparison of options; the snag is that an overwhelming number of plausible options may be available. One problem is finding the option with the best balance of tradeoffs, but there is a logically prior issue. How do you get into a position to recognise what the most important options and their tradeoffs actually are? There are a variety of ways of tackling this problem, but a simple, methodical, interaction-free, step-by-step approach is not one of them. **(11. Tackling Package Options)**

The last briefing tackles a classic problem. Suppose that a certain investment in IT is apparently very attractive and its benefits can be described very impressively in words, but they aren't the kind of benefits that can easily be translated into a cash-flow forecast. How can such an investment be evaluated? Currently decision-makers in the world of IT haven't many good answers to this question, but comparing options is a step in the right direction. Usually the real choice is between a number of options with different gradations of investment, from zero upwards. Once the problem is expressed in that format, it often begins to look much clearer and somewhat less formidable. **(12. Dealing with Unquantifiable Benefits)**

Conclusions

The Reference Model suggests that option-based and level-based work ought to be blended together. An approach to IT planning that consists exclusively of translating plans between one level and another won't generate the tradeoffs between options, that should arise from the inter-action between supply and demand factors.

The briefings in this part of the book don't recommend any decision-making approach in the form of a fixed, detailed model or a firm set of rules or an analytical technique based on certain diagram conventions. Finding the options at the heart of IT strategy decisions, gauging the implications and evaluating the tradeoffs can't be done by applying a predefined method; they call for skill and judgement.

8.   Finding Strategic Options

ISSUES

When important decisions have to be taken, people generally consider their options before making up their minds. Though this may seem a self-evidently rational approach, in many organisations the comparison of options plays very little part in arriving at decisions of IT strategy.

There are two exceptions that prove this rule. Plainly, whenever any proposal is put up for approval — whether it be for a certain project or for a five-year corporate IT strategy — a choice is being offered: either to accept the proposal or not to accept it. But this is like offering a choice between a black car and no car at all — an inadequate basis for decision-making if the situation really demands careful consideration of a variety of different colours and sizes of cars, and perhaps not only cars, but jeeps and lorries too.

Options are also regularly compared in choosing between a number of software or hardware products or tenders from software houses, to meet some need that is already well defined. If a good definition of a certain 'demand' exists, and the only remaining issue is how best to 'supply' it, then of course you should compare and choose between the different possibilities. But in that situation, the main strategy decisions are taken when the demand is firmed up; the supply options which follow are no more than different ways of implementing the strategy.

This briefing suggests that the careful exposure and comparison of options ought to play a much larger part in the way most organisations take IT strategy decisions. Options should not be restricted to yes/no choices and to choices about the details of second-order issues.

If genuinely interesting strategy options do exist in a certain situation, it seems indisputable that they ought to be exposed and compared. The main argument of someone who disputes the importance of options in IT strategy decisions surely must be that, however attractive the *concept* of options may be, there rarely are relevant options of a strategic character to be exposed *in practice*. This briefing aims to demonstrate that relevant options usually are there if you have the insight to find them; and once found, they are indispensable to an understanding of the real issues.

ANALYSIS

For this topic the best approach is to describe a selection of instances where organisations found that the best way to decide their IT strategy rationally was to think in terms of options. Latent options prove to be the key to decision-making in quite a variety of situations.

Options at Rosewood Bank

Rosewood Bank is a small retail bank, with an upmarket image as the place for stylish people to bank. Rosewood's board of directors has a strong inclination to make substantial investments in IT in order to strengthen this image and to offer even more advanced services to the rich clientele. But the expert banking consultant they engaged has been a disappointment. As the chairman of Rosewood puts it, the expert has set out a smorgasbord of all the most sophisticated banking services that advanced technology could support, and he seems to regard that as the solution to Rosewood's problem. Under pressure, he has made some suggestions about introducing all these services in phases, but why assume that Rosewood ought to help itself to the entire smorgasbord? However lavish the smorgasbord, however expert the knowledge that produced it, there must surely be more nuances than this to the strategy-making problem.

Little by little, Rosewood management work out for themselves that they actually have four big options, four different macro strategies.

Strategy A is christened *Improvement*. It says: make far-reaching improvements to the present systems (including perhaps change of hardware, and making some systems on-line instead of batch); this in itself should lead to improvements in the quality of certain customer services; only when this has been done, consider investing in completely new systems to provide new services.

Strategy B, *Selective Expansion*, says: scrap many of the existing systems; build new integrated systems designed both to improve the quality of present services and provide certain new services — but only a few carefully chosen ones (that is, definitely not all those that can be imagined). Concentrate on those new areas that seem to gain most competitive advantage, but without entering unproven or very challenging new areas of technology.

Strategy C, *Hi-tech*, is the same as Strategy B, with the big difference that it aims to include practically all the improvements and extensions to customer services that are at all plausible, making use of whatever technology is needed, however advanced.

Strategy D, christened *Infrastructure*, is rather more subtle. It says: don't commit yourself now to the degree you would if you chose B or C; instead, invest now in infrastructure. Invest in the hardware and software technologies for database and telecommunications that you will probably need anyway; recruit more expert staff; carry out some experimental, pilot projects. Get positioned, so that, as you jostle with your competitors in the market, you are well placed to identify the right new service to invest in at the right time, and to achieve it speedily and effectively.

These four are clearly different possible strategies. Of course, work is needed to flesh each of them out, before there is enough information to choose between them, but once Rosewood management has settled on one of these strategies, many of the more detailed decisions (which items to choose from the smorgasbord; which new customer services to introduce; what decisions to make on the content of technology infrastructure; what order to do things in, etc.) can be made in a rational, consistent, coherent way.

As yet, the Rosewood board is still some way from settling their macro strategy, but now that they have seen the strategy options, everyone can see how inappropriate the smorgasbord approach was.

Options at Woody Pear Homes

WPH (Woody Pear Homes) runs a number of nursing-homes. WPH has some bright managers with good ideas about the way to run nursing-homes profitably; it has expanded in recent years by taking over several less efficiently run nursing-homes.

Two years ago, WPH entered a joint-venture project, with a software house, a hardware supplier and a firm of health care consultants. The joint-venture had two objectives: to produce packaged software that could be sold profitably to other nursing-homes and small hospitals; and to produce the systems WPH needed to run its own business. This was conceived as the kind of aggressive use of IT as a strategic weapon that you read about in books by management gurus. The scheme is that once other businesses adopt the nursing-home administrative systems, based on the software package that WPH was instrumental in designing, WPH will gain some subtle control of those businesses, perhaps leading to takeover or to franchising developments.

Unfortunately, the joint-venture project has fallen far behind schedule and the WPH finance director has now lost most of his original faith in his partners. He considers his strategic options.

Strategy A is to continue with the joint-venture, but only after first reducing its scope, ruthlessly amputating some parts of the systems that seem particularly hard to get right.

Strategy B is to leave the scope of the whole thing intact, but radically change the way the systems are structured, so that those parts that really matter for WPH's own business are fenced off from the rest, and can't be affected by blunders in other areas.

Strategy C gives up hope of ever getting the right systems for WPH's own business to come out of the project. WPH starts a new private project to develop its own systems; but WPH remains involved as consultant to the joint-venture project in order to preserve the chance of achieving the original long-term ends.

Strategy D withdraws completely from the joint-venture; but (this strategy implies) the basic concept of the joint-venture is sound, only the partners are bad; therefore WPH starts all over again with new, more carefully chosen, partners.

Strategy E withdraws completely from the joint-venture; the problem (this strategy implies) was that all the partners had conflicting interests; therefore WPH sets up a new project, with similar, albeit more modest, objectives, all on its own.

Getting these five strategy options defined doesn't solve the problem, of course. Work is needed to examine the implications of each in some detail. But soon the WPH finance director is in a position to tell his board that the main options have been identified and evaluated, and the time has come to bite the bullet and decide which is the least bad. Whatever more detailed actions WPH takes after that (suing the partners? choosing different database software? taking over another nursing-home? hiring computer staff who know about nursing-home systems?) can be taken in the context of the chosen strategy option.

It is not a pleasant time for WPH; it will have to cut its losses, one way or another. But one thing is clear: defining the strategy options is an indispensable step. Otherwise discussions will drift around in circles until some arbitrary decision is taken, that is not necessarily the least bad one available.

Options at Sassafras Magazines

Sassafras publishes magazines about agricultural machinery, computers, printing equipment and numerous other areas of technology. A systems analyst identifies six major demand areas at Sassafras where significantly greater use of IT seems attractive. One is a big new system, processing orders for adverts and scheduling them; another is a new, improved system for keeping records of all the subscribers to magazines;

Sassafras Magazines: Possible Strategies

	Strategy A	Strategy B	Strategy C
Advert Order Processing/Scheduling	✔	✔	✔
Credit Control	-	✔	✔
Sales Analysis	-	✔	✔
Magazine Subscriber Administration	-	-	✔
Reader Enquiry Cards	-	-	✔
Editorial Production Control	-	-	✔
COST	100	150	280

another system processes the enquiry cards sent in by readers wanting information on advertised products; and so on.

Here is what the analyst does *not do*: he doesn't produce a monumental document, describing all the functions of all the new systems, together with detail about all the technical implications and a detailed costing, and then present it to the board, saying (in effect): 'Here is your $1.4m investment programme; take it or leave it. Of course, if you leave it, that will mean I've been wasting my time, these last six months.'

Instead, much earlier, he brainstorms with Sassafras managers through to the definition of three strategic options. *Strategy A* says: do the order processing system; leave out the other five for the time being. *Strategy B* says: commit and make a plan to implement three of the possible systems: the order processing and subscriber records and enquiry cards systems. *Strategy C* is the grand slam — all six possible demands.

In other words, each of the three strategy options is a certain selection from a six-item menu. On any menu with six either/or choices, the number of possible permutations of choices is quite large. That is why the process of brainstorming is necessary in order to identify the three *most plausible* strategy options available. Strategy A is attractive because it is a really powerful, quick strike at the area everybody agrees needs most attention, and it is less risky than the other two. Strategy C, the grand slam, really transforms the company into a formidable competitor for the next decade (if it works of course — you can't be certain). And Strategy B? Well, very often the best buy lies between two extremes.

When three strategy options are exposed this starkly, the obvious next step is to attach figures for comparative investment costs of the three strategies, as well as comparative projected cost savings. This really forces Sassafras top management to decide just how big a commitment they want to make to IT in their business strategy. They may find that a taxing decision to make, but that is far better than being faced with a massive 'take it or leave it' document.

Options at Yellow Mallee Transport

YMT is the public transport authority of the Yellow Mallee urban area. The director of this authority wants to invest in new passenger information systems, in order to give public transport a more stylish image. His idea is to set up sophisticated, computer-controlled indicator boards at key points in the network, showing which trams are coming, which trams are delayed, when to change from tram to metro, and so on.

The hardware of the indicator boards themselves has already been settled. These boards can be made to display their messages according to instructions transmitted to them from a computer in a control room. Also, various sensing devices fixed in the roads, the tram points and the metro lines can send messages about the passage of vehicles into the control room.

The outstanding strategy decision is about how sophisticated the computer system in the control room should be. At one extreme, such a system could be just a convenient way of assisting people in the control room who are responsible for sending out the messages to be displayed on the indicator boards; at the other extreme, the whole system could be so automatic that people in the control room never really had to do anything, not even when bad weather and road works caused all kinds of delays and reroutings.

The YMT team brainstorms through all the different facilities such a system might conceivably offer. After many iterations, and after eliminating a few preposterous ideas, they fit everything into a framework that is conceptually quite neat. A basic minimum system can be outlined, and then eleven distinct 'extra' facilities can be identified; these are facilities that seem attractive but not absolutely vital.

One extra facility, for example, is detection of delayed buses through

Yellow Mallee Transport — Passenger Information System
Possible Strategies

	Strategy A	Strategy B	Strategy C	Strategy D	Strategy E
BASIC SYSTEM	✔	✔	✔	✔	✔
extra facility 1	-	✔	✔	✔	✔
extra facility 2	-	✔	✔	✔	✔
extra facility 3	-	✔	✔	✔	✔
extra facility 4	-	✔	✔	✔	✔
extra facility 5	-	-	✔	✔	✔
extra facility 6	-	-	✔	✔	✔
extra facility 7	-	-	-	✔	✔
extra facility 8	-	-	-	✔	✔
extra facility 9	-	-	-	✔	✔
extra facility 10	-	-	-	-	✔
extra facility 11	-	-	-	-	✔
COST	100	150	180	230	250

Examples of extra facilities:

extra facility 4: automatic detection of delayed buses and display of warnings to waiting passengers.

extra facility 6: automatic change of route information, caused by market day, road repairs, etc.

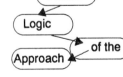

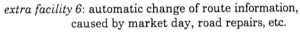

remote sensors on the roads, with fully automatic display of delay warnings to passengers waiting at the relevant halts. Another possible extra facility is to update automatically the advice displayed on the boards about where to make connections from one form of transport to another, whenever there are special conditions such as market day, road repairs and so on. Another possible facility is to set up a special master board at the main bus station that summarises information about bus and tram and metro over the whole city.

As at Sassafras, each strategy option is a certain selection from this menu. Strategy A is the choice of a system with just the basic facilities and no extras at all; Strategy E is the grand slam with all the 11 extra facilities. Strategies B, C and D fall between the two. Strategy B is A plus a certain four of the extras; Strategy C is the same as B but with two more of the extras, making six; Strategy D is the same as C but with three more extras, making nine and excluding only the two most elaborate.

With costs attached to each of the five strategies the *marginal costs* are clear. Calling the estimated cost of Strategy A 100, the range through B up to E goes through 150, 180 and 230 up to 250. So the marginal cost of, say, the first four extra facilities (that is, of B over A) is 50.

How exactly the director makes his choice is a subject in itself. The important point is that, once this analysis of options is available to the director of YMT and his team, they find it inconceivable that anyone could ever think of making this kind of decision any other way.

The Value of Options

These examples show that the definition of options can make all the difference between a rational strategy decision and an arbitrary one. However self-evident this may be, the point is frequently overlooked. There are many cases of Rosewoods, who drift into commitment to an entire smorgasbord; of WPHs, who shy away from choosing the least painful nettle and firmly grasping it; of Sassafras analysts, who design massive families of systems on a 'take it or leave it' basis; of YMT projects, that go round in circles, because nobody can decide what functions to include in the system and what to leave out. So, obvious or not, here is a brief summary of the reasons that options are a vital tool in making strategic decisions.

First, the practice of comparing options improves the chances of taking a good as opposed to a bad decision, because, at the very least, it increases the likelihood of noticing that certain good decisions are available.

Second, the discipline of having to justify a decision by showing its superiority to some other apparently plausible alternative helps to ensure that the important issues in a situation are identified and explored.

Third, in order to get options into a suitable form for comparison, you find yourself forced to summarise, decide what is truly important, and decide what other possibilities are significantly different. This improves the chances that decision-makers decide on the basis of a genuine understanding of reasons and implications, rather than on trust or intuition.

Options-based Progress

SYMBOLS USED

comparing options

description

options

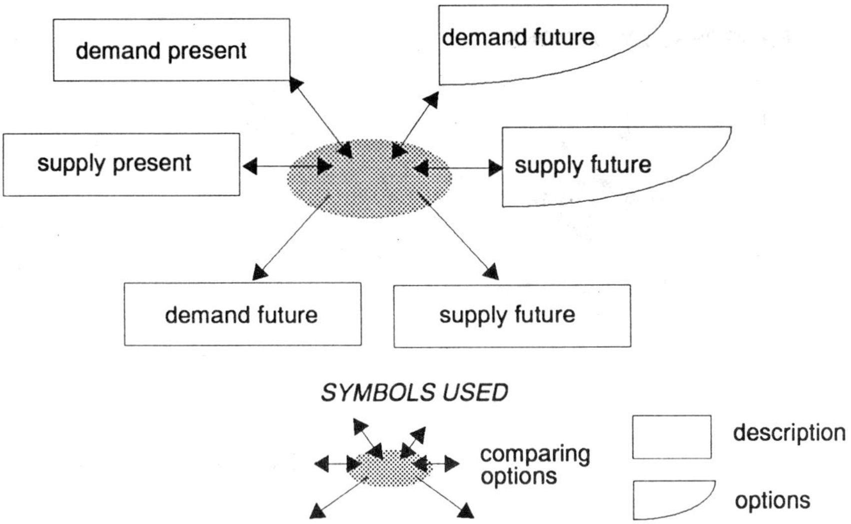

Fourth, by explicitly rejecting certain options, you make it clear what your strategy is not, and that in turn sharpens up your definition of what your strategy actually is.

Lastly, if you force yourself to give reasons for choosing one option over another, then you are much better placed to look back afterwards and see if the reasons were valid. You can learn from experience.

Options, Supply–Demand and Levels

The impressionistic diagram of *Options-Based Progress* shows how progress towards decisions by the comparison of options is a very different thing from the progress that comes by expanding the detail of decisions level by level. Options comparison entails considering both supply and demand in one process. Factual descriptions of the existing state of supply and demand are played off against ideas for options that raise a range of overlapping or mutually exclusive possibilities.

The diagram *Blending Two Means of Progress* suggests how progress towards decisions by the comparison of options is by no means a substitute for progressing through levels by gradually expanding detail. Too much concentration on level-based progress can hinder understanding of

Blending Two Means of Progress

PROGRESS BY OPTIONS

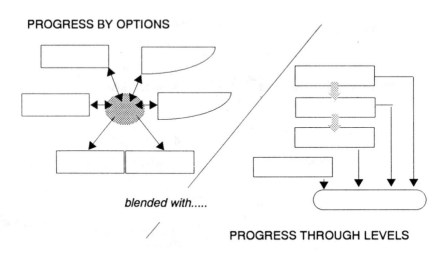

blended with.....

PROGRESS THROUGH LEVELS

the vital tension between supply and demand, but excessive discussion of options can lead to muddle and long delays in actually deciding anything. Each individual case needs a coherent blend of option-based freedom and level-based discipline.

Options and Standard Approaches

If options are such powerful instruments for IT decision-making, why aren't they used more?

Options generally compare different balances of aspirations and constraints — because an ideal goal can rarely be reached at negligible cost or risk or delay. But theories of demand-driven planning tend to ignore this awkward point. Someone who believes that the non-technical 'requirements' of an organisation should be firmed up in detail before they are handed over to the technologists avoids the whole question of finding the right balance of aspirations and constraints.

Most standardised methodologies of IT planning tend to ignore the concept of choosing between options or relegate it to a minor role, buried in a checklist with dozens of other possible activities. This is under-standable because defining and evaluating options don't fit easily into any standard format. As the examples in this briefing show, options arise in all kinds of different situations. They can't be isolated to one specific stage in the planning process (as in: 'Here is the nine-stage planning process and stage 4 is called Option Comparison and this is the format of the diagram we use. . .').

Occam's razor is a famous principle of clear thinking (other things being equal, you should prefer more simple theories to more complex ones). It can be a useful way of thinking about any problem that calls for reasoning, but you can't define in advance exactly how and when you are going to use it. Defining IT options is like that: a very effective and very flexible way of getting to the heart of many IT strategy decisions.

To work effectively with options you need to apply insight. It can be a very demanding task to identify Rosewood's four fundamental strategy options or WPH's five least-bad lines of retreat or Sassafras's three major investment options or YMT's five main options for the scope of their system. You can't lay down standard rules for somebody to follow that will necessarily lead to the right options in any situation.

Of course it would be possible to design some standard diagram format on which people could define options, but this would surely be futile. If you have sufficient insight to identify options effectively, you can easily find the best way of representing them on paper; if not, you won't be empowered to find the right options, just by having a standard diagram to use.

PRACTICAL ADVICE

➤ Hunt out plausible options enthusiastically. If people say there are none, they are probably making unwarranted assumptions because they haven't thought about the case carefully enough.

➤ Search for options that bring supply and demand factors together, as opposed to mere choices between ways of carrying out a decision already taken.

➤ Concentrate on options that pose genuinely different possibilities, as opposed to a simple choice between accepting or rejecting a proposal.

➤ If you come up with a surfeit of options, use common-sense to cut them down and distinguish those that are really significantly different.

➤ Be open to options at all levels: discussing abstract high-level business strategy; finding the pragmatic way of rescuing the entire strategy when it is in serious trouble; deciding the right mix of possible systems to include in a brand new strategy; defining the set of functions to be included in one particular system.

➤ Be wary of those who play down the importance of options and suggest that all will be well if you just follow the predefined steps of a methodology.

➤ Remember that defining the most relevant options, so that the problem is posed economically in a clear, easy to grasp form requires insight and experience, rather than standardised method.

9.   Exposing Options and
         Interactions

ISSUES

The case of Sassafras Magazines has a classic simplicity. The Sassafras
board has to decide between three main strategy options — each a
combination of demand (some computer systems to be undertaken) and
supply (appropriate technology and technical work), with associated
investment costs. Their decision is greatly simplified by the fact that the
demand factors of each strategy option form a *superset* of the option below
it. In other words, Strategy B proposes all the same new systems as
Strategy A, plus something more; Strategy C proposes the same new
systems as Strategy B, plus something more. But Sassafras is a classic
case; many real-life cases are more complex, in that the main strategy
options for consideration don't fit this neat ranking pattern.

Sassafras has another simplifying aspect. Each of the three strategy
options can be understood as offering certain demand factors, from which
the appropriate supply factors *are then derived* — at least, the main
options for decision can be represented in that neat way after all the
brainstorming is done. But Sassafras is a classic case; many real-life cases
are more complex, because the supply factors play a dominant role in
determining what the most relevant demands for consideration actually
are.

This briefing examines four cases where, *to varying degrees*, the two
simplifying aspects of classic Sassafras don't hold; that is to say, the
interaction between supply and demand factors is more subtle. This
appreciation can be put in more down to earth terms. A choice between
plausible options usually involves tradeoffs. The simplest tradeoff takes
the form: the more you pay, the more you get. But option comparison
really becomes interesting when the options and tradeoffs are too complex
to be organised in that pattern.

ANALYSIS

You have one day to spend on the island of Bali. There are places and
things to see (possible demand factors) and there are possible ways of

travelling about the island (possible supply factors). The main supply options are bicycle, public bus services, motorcycle and jeep.

Each of these four supply factors has a price, so they can be ranked in order from that point of view. But this doesn't mean that every step up in order of price brings the same capabilities as the step below, plus something more. The tradeoffs are more complex than that. The jeep is the most expensive and it allows travel to far more places than the bicycle; but the bicycle is still better than the jeep at meeting a demand factor such as following a path through the paddy-fields. The motor-cycle is more expensive than the bus, and you can go places where there is no bus service; but if talking to local people is one of the demand factors, then the bus may rank very high. And so on. With many IT strategy decisions, too, the options can't be neatly ranked in ascending order.

This aspect is often, though not always, linked to a second: the surest way of finding the most relevant strategy options may be to define them primarily in terms of their supply, rather than demand, factors. To define demands first and only then examine possible supply factors can be appropriate in some cases, but in others it may produce a crude over-simplification of the possibilities available. For example, when you evaluate the bicycle supply option on Bali, why not do your best to identify the most attractive set of sights and experiences (demand possibilities) that are available to a strategy based on the bicycle (as supply factor)? Do the same with the other three supply possibilities, and make the best possible case for each. In other words, concentrate on working out strategy options that are primarily defined in terms of different supply factors. Surely that is the way to position yourself best to make the decision in this particular case.

Of course many cases fit neither the Sassafras nor the Bali models of decision-making exactly. This briefing show how the two concepts of awkwardly ranked strategy options and supply-determined options apply to varying degrees in different cases.

Options at Sycamore Supplies

Sycamore Supplies is a wholesaler of stationery and office equipment products, with a network of depots around the country. There is a strong case for setting up new IT systems at the depots. Planners isolate a number of key issues and identify the main options on each.

First is the *invoice/pick* issue. Should you process an order from a customer by first producing an invoice and then going to pick the required goods from the warehouse or (the stark alternative) should you first pick the goods and then produce an invoice? This is a demand-side issue; it may sound like an esoteric piece of organisational detail, but in fact there are quite far-reaching implications. To choose between the two options you have to consider a variety of points. How likely is it that the goods ordered are out of stock? Does this happen with 2% of orders? 0.2%? 20%? Should orders for out-of-stock items be held as back orders to be met later? If so, won't that make the discount calculations (based on total order value) very messy? Can or should Sycamore substitute (say) another brand of paperclips or envelopes, if the brand ordered is out of stock? How probable is it that people will look for goods in the warehouse and not find them, even though they are actually there? These and many more matters arise in making the invoice/pick decision.

The *inventory* issue is fairly closely linked. Here four options are identified: one, don't computerise this part of the administration yet; two, have a simple computerised inventory recording system at each depot; three, have a more advanced inventory recording system centrally (this could show, for example, that an item needed at one depot was available at a neighbouring depot); and four, have a central inventory system that not only records what is actually in stock, but controls it by automatically generating new orders from suppliers.

Another issue is *sales analysis*. Should the new strategy leave this out altogether, or (second option) include a modest, straightforward analysis by product each week or (third option) include a really super facility to extract all kinds of information, based on types of product, types of customer, comparing this month's sales to the same month last year, this year to date with last year's equivalent, and so on.

Another issue is the *core/sundry* question. Whatever shape the computer systems take, you can use them to cover the whole range of products Sycamore deals in, including a very heterogeneous and rapidly changing range of items known as sundries; or you can restrict the full systems to those core products that form 90% of turnover.

The four issues so far are all demand-side and Sycamore managers identify three more, making seven. There are also three main supply-side issues. For example, the options on the *Communications* issue are: either have permanent telecommunications arrangements, between head office and depots, for interactive exchange of data; or transmit data occasionally in batches (e.g. at end of day); or exchange data when needed in physical form (e.g. on diskette). The other two supply-side issues concern the broad character of the computers needed at head office and depots, bearing in mind the complication that there is some hardware already there; they would require too much space to explain in detail.

So, Sycamore Supplies has ten main issues; each one has either two, three or four plausible options. Since every possible combination of choices is a different possible strategy, there are 2x4x2 . . . = 12,288 possible strategies available. Of course a high proportion of these are self-evidently not sensible; for example, a strategy including a high-powered centralised system for the demand-side 'inventory' issue, and the low-powered data exchange on diskette for the supply-side 'telecommunications' issue would not make sense. Nevertheless, determining which single combination of choices is the one strategy that should be chosen is still a formidable task.

Resolving Strategy at Sycamore Supplies

Sycamore managers brainstorm around the issues and finally reduce their real choice to four main possible strategies; each of the four consists of a set of answers on each of the ten issues. *Strategy A* takes the modest options on many of the issues (e.g. no sales analysis, data exchanged on diskette, etc.); call its estimated cost 100. *Strategy D* is the de luxe approach, with estimated cost 300, though it isn't the most extreme possible (e.g. Sundries are out). But Strategies B and C are what make Sycamore a more subtle case than Sassafras Magazines. *Strategy B*, with cost 180, is exactly the same as Strategy A on every issue except one; it takes the lavish approach to sales analysis. *Strategy C*, though it costs 220 (40 more than B), doesn't include this degree of sales analysis. It addresses a different priority: it includes the luxury choice on the inventory issue, together with those choices on the supply-side issues that naturally go along with this.

How do the Sycamore managers whittle things down to just these four strategy options? Here is an extract from their discussions:

'Now we've been over this very thoroughly, and I think we all finally agree that, whatever else we may decide, we definitely go for 'pick first, invoice after'. Although the other approach has its advantages, we think it would lead to chaos in some of the warehouses.'

'Agreed, and that has implications for the 'inventory' issue. I think we ought to invest heavily and have vastly improved systems in that area. We should be prepared to sacrifice other things to achieve that.'

'Not necessarily. Inventory is exactly the part of the strategy where lavish demand choices will entail expensive supply choices: telecommunications networks and so on. I'm more concerned about our lack of management information than our inventory control systems. I think investment in the sales analysis area will produce more benefit; its marginal costs would be all software; there'd be no extra hardware required. I'd be prepared to forgo new inventory systems for the sake of better sales analysis systems.'

'Let's agree then to define four possible strategies. All four go for 'pick first, invoice after' and all four exclude sundries. Those points are their common ground. Then, Strategy A is basic but sensible, while Strategy B

Sycamore Supplies: Possible Strategies

	Strategy A	Strategy B	Strategy C	Strategy D
DEMAND ISSUES				
ISSUE 1: PICKING				
1a invoice then pick	-	-	-	-
1b pick then invoice	✔	✔	✔	✔
ISSUE 2: INVENTORY				
2a not computerised	✔	✔	-	-
2b simple inventory recording at depots	-	-	-	-
2c integrated inventory recording	-	-	-	-
2d integrated inventory recording and control	-	-	✔	✔
ISSUE 3: SALES ANALYSIS				
3a none	✔	-	✔	-
3b modest	-	-	-	-
3c super	-	✔	-	✔
ISSUE 4: PRODUCTS				
4a core only	✔	✔	✔	✔
4b core + sundry	-	-	-	-
ISSUE 5: etc.				
ISSUE 6: etc.				
ISSUE 7: etc.				
SUPPLY ISSUES				
ISSUE 8: COMMUNICATIONS				
8a diskette only	●	●	-	-
8b daily telecomms link	-	-	-	-
8c permanent telecomms link	-	-	●	●
ISSUE 9 etc.				
ISSUE 10 etc.				
	100	180	220	300

Outline
Logic
of the
Approach

is careful but lays stress on sales analysis; Strategy C is careful but lays stress on inventory; Strategy D is lavish but still sensible.'

'Fine. Let's flesh out each of those four to give each of them the most attractive balance of tradeoffs that we can, and suspend judgement on which is the ultimate best choice until we've done that.'

The Sycamore case illustrates the point that strategy options don't have to be ranked neatly in ascending order; Strategy C does more than B in some ways, but less in others. A second feature of the Sycamore case is the way that the supply factors attached to each strategy option are more than merely the necessary consequences of the demand factors; the supply factors themselves influence the discussion of which demand factors should be contained in each strategy option. But this phenomenon is not very pronounced here; in the next case it becomes a little stronger.

Tradeoffs at Black Ash Bank

Black Ash Bank (BAB) is a large bank in a country in Asia. The bank uses conventional telex machines via the public telex network to send messages internally and externally. Over the last ten years a number of more advanced supply-side telex technologies have become available. The bank's managers want to investigate the idea of investing in something more up to date.

Although telex arrangements may seem a supply-side issue, the analysts approach the problem initially from the demand-side. The bank currently sends various types of telex messages: certain types of transaction are done by telex; account statements are telexed to certain clients under certain conditions; then there are pure text messages; and so on. For each of the different current uses, improvements can be imagined in terms of labour saving, speed, reliability, security and integration with other bank systems. Taking account of all this, an inventory of possible improvements in different ways for different types of messages is drawn up.

Then, leaving the demand-side possibilities on one side, *possibly relevant* supply-side options are identified. For example, one supply-side issue is whether branches should use the public telex network to communicate with head office or, alternatively, use the bank's own telecommunications network that already exists for other systems. Another supply-side issue is the type of devices used to key in messages (e.g. conventional telex machines, personal computers, VDUs attached to a mini, and a few other possibilities). Another is whether to have made-to-measure software on a general-purpose minicomputer or the special telex-oriented minicomputer and software sold by the PTT, the national telecommunications authority. So a set of supply-side issues and options can be drawn up.

Then the inventory of demand-side improvements and the set of supply-side issues and options are thrown together. The intention is to define several strategy options for consideration — each made coherent by offering a feasible combination of demand-side improvements with supply-side telex arrangements.

During this 'throwing together' process, all kinds of insights are generated into the relations between the supply and demand factors. For example, if you want to make telexes easy to edit before transmission, the telex machine input option on the supply side is just not adequate. If you want international telexes to be forwarded automatically into the international banking network, that will be a top-end supply-side choice, involving your own general-purpose minicomputer, because the PTT's telex-oriented minicomputer won't do it. On the other hand, some of the improvements in password facilities, that people originally sensed would be quite stiff demands, turn out to be relatively easy to supply. And the special-purpose telecommunications hardware that BAB is on the verge of ordering turns out to be pointless because it won't facilitate any of the demands at all.

The result of this process is the definition of five strategy options, each a coherent, plausible mix of demand and supply factors; each has a different balance of advantages and costs; each is a candidate for choice as the best buy.

Strategic Options at Turpentine Tours

In the BAB case, supply and demand factors were thrown together; they had a kind of equality of status. The Turpentine Tours case is a good example of supply factors actually driving the definition of strategy options.

Turpentine Tours (TT) is a subsidiary of that great promoter of innovation, the Antarctic Beech Corporation (ABC). One of TT's divisions specialises in arranging individual tours for discerning clients who want to do more on holiday than lie on a beach. The Innovation Director at ABC has proposed that some of TT's branches should experiment with a new concept in customer service. To help the culture-oriented client plan a tour of Greece, there will be a special database about all the possibilities, accessible through a powerful PC in the branch.

First and most straightforward, the proposed system can extract 'plain vanilla' tourist information; for example, the timetable for boats from Piraeus to Syros. More exciting, it can also display a quite different genre of information, such as a map of the island of Syros. But the cleverest part is the way it can combine plain vanilla information with map information on one screen. For example, it can show a map of the Aegean, indicating by means of coloured arrows how most boats from Piraeus to Syros continue to either Mykonos or Naxos, while less frequent services go on to Samos. The database isn't merely concerned with boat schedules; it can store information about temples, castles, churches, museums etc. and they can be shown on the maps too. All this is purely an information service; the administration of any bookings will be handled separately by TT's main system.

If all goes well with this pilot project, ABC hope to expand the concept in many possible directions: make databases for other countries (Turkey, Italy, India, etc.); sell the system to other travel agents; add new dimensions of information (e.g. text about the history of places, colour photos).

At an early stage, the ABC/TT workgroup defining the project recognises an interesting dilemma. The database contains two very different types of information that would normally be stored in two different ways. Plain vanilla information about boat schedules can easily be stored using a mainstream database software product. But storing the shape and position of the island of Syros, in such a way that it can be reproduced as a map on a screen, fits most naturally into quite a different and more esoteric sort of database technology, well outside the mainstream.

There seem to be two important options. One option is to store all information in the way that suits it most naturally; so there are *two databases*, a 'fact' database and a 'map' database. The other option is to store all information in one *integrated database*; this entails storing the map information in a rather unnatural, inefficient way, so that it can be integrated with the fact information in the same database. These two options set the agenda for the real decision-making.

Comparing Strategies at Turpentine Tours

At first some of the TT managers can't see how such an apparently technical pair of options can be labelled strategic. Here is the explanation. First, there can be large differences in cost between the two approaches — a reason for deciding at a fairly early stage. Second, there are tremendous implications for the nature of the queries the system can comfortably handle.

The *two-databases option* is ideal if most individual passenger queries can be handled by taking data from either the fact or the map database, but not both. But it is very inefficient if most query answers need to combine data from both databases in complex ways — for example, displaying the map of an island, including any notable temples that are close enough to a port for someone to visit and get back in time for a scheduled boat before nightfall.

The *integrated-database option* is a much more effective way of handling those complex queries with the mixed types of data, but it is much less efficient at handling fact-only or map-only queries.

In short, this inherently supply-side choice of database technology is intimately linked with the whole demand-side scope of the project. The efficiency in handling one type of query has to be traded off against the efficiency in handling another type.

You could, of course, take a simple, demand-driven approach: define all the different types of queries you want to handle and quantify the mix of query types, and only then go on to see which technical option was better. But that would be a very crude way of evaluating tradeoffs. You might find that the already defined mix of query types drove you to choose the two-database option, otherwise certain simple queries would take a ridiculous time to answer, but, as a consequence of that choice, there was a truly formidable programming task to handle certain other queries that combined both types of information. Or again, you might find that, given the defined mix of queries, the integrated database was clearly the only possible choice, even though it was very expensive — but although you were financing this sophisticated system, you weren't really exploiting the potential for intelligent queries that it offered.

ABC/TT find a much better approach to the dilemma. They decide to flesh out and compare two alternative strategies. (More than two actually, but the detail of the others isn't germane to the discussion here.) *Strategy A* is: develop a system where the demand is primarily either fact-type or map-type queries, with only very limited mixed-type facilities; the supply is of course the two-database approach. *Strategy B* is: develop a system where the demand is primarily mixed-type queries that will amaze everyone with their sophistication and power; the supply is the integrated database approach.

Once they see things this way, the ABC/TT team can avoid taking sides between strategies, at least for the time being. Professional pride drives them to work as hard as they can to make the best possible case for each alternative strategy. For example, they note carefully any useful queries that can be handled under one strategy and not (at any sensible cost) under the other. Having worked out the best case they can for each alternative, they are then well placed to decide which is the better strategy to choose for the project.

This case shows a very strong interaction between supply and demand, generating tradeoffs that can only be resolved by treating each alternative strategy as a coherent bundle of supply and demand choices.

Options at Angophora Mining

The Angophora Mining case presents a good example of supply factors dominating the definition of strategy options. Angophora is an international mining company. By the nature of its business, Angophora often enters into complex legal arrangements with national governments, local authorities and joint-venture partners. Suppose the content of all these legal documents could be stored in a really good database system. Then it would be very easy to refer to relevant contractual information about live contracts. Also, whenever any new contracts were being negotiated, the precise wording of both existing and old contracts could be easily accessed for reference.

The range of possible information requirements for such a system is very diffuse. For example, the question: 'What is the text of the *force majeure* clause of contract 721?' is rather straightforward. Answering questions such as 'What are the most important differences in the *force majeure* clauses of our contracts for manganese mining on the seabed and on land?' obviously calls for a more sophisticated system. So does: 'Allowing for both *force majeure* and the financial penalty clauses in contract 721, how much money will we lose, if the revolution in Paraguay causes a month's delay?'

The strategic problem is where to draw the line on such information requirements. What kind of information is it sensible to provide fully automatically? What conceivable requests for information should the system not meet?

With the Sycamore case the range of possibilities was structured as a number of key issues ('sales analysis', 'inventory', etc.), each of which offered two, three or four plausible options. But Angophora's options are all about meeting information needs. How can they be structured? The Angophora workgroup attacks this problem by very carefully formulating fifteen representative questions, similar to the three examples above. Some of the questions are obviously more formidable than others. But they differ not so much in their degree of difficulty, but in their very nature: for example, a question largely concerned with comparing actual progress to the contractually agreed plan is one thing; a question calling for intelligent comparison of texts from two different contracts side by side is another; a question whose answer calls for merging an original contract with the content of numerous extra protocols and addenda is another.

One of the interesting points about the Angophora case is this method of finding a structure for defining options, where no structure is immediately obvious. The strategy finally chosen will involve building a system capable of answering some combination of these fifteen representative questions (and of course all those cognate questions which they represent). If you have fifteen independent two-way choices, the number of possible combinations of choices (ranging from all 'no' to all 'yes') is very large: too many to show as a neat matrix on one sheet of paper.

The next problem is: How can Angophora define a convenient number of relevant strategy options — four, say?

Angophora's Supply-determined Strategies

The product of the strategy study is a document which identifies and compares four strategies. Strategy A aims to build a system that can answer five of the representative questions; Strategy B, eleven; Strategy C, thirteen and Strategy D, all fifteen. But why these four strategies in particular? Why these particular combinations of representative questions?

The *technology supply factors* contained in each of the four strategies expose the rationale for bringing these combinations of possibilities, and only these four, through to the final round of decision-making.

Strategy A has been designed as the approach that will answer as many questions as possible, *without* having to store the content of all the contracts in a massive database of textual information. It entails storing information *about* the contracts, but not their complete texts. It completely avoids the need to embark on text database technology. That is why this strategy is much cheaper than the others; that is why it aims to handle exactly those particular five representative questions.

Strategy D, at the other extreme, aims to provide a system that can answer all the fifteen questions. (The fifteen are actually pre-filtered to eliminate any demands that are absolutely preposterous.) Its four main supply factors are text database, relational database, some artificial intelligence technology and project control software (to compare actual progress against contractual obligations).

An advocate of *Strategy C* would probably say that just removing artificial intelligence from the supply factors will make the project a lot simpler and still allow thirteen of the fifteen questions to be answered; so C has a fair chance of being the best buy.

Strategy B has its own logic too. If you exclude project control software from the supply factors, and concentrate on building a system based on just relational database and text database as the two main supply factors, then you can still answer eleven of the fifteen questions; perhaps this produces the best buy.

In this Angophora case, supply factors turn out to have a dominant role in structuring the strategy problem. In effect, the strategy options

Angophora Mining — Legal System: Possible Strategies

	Strategy A	*Strategy B*	*Strategy C*	*Strategy D*
DEMAND *Which of the 15 Representative* *Questions are handled?*				
question 1	✔	✔	✔	✔
question 2	✔	✔	✔	✔
question 3	✔	✔	✔	✔
question 4	✔	✔	✔	✔
question 5	✔	✔	✔	✔
question 6	-	✔	✔	✔
question 7	-	✔	✔	✔
question 8	-	✔	✔	✔
question 9	-	✔	✔	✔
question 10	-	✔	✔	✔
question 11	-	✔	✔	✔
question 12	-	-	✔	✔
question 13	-	-	✔	✔
question 14	-	-	-	✔
question 15	-	-	-	✔
SUPPLY *What technology is used?*				
relational database	●	●	●	●
text database	-	●	●	●
project control package	-	-	●	●
artificial intelligence	-	-	-	●
COST	100	350	450	600

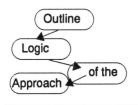

Examples of the Representative Questions:

Question 6: 'What is the text of the *force majeure* clause of contract 721?'

Question 14: 'How much will we lose through the revolution in Paraguay?'

are shaped by their supply factors. Strategy B, for example, is best thought of as 'the strategy that meets as many demands as possible, by exploiting text database and relational database technology, but not project control or artificial intelligence'. But, though Angophora differs from the classic Sassafras case in this important respect, it does have one thing in common: the strategy options can be ranked simply in ascending order — as they cannot for the other three cases in this briefing.

Supply and Demand Implications

The four cases in this briefing show that, in order to decide what is best, you need to compare several possibilities, containing different combinations of supply and demand factors. That isn't just a principle of decision-making about IT; it is true of practically any field of technology. But many people in the IT world don't apply it. Managers are often presented with '*the* set of system requirements' in Sycamore cases, or '*the* telex solution' in BAB cases, or '*the* information product definition' in TT cases or '*the* system design' in Angophora cases; where '*the*' implies '*the one and only worth considering*'.

Often decision-making is structured in stages, so that each stage starts out from a set of decisions reached at the previous stage, and where technology only comes into consideration after several stages. This approach tends to ignore the awkward truth that some of the 'business parameters' or 'information needs' or 'facilities' or 'functional requirements' defined in early stages may fit available technology resources much better than others do. But this awkward truth is fundamental; it means that different aspirations rate differently in terms of feasibility, investment required, risk and so on. This in turn means that concepts such as tradeoffs and 'best buy' combinations of supply and demand factors should be central to rational decisions about IT strategy.

A rigid, stage-by-stage approach is at its weakest in cases such as those discussed here, where the essence of the problem is that supply and demand factors must genuinely interact. Accepting the concepts of tradeoffs and 'best buys' means abandoning the model of making just one definition of requirements in non-technical form, which is translated into technological terms afterwards. It means that non-technological aspirations and technological practicalities often have to be discussed together. This is asking a lot, because there is usually considerable detail to confuse the debate. Skill and insight are needed to unravel the issues and pick out just those stark options that really need to be compared.

PRACTICAL ADVICE

➤ Define strategy options that really expose the interaction between supply and demand factors.

➤ Think of each strategy option as a particular combination of demand and supply factors. Seek out the most plausible combinations available — in other words, those with a good chance of being the 'best buy' combination of attractive demand features with supply features of acceptable risk and expense.

➤ Structure decision-making to avoid false assumptions and arbitrary simplifications. But also encourage elegance to circumvent endless analyses of every conceivable combination of possibilities.

➤ Don't assume that the main strategy options to be found can be ranked neatly in ascending order; sometimes this isn't appropriate. But treat this as a point to be considered specifically; don't just let things take their course.

➤ When it is called for, don't be afraid to stimulate reasoning backward from supply to demand, as a way of refining the neatest combinations of choices. But treat this as a point to be considered specifically; don't just let things take their course.

➤ Design the format for presenting the main strategy options according to the case. Sometimes it may be a simple matrix presenting possible functions like a menu; sometimes the matrix may be structured to show the several different choices on each issue; sometimes demand options may be best represented as possible queries a system might handle; sometimes the main purpose may be to show how demand-side and supply-side options relate to each other.

➤ Discourage everyone from thinking of strategy-making as an exercise in defining the ideal. Promote the ideas of finding the least bad approach, the best justified balance of the ideal and the realistic, the best buy tradeoff between opposing factors.

10. Handling Incommensurable Tradeoffs

ISSUES

Defining strategy options only has a point if you can attach some implications to each that will help in choosing between them. In some cases the tricky part is unravelling the true options; in others, the difficulty comes in the choosing.

At Sassafras Magazines, three strategy options for developing new systems can be translated into cash-flows, containing estimates of the required investment, running costs and cost savings; the issue is then merely to decide which of the possible cash-flows is best for the financial health of the organisation. Something similar is possible at Black Ash Bank, because each of the bank's five strategy options for new telex arrangements has an effect on staff costs and efficiency in the use of telecommunications equipment. Here too, comparing the different cash-flows takes you a long way towards deciding the most attractive strategy.

But there are other cases where, no matter how carefully the details of the strategy options are costed out, the resulting cash-flows are just not an adequate basis for decision. This can happen because one or more factors that should influence the decision really can't be translated into financial terms. This briefing is about the general problem of incommensurables, implications that are relevant to a choice between strategy options but cannot be quantified in common units of measurement.

ANALYSIS

The first three example cases discussed are each dominated by one particular factor that is awkward to measure — respectively, risk, public image and novelty. In the fourth, the challenge is to pick a way through a whole variety of possibly relevant factors.

Strategy Options at Red Cedar

Red Cedar is a project to set up an on-line database information service for a special group of customers: defence industry experts — journalists, strategic analysts and the like. Here the project's demand-side is not the main source of headaches; there is already a rough outline of the kind of information to be stored and the desired facilities for accessing it.

But the means of supplying these demands raise big strategic problems. The project will require database software that can handle text (e.g. articles about global strategy) and graphics (e.g. pictures of guns), as well as highly structured information (technical specifications of different tanks). At the present time, handling this combination of genres of information is not mainstream technology; the most crucial strategy decisions follow from this fact. Red Cedar managers identify the following strategy options:

Strategy A is to develop the new system as part of a joint-venture with a certain supplier of database software, that is keen to use Red Cedar's insight into this area, to develop a new software product for sale to other customers, who also want to store text and graphics and structured information together in one database. Naturally the terms of the joint-venture for Red Cedar will reflect these commercial possibilities.

Strategy B is to use a different software product for this project — in fact, the one and only existing database software that is anywhere near suitable, even though far from ideal for the desired system. Considerable work will be needed to build on this foundation to provide a service to meet all the demands.

Strategy C is to use the same database software product as in Strategy B, but only to implement the most important part of the desired service, leaving out many of the more sophisticated parts.

Strategy D is the flexibility-driven strategy; it commits to a limited project now, containing certain activities that would be needed under any of the other three strategies in any case. After one year, a decision will be made from a better informed position, on whether to go for a form of either B or C; the opportunity for A will probably have passed by then.

Allowing for Risk

Red Cedar management forecast cash-flows for Strategies A, B and C — showing projected investment costs and projected income from customers of the service. They find little difference between the net present value of the projected cash-flows of Strategies A and B. But A seems much more risky than B; after all, joint-ventures are inherently stressful and storing these different genres of information efficiently in one database is quite an ambitious undertaking. Therefore, they decide, if A and B cost much the same and B is less risky, and there is no compensating advantage for A over B, then B must be a more rational choice than A. In the jargon of academic decision theory B is said to 'dominate' A.

Once B and C are compared, B is decisively better than C in cash-flow terms and there is no difference in terms of risk; so B dominates C and C is out too.

It is hard to make a cash-flow for a flexibility-driven strategy like D, but Red Cedar makes the assumption that, at the one-year decision point in D, the choice would be for a B-like strategy. On this basis, it turns out that there is little difference between the net present value of projected cash-flows of B and D. Other things being equal, flexibility is an excellent thing to have in IT strategy matters, because it reduces risk; therefore, Red Cedar decides, Strategy D is the ultimate victor over B.

In this case the decision-making is based on two incommensurable criteria, Cash-flow and subjective perception of Risk. This relatively simple problem is resolved by applying fairly simple decision logic.

Strategy Options at Cedar Wattle City

Cedar Wattle is a zippy, go-ahead city wanting to make a name as the place for stylish modern businesses to be located. The national PTT has suggested to the mayor of Cedar Wattle that the city might care to pay part of the bill for a very advanced, new telecommunications network within the city (the actual technology doesn't matter here). Then Cedar Wattle representatives will be able to claim to any multi-national businesses, wondering where to locate their continental headquarters, that their city has more advanced facilities than any of its rivals.

Plans have been made for a high-speed, high-capacity telecommunications network, linking the eight main telephone exchanges of the city together. The city will pay for this infrastructure; individual businesses will pay for the spurs from their buildings to the nearest point on the network.

There are various strategy options. *Strategy A* is to invest in the whole network as sketched; *Strategy B* is to invest in about half the network; *Strategy C* is to invest in just one line between the city's science park and the middle of the downtown prestige offices area. *Strategy D* is not to do it, at all. How should the mayor go about deciding?

There are two main decision criteria in this case: finance and image. Investigating the financial aspects of each strategy option can get quite complicated because the costs of setting up and maintaining the network will depend on the technical details of the network. The technical details of the network will depend on the assumptions made about volume and patterns of usage. Actual volume and patterns of usage will depend, in part, on the premium tariffs that are charged. The tariffs paid will go to offset the costs. But nobody knows the optimum tariffs to set in order to recover the costs.

But this isn't intended to be a money-making venture anyway. The point of the whole strategy is to have something to boast about to any multi-national businesses, wondering where to locate their continental headquarters — not to invest the city's money in a way that generates the greatest immediate immediate financial return. The objective is to establish Cedar Wattle's image as the place to go for high-technology. But what units of measurement can be applied to image?

Marginal Cost, Marginal Image Gain

The question is really: Which strategy option is the best buy, in terms of the amount of positive image gained in exchange for money lost financing an uneconomic service? Any assessment of image value has to take account of factors like the following: facilities offered by other competing cities in the region; how the proposed network technology rates by world standards; ability of the network to support futuristic facilities, such as videoconferencing and telecommuting, that companies like to talk about, without actually doing; possible vulnerability to rivals who say the network is just a toy, not a serious service; and so on. These things are all tough to quantify.

The mayor decides that the last of the factors just listed is crucial. A line which just links two points (Strategy C) can be derided too easily by critics as a mere experiment or gimmick, rather than a genuine infrastructure. Although there is a significant (but hard to measure) marginal cost to B (half the network) over C (one line), that marginal cost seems to be worth accepting, because B meets the image goal adequately whereas C does not. Further, the significant (but hard to measure) marginal cost of A (whole network) over B (half the network) may bring some marginal increase in image, but (in the mayor's judgement) this marginal increase is very small; so the marginal cost of A over B does not seem to be justified.

This puts Strategy B ahead of A or C. The rough estimate of its net costs shows that B can be paid for within the city's total budget; therefore it wins over its last rival, Strategy D (do nothing).

In this case the incommensurables are Finance and Image. Image is judged to be the crucial one; the cash-flow estimates only play a secondary, fail-safe role, ensuring that the project doesn't bankrupt the city. The decisions between the strategy options are made primarily by forming subjective judgements about their marginal image value, rather than by attempting to measure image directly.

The Strategy Problem at Red Rivergum

Red Rivergum is the codename of a new service introduced by Red Box

Data Services. It provides ecologists with access to an on-line database that contains both recent news and reference information. This poses more intricate strategic problems than the on-line service at Red Cedar. Nobody in the Red Rivergum team is at all sure what an on-line database service for ecologists should be like: what sort of information it should offer, what access facilities it should provide, what exactly the target market is, and so on.

So the general approach is to set up an experimental, free service and to be as bold and innovative as possible, at as little cost as possible. After that, the experience gained will be used in order to develop a real industrial-strength service that will actually make money.

This is another strategy case where the problem is what to choose to do out of an enormous range of possibilities. There is a strong motivation to be as original and creative as possible in spotting new things to do; but, on the other hand, there isn't a great deal of money available for investment in what is a throw-away experimental service, that will generate zero income. In effect, Red Rivergum need to find the strategy that best reconciles the two incommensurables, Novelty and Cost. After a great deal of brain-storming, Red Rivergum finally produces a project proposal that suggests the best buy.

Simplifying by Capping

The project proposal starts by setting some constraints in the form of two financial ratios. Firstly, the *total budget* for the whole experimental project should not be more than 20% of the estimated *capital cost* required for setting up a real service (the real service's *running costs* are excluded from this calculation). The second constraint is that the *software costs* for the experimental project (most of which are the costs of work done by programmers) should not be more than 10% of the estimated software costs for the real service.

This helps to simplify the problem, because it sets a cap on the amount of innovation that can be included; if one exciting but expensive idea is included, some others may have to be excluded. Now the issue becomes how to optimise the amount of relevant, useful novelty within the defined financial constraints.

One of the problems in choosing between options for novelty in an experimental service is that many of the concepts ('on-line text database' and 'current awareness service' and 'high-quality graphics') can easily sound glib and bland; they need to be broken down and clarified. One aspect of all strategy cases where options are defined is that after the choice is finally made (say, Strategy B), it is also quite clear what is not being chosen (all the things that make Strategies A, C and D different

Using Catalogues to Define an Experimental Database Service

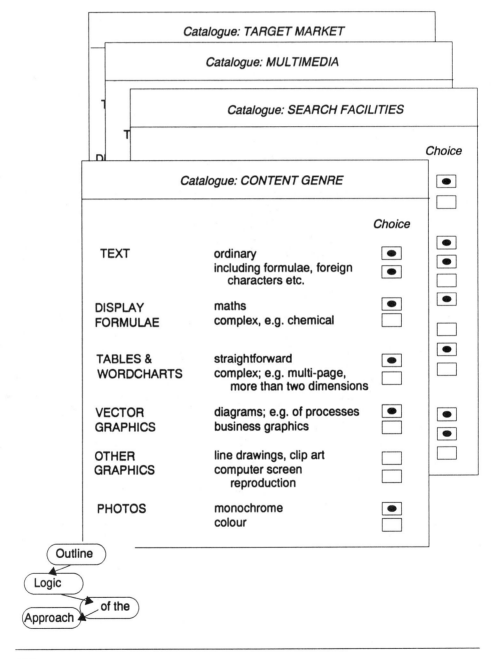

from B). To combat the glibness of terminology and really seek out the best combination of novelties feasible within the constraints, the Red Rivergum planners give special attention to making very clear what they are not going to undertake.

Red Rivergum's final definition of project strategy, after all the option-comparing has been done and the choices have been made, contains a number of 'catalogues'. Each catalogue breaks down one particular aspect of the project into a list of conceivably relevant possibilities — each clearly marked, to show whether it is included or not. For example, there is a catalogue headed 'Content Genre', which shows the nature of the information that will be included: ordinary text; display formulae; diagrams; photographs and so on. The more of these genres the service includes, the more valuable it will probably be; on the other hand, the more it attempts, the more it will cost.

There are other catalogues defining, both specifically and by exclusion, such things as: the facilities for searching for information in the database; whether information can be printed, its timeliness and speed; the type of people the service is aimed at. One catalogue contains nearly all exclusions, in order to show that the service isn't concerned with multimedia possibilities, such as supplying information in the form of audio or moving video or computer software or images that can be viewed from various angles.

Thus the set of chosen items in the catalogues represents the final view, after much brainstorming, of the features of a Red Rivergum service that contains as much relevant Novelty as possible, within the self-imposed Financial Constraints.

Casuarina's Strategy Problem

In each of the three cases so far one hard to quantify factor has been set against financial considerations. The last case in this briefing describes the difficulties arising from the interaction of *several* different non-financial incommensurables.

Casuarina is already very well-known as an agency for temporary office staff. It has a strong network of branches and there are now big plans to move upmarket to place clerical staff such as book-keepers and customer order clerks on a permanent basis. Casuarina even intends to go for specialised markets such as travel agency staff, computer programmers and analysts, insurance specialists and so on. There are two main components in this business strategy. One is a marketing campaign to change the company's image. The other is the development of elaborate computerised facilities, that will support Casuarina staff in their challenging task of matching jobs and candidates in the new markets.

The IT workgroup identifies about fifty different possible demand-side elements (functions or possible sub-systems, they might be called). There are some fairly obvious ones: 'Registration of Candidate', 'General Job/Candidate Matching', 'Nominal Ledger' and 'Statistical Overview', for example. And there are more esoteric ones. For example, there is a sophisticated procedure for matching candidates who are specialists in the oil and natural gas sectors of the economy to appropriate jobs; this makes use of a knowledge base of technical terminology. Analogous facilities are planned in eight other specialist areas: computer staff, for example. There is an electronic bulletin board facility, making available hints, news and so on, via the telecommunications network to staff in different offices. A system for tracking complaints, liability claims and legal actions is another facility demanded. An automated system for training Casuarina's own staff is another. A facility for distributing and cataloguing libraries of slides showing the locations of available jobs is yet another. And so it goes on.

The strategic problem is this. Casuarina *could* make a master plan to produce one highly integrated family of systems that fully met all fifty demands. But this would surely be over-ambitious; it would take far too long to plan and then implement; and there would be a strong chance of things going wrong — not necessarily through incompetence, but simply because there are too many uncertainties. Or Casuarina *could* choose just a tiny subset of all the possible features, just enough to be able to operate but not more, and implement that subset as efficiently as possible. The trouble here is that, if you wanted to add in most of the other features afterwards (which you certainly would, in order to achieve the strategy of the upmarket image), then you would probably have to scrap all the simple systems you had just built. That is the way investment in IT systems usually works. So Casuarina need a strategy that lies between the two extremes. But how is it to be found?

Casuarina's Approach

The fifty facilities are drawn up in a list, structured as naturally as possible. The analysts and managers of Casuarina have a session to brainstorm through the list; they agree to allocate one out of the letters A, B, C and D to each facility demanded.

Option A has a simple meaning: the facility is included in the initial version of the new set of systems.

Option B means that a firm commitment is made now to include the facility in the Casuarina set of systems. From the very beginning, the overall design of the systems includes the facility. In the initial version of the new set of systems, there is (conceptually) an empty spot reserved for the facility. The facility is slotted in neatly as soon as convenient thereafter.

Option C is like Option B: an open place is left for the facility in the whole design, so that it can be slotted in later. The difference is that it won't be slotted in automatically like a B facility. Casuarina will wait until it has a successful system including all the A and B functions. At that point, it will examine each C function individually to decide whether it should still be slotted in, or whether perhaps things now look different.

Option D facilities are excluded from consideration in the design. This doesn't mean they are rejected and will never be done. It may mean that, by its very nature, the facility can be treated as a separate little project to create its own separate sub-system. Alternatively it may be advisable to wait and get a clearer view of the shape of the desired facility, after the main family of systems is well established.

Thus, once Casuarina management have allocated an A, B, C or D to each of the fifty facilities, they will have a solution to their strategic problem. But, after brainstorming for a number of hours, everyone realises that they have glossed over one fundamental aspect of the problem. The set of fifty A/B/C/D choices needs to be *coherent*.

For example, one person in the group, Anton, keeps voting for Cs and Ds, because he wants to avoid immediate commitments, play safe and *minimise risk*. Bernard is voting As for all the most extravagant facilities, because he thinks that is the best way to establish the *upmarket, new image* of the business in the market. Colin votes Bs for almost everything, because he believes that the most important thing is to get the *architecture* of the whole thing right from the very start. David always votes A for facilities that concern the branches and D for head office facilities; he feels that the *culture* which has made Casuarina such a profitable business has always been that the branches should get the best of everything before head office gets anything at all.

They end up trading votes, making compromises, and achieving a thoroughly incoherent, khaki-coloured strategy, that doesn't really minimise risk, establish the upmarket, new image, set up a stable architecture or properly reflect the culture.

Identifying and Resolving the Factors

There are four incommensurables here: Risk, Image, Architecture and Company Culture. How should Casuarina resolve them? This is an involved problem without any simple solution. An excellent start is to recognise that the four incommensurables actually do exist. Bring them out in the open and discuss them before getting involved in the As, Bs, Cs and Ds of individual facilities. It may be possible to resolve part of the

Casuarina: Making a Coherent Selection of Choices

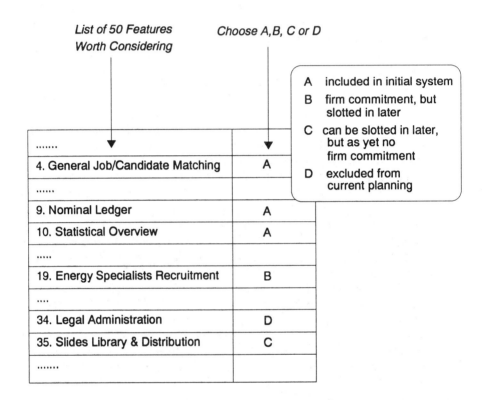

List of 50 Features Worth Considering

Choose A, B, C or D

A   included in initial system
B   firm commitment, but slotted in later
C   can be slotted in later, but as yet no firm commitment
D   excluded from current planning

....	
4. General Job/Candidate Matching	A
......	
9. Nominal Ledger	A
10. Statistical Overview	A
.....	
19. Energy Specialists Recruitment	B
....	
34. Legal Administration	D
35. Slides Library & Distribution	C
....	

To make 50 COHERENT Choices:

First, agree firm guidelines on the relative importance of factors such as:
. Risk
. Image
. Architecture
. Company Culture.

Then make the choices.

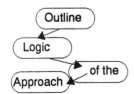

Outline

Logic

Approach   of the

problem in that way; for example, to agree that the Culture factor should be ignored, and therefore may not be advanced as an argument in any subsequent discussions.

With luck firm principles may be agreed about the relative weight of these incommensurables. For example, firstly: there must be something really advanced in the very first version of the system in order to capture that *upmarket, new image* right from the very start; but this only implies selecting a small portion of all the possible esoteric facilities; the others can wait. Secondly: apart from this, *minimise risk* must be the watchword. Thirdly, only pay attention to *architecture* and *culture*, if there are cost-free ways of doing so, without compromising the first two principles. With an agreed set of principles in this form, it should be much easier to go through the fifty facilities, allocating the letters to take *coherent* account of the incommensurables.

It may be a good thing to draw up several different sets of principles about the incommensurables and explore their implications in terms of the systems' facilities as strategy options. The great thing is to compare the options that are both relevant and coherent.

Summing Up

There are no rigorous techniques to be followed for situations like these; they can't really be handled by a predefined step-by-step approach. Nevertheless the four example cases do illustrate certain handy concepts that often help in getting part of the way.

Red Cedar shows the concept of one strategy option *dominating* another: Strategies A and B differ in certain ways; B is better than A in some ways or under some circumstances; but A has no obvious advantages over B; therefore the problem can be simplified by knocking out A.

Cedar Wattle City shows the concept of *marginal difference*: the marginal advantage of Strategy B over Strategy C is judged (by inspection, rather than calculation) to be worth the marginal cost.

Red Rivergum shows the concept of *simplification by capping*: starting out from the assumption of a maximum budget and other constraints, simplifies the range of choices considerably.

Casuarina shows the concept of deciding between *different general principles* first in order to simplify the choice between specific options.

Plainly such cases can't be handled adequately by first defining the demands and then planning the detail of the supply; that is just too crude. If somebody offers you a new standard method for defining IT strategy in an organisation, test the method out by seeing whether it could do justice to the Red Cedar, Cedar Wattle City and Red Rivergum cases. If those tests are passed, let Casuarina be the ultimate trial.

PRACTICAL ADVICE

➤ Accept that the rational analysis of a strategic situation may sometimes throw up options whose implications are incommensurable. In such cases, it follows by definition that you can't demonstrate by tight reasoning or calculation that one particular option is superior to another.

➤ Don't be tempted into making arbitrary, simplistic quantifications of factors like risk and prestige and public relations.

➤ But don't exclude a factor from consideration, just because it can't be quantified.

➤ Even if some of the implications are incommensurable, do your best to define and summarise the possibilities and implications as clearly as possible.

➤ Look out for opportunities to simplify the problem with any one of the following techniques: finding one option that dominates another; focusing on marginal differences between options; simplifying the range of options by capping; and deciding between different general principles before considering more specific options.

➤ Don't try to tackle problems involving incommensurables by applying the simple approach of first defining demand, and then filling in supply details. It just won't work.

11. Tackling Package Options

ISSUES

A piece of 'packaged' software resembles a postal package in the following respect: you can't accept a package, unwrap it, take out the items you want and hand the residue back over the post office counter. You have to take it or leave it. But with packaged software things are more complicated; you may well be able to ignore some of the items you don't want or pay for them to be taken away. You may even be able to add in extras not contained in the original package — albeit, usually at a substantial price.

Packaged software is available to meet the demands for application systems in specific industries or to provide general applications that are required by many industries. The package may be relatively cheap, but then it may not do precisely what you would like, and modifications to minor details may cost more than the whole standard package. In this way, cases where package options are involved often provide excellent examples of complex interactions between supply and demand factors. In more abstract language, it can be said that with packaged software there is no simple relation between the extent of the demands and the extent of the investment required to supply them; small marginal increases in demands may result in large marginal increases in supply costs. Therein lie the complications for the decision-maker.

The essential difficulty is deciding the best tradeoff between packaged and bespoke (i.e. 'made to measure') software, but before that matter can even be considered, there is another difficulty. How do you get into a position where you can identify what the main options and their tradeoffs actually are? This briefing explores the issues raised by packages.

ANALYSIS

If packaged software is not a relevant option, it follows that, if you are to have a computer system at all, you have to develop the software yourself. Many of the other briefings show that simply to ask people their desires for systems, collate them in a 'requirements' document, and then go ahead to work out the appropriate technical design may not produce the most cost-effective result. In very many cases, at least three strategy options, usually more, can easily be sketched out. Perhaps Strategy A meets the most important requirements and prunes out the others, making it relatively cheap and quick; Strategy C meets all the desired requirements (except a few that are really wayout), but is correspondingly expensive; Strategy B stakes a claim to the middle ground somewhere between A and C in terms of what it delivers and what it costs.

Often it takes hard, skilful work to arrive at the (say) three most relevant candidate options and then to choose between them. The trouble with packages is that they can easily generate a vast new range of plausible strategy options that have to be taken into account.

The Complexity of the Range of Options

Suppose, for the sake of discussion, three strategy options have already been sketched out, all based on the idea of having bespoke software specially written: Strategies A, B and C, the modest, moderate and ambitious strategies respectively.

You survey the market and find that there are, say, four packages available that seem worth considering (W, X, Y and Z). Very likely the price of each package will be attractive — perhaps around the cost of Strategy A, but offering systems as extensive as B or C. On the other hand, being generalised, some features of a package won't be quite what you need for your company; and maybe a few things regarded as so essential that they belong even in Strategy A aren't included in all the packages. And all four packages differ from each other in various awkward to summarise ways. Now there is a choice between seven possibilities: A, B, C, W, X, Y and Z: each one with its own attractions and disadvantages in terms of demands met and supply implications (particularly cost and time).

But this is only the start of the complications. If the W option is so much cheaper than C, perhaps the very best strategy would be to buy package W, but also pay its suppliers to modify it and add some features; that might produce a system that does as much as C but still costs less and is ready earlier. Of course, the same concept can be applied to X, Y and Z too; so the seven options have now become eleven.

But this is a gross over-simplification; the option of buying package W and modifying/supplementing it actually has to be broken down into several sub-options: modifying the package very modestly or using it as a mere starting point for far-reaching extensions, or one out of three or four possible points between those extremes; then similar possibilities exist for package X; and so on.

In other words, anybody looking down from Mount Olympus on this situation, with infinite time available, could work out that there were dozens of plausible strategy options to be found — each one different in important ways from all the others; each one with its pros and cons that made it a serious candidate to be the 'best buy'. Unfortunately there normally isn't time to make this kind of Olympian survey. This conflict between the profusion of options and the practical constraints of evaluating them is the essence of the problem.

Unacceptable Simplifications

In this kind of situation, people sometimes turn away from the complexity of the possibilities altogether. A document is produced making a firm, non-negotiable statement of what is expected from a system; package suppliers are told that only proposals fully compliant with these demands will be considered. As a result, most of them quote for the work of modifying and expanding their package, as well as for the package itself. When the proposals are in, the best proposal received is to be accepted.

This approach simply ignores most of the options discussed so far. Suppose 20% of the total cost quoted by the supplier of package X actually goes to pay for the last 2% of the non-negotiable functions demanded. Would those demands really have been set as non-negotiable, if it had been known that they cost so much? The simplifying approach adopted prevents that question ever being asked; it prevents consideration of the option of meeting 98% of the demands for 80% of the price.

Casting demands in concrete first, before you even consider supply possibilities, is an unacceptable simplification. On the other hand, any more detailed attempt at exposing options, seems to require an almost infinite amount of time. There are two big problems here in reconciling supply and demand factors: one is actually identifying the most important strategic options in a neat, economical way; the other is choosing between them.

White Cypress, White Gum, White Mallee and White Wattle are four manufacturing companies faced by much the same problem. Each company needs a comprehensive range of new systems to control inventory, production and related functions. Standard software packages are available and, at first sight, represent much cheaper and quicker solutions than commissioning development of bespoke software. But how do you navigate around the whole set of possibilities the packages raise? The four companies take four different approaches.

The White Cypress Approach

White Cypress is the least sophisticated company. Its managers avoid the time and expense of preparing a detailed definition of requirements in isolation. They start by investigating the most prominent package on the market from Supplier A. Judging by its documentation, most of the things the package does are indeed things that White Cypress would like to have in a computer system; and there are only a few minor things that White Cypress might ideally like which are not in the package. Supplier A confirms these judgements.

The managers of White Cypress also ask a software house, Supplier B, that doesn't have a package, how much it would cost to write a software system covering much the same ground, but made to measure to White Cypress's exact requirements. Calling the package price 100, the bespoke price is 350; also the package can be delivered tomorrow, whereas it would take one elapsed year to program the bespoke system.

The other supplier they contact, Supplier C, also has a package at a cost of 100, but he is far less positive. He estimates that to produce the system White Cypress really want, his package would have to be greatly modified at a cost of 400. So Supplier C's modified package would cost 500 in total, as compared to Supplier B's totally bespoke system at 350 and Supplier A's 'more or less adequate' package at only 100.

The White Cypress managers are aware that they haven't investigated every possible detail that might be relevant to their decision, but they decide that they know enough to make a pragmatic decision. The package of Supplier A is chosen.

The White Cypress Experience

As soon as the package is installed, it becomes clear that some of the minor things that White Cypress managers noticed were not in the package are in fact vital to their particular business. A group of managers refuse to use the system until certain things are changed. After much argument they scale down their demands to a list of five non-negotiable points for immediate action: the safety stock level must be held on the stock record; it must be possible to record stock held at more than one location; cost values must be eleven digits, including four of decimals; bulk issue parts should not be handled through the material requisitions procedures; it must be possible to record certain stock items in units of a thousand. The cost of programming these changes is 40, although the amount of the software that actually has to be changed is probably less than 1%. The work takes twelve weeks.

The system goes live, and immediately some even more important requirements emerge. After two months, the White Cypress factory manager has a list of ten major points that everyone is convinced must be altered, absolutely irrespective of what it may cost: safety stock should be allowed for in material requirements planning; each stock transaction should be costed; inventories should be valued at actual cost; and so on.

Making these changes costs another 100 and takes another 20 elapsed weeks.

This example illustrates a number of typical features of the package versus bespoke dilemma. First is the price gap in the initial investment; a ratio of 3.5:1 between package and bespoke is not exceptional. Second is the relatively huge cost of changing small portions of a standard system; 40% extra to change 1% of the system is not exceptional; modifying a substantial amount can easily cost more than starting from scratch. Third is the great difficulty of judging beforehand what the exact differences are between the standard system and the system you genuinely need.

It is very difficult, even with hindsight, to find a realistic, well structured approach to the whole problem. White Cypress managers have to scramble about in an undignified way, hold angry meetings, deliver ultimatums and work many bad-tempered hours of overtime — and yet they end up with a tolerable system at a cost of 240. Who is to say whether they would really have done better if they had handled things differently? On the other hand, the unsubtle White Cypress approach can reasonably be criticised as too risky. The set of vital changes discovered after signing the order might have cost 150 instead of 40 and might have delayed the system by a year instead of 12 weeks. The second batch might also have cost more and taken longer. White Cypress surrendered control over these factors.

The White Gum Approach

White Gum is a gem of a case showing what can happen if you try to be too methodical. The production director at White Gum knows only too well the anguish that can result from a White Cypress-like approach to the problem. He has seen several companies like White Cypress who have cut corners on defining their requirements first and come to grief because they had nothing against which to compare the actual facilities offered. On the other hand, he is well aware that simply defining a set of inflexible requirements in isolation and telling a supplier that the only acceptable proposal is one that meets 100% of those demands is not the way to arrive at the best buy.

He goes on to reason as follows. Considering a package for a manufacturing company can be a very complex matter of matching supply and demand. On the demand side are the functions and features that are essential, nice to have, interesting or irrelevant. On the supply side are the possibilities contained in the packages that are on the market. Surely the sensible thing to do is to collect as much information as possible about these supply and demand factors, and make it as well structured and easy to cross-relate as possible. With a well organised definition of White

Gum's demands and the supply possibilities offered by, say, five suppliers of packages, it must surely be possible to work out the optimum solution to this matching problem.

His team produces a very impressive, highly structured, 'invitation to tender' document. In essence, it describes an ideal system for White Gum. It identifies 119 discrete functions and organises them in a multi-level hierarchy; thus function 5.3.2.1 states that 'the requirements planning period must be structured as 65 weekly time slots'. The package suppliers are asked to give the following information about each of the 119 functions. Is it (1) fully satisfied by the package (if so, give reference to package documentation where described)? Or is it (2) partially satisfied by the package (if so, give reference)? Or is it (3) not satisfied at all?

Then, for those functions where answers (2) and (3) are given, suppliers are asked to state whether it is (a) possible to modify or expand the package to provide the function fully (if so, give costs), or (b) possible to modify or expand the package to provide the function partially (if so, give costs), or (c) impossible to modify or expand the package to provide the function.

White Gum's idea is that once five different suppliers have supplied tenders, all containing this information, structured in this consistent way, then White Gum will be able to process all this data to arrive at the best buy: almost certainly, choosing one particular package and some but not all of its possible modifications. In this way White Gum should be able to find the 'best buy' combination of functions and price.

The White Gum Experience

The production director at White Gum has prepared the ground for a truly magisterial survey of his strategy options. The only problem is that he is still waiting for a supplier to send him the information he wants in the detail and the format he wants. Unfortunately the time needed by a knowledgeable pre-sales consultant to do the work White Gum are asking for would cost more than the whole purchase price of a typical standard package; since there is only a one-in-five chance of getting the order, this is not an attractive business proposition for the package supplier.

Suppose that, instead of White Gum, a manufacturing company with one factory employing 500 people, the prospective client is a huge oil company needing a package to be installed in hundreds of locations world-wide. Then, the White Gum approach could be sensible — provided the number of functions is still 119; with 119,000 functions, exactly the same problem might well arise. The important general point is that if you do try to tackle the package/bespoke dilemma by really clamping down on detail, there is a grave danger that the detail — no matter how well structured — will get out of proportion to the size of the problem. The White Gum case suggests the need for the bold generalisation, the judgement that certain detail can be filtered out at the decision-making stage, the calculated leap in the dark.

The White Mallee Approach

One aspect of the package/bespoke dilemma is that certain features in a company's new system may be regarded as essential, while others are merely desirable — welcome if provided by the package, but probably not to be paid for as extras.

White Cypress wait until they are already committed before worrying about this distinction, by which time they have so many pressing problems that there is no time to think about functions that are desirable but not essential. White Gum play their cards close to the chest: they want to get all the structured, costed information in first — before deciding on essential/desirable distinctions. White Gum are entirely rational in this, because, in reality, the distinction is a considerable over-simplification. A certain feature may not be literally essential, but may be irresistible at a marginal cost of only 1, worth considering at 5 and out of the question at 10. Another feature may not be literally essential, but is still quite desirable even at a marginal cost of 10; and so on. The White Gum approach can handle this in theory, but, as the example shows, not in practice.

The managers of White Mallee, profiting from White Gum's embarrassment, reason as follows. Admittedly dividing up possible functions for a system into just two categories, essential and desirable, is a big simplification; but unless that nettle is grasped, there is no chance of making progress. The main features White Mallee need can be summarised as a list of thirty brief, general points, of which half are called essential and half desirable. The fifteen *essential* features contain items like: hold stock quantities at multiple locations, hold bill of materials information, hold schedule orders on suppliers, and so on. The fifteen *desirable* features contain items such as: simple demand forecasting, generate supplier orders automatically, ABC product analysis, and so on.

This approach works quite well. Compared to the attempts of White Cypress and White Gum, the approach is like a hot knife through butter. The list of *essential* features is a fine tool for sorting out those packages that are basically right for White Mallee and those which are not. Since quite a few packages meet all or nearly all the essential features, the list of desirable features can be used to reduce the list substantially further. Thus White Mallee arrive fairly rapidly at a shortlist of two and a reasonable estimate of the likely amount of package modification and cost involved. But this is only the first stage.

They then enter a second stage of more detailed discussions with the two suppliers to check out much of the detail that is merely summarised by the initial, broad brush comparison of points, and to examine the implications of paying for some of the items that are on the desirable list but not in the package. During these detailed discussions one supplier establishes a clear lead over the other and is therefore chosen.

Thus White Mallee's two-stage approach is an efficient way of getting to the right package and the right combination of functions. Note, however, that a great deal depends on the initial list of essential and desirable requirements. Summarising the features of a complicated manufacturing system in this way isn't easy. If the person drawing up the list makes the right judgements about what is essential, desirable and not worth mentioning, then the approach can be very effective indeed. But if the wrong judgements are made, the whole decision-making procedure can be blown off course.

The White Wattle Approach

White Mallee benefits by taking a two-stage approach. White Wattle's approach to decision-making actually contains three stages.

First of all the Production Director and his advisors write off for the standard documentation of a fair number of packages. After studying that information and thinking carefully about White Wattle's needs in outline, they form the provisional view that the new White Wattle system can be met primarily by packaged software, except for two special parts of the system, sales forecasting and material costing, that probably have to be bespoke. That is Stage 1.

Then they produce a document, called 'Provisional Definition of Requirements', outlining the kind of system they probably need and giving some nuances of the differences between essential, desirable and other types of requirements. Suppliers are invited individually to come and brainstorm informally, on a non-binding basis, about the way their products match up to the ideas in the document. This feedback deepens White Wattle's understanding of the likely awkward issues and, at the same time, helps firm up the provisional view from Stage 1. That is Stage 2.

Then in Stage 3, White Wattle produces the invitation to tender document, which prompts formal contractual proposals from suppliers. This document benefits greatly from the work of the previous stages. It leaves out unrealistic demands, it states that certain parts of the system will have to be bespoke and, on those key issues that are likely to be the real battleground between competing packages, it carefully explains what is and is not required. After that, evaluating suppliers' responses, to decide which one to choose and how much bespoke work to invest in, is relatively straightforward.

Again, as with the White Mallee case, a lot depends on the effectiveness of the people involved in the early stages. They need to be shrewd enough to sense which issues are likely to be most decisive and home in on those during contacts with suppliers. They need to avoid wasting time on the things the suppliers want to talk about or on things that are interesting to discuss but unlikely to influence decisions.

Conclusions

What do these four cases demonstrate? First of all, the theoretical view that packaged software opens up a whole variety of difficult to handle options is indeed true in practice. The problem is just as formidable as it sounds in theory.

Second, there is no reliable, standard way of handling the problem. In three of the cases, White Gum, White Mallee and White Wattle, management think quite hard and came up with different ways of structuring decision-making — in two of the three cases with some success. It wouldn't be too hard to devise some variations on the two successful approaches and find plausible reasons for adopting them in certain cases. The important thing is to understand the essence of this kind of problem and find the approach which best does justice to the particular case.

Solutions to the problem of structuring this decision-making will vary depending on whether there are two possible packages in contention initially or ten, how significant the deal is likely to be to the supplier (20% of annual turnover or 0.02%), whether there are good reasons to expect this company to have significantly different needs from others in the same industry, and (if so) what the reasons are, and so on. Any detailed standard approach to package selection which brushes aside such differences may easily share the fate of White Gum's approach: admirable in theory, almost worthless in practice.

There may not be a credible standard way, but there are some fairly certain general principles. First, simply defining requirements and then choosing the supplier that makes the best proposal for meeting them is unlikely to result in finding the 'best buy', since it ignores the possibility of trading certain demands against the costs and complications of supply.

One necessary concept in avoiding White Gum's fate seems to be accepting the need to make broad, simplifying statements about demands

— a delicate task, since there is a danger of simplifying out factors that are actually crucial.

The other fairly common factor in successful package selection seems to be a carefully controlled multi-stage, decision-making structure, as with White Mallee and White Wattle — rather than one big, concentrated process, or indeed a sprawling, ill-controlled, spread out process.

PRACTICAL ADVICE

> ➤ Bear in mind that, when the possibility of using packaged software exists, defining demand first and only then studying the supply possibilities is not adequate. Interaction is needed between the supply and demand possibilities.

> ➤ Be aware of the full complexity of the situation. The possibility of modifying packages considerably increases the number of supply–demand options available. Treat the whole process as an exercise in discovering and narrowing down options.

> ➤ Don't look for any one standard way of resolving the supply–demand complications in cases where packaged software is a relevant factor. Be open to different possible approaches and decide what is most appropriate for the given situation.

> ➤ Take account of the tradeoff between comprehensively checking out details and evaluating tradeoffs, on the one hand, and producing results in a reasonable time, on the other.

> ➤ Don't forget that the readiness of the supplier to participate fully in your investigations may well be a constraint.

> ➤ Don't be afraid to set up a carefully controlled multi-stage, decision-making structure, if that seems most efficient. But make sure that you control the iterations yourself, and that you are not blown off course by awkward issues that should have been handled earlier.

12. Dealing with Unquantifiable Benefits

ISSUES

If you can't make a credible quantification of the benefits of some investment in IT, can it ever be rational to go ahead? This problem has long haunted IT management and is still a long way from being resolved. In fact things have got worse over the years as attention has shifted from systems that automate clerical tasks towards systems with less tangible ends, such as 'strategic advantage'.

Consider two limiting cases. First, the decision-makers at Sassafras Magazines are very fortunate. They have three strategy options, ranging from modest to extensive. For each, the costs of the new systems can be estimated and so can their benefits, primarily staff savings and savings of the costs of the present, very inefficient, bureau-based computer systems. Discounted cash-flow analysis is the main tool for deciding between the three strategy options.

Over at Angophora Mining, they are trying to decide whether and how to invest in a system that will store the texts of legal contracts in a computer database. Four options are identified. The costs of building each of these four possible computer systems can be estimated, to roughly the same degree of accuracy as with Sassafras; but what benefits can be added into the cash-flow? There aren't any staff savings or savings of the costs of present computer systems. Among its main benefits, the new system is expected to help Angophora legal staff negotiate more confidently and avoid signing contracts that contain mistakes. But how is it possible to put a cash value on that kind of benefit? And without quantified benefits how can any choice be made?

This briefing assumes that every sensible drop of financial quantification has been squeezed out of both these cases, including, where it is plausible, assessment of matters such as increased market share, better control of bad debts and so on. In the one case, Sassafras, there is clearly sufficient evidence available to make a sound decision; in the Angophora case there is not. The problem is what to do about Angophora and similar cases.

ANALYSIS

This is one of those problems where there is no straightforward solution to be found. But useful progress is possible by eliminating some of the minor confusions scattered around the periphery of the problem area. After that the issues can be seen more clearly and pragmatic solutions suggest themselves.

Clearing the Ground

One logical confusion is almost embarrassingly simple, but it has vitiated many a debate. Discussing how to *measure* benefits is a totally different thing from discussing how to *achieve* benefits. If you were discussing the merits of different ways to measure heat (techniques for designing thermometers, say), it would not be at all relevant to bring in the technology of electric fires and designs of central heating systems and ways of insulating houses; those things are all concerned with creating heat or using it efficiently, but not with measuring it. Similarly, a person's ideas on how to improve the efficiency of a data centre or how to develop software more quickly and reliably or how to spot opportunities for innovation may or may not be good ideas — but they are nothing to do with the subject of measuring the benefits of an awkward case like Angophora.

Articles or books on measuring benefits are often padded out with matter that is irrelevant. They may suffer from the confusion just described or contain statements that are self-evident or meaningless or too abstract for any practical application. Advice about the importance of treating your information systems as an asset, or treating IT as an investment not a cost item, or thinking strategically rather than tactically, or ensuring each project has a 'champion' to 'sell' its benefits, or remembering to count in increased profits as well as reduced costs, or monitoring results against forecasts, or concentrating on the 20% of cases that yield 80% of the benefits, or learning from surveys of the results of strategic systems is usually beside the point. Material like this rarely helps you get any better grasp of the issues raised by a case such as Angophora's.[1]

Relative Quantification Difficulties

To talk as if the Sassafras and Angophora cases were quite different in kind is a useful but ultimately misleading simplification. On the surface, the benefits of one are definitely quantifiable, the benefits of the other definitely not. But in fact you *could* make estimates of the Angophora benefits if you really had to; the trouble is that they would be terribly speculative. You would be reasoning in terms like this: the probability of a serious mistake in negotiating a contract is 1% and the cost of such a mistake might be $1–10m; this system will reduce the probability of a mistake from 1% to 0.1%; from this and similar data a value can be calculated for the system. If a sceptic asked for evidence to show that the cost of mistakes in contracts actually was in the range given and the change in the probability of a mistake actually was the percentage, it would probably be hard to give a satisfactory answer.

But the Sassafras figures aren't absolutely certain either, and some of them are more speculative than others. For example, the savings in labour costs are more difficult to forecast than the savings from leaving the present computer bureau.

In fact, benefit estimates can be placed along a continuum, with degrees of uncertainty graded off pretty continuously. This is a useful insight for two reasons. First, different people have different motivations towards quantification; some will go quite a long way along the notional continuum before admitting that the estimates are so uncertain as to be futile; other people will lose faith in the value of the numbers much earlier. Second, different people may have different opinions about where a given benefit estimate is located along the continuum of uncertainty. One person may think that the estimates just given of Angophora's savings through avoiding mistakes are so arbitrary that they are worthless, but find other estimates made of benefits achieved through negotiating contracts with more favourable terms to be quite convincing. Somebody else may think exactly the reverse. Reconciling such opinions may be a delicate job, but at least the concept of the continuum of uncertainty helps explain what is happening.

This can be a big help if you're trying to keep order in a meeting between people with different temperaments. It can also help you avoid a more subtle snare. Sometimes people find extremely ingenious ways of expressing in financial terms benefits that nobody else could even begin to quantify (perhaps cleverly translating into money such factors as staff leaving because their work is so dull; perhaps showing how a reduced elapsed time for a certain activity can save money, even if the actual amount of work remains the same). The very ingenuity of the case presented may evoke admiration and disarm scepticism. But it shouldn't; the underlying assumptions still need to be appraised, and if they seem arbitrary or unbelievable, then no amount of ingenuity in the subsequent reasoning should rescue the case.

Discrete or Continuous Choices

Quantifying the expected benefits in order to decide whether to undertake a project to build a system is one thing; trying to quantify actual benefits for a system already operational is quite different. In one way, quantifying the benefits of a possible new system may seem the more difficult, because less information probably exists; but in another way, it is less demanding — and for an important reason.

If you are estimating the benefits for an existing operational system, you normally want to arrive at a figure: subject to a margin of error no doubt, but still a number somewhere between zero and infinity. When estimating the benefits in order to decide whether or not to carry out a new project, all you really need is enough information to help you make that decision. If the breakeven point between doing and not doing the project is, say, a net present value of $1m, you need to find out whether the benefits are more or less than $1m; whether an accurate estimate would be $2m or $20m is probably irrelevant to the distinction.

This briefing concentrates on the problem of estimating benefits as the basis for decision-making and ignores the problem of benefit quantification for an existing operational system, interesting though that can be.

First of all, it is not entirely valid to suggest that an estimate need only be made for the yes/no decision. The Sassafras and Angophora cases offer four and five options respectively (counting 'do nothing' as an option), differing in scope, each with its own costs and benefits. The real task in these and many other cases is to compare the benefits of four or five options.

But is that a fair account of the problem? Is an IT decision normally a problem with discrete choices? If you are offered a treacle factory by the liquidator of a bankrupt company, there may well be just two discrete choices, to buy it today or not; but if you are thinking of buying shares in a treacle manufacturer, there is a continuous range of choices, to buy any quantity from zero through to quite a large number.

Fortunately most IT strategy problems can be reduced to a small number of discrete choices (albeit more than two). For example, you may be able to see by inspection that although there are several strategy options available for Angophora, which offer a little more than Strategy B and a little less than Strategy C, none of them would have much chance of being judged superior to both B and C, no matter how carefully you estimated the costs and benefits.

This model of possible decisions arranged in a small number of discrete steps is a very useful element in approaching many cases.

Applying Stepped Decision Logic

Sometimes, this stepped decision model makes it possible to knock out certain options, without making any very bold assumptions about cost and benefit figures. For example, it may be possible to avoid quantifying the total benefits of Angophora's Strategy D, if the reasoning goes as follows. The extra cost of D over Strategy C has a net present value of $200,000. By comparison with C, D provides the ability to make certain queries that are based on artificial intelligence techniques. How many such queries are expected? 500. Are they worth $400 each? Impossible. Therefore C is superior and D must drop out. But if there were 50,000 queries at $4 each, the situation would be quite different. Strategy D would be manifestly superior to C.

Thus it may be possible to avoid the painful task of putting a financial value on the total system, by concentrating on the quantification of *marginal benefits in non-financial terms*. Angophora can ask how many of the special queries there will be, just as Casuarina, the employment agency, can ask how many more job-seekers will be matched to jobs under its Strategy C system than under the Strategy B system.

These things may still be painful to estimate, but may well be more approachable than cold financial figures. Probably the whole problem can't solved in this way, but it is often possible to knock out one or two options, and that can be a useful step forward.

Justification by Portfolio

Now for the real meat, such as it is, of the debate on awkward benefits. When you look at them carefully, most of the credible solutions that are available to the problems discussed actually amount to *justifications for not quantifying the benefits*.

Red Rivergum is a project to set up an experimental service providing ecologists with access to an on-line database, containing both recent news and reference information. The costs of the project can be estimated, but the financial benefits are very awkward; since the experimental service is to be free, there will be no income. Even if everything is a great success, the system and database for the experimental service will be thrown away and replaced by a much more extensive, much more solidly built service. The real benefit of the system, even if it succeeds, is counted in the experience, knowledge, market feedback and technical expertise it brings to Red Rivergum and its parent, RBDS. How can you put a figure on such things? At first sight, this seems at least as challenging as the Angophora case.

There is a vital difference. The Angophora case has two problem aspects: first, assessing the financial benefits is difficult; second, without an assessment of the financial benefits, there seems to be no basis for any rational decision on whether to do the project (and if so, in what form). That is the awkward combination. But at Red Rivergum, the factors are: first, it is very difficult to assess the financial benefits; second, it is still feasible to make a rational decision whether to do the project (and if so, in what form), *without assessing the financial benefits*.

Red Rivergum's parent, RBDS, has already decided, for broad strategic reasons, that it must invest in projects that gain experience of innovation. Red Rivergum's is just one of many possibilities. Therefore, the important test in deciding whether or how to do the Red Rivergum project is: How does this particular project compare with other projects that might be done in order to gain experience of innovation? If there are proposals in ten other parts of the company for similar on-line services but in different knowledge areas, RBDS surely won't undertake them all, and some way of choosing between them must be found. But if the champions of the Red Rivergum project can show that their project experiments with certain aspects of an on-line service (for example, in the area of the user interface), which are both very important and not covered by rival projects in RBDS, then that kind of argument can justify the Red Rivergum project.

Something important has happened here: in this case a rational decision can be made without translating the project's benefits into financial terms. Now the issue arises: Is a pure experimental project an exceptional case or are there many other cases where good reasons can be cited for sidestepping the matter of financial quantification of benefits? The issue is important, because this seems the most promising approach to an otherwise intractable problem.

Justification by Inseparability

In the Red Rivergum case one important detail is implied, without being fully explored. The whole Red Rivergum project contains both investment in technology and investment in work by non-technologists; e.g. experts on ecology collating information, indexing it, marketing the service and so on. But nobody suggests the option of doing the project by other means, in a way that excludes the technology. You can't have an on-line database service without using technology; the very identity of the projected service as a business entity depends on the technology. This factor makes the Red Rivergum case different from those of and Angophora, where magazines could still be published and contracts could still be negotiated, even without any new computer project. Are there perhaps some other cases, that may lack the experimental dimension, but where the argument applies that the computer system is an inseparable part of a business entity?

Candlebark Insurance has planned a system to maintain sophisticated statistics about multi-national clients who have Candlebark policies in many countries. This system serves a small Global Clients department of expert personnel at head office, whose concerns are to ensure that this important but tricky insurance business is as profitable as possible, and also to expand its scope. Here is a line of reasoning justifying the Global Clients computer system.

Candlebark could easily abolish (or not set up) the Global Clients department; the insurance policies concerned could still be administered by Candlebark's local company in each country. But Candlebark can attach a value to the Global Clients department; this value is the difference between the average profit on all Candlebark's policies throughout the world and the slightly greater average profit expected from all these international policies. Suppose such calculation suggests a value of $1m per year.

Candlebark management needs to check that all the costs of the Global Clients department added together come to less than $1m per year. If they do, then having an Global Clients department is a good idea; otherwise not. The relevant costs include salaries, substantial travel expenses and the computer system — since it is inconceivable that the department could function without the exceptionally incisive statistics about these special risks — and obviously out of the question to produce them by hand.

In other words, there is no point estimating the value of the benefits of the computer system in isolation, since there is no sensible question to which this would be an answer. The sensible question is whether the Global Clients department as a whole, including its computer system, is justified or not. The question is answered by looking at the financial figures for the department as a whole.

This suggests a second class of systems to join the systems, like Red Rivergum, that are justified by their place in a portfolio. This new class contains systems that can't sensibly be disentangled from the business entity they support; they are justified by their *inseparability* from a business entity that can itself be justified.

Suppose the head of the Global Clients department has to choose between Strategy A (a just acceptable system, cost $0.3m) and Strategy B (a system with some attractive extras, cost $0.5m) and Strategy C (a de luxe system, cost $0.8m). Given the logic so far, he can start by checking that the whole department can be justified, given that the computer system will cost at least $0.3m. Provided this test is passed, Strategy A can be said to be justified. He can then assess the marginal benefits of B over A and of B over C. In other words, the problem can probably be solved by combining the Inseparability argument with the Stepping technique.

Applying the Inseparability Argument

Like Red Rivergum, Candlebark Global Clients is a classic case in a rather pure form. The Inseparability argument can be called in to some degree in many other cases. The argument is at its most convincing when the inseparable business entity is a department that is truly discretionary (like Global Clients, which could be closed down at any time) or a service (not necessarily experimental) that is inherently technology-based.

But the inseparability argument can be applied to many other types of business entity. The *entity*, from which the system is inseparable, might be a rather vague policy (such as giving the people in the branches more power) or a more exact, but general policy (such as establishing a place in the Danish insurance market with a certain premium income within a certain number of years) or it might be 'management' (it might be unreasonable to expect anyone to manage effectively without certain decision support systems).

Or the entity from which a certain IT investment is inseparable might be the business as a whole. For example, a manager at the Murray Pine Organisation might argue as follows. To remain in business we need to have people working in offices. It would be absurd to cost out the option of making people work in offices without heating or carpets or coffee machines or toilets. Those things are simply inseparable from the very idea of a modern office; and the offices are in turn inseparable from Murray Pine's policy of staying in business, rather than going into liquidation. Making people work on old-fashioned word processing equipment is just as absurd as making them work in offices without heating or carpets. Therefore, the proposed acquisition of 200 PCs and Word-Perfect packages together with laser printers is justified; there is no need to make a financial estimate of the benefits.

When you study techniques that consultants and academics and gurus propose for tackling the problem of awkward benefits, it often turns out that, lurking behind the grand talk of strategic value and business value and platforms and threshold investments, what is proposed is simply a variation on the inseparability argument.

Implications for Decision-making

If a royal commission were ever set up on the general problem of awkward-to-measure IT benefits, it could probably divide all the ideas for investigation up into two distinct parts. In one part come ways of meeting the problem head on; ie finding a clever way of actually putting a plausible value on a system's benefits, hard though it appears at first sight. The trouble here is the difficulty of finding useful, *generally-applicable* techniques for doing this. The second part is concerned with finding ways of making rational decisions, while *avoiding the need* to put a value on a system's benefits, in isolation. Three main concepts have emerged in this briefing: the Stepping model, justification of projects by Portfolio, and justification of projects by Inseparability.

And what about Angophora Mining's legal information system? That is a deliberately chosen tough nut to crack, so it would be unrealistic to expect a perfectly convincing solution.

The head of Angophora's legal department faces five strategy options (one of which is to have no system at all). Strategy A is the cheapest of the four options for building a system, because it stores information about contracts, rather than the complete texts of contracts. The head of the legal department puts up a strong case for Straegy A, based on the Inseparability argument ('In this day and age . . . governments are making fewer concessions to big business . . . such a system is an essential component of the infrastructure of my department . . . etc.').

Once the point is accepted that adopting Strategy A is better than having nothing at all, he sets out to show that other strategies are even better than A. B certainly costs much more than A because it involves maintaining a large text database. By looking around the company, he shows that this particular technology, text database, could be relevant to several other departments, although none as yet has any experience or understanding of it. With this variant of the portfolio argument, he shows that B is more beneficial to the company than A.

Then, using the stepping technique, he goes on to show that the marginal advantages of C over B far outweigh the marginal cost of C over B. On the other hand, the stepping technique shows that D can't be justified over C. Therefore Strategy C must be the most rational choice. QED.

The head of the legal department may be right or he may be wrong in his contention that Strategy C is the choice that will most benefit the interests of Angophora's shareholders, but at least the logical pattern of his argument is respectable. Starting from a position where it was hard to find any basis for reasoning about the relative merits of the options, he has managed to develop a plausible piece of reasoning. There is therefore a good chance that a rational decision can be made.

PRACTICAL ADVICE

➤ Don't be seduced by claims to have solved the problem of quantifying benefits, if they simply rest on arbitrary, unverifiable assumptions; anyone can quantify anything, no matter how insubstantial it is, if he makes enough bold assumptions.

➤ Strip away advice on how to gain benefits, by being more efficient or finding more attractive projects; those ideas are quite separate from techniques for measuring benefits.

➤ Don't assume you need to quantify all benefits; you only need quantification in so far as it helps you decide between options. That is a welcome simplification.

➤ Apply the Stepping technique as one tool for tackling the problem of difficult to appraise IT investments. If the absolute costs and benefits are hard to compare, it may still be feasible to show that substantial marginal benefits are available at apparently low marginal cost. Prune down competing possibilities in this way.

➤ Where possible, employ the notion of justifying a project by its place in a balanced Portfolio of projects. It may well be more feasible to justify the policy of having the Portfolio than to justify the individual project.

➤ Explore the argument of Inseparability. It may be impossible to justify a certain project in isolation, but feasible to justify it as an inseparable part of something wider that is justified. Look for different angles to apply this concept. At the same time, appraise its use critically.

Part III:

Problems of Commitment and Flexibility

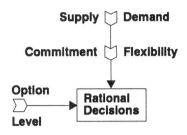

Supply ⬡ Demand

Commitment ⬡ Flexibility

Option ⬦ → Rational Decisions
Level

BRIEFINGS AND MODEL

The briefings in Part II concentrate on approaches to the problems of IT decision-making. In Part III the briefings return to the analysis of the problems themselves.

The Reference Model identifies two main sources of tension at the root of the problems tackled in IT decision-making: Supply–Demand and Commitment–Flexibility. The briefings in this part of the book are concerned with the Commitment–Flexibility Tradeoff. This tradeoff is often found to be tangled up with the Supply–Demand Interaction in an intricate way.

Introducing Commitment and Flexibility

Comparing options with different tradeoffs between supply and demand is an excellent technique, but suppose that option A is something that can be done in two years and option B is something that would take five years. Deciding between those two options necessarily involves deciding how far ahead one should make plans — two years or five; in effect, this is deciding how much commitment to make, or, put another way, how much flexibility to sacrifice.

The first briefing looks at the question of how far ahead to set a planning horizon. Why not have a ten-year strategy? What are the pros and cons of taking a short-term view? From this discussion it emerges that setting a planning horizon is a strategic decision in its own right, which can play an important role in determining the nature of an organisation's whole strategy. **(13. Setting a Planning Horizon)**

This leads to more issues for the next briefing. The degree of commitment is generally related to the distance of the planning horizon chosen, but it can be affected by other factors too. If you make a plan for a certain number of years ahead, you are presumably committed to it, but what does it really mean to be committed to certain IT investments in the future? Commitment surely means that you expect to suffer penalties, should you ever break the commitment. Decisions about the degree of commitment that should be accepted are themselves strategic decisions which need to be made explicitly rather than allowed to develop through unnoticed assumptions. **(14. Assessing Commitment)**

Four Examples

The first two briefings discuss the general concepts related to the Commitment–Flexibility Tradeoff. The remaining four briefings in this part of the book raise some more specific issues, where the logic of the discussion is dominated by the tradeoff between commitment and flexibility.

Some decisions about technology, particularly in the database and telecommunications areas, are best treated as decisions about an infrastructure, that transcends individual projects. But in practice it can be very hard to draw the line between technology decisions at the infrastructure level and decisions that should be left to project level. The more investment in infrastructure, the more commitment and, perhaps, the greater the embarrassment later, when individual projects call for technology supply factors that were not allowed for in planning the infrastructure. The less infrastructure, the more flexibility, but then the less chance there is to benefit from economies of scale and possibilities for integration. **(15. Technology Infrastructure)**

That briefing is concerned with supply-side factors, and there are analogous issues on the demand-side. If an extensive database will store information for a number of different future systems, how do you coordinate developments? Probably some aspects of the database need to be firmed up at an early stage, independently of individual projects. Perhaps a distinction can be made between a shared information infrastructure and other information that is more system-specific in character. There are many opportunities to go wrong here — that is to say, opportunities to drift unawares into an unfavourable degree of commitment. **(16. Information Infrastructure)**

One common approach to the planning of an organisation's use of IT is to develop a framework defining all the main functions and the main bodies of data and the relations between them. This framework is intended to ensure that the development work on individual projects can be carried out in a coherent, well coordinated way. This may sound a very sensible thing to do, but interesting issues arise when things are considered in Commitment–Flexibility terms: the more robust the framework, the less scope may be left for flexibility. (17. **Strategic Information Systems Planning**)

People occasionally talk as if modern database technology can store information so very flexibly, in such a generalised form, that it can be used to meet many demands quite different from those originally envisaged. If a database were really so flexible, then many strategic decisions could be reversed whenever necessary at little or no penalty. This would mean in effect that the Commitment–Flexibility Tradeoff was of little consequence: you could combine the economies of scale of commitment with the freedom of flexibility. Examining this issue carefully is a useful way of gaining new insight into the Commitment–Flexibility Tradeoff. (18. **Database: Flexibility and Constraints**)

Commitment–Flexibility and Supply–Demand

The issues discussed in these briefings show how the Commitment–Flexibility Tradeoff is mixed up with the Supply–Demand Interaction. If it were possible to firm up long-term demand reliably first, and afterwards proceed to firm up the required supply-side arrangements, then you could reasonably commit to a substantial infrastructure or framework, without worrying very much about any Commitment–Flexibility Tradeoff.

The trouble is that the potential supply and demand factors are too uncertain and interact too awkwardly to permit any reliable once-and-for-all definition. Given that fact, any infrastructure decision has to rest on judgements, rather than firm data, about the demand and supply factors likely to emerge over the years ahead. In other words, it has to trade off commitment and flexibility.

13. Setting a Planning Horizon

ISSUES

Suppose you were offered a choice between *Strategy A* (a certain bundle of system developments and technology investments over a two-year period) and *Strategy B* (a certain bundle of system developments and technological investments over a five-year period).

Comparisons of strategy options, whether at organisation or individual system level, can become complicated when the alternative options have different timescales. You can't compare the two by taking a five-year view of each, because Strategy A is silent on the question of what will happen in years 3, 4 and 5. You can't sensibly take a two-year view, because that would ignore much of Strategy B's content.

This kind of choice needs careful handling. 'Shall we go to the cinema or go to the theatre tonight?' is a straightforward either/or choice, but in 'Shall we go the cinema tonight or shall we buy a subscription ticket to a winter season of symphony concerts?', the two choices offered are not simple alternatives. They mix up two different issues in the apparent form of one question. 'How shall we entertain ourselves?' is one issue and 'How far ahead shall we plan our entertainment?' is the other issue. Thus in the choice between two-year Strategy A and five-year Strategy B the issue 'How far ahead should we set the horizon of our IT planning?' needs to be recognised as a question distinct from: 'What should be the content of our IT plans?'

Should the IT planning horizon be placed as far away as possible, because the more detailed the planning, the better? Or should it be as near as possible, because the less you forecast the future, the less chance there is of making expensive blunders? That is the dilemma addressed by this briefing.

ANALYSIS

The best way to get to grips with the issues is to start with some simple examples of different features of IT planning that illustrate the dilemma well. These lead to the definition of some classic tradeoffs in setting a planning horizon. This in turn suggests some conclusions about the way to handle typical cases.

Examples of Hardware Planning

A survey of Apple laser printers in the October 1990 issue of *MacUser* reported that the Laserwriter IINT cost $4,499 and the Laserwriter IINTX, a more powerful printer, cost $5,995, a difference of $1,496. If you bought a IINT and decided later to upgrade it, it could be modified to function like a IINTX but the cost of the upgrade was not $1,496 but $3,699.[1] On these figures, deciding whether a IINT or a IINTX is the printer you really need is important. If you buy a IINT now, discover a few months later that it is not powerful enough and so upgrade it, then (unless prices have changed in the meantime) you end up paying $8,198 to arrive at a printer you could have bought for $5,995. On the other hand, if you buy a IINTX now and realise later that it is more powerful than you need and a IINT would have done just as well, then you have wasted $1,496. This kind of price structure is very common with computer hardware products.

Sycamore Supplies, the wholesaler of stationery and office products, needs a minicomputer system in the accounts department at head office. Sycamore could buy a certain configuration (call it the CTS355) to meet the current needs at a certain price (call it 100); the main alternative configuration (the CTS500) costs 150. The CTS500 has a much more powerful processor, enabling it to serve many more terminals, and it has far more disk storage. If Sycamore can be sure that the CTS355 has ample capacity for the foreseeable future, then of course it will be irresponsible to waste money on the CTS500. But if Sycamore buys the CTS355 and discovers soon afterwards that more disk storage is needed, then the cost of the next disk upgrade is 50, bringing the total cost for the upgraded CTS355 configuration to 150. Even then Sycamore would have less disk storage and would be stuck with a less powerful processor than if it bought the CTS500. Of course if Sycamore buys the CTS500 now, it may never make full use of it; the much cheaper CTS355 may be perfectly adequate.

The kind of decision logic illustrated by these two examples affects a great deal of IT planning. There is a strong incentive to decide just what you need with some precision a fair distance into the future, because that gives you a better chance of making wise purchases and avoiding embarrassing mistakes.

Advantages of Systems Planning

With the development of software for application systems, there is usually no published price list showing the relative costs of initial commitments and upgrades; but in practice the same price patterns are found as with hardware. The extra cost of upgrading software to add or change system functions can be staggering compared to the costs of the original system or compared to the costs if all the desired features had been included in the system from the start. There are many anecdotal examples of application systems costing much more in minor 'maintenance' modifications over the years than they cost to build originally.

This is a general characteristic of any piece of technology consisting of many parts fitted together in complex ways. Suppose you ask an aeronautics engineer to design and build a propeller-based engine and then, after it is working, you decide that you would rather have a jet engine; you then insist that the jet engine be made by modifying the propeller-based one. It wouldn't be surprising if the total costs were at least double a reasonable estimate for designing and building a jet engine from scratch. This analogy fits the history of some computer systems quite well. Clearly, there is a considerable incentive to take a sufficiently long-term view of the scope of any one application system, to be able to decide whether the organisation really needs a jet engine or a propeller-based engine, as it were.

The argument applies all the more strongly to families of application systems. Modifying a system to allow one data item in one system to be processed in a new way can be surprisingly expensive, but the complications can become far greater if a piece of data hitherto used by one system now has to be used by several, or if two systems that function independently now need to share a considerable amount of information. In such cases inconsistency can arise in many different ways: a data item such as product or customer may be understood slightly differently by the departments using it; a data item may be a different length or have a different coding scheme in different systems; the rules for checking update validity may differ between systems; the data may be updated at different times, daily in one system and interactively in another. It can require tremendous effort to recognise and deal with all such inconsistencies after the event; it can be frustrating to realise how much easier everything would have been, if only things had been planned more carefully from the start.

Therefore there is a strong incentive to plan far enough ahead with sufficient precision to map out which systems and which information are likely to need to be fitted together in the future, and how this is to be done.

Problems with Long-term Planning

The examples of hardware planning given above present both sides of a tradeoff; belated upgrading to meet needs greater than expected is an evil to be avoided; so is the overkill of investment in hardware that isn't really needed. Some people talk as if belated upgrading was something to be avoided at all costs, while overkill hardly mattered at all. Circumstances vary, but as a general attitude this is not very rational. For one thing, money wasted on overkill can be considerable. For another, there is a general problem with all 'playing-safe' strategies: How safe is it sensible to play? The CTS500 is safer than the CTS355, but then the larger, more expensive CTS600 is safer still, and what about the ultra-powerful CTS850? Who knows whether Sycamore might need that CTS850 if it took over another big company?

Opting for overkill and trying to forget about the possible waste of money doesn't really provide a satisfactory escape from the honourable course of carefully examining the wants and needs and demands of the actual case. But now the question arises: How far into the future should you plan in order to have an adequate basis for these decisions? If there is such a premium on knowing exactly what you need, why not always plan everything in great detail a long way ahead — seven years, say?

With a distant planning horizon, it appears, you can carefully estimate all the likely demands over a long period, and therefore take the best possible decisions about investment in the necessary supply resources. You can avoid ordering the equivalent of a propeller-based engine — a IINT or a CTS355 or stand-alone application systems — and finding you have to upgrade later in a way that (seen in retrospect) is far from cost-effective. Equally, a good distant planning horizon should save you from the overkill of a jet engine you don't need — a IINTX or a CTS500 or a completely integrated database, when cheaper alternatives would have served just as well throughout the whole planning period.

This line of thought seems to suggest that the further ahead a plan extends in reasonable detail, the better. But the matter is not that simple. As an aphorism attributed to Churchill puts it: it is always wise to look ahead, but difficult to look further than you can see.

Suppose you ask a five-year-old to define toy requirements for the next seven years, so that, armed with this demand projection, you can go and strike a deal for a volume discount with your local toyshop. However logical, this is obviously impractical: the child doesn't fully grasp what is going on; the development of the child's tastes, the influence of other children, the emergence of new toys are all unpredictable factors.

But these forces against the long-term planning of toy procurement have their parallels in the world of IT strategy too. Many people only become knowledgeable and perceptive enough to articulate certain demands for certain system features required in, say, year 3 of the seven-year plan, when they have the experience of the first two years behind them; and these new perceptions of IT possibilities may well run counter to the contents of the original plan. Developments in the organisation's market or in society in general, that occur after the seven-year plan is drawn up, may lead to changed ideas about IT systems. Technology developments may invalidate some of the plan's assumptions and suggest new possibilities. These and many other uncertainty factors, together with sheer human fallibility, can easily erode the validity of a long-term plan.

Plans with distant planning horizons are often very vulnerable. The plan may involve buying computers in year 1 whose capacity is only fully utilised in year 4; it may involve implementing certain design decisions about systems in year 2, whose true rationale only becomes relevant when they share data in year 4; and so on. The plan may be an almost perfect one provided its judgements about all the possible uncertainties prove correct, but may be vulnerable to so many uncertainties over its life, that it is unreasonable to expect that things will turn out exactly as foreseen. That being so, the planning may well turn out to be far from optimal, and if the plan extends to a distant horizon, there is plenty of scope for it to become progressively more sub-optimal over the years. By year 3, there may already be signs that the hardware purchase made in year 1 and the system design implemented in year 2 won't fit into the developments of year 4 as neatly as originally envisaged. In fact, despite all the effort that went into the long-term plan, some of its content may appear to be simply wrong.

The Classic Horizon Tradeoff

So the decision on how far ahead to plan is affected by a tradeoff. If your planning horizon is too close, you can't invest cost-efficiently, either in technology products or in the structures of systems and databases. But if your planning horizon is too distant, your predictions and projections will be inaccurate; then you will make wrong investments and design decisions. In addition, you will waste all the time that was spent in up-front planning activities and lose credibility with other people in the organisation who have less understanding of the difficulty of IT manage-ment issues. Moreover, other things being equal, a long-term strategy is generally more ambitious than a short-term strategy; it contains more activities, related in more complex ways, therefore the scope for disaster, if it goes wrong, is all the greater.

This classic tradeoff is met time and again in IT strategy problems at all levels. In practice more people go wrong more disastrously by making the mistake of taking an unrealistically long-term view, without being aware of its disadvantages; therefore it is useful to summarise the problem from that angle.

First, the more long-term and detailed an organisation makes its IT planning, then the more cost-efficient its IT activities can be in the long run — in theory, that is, if the plans are all implemented effectively.

Second, the more long-term and detailed the plans, the greater the chance that, for a variety of reasons, the plans won't all be implemented effectively.

Third, the more long-term and detailed the plans, the greater the damage, should it turn out that the plans in fact are not all implemented effectively.

Conversely, the less you plan ahead, the less the practical chance of the plans going wrong in the short term, but the less the theoretical chance of IT activities being cost-efficient in the long term.

As with most tradeoffs, there are no standard answers; the factors in each case have to be assessed on their merits.

Horizon Implications in Generic Cases

What does it all mean in practice? There are some generic cases where the horizon issue plays a vital role.

First of all, Snowgum Supplies represents the emergency case. The company is in bad shape financially and organisationally and so are the information systems. Snowgum is under pressure from its creditors and, because of its poor systems, the company is never quite sure how much it owes to whom. In this case, a plan with a distant planning horizon would be a pointless luxury; Snowgum needs a rescue plan. For better or worse, things are bound to be very different in a year or two. At the moment, there is little point in making clever projections about the optimum hardware upgrade path and planning telecommunications or database infrastructures, whose purpose would be to support new systems much further down the road.

Managers at Sassafras, the magazine publishers, examine all the demand factors — the features people would like to have in new systems to support the administration of the publishing business. They study the supply factors — the way those systems could be achieved. They produce a cost–benefit analysis that looks favourable. The natural way of organising projects to implement all the features demanded would entail a timescale of about three years. The following question then arises: Theoretically, a three-year planning horizon seems attractive for this situation, but are there any special uncertainty features to suggest that a three-year horizon is too ambitious? In the case of Sassafras the judgement is that there are not, so three years is the planning horizon taken.

Sassafras is a relatively unusual case, since all the system demand that seems worth meeting can be met within a realistic planning horizon. The Ironbark Insurance case is more representative; here there are just too many attractive possibilities for using IT to reduce administration costs and to improve service within the company. To supply all these demands properly would require an ambitiously long timescale, perhaps with quite complicated integration of activities. There are serious doubts whether sufficiently accurate plans could be made for such complex work over such a long period. In other words, demand-drive suggests one strategy horizon (distant) and supply-caution suggests another (not-so-distant). The rational approach is to bring the horizon issue into the open as a major strategy point to be resolved and to find the least bad compromise solution. This may mean accepting some risk by working to a longer horizon than ideal, and at the same time excluding some demands that taken in isolation, without the horizon constraint, would have been desirable.

Then there is the situation exemplified by Antarctic Beech, the company considering investment in innovative new products and services, based on the use of IT. Here there are special uncertainties making a relatively close horizon advisable. For example, the required shape of the systems and their value will be highly dependent on the market's response to the innovative products and nobody knows what that will be. Antarctic chooses a two-year planning horizon and intends to reassess its strategy after that time.

Another common source of short-term uncertainty is vulnerability to changes in the policy of government or other regulatory authorities. This is a factor for some of the subsidiaries of Candlebark Insurance on the mainland of Europe, which discourages them from setting distant planning horizons. With special uncertainties like those of Antarctic Beech and the Candlebark subsidiaries, it seems sensible to keep the horizon as close as possible, without being totally negative about meeting demand or permitting outrageous inefficiencies of supply.

Plainly the choice of strategy in these cases is largely based on judgement. Decision-makers have to take a view on which factors in the prevailing situation are most relevant and they have to assess the implications for the appropriate planning horizon. Because this is so much a matter of judgement, some standardised approaches to IT planning avoid recognising the planning horizon as a management issue at all. Either they assume that five years is always the right period or they assume that the right period is however long as it takes to meet the demands for all the possible systems. The essence of this briefing is that such assumptions are quite unwarranted.

The Horizon and Psychological Issues

Pink Gum Products, the medium-sized manufacturers, decide to make a fresh start with new systems on a computer installation of their own. Analysts and managers draw up quite a menu of requirements for systems they think could help the business — enough system developments to stretch to a very distant horizon. At the same time, there is one huge uncertainty factor: nobody can be sure how well the company culture will accept the discipline of working far more extensively with computer systems, in such matters as planning production, processing customer orders, controlling suppliers and so on. This is just as great an uncertainty factor in the strategic analysis as Antarctic Beech's uncertainty about market response to their innovative products.

Pink Gum decides to set the planning horizon at two years; this means that less than half of all the systems that might conceivably be automated are included in the planning.

There is an important psychological difficulty here. If you tell a Pink Gum manager: 'I'm afraid the new system you wanted isn't in the plan. It seems a good idea and we may well do it at a later time; but we've settled on a two-year horizon, so we obviously can't do everything; and there are other systems of more fundamental importance', he may well think that what you actually mean is: 'Your system is out. Forget it.'

You have to explain that, just because something is excluded from the current plan, that doesn't mean it will never be done. It just means that there is no commitment to do it in the present, relatively short-term plan. It can sometimes be very difficult to get this point across. One approach is to explain that setting a planning horizon is unavoidable, and the particular possibility under discussion is currently 'below the horizon'. Of course to say an oasis is below the horizon is not to deny that it exists; indeed as you progress across the desert, you get nearer to more and more places that were originally below the horizon.

Strategy Implications

The logic of tradeoffs discussed in this briefing suggests that the question of how far ahead should one should plan requires attention in its own right as an important IT strategy issue. There is no self-evidently appropriate answer; it depends on the specific situation.

To return to the starting example, if I vote for Strategy A (a certain bundle of system developments and technological investments within a *two-year* timescale), I choose *not only* that particular bundle of system developments and technological investments, as opposed to those in

Strategy B (a different bundle within a *five-year* timescale), but I also choose the principle of a two-year planning horizon, as opposed to five years. Therefore deciding between two strategy options involves more than assessing the inherent nature of the supply and demand factors they contain; it involves judging the appropriate planning horizon. That means weighing up the potential benefits of commitment to a long-term plan and the implications of any uncertainty factors that make planning vulnerable.

Moreover, once the planning horizon emerges as a separate variable, more alternative strategies may spring to mind. For example, perhaps the best strategy of all is one containing the same things as those in Strategy A's bundle, plus a couple more — but all spread out to a planning horizon three years away.

PRACTICAL ADVICE

➤ Bear in mind that progress through piecemeal modifications is invariably more expensive than implementing one grand scheme.

➤ But fight any suggestions that the further ahead one plans the better it will be; there are drawbacks attached to long-term planning too.

➤ Focus on the essential tradeoff: unless you plan far ahead you can't invest in IT efficiently, but the further ahead you plan, the more vulnerable your planning is to the forces of uncertainty.

➤ Concentrate on the planning horizon as one of the most fundamental issues of your IT strategy. It shouldn't be merely a practical consequence that derives from other decisions.

➤ Decide your policy by comparing your own situation to certain model cases: the emergency case where long-term planning is an impossible luxury; the case where the maximum sensible demands can still be met within a prudent timescale; the case where the maximum sensible demands call for a timescale that is unacceptably ambitious; the case where powerful uncertainty factors suggest a relatively close horizon.

➤ Be prepared for misunderstandings and hard feelings that may arise through demand possibilities that have to be placed 'below the horizon'.

➤ Find the most appropriate horizon, the one with the best balance of tradeoffs for the particular case. Consider different strategy options based on different planning horizons.

14.   Assessing Commitment

Making a four-year plan for IT investments and activities seems to be a bolder step and a greater commitment than working with a two-year horizon. But is it? Certainly, the planning horizon has some influence on the degree of commitment that an organisation takes on, but there are more subtleties to this notion of the commitment that results from IT decisions.

Compare a ten-year plan to redecorate the interiors of all the rooms of the Palace of Versailles — divided up into, say, 10,000 sub-activities — with a ten-year plan to build a tunnel under the English Channel, also divided up into 10,000 sub-activities. There is one big difference between these two plans. Suppose both projects are cancelled after nine years with 9,000 activities completed. Very probably this means that the tunnel project will have been a total waste; a tunnel with one tiny segment missing is of no use at all. But a palace that is 90% redecorated very probably has most of its rooms already completely redecorated. Admittedly, if both projects were cancelled after, say, six months there would probably be nothing of value from either, but even a couple of years into the Versailles project, some of the rooms may be ready. Thus even if the projected cash-flows are identical, the Channel Tunnel seems to represent much more of a commitment than the Versailles project.

Probably the Versailles project offers more flexibility than the Channel Tunnel project too. Half-way through the tunnel project is probably too late to make major design changes, but half-way through redecorating the palace it may still be possible to revise the plans for the wallpaper in the East Wing, without major disruptions.

These notions of commitment and flexibility apply to planning activities in the field of IT as well. If somebody presents, say, a four-year IT strategy, it seems sensible to ask whether this represents a Channel Tunnel-style commitment or only a Versailles-style. Some investments in IT, such as gradually installing PCs throughout the organisation, may be more like Versailles, whereas other investments, such as setting up a telecommunications infrastructure, may be more like the Channel Tunnel.

Commitment and flexibility seem to be important aspects of IT decision-making but many of their details need to be thought through. This briefing sets out to put a sharper edge on these concepts.

ANALYSIS

A good start is to look at a relatively simple case, showing the difficulties that arise when the dimension of commitment is left in the air and undefined. Through other examples, the idea of a tradeoff between commitment and flexibility gradually takes shape. This leads to the question whether the definition of an all-embracing framework for the whole organisation can necessarily achieve the benefits of commitment while minimising its disadvantages.

Rosewood's Four-stage Plan and its Implications

At Rosewood Bank, the director with special responsibility for IT is explaining to his colleagues on the board how he and his staff have conceived a four-stage plan to develop a new generation of application systems. Although each stage has roughly the same elapsed time, the size and cost of the applications to be implemented in those stages is roughly in the proportions 1:3:1:1.

He explains that a proper understanding of the logic of this four-stage structure is of the utmost importance. The first stage is to be seen as a 'quick strike' or an 'appetiser'; it proves to the organisation as a whole that stimulating new developments are afoot, without running too much risk of disaster through being over-ambitious. The second stage contains the big 'bread and butter' systems. The third stage includes some systems for the connoisseur; it generates high added value, takes advantage of the investment in systems of the previous stages and exploits the rising level of enthusiasm for IT within the organisation. The fourth stage tidies up a variety of loose ends from the previous three, and adds some other features that may be relatively esoteric but which sophisticated users who have experienced the previous stages will doubtless insist on.

One of his more feisty colleagues begins the questioning:

'You sound as if you already have a certain clear view of a whole collection of application systems that the company needs. You are suggesting that the best way of achieving that goal is to split things into four stages over a number of years in the way you describe. Your intention is that we should agree today on two things: one, that we do need the collection of computer systems you have described, and two, that your four-stage approach is the best way of achieving them. Right?'

'Right.'

'That's clear then. At first I was confused and I thought you meant something completely different. In your explanation of the stages, you seemed to be laying great stress on psychological factors with concepts like appetiser, proving something to the organisation, enthusiasm, insistent sophisticated users and so on. That led me to think that your plan was a lot more flexible than it is. I thought, for example, there was some scope for choice about what should happen in later stages, according to how appetising or otherwise the first course had been. I thought that the scope of the systems of stage 3 might depend on which departments had produced connoisseurs and who was still hungry after digesting the bread and butter stage and who'd already had more than enough. I thought the shape of the esoteric fourth stage demands might only become clear after the third stage. But none of this is so. By your previous answer you've closed off all that kind of flexibility.

'Well . . .'

'You can't have it both ways. Either you're asking us to make a long-term commitment now to a certain defined set of systems, with all the advantages and disadvantages of making long-term commitments — or you're asking us to adopt a strategy of commitment to one short stage at a time, such that at the end of each stage, there will be significant flexibility about what, if anything, happens in the following stage.'

Since the IT director hasn't thought about the matter from that angle before, he is stuck for any convincing response.

Commitment as Dimension

Some dimensions of a plan are so important that they need to be recognised explicitly. Suppose an entrepreneur asked your opinion of a five-year business plan for a company to manufacture and market a consumer product, a new way of opening wine bottles, say. Suppose the plan all seemed very plausible, but it said nothing about the matter of competition from other companies. That might not make it a bad plan; the entrepreneur might be able to find good arguments to show that competition wouldn't be a problem; or perhaps a further detailed study would show that competition wasn't in fact an important threat; or maybe the content of the plan is in fact already heavily influenced by the entrepreneur's assessment of competitive factors, but they just haven't been spelt out. It is uncertain whether these or any other possibilities are the case, because a vital dimension, competition, has not been dealt with *explicitly* in the plan. Another entrepreneur's plan might cover the dimension of competition very well but ignore taxation; or in another case inflation might be a missing dimension.

What the feisty board member at Rosewood has really pointed out is that the IT director's plan completely ignores a certain vital dimension of IT decision-making — commitment. As a result, the plan is so weakly defined that it can be understood in any number of different ways. Which of the two options posed by the board member is better or whether some other option, handling commitment in a more subtle way, would be preferable doesn't matter here. The important point is that, just as you can't sensibly discuss a business plan for a consumer product without taking some notice of the dimension of competition, so you can't sensibly discuss IT strategy without recognising the dimension of commitment.

Commitment to a Project in Year 4

The notion of commitment needs more careful examination. In a sense, no organisation is ever irrevocably committed to its IT plans; the chairman of the board always has the flexibility to change whatever is in the plan — but of course that may mean accepting some penalty. Thinking clearly about the concept of commitment entails bringing in this notion of penalties for abandoning the commitment.

Saying: 'We shall probably take a vacation in Colorado next year' does not necessarily take on much of a commitment; the speaker still has complete flexibility to go somewhere else instead. Saying: 'We shall take a vacation in Colorado next year and here are the bargain, non-refundable plane tickets we've bought' deserves to count as commitment; now it is still possible to take a different holiday, but only by sacrificing the cost of the plane tickets.

Similarly, just to write down: 'Candlebark Insurance has a four-year IT planning horizon and we shall carry out the Textbase system development in Year 4' may not necessarily mean a real commitment to Textbase. But if Candlebark's plan calls for some investment in year 1 that wouldn't be made (or would be made differently) except for the fact that Textbase was planned for year 4, then that counts as a commitment to Textbase.

Textbase is a new application system storing and accessing textual information about holders of the company's insurance policies — information such as 'He is fifth in line to become the Earl of Burnley' or 'This company was involved in an ugly takeover battle in 1987'. Information of this sort can't be handled effectively with normal structured fields in a database (e.g. a one-character code to record 'sex', a four-digit code for 'industry-sector' and so on). For that reason, the application doesn't suit mainstream relational database technology very well. Its demands imply supply factors that are out of the mainstream.

The Textbase system won't stand alone; it has to fit in with the large-scale systems being developed in years 1, 2 and 3, using mainstream database technology to process great quantities of customer transactions. A certain database management system (DBMS) software product has to be chosen as the basis for the main transactions systems to be developed first. If there were no Textbase system coming along later, Candlebark's technical people would have a slight preference for the DBMS A product over DBMS B. Both meet all the main requirements, but DBMS A is very clever at recovering from failures if a telecommunications line goes down in the middle of a transaction; DBMS B is adequate in that regard, but not quite as fast. But nobody has ever heard of text data being stored in an application system based on DBMS A, whereas the suppliers of DBMS B offer a special extension to their software, specifically intended to make text storage and access feasible — just what Textbase will need in year 4. So DBMS B is chosen; the Textbase factor is decisive.

When the information structures of the database are being drawn up, empty boxes are left in appropriate logical places to accommodate the text information that will be coming later. When the experts make their technical decisions about how to organise data storage for optimum efficiency, they make rough assumptions about the volumes of this textual information. In short, things are done in years 1, 2 and 3 that only make sense because of the intention to do Textbase in year 4. That is commitment.

Non-commitment to a Project in Year 4

The rival insurance company Stringybark Assurance also has a four-year plan. They also plan to set up transaction systems in the first three years, followed by text storage facilities in year 4. Despite this, Stringybark actually go ahead concentrating on the transaction processing without giving any serious attention to Textbase. They choose DBMS A rather than DBMS B, and are delighted by its superior approach to transaction recovery. Moreover, because their technical people don't have to include the text storage requirements in their design calculations, they save effort and make more efficient use of hardware too.

When asked about the Textbase system contained in the plan for year 4, the MIS manager of Stringybark says: 'Well, that's still a long way off. Maybe, we'll have a separate text database linked to our main database in some simple way or maybe the suppliers of DBMS A will be offering a special text extension by then (like DBMS B already has) or maybe, when we look at the requirements in more detail, we'll find that you can store the text data somehow in the main database, after all. Don't worry, we'll find a way.'

Clearly, Stringybark is not actually committed to Textbase at all, in any real sense. Everything they are doing now is what they would be doing anyway, even if the idea of doing Textbase had never occurred to anybody. If all their plans for year 4 are like this, then it is really misleading to say that they have a four-year plan; they have a three-year (or less) plan, supplemented by mere notes on later possibilities.

Put like this, it sounds as if Candlebark and Stringybark are playing the roles of the wise and foolish virgins in the Bible. In fact, Stringybark may be the more sensible. Suppose its MIS manager has judged correctly that, given the volume of transactions and their complexity, then the crucial issue for those main systems is recovery, and that it would be unwise to make any compromise on that aspect. Suppose he is also right in judging that the whole technology of text storage is in a state of flux and that therefore commitments in that area should be put off as long as possible. Suppose he suspects that a really careful examination of these text requirements might show that a totally different technology such as expert system was the real answer. If all that is so, then avoiding commitment to Textbase may be an intelligent move.

The Commitment–Flexibility Tradeoff

Commitment means a non-refundable air ticket to Colorado or the choice of a DBMS that only makes sense if you actually do carry out the Textbase project in Year 4. The good side of commitment is that a non-refundable air ticket usually costs less than a normal one and choosing the right DBMS now can save you from unpleasant complications in Year 4. The bad side is that you give up flexibility. To be more precise, if you do change your plans — go to Bermuda instead of Colorado, scrap Textbase — you incur a penalty. You are stuck with a worthless air ticket or a DBMS which would not be your first choice for the systems that you actually are doing.

As so often in IT strategy, there is a tradeoff. You can't normally *both* have a carefully integrated, long-term company IT strategy, with all its features beautifully optimised and dove-tailed, *and at the same time*, assure the board of directors that there will be frequent review points, providing the flexibility to make all kinds of revisions and additions to the plans without any trouble at all. That will almost always be a contradiction. The real task is to discover how to get the right balance between commitment and flexibility.

Quite often people who are enthusiastic about a particular project (especially software houses hoping for a contract to develop the software) do try to have it both ways. The sales pitch runs like this: 'We've planned the project in eight development phases: outline functional design, detailed functional design, outline technical design and so on. At the end of each phase, we shall make a very careful estimate of the costs of the next phase; therefore the end of each phase forms a decision-point, where you can, if you so wish, decide to halt the project. This arrangement saves you from making a firm commitment now to an expensive multi-year project.'

The point conveniently ignored is that if you do decide to stop after phase 3, because the estimate for phase 4 is so outrageous, then your organisation has to write off all the costs of the first three phases and you, personally, have to explain to your colleagues and superiors why the money has been wasted. No, starting on phase 1 of a project unavoidably makes a commitment, and that is a rash thing to do unless you have a reasonable idea of the costs of the whole thing. If you scrap a project, a penalty has to be paid and, barring nuclear war or the earth being hit by an asteroid, somebody generally deserves to be blamed.

A Framework at Corkwood

Many people active in IT strategy affairs advocate the development of a 'framework' (or blueprint or architecture or strategic information plan, etc.) which sets out the essential structure of the most important systems and databases and processing of an organisation, leaving the work of detailed design and development to be done within individual projects, after the overall framework has been agreed. Leaving aside the way it may be worked out, the value of such a document can be appraised in commitment–flexibility terms. The rationale of the framework approach is roughly as follows. Integrating many systems and databases is a complex matter. You might try to firm up every detail in one massive planning process at the beginning and commit to the resulting plan before starting to develop anything, but in fact matters are far too complex for that to be realistic. Therefore you should define and firm up a framework covering just those things that really need to be firmed up in advance. Once the organisation has committed to that framework, then work on individual systems within the framework can proceed independently.

Good work can be done with this approach, but there are also many opportunities for drifting into hazy assumptions, as the case of Corkwood Bank shows.

The IT planning manager at Corkwood Bank has produced a framework for the future. In essence the framework consists of a design for a whole family of new systems making use of a certain pattern of databases, and running on certain configurations at various locations. The term 'framework' is well justified: the whole design stresses the integration of different elements in one coherent structure, and the whole thing presents an outline of the key parts of the structure; it doesn't attempt to provide full detail about any individual part. Once this framework is accepted as the basis for the company's future developments, work on any project can push ahead, safe in the knowledge that, as long as it occupies the assigned place in the framework, it can be integrated within the whole structure.

Uncertainty about Commitment

But the board of Corkwood Bank has its curmudgeonly elements too:

'I can easily think of four different ways of interpreting this framework of yours. First of all, it might be intended as the design for the set of systems that you are now asking the board to commit to; all the work that follows will just be filling in detail within that framework. That would mean that you are telling us that, provided we commit to these seventeen systems today, you are sure that this is the best possible design for fitting the seventeen together — and that you've optimised it for that very purpose. If you are saying that, then something important follows inescapably: should we decide later that some of the seventeen are not required, or should we decide in two years that certain other systems are needed, we may well find that we have the wrong framework and, as we all know, significant changes to a framework can waste a great deal of time and money. So in effect, by committing today, we'd be giving up a great deal of future flexibility.'

'But perhaps I should interpret your framework quite differently. Perhaps you are saying that this framework embodies certain fundamental features of the business, present and future, and therefore it should, by this very fact, accommodate all future demands for systems — whether these particular seventeen or some other seventeen or ten systems or thirty. With this approach, you are not asking us to commit to all the seventeen systems shown; they are simply plausible, realistic examples of systems that we might one day, but not necessarily, commit to. You may find it much easier to defend this interpretaton of your framework; but if you do take this line, please will you provide us with a two-coloured diagram to distinguish the 'fundamental' parts we have to commit to, from the 'plausible example' parts of the framework, where no commitment is entailed at present. Then we shall scrutinise the fundamental parts very thoroughly indeed.'

'Or I suppose, there's a possible third interpretation. Perhaps you are putting your framework forward as an ideal vision and you are asking us how much out of all this total vision we the board wish to commit to now, and how much of it should be left out,'

'I can even think of a fourth interpretation. Perhaps your framework is intended as just an example to prove that there is at least one straightforward way for IT to achieve the things the business needs; having confirmed that the board does indeed want these things, your team will consider what is the optimal approach. That could be the same 'framework' or something totally different. In that event, our only commitment today would be in authorising you to do that further work.'

If the framework diagrams are based on an uneasy, ill-defined *mélange* of purposes, it will be hard to have any rational discussion about them at all. Somebody who presents a framework without thinking about the commitment dimension is likely to handle this line of questioning as unconvincingly as an entrepreneur who makes a business plan without considering the matter of competition.

The 'Step by Step' Confusion

Sometimes people like the IT Director of Rosewood Bank or the IT planning manager at Corkwood Bank create the illusion of sensible planning by talking about a 'step by step' approach. One of the advantages of recognising commitment as a dimension is that it helps cut through some confusions that arise from such unclear use of language.

'Step by step' is a metaphor. The metaphor can be used to describe the following policy: 'We know exactly what we want to achieve. Our policy is rather like taking four firm strides in a straight line towards it. That is the surest way of getting there.' In other words, there is *already a firm commitment* to a certain goal.

But the 'step by step' metaphor can also describe the following policy: 'We have a provisional goal. Instead of jumping straight to it, we shall take a series of discrete steps in that direction. After any step we shall have the freedom to stop or to take further steps in some different direction.' In other words, there is *no firm commitment* yet to a certain goal.

Plainly, if you do use the expression 'step by step' about a policy, it is advisable to clarify the nature of your commitment.

Some Implications for Decision-making

The logic discussed in this briefing can cut quite deep into the IT planning of many an organisation. Just because there are desktop-published reports and presentation-graphics slides showing an N-year IT plan, that doesn't necessarily mean there actually is an N-year commitment in any real sense. You can only tell that by looking at the plan's content and asking awkward questions.

If the plan is like a plan to build a Channel Tunnel, something that only makes sense if you do the whole thing, then there is indeed an N-year commitment, for better or for worse. But it may be possible to see that, even if plans were abandoned or radically changed in, say, year $N-2$, most of the work done would still be valuable and even cost-efficient in retrospect; if so, then, whether for good or ill, there is no genuine N-year commitment there.

It may sound as if the only value of these concepts is to generate criticisms of work done by other people. If plans and proposals and frameworks are in fact based on unstated assumptions or have unrecognised implications, criticising them can only do good. Even so, understanding the tradeoff between commitment and flexibility has more positive value too. In IT strategy, it is surely rational to minimise commitment — provided there is no major disadvantage attached. The greater the commitment, the greater the dependence on everything turning out exactly as expected and the greater the restriction on flexibility in responding to the unexpected. The world of IT contains many uncertainty factors, some of which you just can't control, no matter how competent a manager you are, so reducing your dependence on the correctness of forecasts is a wise policy.

If you had to redecorate all the rooms at the Palace of Versailles, you might plan to do it one room at a time or you might judge it more efficient to do everything in parallel — first clean all the woodwork of all the rooms, then paint all the woodwork, then put paper on all the walls; and so on. With an extreme form of this parallel approach, there would be a big commitment involved; if the project were abandoned after nine of its ten years, none of the rooms would be completely ready, all would be 90% ready. But by deliberately planning to redecorate a room at a time, you could greatly reduce commitment. Then if the Ministry of Culture ever cut off funds, at least some of the rooms would be ready. Thus there can be several ways of doing the same thing, each with different degrees of commitment.

You may well find a genuine four-year plan for the use of IT in an organisation, in which the activities in year 1 are indeed closely related to the activities in year 4, but where questions can be asked, such as: 'Is it really necessary to make a four-year commitment? Isn't there another way of organising roughly the same things, that only requires a two-year commitment? For example, why not postpone firming up the choice of client–server technology? That may seem to be a little less cost-effective, but doesn't the freedom to revise plans after two years, without incurring a high penalty, have a value, too?'

This can be put in more abstract terms. The example of Candlebark and Textbase illustrates another important feature of the commitment issue. The reason commitment becomes an issue at all really goes back to the familiar problem of the interaction between supply and demand factors. Candlebark commit to a particular DBMS, a supply factor, in Year 1, because they believe that is the best way of providing Textbase, a demand factor, in Year 4. By doing so they enter a commitment to meet that demand far in the future. Therefore the more that present supply can be uncoupled from distant demand, the easier it becomes to get a favourable balance of commitment.

Whether and how this can be done in any particular case are matters that the skilful IT decision-maker has to assess for himself; there is no standard checklist, no format of modelling diagram, no multi-step procedure that can provide real insight into the tradeoffs between commitment and flexibility.

PRACTICAL ADVICE

➤ Remember that commitment is a fundamental dimension that nearly all strategic decisions in IT have to take into account.

➤ Assess the degree of commitment contained in any plan. Genuine commitment means willingness to pay a penalty for changes of plan.

➤ Since developments in IT are so unpredictable, there is a lot to be said for being economical with commitments. Other things being equal, minimise commitment, except where it provides a clear advantage.

➤ But very often, the only way to achieve certain things effectively is to make certain commitments earlier. Make sure everyone realises that this kind of commitment is taking place.

➤ Be constantly aware of the tradeoff: the higher the commitment, the lower the flexibility; the lower the commitment, the greater chance of uncoordinated, sub-optimal use of resources. A big part of IT strategy consists of getting that tradeoff right.

➤ To handle the tradeoff in any specific case, study the technological implications that may argue for commitment; but also size up the whole range of possible uncertainty factors, on both the supply and demand sides, that call for flexibility.

➤ Be particularly cautious about the degree of commitment and underlying logic implied by large-scale frameworks and other organisation-wide plan/design documents.

➤ Look for ways to reduce commitment and increase flexibility in any plan, if it can be done without disadvantages.

➤ Get used to making the distinction between the duration of any IT plan and the amount of commitment a plan implies. One five-year plan may be all solid commitment; another five-year plan may contain much less actual commitment, because many of its activities could be scrapped or altered at little or no cost. This distinction is part of the essential grammar of IT strategy-making.

15. Technology Infrastructure

ISSUES

It seems sensible enough to make certain fundamental decisions about technology at a level that transcends the planning of individual systems. Candlebark Insurance, for example, chooses the Oracle DBMS software product as the one to be used for all its systems that need database technology; Oracle becomes part of the Candlebark technology infrastructure.

Having chosen Oracle, Candlebark invests in the development of expertise in this technology: a permanent group of experts on the finer points of the Oracle product is set up; many people are sent on Oracle courses; general-purpose, company-specific software is developed that dovetails with the Oracle software; standards are defined for using the Oracle facilities; and so on. The developers of each new Candlebark system will profit from this investment. Whenever any new system is being designed, the presumption is that Oracle will be used to organise the system's data. Holding a new DBMS comparison contest during the design stages of every single new project is definitely not desirable.

Besides database software, other choices typically treated as technology infrastructure decisions, transcending individual projects, are: the mainframe hardware supplier, CASE (computer-aided software engineering) technology, and the communications arrangements linking different locations in an organisation. In all these cases it seems natural to make decisions at a level higher than individual systems, so that each new system can benefit from an infrastructure that is already established.

This briefing offers no opinion on whether Oracle is a better software product than Ingres, DB2 or a legion of rivals. Moreover, the general idea of having a technology infrastructure is hard to fault. What, then, is there to discuss?

If a decision about technology infrastructure is determined by purely technical factors, then of course technology expertise is all that counts, and the decision can remain the province of the technologist. But suppose certain infrastructure decisions raise strategic issues with much wider implications; for example, suppose they bring into question the whole structure of an organisation's IT planning procedures. Then some rather awkward issues might emerge. This briefing explores in that direction, and uncovers a number of difficulties and tradeoffs.

ANALYSIS

To approach the really tricky issues, start out with the following *naive view* of technology infrastructure planning. First you summarise the demands of the main systems the organisation will need for a reasonable period into the future. Then, using these demands as the basis, you decide on the most appropriate choice of technology infrastructure (e.g. the Oracle DBMS) to supply those demands. Having made that decision, you invest in that technology. Then, as new development projects are set up, they benefit from that infrastructure investment. Unravelling the issues in technology infrastructure is best done by seeing what is wrong with that naive view.

The General Problem of Infrastructure

Think of the planning of an individual new system (e.g. to produce statistics about the premiums and claims of an insurance company) rather like the planning of a large new building (e.g. a mansion in the country). The planner of a country mansion can usually take certain infrastructure for granted: the roads, electricity, sewers in the area and so on. Planning a new computer system is easier if you can take certain infrastructure for granted (database technology, telecommunications technology, etc.) and devote most of your attention to the details of the application itself. In both cases the planning problem is manageable; you know more or less where you start out from (the infrastructure is already given) and you know what you want to achieve (a building or a computer system using that infrastructure).

Now suppose that instead of planning a new building you have to plan the infrastructure itself for an area of countryside. As yet there are few buildings there; to plan the infrastructure you are forced to make some assumptions about the buildings that may be there in the future — mansions, hospitals, sports stadia and so on. You have to make some assumptions about building decisions that other people may make at a later date. Unless you make those assumptions, you can't determine the appropriate infrastructure. But other people's decisions about buildings in the future will be based on decisions you will have already made about infrastructure; if a site for a new hospital is needed, the site with the best infrastructure may well be chosen.

Thus *your* decisions about infrastructure are based on assumptions about *their* future decisions about buildings, which, however, will be based on *your* decisions about infrastructure. So, as the planner of infrastructure, you have one of those very awkward problems with no clear starting-point.

Without some assumptions about the buildings other people may decide to build, there is no basis for making any decisions about the infrastructure you should commit to; the more detailed these assumptions, the greater the commitment and the more chance of optimising the infrastructure. But, also, the more assumptions that are made, then the more vulnerable the planning will be to assumptions that turn out wrong — a very real danger, since all the assumptions are about decisions other people may make of their own free will, in the future.

The Infrastructure Problem in IT

The planner of the IT infrastructure in an organisation is often in a similar situation. Candlebark Insurance has five main business areas for information systems, all of them using infrastructure technologies, such as DBMS and telecommunications network. Using several different, incompatible database technologies within Candlebark is no more desirable than using several incompatible electricity supply technologies in the same area of countryside. The natural course is to select one database technology and make a commitment to it.

But different application areas within Candlebark have different characteristics. Study of these characteristics and of the available DBMS products shows that the ideal DBMS product in one area is not ideal in another. Tradeoffs and compromises are needed if the ideal of a common infrastructure is to be achieved.

But final decisions about all the future projects and all their relevant characteristics haven't yet been made. Therefore there is insufficient data on which to base an infrastructure choice. On the other hand, it is difficult to firm up decisions on some of the projects while the infrastructure remains uncertain. This is the IT version of the classic general problem of infrastructure.

The only way of resolving the tradeoffs and avoiding the difficulty of facing a problem with no clear starting-point seems to be the following: once every three or five years (say), define all the key demands of the main systems in all five application areas — in one discrete planning process; on that basis decide the infrastructure.

In practice, it is probably not sensible to synchronise all major decisions in all application areas that may be relevant to infrastructure, in one tidy cyclical planning process. Remember everything has to be planned in sufficiently fine detail to permit plausible choices between Oracle and Ingres and DB2 and all the others. The requirements in different business areas will change at different rates, in unpredictable ways — according to changes in technological possibilities, changes in the external business conditions, changes in perceptions of user requirements and various other possible sources of uncertainty. This kind of monolithic IT planning in an organisation often turns out to be just as futile and inflexible as the centralised planning of a command economy.

But if that approach won't work, then there is no other way available of realising the naive view of infrastructure planning given at the beginning. All the possible alternative approaches are pragmatic compromises of one kind or another.

For example, one compromise approach is to define a substantial infrastructure (e.g. choosing Oracle and making a strong commitment to it), but on the basis of a deliberately rough assessment of the demands of the relevant systems. This has the big advantage that it avoids spending time on lengthy planning procedures that may well turn out to be futile anyway. The big drawback is that the rough assessment can lead to decisions that are simply wrong in embarrassing, obvious ways. Some feature of Oracle, which seemed to be of decisive importance, turns out to be irrelevant to the company's real needs, whereas it becomes obvious that some unique feature of a rejected product would have been of great value.

Possible Compromises

There are other possible compromises, other ways of moving away from the naive view. They all entail reducing the importance of infrastructure planning and shifting more of the decision-making to the planning of individual systems.

Go back to the basic principles of infrastructure. When a big commitment has been made to (say) Oracle, a wise management will still allow the possibility that for a certain new system an alternative technology outside the infrastructure (IMS, DB2, Ingres, VAX Rdb, say) may still be used — if there are overwhelming reasons for it. But they have to be overwhelming reasons: an advocate of using IMS for a certain new system might have to demonstrate that building the system with IMS rather than Oracle would cut costs and timescales in half; merely showing that a deviation from use of the normal infrastructure would save a project 10% or 15% would not be good enough. After all, the whole logic of fixing on a certain technology infrastructure for the organisation as a whole is that, though it may not be optimum for every single system, it is on balance, more effective than trying to find the optimum for every new system in isolation.

One compromise approach to infrastructure varies this model by making the infrastructure itself much more flexible, without of course toppling over into anarchy. For example, Candlebark might lay down 'Our infrastructure contains three DBMSes — no more, no less, each rather different in character: Oracle, IMS and IDMS/R. For each application system, we use the most appropriate one out of those three.' With this policy there is less need for detailed assumptions at the beginning about the systems that will use the infrastructure, because the company is placing a three-way bet. If Oracle turns out to be unsuitable for the Global Clients application system, say, maybe IDMS/R can handle it. The disadvantage is that the company has to invest three times as much in technical support staff, courses and all the other things — or else, of course, dilute their quality.

This suggests another compromise approach — reducing the scale of the investment in the infrastructure. The cost of obtaining the technology itself (in this example the DBMS software) may be more or less fixed, but the investment in a group of in-house technical experts, the batches of people sent on courses, the development of detailed technical standards and so on are all areas where different degrees of commitment are possible. Of course, the further you go in this direction, the less you gain of the advantages that the infrastructure is meant to bring; you leave each individual project more to do in terms of decision-making and sheer work. On the other hand, you reduce the chances of making substantial commitments to the wrong infrastructure solution; and you may consider it beneficial that individual decision-makers on each project are given more scope for flexibility and creativity.

A more radical compromise approach is to leave out certain technology areas that might plausibly be contained within the scope of the infrastructure. Database technology is unlikely to be a good candidate for this approach, except perhaps in a very decentralised organisation. Word processing is a more plausible possibility. Some companies choose one particular word processing package (WordPerfect or WordStar, say) and make it part of their infrastructure. That may be a very sensible policy, but a company might easily decide there was no great harm in allowing different people to use different word processing software. This might have the advantage of freeing energy for making commitments on other matters (in the telecommunications area, perhaps) where the benefits of an agreed infrastructure were far more significant.

Decisions *In Medias Res*

The discussion so far of alternative approaches to infrastructure is simplified in one respect. It covers the different policies on infrastructure an organisation may choose between, if it has a completely free choice. But there is often an additional complicating dimension: the strategic decision about technology infrastructure isn't taken in a green field; it is taken *in medias res*.

For example, Yellow Carbeen already has a large family of systems using the IMS database software. Though this technology would not be its choice today, completely replacing IMS by something new is judged to be impractical.

The company formulates the following policy. In principle, all new application systems will be developed within the environment of IBM's DB2 database software. The only acceptable argument against using DB2 for any new system is the need for that system to be integrated with any existing application systems, that are based on the older IMS software. The IMS-based systems will continue to run and indeed will be enhanced when necessary. But if an existing system needs to be so drastically altered that it is, in effect, redesigned and rewritten, then it will be redeveloped using DB2.

Sensible or not, this is a clear policy on the issue of the amount of choice offered to individual projects. In effect, there is practically no choice available to the planners of any individual new project. The above rules have to be followed and they determine whether the choice will be DB2 or IMS; arguments about the nature of the processing or the security features or the data structures demanded by an individual project don't come into it.

Variants of Infrastructure Logic

The example of database technology used in this briefing is the neatest single one for bringing out most of the infrastructure issues, but some other technologies raise other issues. Database management is a relatively well established technology; there is often a case for introducing less familiar technologies at infrastructure rather than project level. Here the logic of infrastructure investment becomes slightly different.

For example, rather than try to define a cost-justified new project using the technology of expert systems, Candlebark invests in a small group of staff who first prime themselves with knowledge of that technology, then start giving seminars throughout the organisation to stimulate interest and only after that, look seriously for real applications. The logic of this approach rests on two assumptions: first, that the new technology will indeed be relevant to the organisation in the long run (because the investment in infrastructure without apparent return is justified on a longer view) and second, that the hurdle to be surmounted by the very first application is too great for it to be cost-justified individually (that is, the investment in infrastructure is necessary as well as justified).

This logic may be even stronger in cases where the infrastructure stimulating an innovative technology requires investment in hardware facilities as well as just specialist expertise. For example, this argument might apply to an infrastructure-justified internal service intended to stimulate awareness of the possibilities of on-line databases providing access to large quantities of texts.

In the discussion so far it has been assumed that an organisation has to decide, albeit with various nuances, which technology is best taken as its standard, but the concept of 'the best technology to take as a standard' contains two distinct components. You could choose a certain infrastructure technology, because you believe it is the best one *for what you want to do*; for example, your organisation needs advanced distributed database facilities and so you select a database software product that is strong in providing such facilities. But you could choose a certain infrastructure technology, because you believe it is the best one *to take as a standard*; for example, your organisation possesses a range of incompatible hardware and you judge it important for common systems to run at different sites. To achieve that aim, you lay down that all new systems are to be based on the Unix operating system, because Unix is the best established, most widely used operating system. You might quite rationally choose Unix on these grounds, even if you considered that as an operating system it had many weaknesses and was inferior to other rivals.

There is potentially a tradeoff between two conflicting factors here. In the examples discussed in this briefing so far, the intrinsic nature of a technology has probably weighed greater than its standard nature; but the situation can be different in one important infrastructure field — telecommunications. In choosing between the various technical standards for a network (OSI or SNA or TCP/IP, for example), you might very well devote most attention to assessing each possibility in terms of factors such as its existing degree of acceptance, whether it is stable or in a state of flux, whether powerful standardising bodies are promoting it, what future trends in the industry may be and so on. These factors could easily be more important than judgements about the inherent quality of the technology.

Generic Decisions

The discussion of alternative compromises to the naive approach to infrastructure has exposed a set of generic issues that usually need to be addressed.

One issue is the degree of detail to go to in defining the demand from actual and projected systems before taking the plunge and opting for one infrastructure technology rather than another. This has to be decided both absolutely (how much time to spend, how much paper to produce) and specifically (some areas may well need far more detail than others, because they may have a more decisive effect on infrastructure decisions). Clearly, whatever is decided here needs to be consistent (to put it no higher) with the arrangements for resolving all the other matters of IT strategy.

Another family of issues is the scope of the technology infrastructure itself. What areas of technology should it cover and what should it deliberately exclude? (Database? Word processing? Expert system technology?). A second scope issue is how flexible or rigid the infrastructure should be ('You must use Oracle' or 'You must use one out of Oracle, IMS and Sybase' or 'You must use a DBMS which supports the industry-standard access language SQL'). A third scope issue is the amount of investment in the infrastructure ('We've chosen Oracle and budgeted $1.7m per year to support it on a system-independent basis' or 'We've chosen Oracle but virtually all associated costs will be incurred at the level of individual projects').

Policy on the scope of the technology infrastructure may have quite far-reaching implications. For example, if Candlebark standardises very rigidly, and makes huge investments in its technology infrastructure on a trans-system basis, then (you would hope) the marginal cost of meeting demands for systems which happen to fit into that infrastructure quite neatly will be rather low; on the other hand, the marginal cost of meeting demands for quite minor system details that don't suit the characteristics of the chosen infrastructure may be alarmingly high. The arch-rival Stringybark Assurance, on the other hand, with a much more limited infrastructure, ought to have higher development costs for each new system on average, but have less trouble dealing with awkward system details. In this comparison, Candlebark is managing its IT in a more supply-driven way than Stringybark.

Strategic Implications

Technology infrastructure is essentially a supply factor — a means of meeting certain demands. If there are awkward difficulties in planning this supply factor, what are the implications for IT strategy as a whole? The naive view of infrastructure planning reduces the problem to two issues: What are the demands placed on the infrastructure? What is the best technical solution to supply the demands? This doesn't really work; it glosses over the fact that supply and demand interact and it ignores the concept of a tradeoff between commitment and flexibility.

What kind of considerations, arguments and factors should help you decide about the more subtle infrastructure issues — for example, how far to go in defining demand detail before firming up commitment on supply factors? The important thing is to realise that there are no generally applicable rules; what counts is the insight to identify what is most important in the particular case.

Candlebark Insurance goes an unusually long way in defining certain application characteristics before choosing the DBMS. There is one particularly large application, with some very demanding on-line transaction processing features. It is worthwhile to do a lot of work to identify the best possible technical solution — fending off the potential danger of monolithic planning rigidity as far as possible. But over at Stringybark Assurance, there is a wide variety of possible new applications, none particularly demanding; probably any of four or five alternative DBMS products would be about equally good. At Stringybark there is a lot to be said for getting practical experience of modern DBMS applications as quickly as possible, rather than taking very long over planning on paper.

These are merely examples of the kinds of factors that can influence the approach to infrastructure planning; many other relevant factors might point to different conclusions. Trying to set out a standard inventory of all such possible factors and their comparative weights as part of a step-by-step method for infrastructure planning would be about on a par with the labours of Sisyphus. As with many of the other matters that affect IT strategy decisions, the best advice is simply to be aware of all the issues involved and avoid unwarranted assumptions.

PRACTICAL ADVICE

➤ Accept the necessity for an up-front investment in planning and developing technology infrastructure. This should make it easier to develop individual systems effectively.

➤ But keep in mind that a technology infrastructure, like any up-front investment, is highly vulnerable to uncertainties and unforeseen developments along the way.

➤ Strive for the most favourable tradeoff between the commitment entailed by investment in infrastructure and the flexibility needed for project-level decisions. Note that this tradeoff decision is a different strategic decision, perhaps even a more important one, than the choice of the actual infrastructure technology.

➤ Carefully consider the following variables to help achieve the right balance: how cursory or comprehensive the up-front investigations are; how many choices the infrastructure leaves open to individual projects; how much financial commitment is made at infrastructure level as opposed to project level; how many matters are encompassed by the infrastructure.

➤ Distinguish between infrastructure investment that is motivated by cost-effectiveness in meeting known demands, and infrastructure investment in new technology and services, intended to stimulate new supply and demand possibilities.

➤ Recognise that standardisation is one, but only one, aspect of infrastructure. Treat it as a discrete issue.

➤ Strike the right balance and evaluate the possibilities by considering the relevant features of the specific case. There is no standard method.

16.   Information Infrastructure

ISSUES

The Eucalyptus City Project is under way; a complete new city is under
construction, Brasilia-style. Soon the city will need computer systems to
help administer its government and services. Early views suggest that
about twenty separate application systems will be developed: one for
collecting local taxes, one for monitoring the maintenance of the drains,
one for billing citizens for their use of electricity, one for planning public
transport and so on. This seems an excellent opportunity to gain the
benefits of integrated information systems, all sharing the information
held in one city database.

A good discipline is to ask what such abstractions as integration and
information-sharing mean in practice. As a simple example, most application systems at Eucalyptus need to record which streets and highways
exist in the city; a successful database system should allow that information to be stored in just one place in the database, and be accessible to all
the application systems that need it.

The Eucalyptus planners set up an *information infrastructure* in
database-form right at the beginning, containing shared information,
such as that about streets and highways, and this database (or family of
databases) is meant to develop in a well controlled way as new application
systems are gradually developed. Stating this desirable objective is easy,
but how is it to be achieved?

In situations like this the main difficulty is often in keeping a sense
of direction, since various parts of a database are shared in various
different ways by various application systems in quite complicated patterns of usage. It may be hard to design the database structure in a way
that is detailed enough to do justice to the complexity, yet clear enough
to be a basis for taking reliable planning and design decisions. In the
Eucalyptus case, order will be imposed by employing a simple distinction:
data items that are needed by several application systems are to be
regarded as belonging to the information infrastructure, and those
needed by only one system count as non-infrastructure data items.

This briefing looks at some issues of principle associated with this
concept of an information infrastructure. They have nothing to do with
database technology itself. Familiarity with concepts such as two phase
commit protocols or location transparency or query-by-example is quite

unnecessary to follow the arguments. The issues and problems are all matters of clarity and logic.

ANALYSIS

Start by getting clear what the information infrastructure approach is trying to avoid. You might begin the Eucalyptus City programme of IT developments with a project to build one application system with just the data it required in a database, without taking any account of the needs of any systems that might come later. Then you could go on to the second application system, making whatever expansions and retrospective amendments to the database seemed necessary; and proceed in this fashion through (say) twenty application systems. The Eucalyptus planners see many disadvantages with this approach; they intend to apply more sophisticated principles.

The best way to examine the issues that arise in planning the sharing of information in a database is to see the difficulties with the crude project-by-project approach, then go on to see how a naive infrastructure approach might promise to do better, then see the difficulties that arise with the naive infrastructure approach, and so on.

The Essential Tradeoff in Information-sharing

The crude project-by-project approach does have one advantage — it allows you to put off certain commitments. Nothing done in application systems numbers one or two presupposes that you will necessarily implement application system number three. Should you decide you don't need this system after all, it can simply be crossed off the list, without adverse consequences. In certain circumstances this avoidance of commitment can be of great value; uncertainty factors on the business and technological planes sometimes make it rash and irresponsible to formulate detailed assumptions about the shape of many future systems.

But the flexibility of the project-by-project approach is bought at a heavy price. As the successive application systems proceed, things get more and more messy and awkward. By (say) application number five the database structure resulting from the first four systems is already so intricate that modifying it again to meet the new set of needs of the fifth is a very tough job; and it will be practically impossible to work through in this fashion up to application number twenty. However skilful the work done, words like 'infrastructure' or 'blueprint' or 'framework' can't reasonably be used to describe the resulting database structure. The analogy of a battered, frequently erased 'palimpsest' is more appropriate.

In most (not necessarily all) cases where a significant degree of information-sharing is required, the disadvantages of the project-by-project approach are so great that they outweigh the attractions of avoiding commitment in the face of uncertainty.

Some form of coordinated, farseeing approach is usually desirable, but there are important implications. Building any kind of outline structure, within which the things that really count, the application systems, can be built, entails an initial investment. Some definitions of the nature of the coming applications have to be made; otherwise there is no basis for deciding what the nature of the database structure should be. In other words, commitments must be made that certain systems with certain characteristics are indeed intended for the future.

The extreme approach is to conduct a very detailed data modelling exercise covering (say) all twenty possible applications, firm up that detail and thus design a complete database embracing all the pieces of information and all the relationships between pieces of information that will ever be needed by all the application systems. Only then does work begin on the software for the first application system. This approach is normally quite impractical in real life, because accurate planning to that level of detail is just too onerous. The difficulty is analogous to that of trying to make detailed plans for the entire Soviet economy, while sitting in an office in Moscow.

So the real challenge is to steer between the two tendencies. On the one hand, commitment has to be made at the beginning to some definition of the relevant information; this is essential if the database is to develop within a genuine structure rather than as a mere palimpsest. On the other hand, the more that is defined at a general level, prior to the individual projects, the more possibilities there are for making assumptions that turn out later to be inaccurate; any commitment to detail has to be made as economically and elegantly as possible, avoiding matters that are not vital to the health of the database's structure. This is the essential, generic tradeoff in the planning of information sharing. Eucalyptus City's information infrastructure represents one of the commonly found approaches to the problem.

A Naive Approach to Infrastructure

Eucalyptus City adopts an approach that seems plausible, though, on closer examination, it can fairly be described as naive infrastructure.

Plainly some pieces of data have a more general character than others. If the name of a certain street is changed from 'Rat Lane' to 'Avenue of the Martyrs of 28 September', that will have some effect on quite a few of the twenty application systems. If the diameter of a certain sewer is changed from '1.81 metres' to '1.95 metres', that may well affect only one application. The Eucalyptus planning team makes the following rules. There are two types of data items in the database: *infrastructure* data items and *application* data items. Infrastructure items are by definition relevant to more than one application and belong in the infrastructure part of the database; 'Street Name' is one example. An application data item is relevant to only one application and belongs in those parts of the database specific to individual applications; 'Sewer Diameter' is an example.

This provides a firm criterion for labelling every piece of data as either infrastructure or application. The distinction matters very much, because the two types of data item are handled differently on four main issues. The first issue is the time at which the piece of data is actually firmed up as a fully defined component of the database structure. The infrastructure part of the database, including data like 'Street Name', is set up at the very beginning; but the application parts of the database, including items like 'Sewer Diameter', are slotted in neatly over time as application systems are developed. Call this the *definition moment* issue.

Second, there is the question of *development responsibility*. The infrastructure part of the database is set up by a special team at the start, not specifically concerned with any one of the applications. The twenty applications, together with their application-specific data, may, at least in principle, be developed by twenty different teams, whether staff belonging to the appropriate departments of the city administration or teams from software houses under contract.

Third, in this approach, is *software structure*. In the structure of the software of the Eucalyptus systems, infrastructure information is only ever updated by special self-contained infrastructure modules of software, whereas application information is only ever updated by special application modules of software.

Fourth is *update responsibility*: infrastructure information is normally updated by clerks in a special 'infrastructure' department within the city's administration, whereas application information is the responsibility of staff within the appropriate department concerned with the application.

In summary, this approach consists of a criterion (just about the simplest you could think of) for assigning every item of data to one out of two possible categories — *infrastructure* or *application* — together with four important issues (*definition moment, development responsibility, software structure, update responsibility*) which show how it really does matter which category an item is assigned to.

**Infrastructure and Application Data:
a Plausible but Inadequate Model**

	Infrastructure Data	*Application Data*
CRITERION		
relevant to how many applications?	more than one	only one
ISSUES		
development moment	when database first set up	when application developed
development responsibility	database infrastructure team	individual application team
software structure	updated by special infrastructure software	updated by application software
update responsibility	database infrastructure department	staff in department concerned with the application

Problems with 'Relevance'

What is naive about this approach? First of all, the *criterion of relevance* is vulnerable. Suppose you made a complete list of all the data items and used twenty columns to show which out of the twenty applications each item was relevant to. It is true of course that (assuming no pointless data was listed), every item would have either one entry or more than one entry across the application columns.

But to say that data item SID, 'sewer inspection date', is 'relevant' to application 15 is to say something rather vague: it could mean that data item SID is updated within application 15; or it could mean that, although data item SID is not updated within application 15, neverthe-less application 15 depends heavily on data item SID (e.g. SID is used in some logic that governs the processing of application 15); or it could mean that application 15 contains a facility giving a user the option of looking up the value of SID — and if so, it must be present and correct; or it could mean merely that application 15 contains a facility for looking up the value of SID — but if SID is not present, there is little damage done.

Therefore, including the null option, there can easily be five gradations of relevance, for any combination of data item and application; reducing these to two (relevant or not relevant) could well be a gross over-simplification with undesirable consequences for the way the four issues of definition moment, development responsibility, software structure and update responsibility work out.

There is another vulnerable point. Either a data item is 'relevant' (in whatever sense) to only one application or to more than one application; whether it is relevant to two or to seventeen applications is ignored, because both cases are regarded as 'more than one'. This works very well in the case of 'Street Name' (clearly relevant to lots of applications in various degrees) and also in the case of some highly technical piece of data about a sewer, that could only possibly be of relevance to the Sewer Control application system. But what about the data item SID, 'Sewer Inspection Date'? There may well be a city policy that the scheduling of sewer inspections should be coordinated with other road maintenance; this data item could therefore be relevant to the Road Maintenance application as well. But this seems to be a very different case from 'Street Name', which is used in all kinds of ways by all kinds of applications from property tax through sewer control to public transport: an obvious candidate for the information infrastructure. SID, by contrast, seems to belong naturally to one particular application, but is also used by one or two closely related applications in a certain easily definable way. It will end up in the infrastructure merely by blind application of a crude rule; not because it necessarily has to be there, when you consider the issues of definition moment, development responsibility, software structure and update responsibility.

Going Through the Issues

The first of the four issues making up the naive Eucalyptus approach is *definition moment*. This suggests another couple of problems. If the division of data items between infrastructure and non-infrastructure data is made at the beginning, can it ever be changed, as a result of, say, altered decisions about applications or sheer human error? If it can and numerous changes are actually made, the infrastructure may well become a palimpsest rather than a genuine infrastructure. If it cannot and lots of sensible changes have to be refused, then the infrastructure may become a kind of historical relic with no inherent logic, regarded with increasing scorn by those who have to work with it.

There is a related issue. At the time the infrastructure is set up, no applications yet exist, therefore, strictly speaking, no data items are yet relevant to one, still less more than one, application. You could interpret the infrastructure criterion by saying that as time goes by, more and more applications are implemented, so more and more data items meet the criterion of being relevant to more than one application, so items cross over from the application part of the database to the infrastructure part. But this is surely chaos not infrastructure.

Therefore the only way of interpreting the criterion is to take the criterion 'relevant to more than one application' as meaning 'relevant to more than one of the twenty intended applications, whether already implemented or not'. But this still brings a couple of difficulties. It implies you have a clear enough view of all twenty applications to be aware of all the data they will need, and you have committed to their features in detail — even those still five years way.

The fourth issue identified is *update responsibility* at the organisational level. The Eucalyptus approach identifies two categories of data and suggests that the updating of infrastructure data is the responsibility of a special trans-departmental group, whereas updating application data is done by people in the appropriate department.

Again this is vulnerable to the charge of over-simplification; you probably need more than just these two choices. For example, you might very well want the computer system to enforce the following pattern of responsibilities. Some very general data items (e.g. 'Street Name') are maintained by a central group of people who know nothing about the applications. Some data items (e.g. relating to inspection planning) are maintained by a group of people who are closely involved with several departments whose responsibilities overlap in certain areas. Some data items (e.g. relating to inspection results) are maintained by one and only one person in a department. Some data items (e.g. Sewer Diameter) can be updated by anybody within a certain department. Those four possibilities probably represent the absolute minimum; there could easily be more.

All this illustrates a rather fundamental problem. A distinction between two categories of data item, infrastructure and application, however subtly made, is really an approach to the problem of commitment. There is a clear commitment to the infrastructure items from the start, but commitment to the application items only arises when the application systems themselves are firmed up. But, if the two categories of data item are defined in this way, there is no real guarantee that they will map neatly onto the patterns of *definition moment, development responsibility, software structure* and *updating responsibility* that are desirable. Two data items could each be highly specialised and quite inappropriate candidates for an infrastructure, but require very different patterns of (say) updating responsibility.

Analysing What Has Happened

Plainly, if a number of different systems are going to share data in a database, some coordination is needed. Since it can easily happen that various parts of a database are shared in various different ways by various systems in quite complicated patterns of usage, this coordination can be very taxing.

The most obvious answer is to study all the intricate patterns of relationships between data items, within one design process once and for all, in order to produce a detailed, correctly designed structure for the database. Once that is done, coordination of individual system developments should proceed smoothly. But unfortunately the initial work to design and set up the database can take a very long time, paralyse the development of application systems in the meantime, and even when it is ready, give up the flexibility to react to unexpected events and needs.

The problems really arise because the problem of matching supply and demand is intertwined with the tradeoff between commitment and flexibility. If it were feasible to *commit to* all the data items of the entire database right at the start, then that would provide a firm definition of demand; the job of supplying that demand by building a database would then be a purely technical one, and there would be no call for flexibility in varying the demand. But very often it is not feasible to define demand so firmly from the start. There is the practical impossibility of carrying out the detailed work of defining all the individual systems of the future. Also, as many other briefings show, very often certain demands raised by systems are so tricky to supply, that it may be sensible to modify the demands to take better account of the supply possibilities.

Given that defining the complete database at the very start is not possible, one very natural compromise is to recognise two classes of data items — such as infrastructure and application. Then the initial work need only firm up the structure and detail of the infrastructure part.

One interpretation of the Eucalyptus City case is that the planners understand the outline of the problem: you have to start by defining some structure for the database but you can't design the complete thing in every detail. They recognise the need for a reduced, compromise approach, but they go wrong by building an approach around assumptions that still under-estimate the difficulty of the problem. They assume that some simple, firm criterion can be laid down to determine incontrovertibly whether each data item should belong to the infrastructure or the application category. They assume unjustifiably that all data items in each category should be handled the same way, in terms of the issues of definition moment, development responsibility, software structure and update responsibility.

These mistakes are understandable, because the alternative seems to be to abandon firm rules and rely on the intuition and judgement of skilled practitioners. The trouble is that any firm, simple rules are always likely to encounter the kind of problems seen in this case. Of course complexity is a factor; in a situation with many fewer application systems, the Eucalyptus infrastructure approach could be quite respectable. This may suggest that there is no good way to resolve the issues that arise in information sharing. It is certainly hard to believe that there is any one good standardised method that can take proper account of the tradeoff considerations to provide a satisfactory answer almost every time.

It is well worthwhile to be aware of the false assumptions that can arise. The more clearly you see the potential traps, the easier it is to apply common sense and find a solution that avoids them. In very general terms, the right approach is to get a clear view of the real dilemmas and issues of the specific case, to understand the interplay of the supply–demand and commitment–flexibility phenomena and to identify the best buy or least bad choice.

PRACTICAL ADVICE

➤ Acknowledge that if a database is to be shared by several application systems you have to start by defining some structure for the database as a whole; otherwise successive developments won't fit together in a well coordinated way.

➤ Allow for the fact that you can't design the complete database in every detail from the start. Define only what needs to be defined in order to produce a sound structure.

➤ Be influenced by the tradeoff between commitment and flexibility. The more up-front definition, the greater the commitment. The more uncertainty factors exist, the less commitment you should make.

➤ Consider the simplifying approach of adopting a simple rule: draw a line between the information in a database which belongs to in-dividual projects or systems and that part which serves as a common 'infrastructure'.

➤ Be conscious that a simple rule that helps determine what features of the database to firm up at what point may not apply to other related issues: choices on the issues of definition moment, development responsibility, software structure and updating responsibility may not hang together neatly.

➤ Remember that if the complexity of information sharing passes a certain point, it may be too great a simplification to distinguish infrastructure from project data or to rely on any other firm rules to tackle the issues. Pragmatic judgements may be unavoidable.

17. Strategic Information Systems Planning

ISSUES

This may sound a pompous title, yet many people use it without embarrassment. Sometimes the four words are arranged in a different order. James Martin has a book called *Strategic Data-Planning Methodologies*.[1] Such phrases invariably stand for versions of a certain general approach to planning an organisation's use of IT.

The rationale of the approach runs as follows. Any substantial organisation will develop a large number of application systems, and the systems will share data from many databases or segments of databases. Coordinating all these developments is a formidable problem. Therefore, why not develop a kind of master framework (also called architecture or blueprint)? This framework will summarise all the systems and database segments. Essentially it will be a matrix, showing which pieces of database are used by which pieces of system. With such a framework it will be possible to carry out development work in a well coordinated way. Projects can be planned to develop application systems or to set up segments of database, in the sequence that best suits the whole grand design. The people on any particular project will know that, provided they keep within the terms of reference implied by the framework, their work will fit neatly together with work done on other projects.

This concept is so seductive that some people go much too far and present the approach as if it were self-evidently the only way for any large organisation to take its main decisions on the use of IT. Leaving aside relatively unimportant details of nomenclature and diagram formats, many standardised approaches to IT planning are directed towards developing such a framework. The term SISP (for Strategic Information Systems Planning) is as convenient as any for this general pattern of approach.

In reality, the SISP approach is subject to a good many qualifications, which in certain circumstances can render it quite inappropriate. On the other hand, healthy scepticism about the claims made for SISP need not cause it to be dismissed outright in every case.

This briefing looks critically at the SISP philosophy and reveals some of the snags that are often glossed over. It identifies the main issues that determine how appropriate SISP is in any particular case.

ANALYSIS

Martin's book is a useful basis for a critical examination of SISP-style approaches. Some consultancies and other computer services companies offer their own methodologies in similar vein, but the documentation is often opaque. Martin sets out the main concepts quite clearly, so there is time to think for yourself about how valid they are.

The Peril of Unnoticed Assumptions

Martin's book starts with the observation that if you had to build a battleship you would make an outline design for the whole thing first and then fill in the details; the same applies to 'corporate information engineering'. This sounds a persuasive point, but closer examination shows that the analogy begins *after the important decision has already been taken:* the decision to build the battleship. That is the real moment of strategy decision. Not all countries need battleships: for some, it may be more sensible to have no battleship, but a number of frigates and destroyers; for others, submarines may be a better choice.

Decisions on the *pattern* of a country's fleet are certainly strategic, and so are decisions about the *degree* of coordination of an organisation's systems and databases. The battleship analogy almost smuggles in the idea that it is self-evidently right to try to make an organisation's entire range of systems and databases fit together as neatly as the guns, electronics or other subsystems of one battleship. This may be sensible in some cases, but in other cases, it could be preferable to allow different operating units to speed ahead developing the systems they need without interference; or to insist only that some tiny percentage of all the organisation's data be regarded as shared; or to identify, say, three great families of systems, each one internally coordinated, but related very loosely, if at all, to the other two.

This example illustrates one of the perils of SISP work. Assumptions, that may or may not be justified, but certainly have far-reaching consequences, can easily creep in unnoticed at many points.

The Commitment–Flexibility Tradeoff

The arguments in favour of an overall framework for an organisation's systems and databases can be summarised as follows. Designing everything in one great process would be far too complex a task. Developing a number of discrete modules of manageable size seems far more sensible.

But if these modules are developed absolutely independently, they won't fit together. Therefore a framework is needed, within which the modules can be developed separately and yet still cohere with the whole structure.

That companies often do run into great difficulties and inefficiencies as a result of badly planned, uncoordinated developments is an incontrovertible fact. But the phenomenon is so well known and so universally condemned that there is a danger of over-reaction to it. Can it be true that coordination in pursuit of coherence is unalloyed virtue — the more of it you have, the better?

There is really a tradeoff here. The more highly you prize coherence, the more detailed you will make the framework and the fewer decisions you will leave to be resolved by those who work on individual modules within the framework. On the other hand, the more you wish to encourage creativity in the designers of individual modules, and to preserve freedom to cope with unforeseen business or technology developments, and to minimise damage from possible inaccuracies in the up-front planning, then the less detailed and prescriptive you will make the 'framework'. A balance has to be struck between commitment and flexibility.

In Martin's first chapter, the advantages of coordination are stressed through several brief analogies: a telephone system needs a common directory; an orchestra needs a conductor to ensure everyone is playing the same symphony; a house needs to be built on foundation stones not on sand. Once you see that coordination is only one half of a tradeoff, rather than an absolute virtue, these comparisons can readily be criticised for obscuring the tradeoff. A list of telephone numbers is trivially simple in structure and therefore easy to design and easy to amend later — very different from a database. The score of a symphony defines what is to be played in great detail; the players in the orchestra aren't supposed to regard it as a framework for improvisation of their own or as a robust structure to withstand unexpected events in the concert hall. Good foundations may ensure that a house stands firm on the same spot for decades, but they don't provide any guarantee that the house can be significantly enlarged or altered during its life.

Making an elaborate SISP framework generally has a point only if a firm commitment can be made to plans that extend quite a way ahead — typically the next five years. There is little point in doing that unless you are confident of making reasonably accurate projections of the main demands and main means of supplying them for the period covered. Suppose a colleague says: 'One thing's for sure. This industry and the way it uses IT are going to be revolutionised over the next five years in ways nobody can even dream of today.' If you agree with that opinion, it would be irrational to firm up an elaborate framework of IT plans for the next five years.

In general, the more confident you can be of making accurate forecasts of all the main factors, the more sensible you are to invest in commitment at the expense of flexibility; and the less confident, the less sensible. And the more you are prepared to invest in commitment at the expense of flexibility, the more appropriate is a framework based on the SISP approach; and the less commitment, the less appropriate is SISP. Plainly the variables in this little piece of logic will vary considerably from case to case. Therefore the relevance of the classic SISP approach will vary from case to case too.

Representative Examples

Ironbark Insurance, a representative example, produces a SISP framework. The main working document is essentially a huge matrix. One dimension, the columns, represents groups of data selected by the criterion of naturalness (or 'logic' or 'structure' to be more grand). For example, the data about *Policies* can be separated very naturally from that about *Claims*. Policy data can be separated naturally into those items that are standard to all types of policy (e.g. 'name of policy-holder') and those that are risk-specific (e.g. 'car registration number' is only relevant to motor insurance). Within Claims data there is a natural breakdown between that which describes the incident causing the claim (e.g. 'date of accident') and accounting data (e.g. 'value of initial payment').

The other dimension of the matrix, the rows, represents different functions within the company and, in Ironbark's case, these functions are grouped together by what is called 'business location'. For example, the matrix has rows for the functions 'policy administration', 'claim administration' and 'agent administration' — and those three all appear below the heading 'branch office'. The functions at each location can always be structured to further degrees of detail; 'policy administration' can be broken down into 'new policy', 'renew policy', 'end policy' and so on, but Ironbark analysts try to avoid proliferating rows on the matrix. Entries in the cells of the matrix show which functions need which data.

Sheer physical distinctness is one but not the sole criterion for making the natural breakdown into business locations; the accounts department and the board of directors can be seen as separate business locations, even though they work in the same head office building. But, if there are a dozen branch offices, each playing much the same role in its region of the country, the matrix need not show each one separately.

One information analyst at Ironbark argues that 'business location' and 'function' should be separate *dimensions*. This would mean, say, that the function 'policy administration' would be treated as a distinct thing

Strategic Information Systems Planning Matrix

IRONBARK INSURANCE

BUSINESS LOCATIONS Functions	Database Groupings						
	Policy (Standard)	Policy (Risk Specific)	Claims (Incident)	Claims (Accounts)	Agent (Accounts)	etc.	etc.
BRANCH OFFICE							
Policy Admin	■	■					
Claim Admin			■	■	■		
Agent Admin					■		
etc.							
etc.							
HEAD OFFICE - BOARD							
Management Information		■		■	■		
Five-Year Modelling		■		■			
etc.							
HEAD OFFICE - ACCOUNTS							
Audit				■	■		
Government Returns		■	■	■	■		
etc.							
ETC.							
etc.							

Outline → Logic → of the → Approach

that could crop up in several different business locations: branch office, agent's office, etc. Most people at Ironbark consider that, although this may be a valid point from a purely logical point of view, it would entail drawing up *three-dimensional matrices* and these would be too awkward to work with. With Ironbark's two-dimensional matrix, as with any model partly based on multiple criteria, potential conflicts and compromises arise. This may not matter, provided people understand that the model is summarised and impressionistic rather than rigorous.

Ironbark's complete working matrix makes it plain that the entries showing what data items are used for what purpose are not spread at random; they form distinct clusters. From this clustering, Ironbark are able to see by inspection that they have certain large chunks of system to implement; each of them will automate certain functions and add certain parts to the company-wide database.

Martin's book provides three comparable examples. A large bank draws a matrix mapping 21 'subject databases' against 120 'processes'; on average each process uses 8 of the 21 subject databases. A manufacturing company has a matrix of 24 subject databases against 37 processes; in this more sophisticated example each cell can have several different values — recording such information as whether the process creates, updates or looks up data. IBM's BSP approach is described as requiring several matrices, whose effect is actually to produce a five-dimensional structure; the dimensions are (1) business processes; (2) DP systems; (3) data files (or databases); (4) executives responsible in the organisation; (5) situation now / situation desired.

The 'Green Field' Assumption

The more detailed these matrices get, the more the SISP approach comes to depend on one assumption, that may never be explicitly stated. The approach works at its best if a certain strategic decision has already been taken before the SISP work starts — the decision that everything needs to be developed anew and all the existing systems have to be phased out and replaced. The further away this 'green field' policy is from being a sensible policy in the circumstances, the less effective the SISP work will be.

Suppose Ironbark decides that the recently completed Claims system can stand, but everything else needs to be redeveloped. You might think that a SISP approach could still work well, but even in this very simple case, there could be problems. The scope of the actual Claims system probably won't be identical to the ideal one that SISP would have defined, and it may interact with the other systems in slightly different ways. Therefore, to allow for this, the other systems can't be identical to the ideal ones that SISP would have defined either. Thus the very simple constraint of not scrapping the Claims system can exert awkward little pressures at many different points in the framework.

Now take the case where there are numerous systems and portions of systems that don't deserve to be scrapped, plus, even more awkwardly, numerous systems and portions of systems where redevelopment is an open question pending further detailed investigation. Trying to follow the generalised SISP methods appropriate to a green field case, while at the same time coping with such awkward constraints can be a very wearisome task.

The Problem of Detail

There is another big problem suggested by the examples. In theory, work proceeds at a summary level (for a large bank, 21 'subject databases' against 120 'processes') and the framework product is at this summary level. But it may not be practically possible to work with that level of detail. For example, in order to visualise the nature of one of the subject databases, you have to think of a few specific examples of actual data items it contains. In order to debate whether a certain subject database should be split in two or merged with another, you may need to go into considerable detail about the data items it contains.

Also the main purpose of the framework is to set the scope within which individual projects can safely work and still be sure of fitting in neatly with all the others: just giving the names of the processes and the pieces of database that a project is concerned with is unlikely to be enough for that. Many pages of definition may be needed to describe just how one project fits in with all the others, including how it depends on certain data from others and how others depend on it.

These issues of detail produce some dangers. One danger is that a superficially impressive framework turns out to be defective six months into a five-year implementation period, because the relevant detail wasn't assessed sufficiently carefully during the SISP activity. The opposite danger is that the people involved in the SISP work sense the need for investigating detail in order to ensure that their framework is reliable, but sink ever deeper into a swamp of data analysis, because they are never quite sure where to stop. Meanwhile the framework product degenerates into documentation so complex that it becomes, as they say, unreadable at any speed.

The conclusion? Don't consider starting a SISP without getting a realistic view of the amount of detail that is likely to be required to support a worthwhile framework. Then decide whether that is still sufficiently manageable to produce a document that is readable and useful. If that test is passed, check that it will be feasible to impose controls on the SISP work to ensure that the detail doesn't overflow those limits.

Martin gives some further examples in which the modelling of data and of the activities within processes gets very detailed. Essentially, a matrix is produced that is far too extensive to be of use as a document on paper. Plainly it is no longer possible to rely on human judgement to notice how the entries in matrix cells form natural clusters. Logically enough, Martin suggests some techniques based on formulae to automate this analysis.

For example, if piece of data A is used by 20 different activities and piece of data B is used by 19 out of those 20, the 'affinity factor' of A to B can be said to be $19/20 = 0.95$. An affinity factor this high suggests that the two items belong together in the same part of the database. Once started along this route, you can use a computer program for all the calculations required by complicated formulae devised to find optimum ways of dividing things up. Subjective weightings can be applied and fed into the formulae too. Other people besides Martin have published other formulae for similar purposes.[2]

The question arises: If you are involved in all this trouble and detail, can you really claim to be taking strategic decisions as opposed to doing detailed design work? In most cases the answer is probably no; but it is not impossible; it all depends on the case.

What Are the Real Strategy Issues?

Classic SISP works best if the 'green field' assumption is accompanied by another. If there is one natural set of system demands whose scope is not subject to significant debate, then SISP is a reasonable approach towards breaking this body of demands up into convenient pieces for implementation. If there is no complex interaction between supply and demand factors, and little scope for tradeoff between flexibility and commitment, then one of the few strategic issues remaining may be how to split things up for implementation; and SISP can help with that problem. But SISP is of little help with issues such as whether or not to meet a certain demand or how much commitment to accept in the face of uncertainty.

A SISP-like approach is relatively ineffective when the real strategic issues are not how to divide up the whole body of things to do, but rather what things should be done. For example, the managers of any company in banking or manufacturing or publishing may feel that they need to catch up and surpass others in the industry in imaginative use of IT. There is a useful distinction between cases where the main stress is on finding the best way of dividing up a well understood body of things (as with all Martin's material) and cases where the main stress is on deciding what the new things are that should be done. If you adopt a really open approach to new ideas for using IT and only come on to the dividing-up puzzle much later, it is rarely sensible to do much detailed SISP work, because the analysis and assumptions of your matrices will be relatively tenuous and uncertain.

Yet another classic SISP assumption needs to be mentioned. The matrices work best as a framework when all the data and its access and its processing correspond to the normal patterns of mainstream database technology. With a large publisher like Murray Pine, for example, that is true of those systems that control subscriptions to magazines, but not of those that store magazine texts for access in an on-line database. With applications like text retrieval or CAD (computer-aided design) or GIS (geographical information system), the SISP matrix is often so trivial that it is worthless or so complicated that it is also worthless (at least, as a document for strategy decisions). So, in deciding whether to use a SISP approach, you also need to judge the extent to which the use of out-of-the-ordinary database technology raises issues for your organisation; the more of it there is, the less use SISP will be.

It follows from all these qualifications, that a well run SISP activity needs to be based on some pre-existing awareness and agreement on what the main strategic issues are and what assumptions can be safely made.

Data Distribution — a Third SISP Theme

As the previous paragraphs suggest, deciding what systems are needed and deciding how to divide the work up into projects are two rather different things; the one may be more relevant than the other in a certain situation. There is a third large theme that often creeps into discussions of SISP — data distribution. Like each of the other two, this may be at the heart of the strategy problem in some cases or have hardly any strategic impact in others.

The classic SISP matrix sets database groupings against business locations and functions in the most *natural* possible way. For example, at Ironbark Insurance all the data items concerned with insurance policies naturally form one very large piece of the pattern, that can be conveniently broken down into Policy (Standard) and Policy (Risk-specific). Data concerned with claims is another large piece in the pattern.

The most natural pattern for the data is generally the neatest, least confusing and most insight-generating for discussions; but the most efficient physical arrangement of data for the real-life computer systems may be quite different. For example, when the systems are actually implemented, it may be best to have some data physically stored in a database at each branch of the insurance company and other data stored in a head-office database. Thus some policy and claims data items may be held in one place and other items in another place, and others, perhaps, in both places. In arranging these patterns of data items, there can be other criteria besides naturalness; for example, estimates of transaction volumes and costs of transmitting data from one location to another may be relevant.

This raises a new motivation altogether for a SISP exercise. Some decision-makers might reason: 'We don't really need SISP to decide how to divide things up into separate projects, because that's not our main problem. We certainly need to think very creatively about the kind of systems we ought to have in the future, but we can find better ways of doing that than following a SISP approach. However, we are seriously worried about the way data and processing should be divided over the different locations. Therefore, we will carry out a SISP-like activity whose primary purpose is to resolve that particular issue.'

Is Data Distribution Really a Strategy Issue?

Some SISP studies devote considerable attention to data distribution issues. Since data distribution issues seem to be both fairly detailed and fairly technical, this may be thought surprising. It is useful to consider how it can be justified.

Suppose you have produced a detailed logical data model, with carefully notated entities and relationships and attributes and so on. For a whole insurance company it will certainly run into hundreds of pages. To convert this *logical* data model into the optimum design for the *physical* distribution of data may well require a very awkward reshuffling of all the items into different patterns. Arriving at even one pattern that contains no obvious mistakes may be a very laborious process, but there may be any number of plausible patterns to be found. If you work at the level of detail of the data model, how can you ever be sure that you find anywhere near the best available arrangement?

Therefore, in order to solve major data distribution problems, it is usually best to operate at the summary level by considering *groups* of data items rather than individual items. The classic SISP matrices can be made more complicated or extra matrices can be drawn, in order to represent the location dimension of the planning.

But this conclusion doesn't directly answer a different, more important question: Are data distribution problems matters of *strategic* decision? In other words, should decisions about data distribution be seen as the business of technology experts or should they result from strong interaction between the experts and other parties taking a wider view?

Distribution decisions can certainly be very demanding. Martin's book lists five generic properties of data that argue for distribution and eight that argue for centralisation, nine different varieties of distributed data and nine generic problems with distributed data. A table presents thirt-three generic factors relevant to deciding how a given piece of data should be distributed. And that book dates from 1982; many new possibilities, issues and problems have arisen since then. But 'very demanding' doesn't necessarily mean 'strategic'. Indeed, the more technical parameters there are to be tuned, the less reason there is for the useful involvement of non-specialists, it may appear.

Moreover, there is a strong motivation to classify data distribution as a supply problem, to be approached only after the demand for the information is fairly well defined. This arises from the vald point that in a well made system, people should not have to know or care where the information they access is actually stored — any more than a telephone user should have to know anything about the exchanges that route his call.

There are cases where these arguments are decisive because there are no strong arguments to set against them. If so, regarding data distribution as a matter of genuine strategy decision is an unnecessary and misleading distraction.

When Data Distribution Is Strategic

In other cases data distribution does have serious strategy implications. There may be strong feedback from supply to demand. For example, the demands of the Global Clients department of Candlebark Insurance define which information should be accessible to which people with what degree of currency. They are ambitious demands because up to date information, originating from many different sources, must be accessible to people in many different places. Studies of possible distribution patterns for the data to supply these demands reveal that, if only the demands can be made slightly less exacting, the data distribution can be simpler and more cost-effective. To have certain business statistics (e.g. premium income year to date) current as at close of business yesterday rather than on an up-to-the-minute basis may be regarded as a small concession in return for a much simpler pattern of data distribution. In other words, data distribution may be a strategic issue because it leads to a tricky interaction between supply and demand.

It may be a strategic issue too for a different type of reason. For example, there may be good *psychological* reasons that certain offices of Ironbark Insurance should have responsibility for maintaining data stored at their own computer installations — even if this is not quite the recommended solution from a cold, technical optimising calculation. Conversely, perhaps staff at certain offices are so distrusted that they should have the absolute minimum of responsibility for on-site equipment and systems — even if this contradicts theoretical optimisation.

Perhaps it seems a worthwhile objective to make any distribution of data as *flexible* as possible, in order to contend with the unpredictable; for example, at certain locations data might be stored to encourage people to use initiative to find unforeseen ways of accessing and using it. Or perhaps that is just what you want to avoid happening — even at the expense of a sub-optimal distribution for handling day-to-day processing.

To sum up, data distribution may or may not be a strategic issue in any given case. Deciding whether it is involves weighing up the kind of factors just discussed. The rest of this briefing discusses how to proceed in those cases where genuine strategy issues do exist.

From Demand Matrix to Supply Design

How do you actually make the jump from the pure non-technical matrix showing the information desired by various parties to an actual, outline technical design for the distribution of data and processing?

Some standardised SISP approaches duck this problem. The handbook may set out many generic pros and cons of data distribution in lists similar to those in Martin's book, but there may be very little guidance on *how* to take account of them.

Martin, with admirable logical consistency, presses on by proposing detailed step-by-step methods of getting from demand matrix to supply design. These include extensive three-dimensional matrices, whose cells may take multiple values to represent various factors affecting the way each data item is used. Formulae are proposed to process considerable volumes of raw data from these matrices, quantifying the factors of the whole problem in order to arrive at an optimal design.

But the more a distribution decision deserves to be called strategic, the less appropriate detailed formulae seem to be. The circumstances where distribution is genuinely a strategic issue — feedback between supply and demand; weighing psychological factors against technical efficiency; and weighing flexibility against efficiency — all share certain traits. They call for a recognition of different options in order to find the best buy; the best buy has to be judged by weighing up a variety of technical and non-technical factors. Therefore the progress from the definition of the information desired to the chosen pattern of data distribution is likely to require iteration.

One good approach is to begin with a rough draft document, a summarised, non-technical matrix, as a basis for discussion with a technology specialist. It may well be that some rather vital parts of these non-technical demands have big supply-side implications, setting the tone for much of the technical design. Some less important demands may prove too awkward to be worthwhile; conversely, some areas where the demands are rather moderate could possibly be expanded without major supply problems. In the course of several iterations of discussions about drafts it should become clear whether certain non-quantifiable strategic factors, such as psychology and flexibility, have any great effect on the choices between possibilities.

Intermediate Drafts of Data Distribution

The concept of working iteratively with draft designs can be developed into quite a powerful technique. To see the whole problem as a translation from a pure demand document, the data/function matrix, to a pure supply document, the database internal schema, is to over-simplify. Why not work through several intermediate draft designs for data distribution that are more supply-oriented than the matrix but more demand-oriented than the internal schema?

For example, one early draft might suggest an outline pattern of distribution based only on some simple principle such as 'each data item should be stored as close as possible to its creator'. A later draft might be based on more detailed quantification of transaction volumes, but it might still ignore certain complications. A later draft still might show that, for reasons of system reliability, duplicate versions of certain data should be held in certain places. This use of intermediate drafts provides a basis for iteration that makes it easier to approach strategic factors. For example, the decisions that are really strategic might be resolved well before the end; the issue of how to achieve reliability by duplicating data might be left as an important but not strategic issue.

There are associated dangers. It may seem platitudinous to aver that the terms of reference of any given draft model or matrix need to be crystal-clear, but sometimes bad IT decisions flow from charts that arrange information in groups and locations, without making it plain what the arrangement signifies. Does the information for some reason, *have to be physically located* in certain places or does it *seem to belong naturally* in certain places or, in some weaker not totally clear way, should it be seen as *logically but not necessarily literally located* in the places shown? As so often, half the battle is seeing the potential snare and carefully defining just what you are claiming and what you are not.

SISP, Distribution and the Future

Although all the issues raised by SISP were both important and potentially confusing throughout the 'eighties, technology development may well amplify their importance during the 'nineties. One big area of excitement is client-server architecture, where a PC and some other computer (more powerful PC, minicomputer or mainframe) share the work associated with database access in more sophisticated ways than hitherto. Another big development is the truly distributed database, where information is stored on a number of interconnected minicomputers and mainframes, permitting a person at a terminal to access information without needing to know where it is physically located.

Practitioners of the SISP approach will probably need to pay relatively more attention to the formidable distribution questions and less to the problem of how to divide up a known body of system developments into convenient projects. In any event, the rule remains: the more intensive your SISP work, the greater the level of commitment and the greater the chance of achieving the benefits of a robust framework — but also the greater the loss of flexibility to do those things that don't happen to fit into the framework.

PRACTICAL ADVICE

➤ Don't assume that a Strategic Information Systems Planning (SISP) exercise is self-evidently necessary for every large organisation. Compare the situation of your own organisation to the classic situations that SISP handles effectively.

➤ Decide where you stand on the following generic tradeoff: the more confident you can be of making accurate forecasts of all the main factors for (say) the next five years, the more sensible it is to invest in commitment at the expense of flexibility; and so, the more appropriate is a framework based on the SISP approach. And the converse is true as well.

➤ Evaluate another tradeoff. Really classic SISP means completely redeveloping everything in the field studied; SISP is awkward to apply in cases where a messy combination of old and new is appropriate. Where does your case stand on this issue?

➤ Control detail. Before you start, get a realistic view of the amount of detail required to support a worthwhile SISP framework. Set up controls to ensure that the amount of detail doesn't overflow those limits.

➤ Make a judgement of what the really difficult problem is. Is it essentially how to divide up the required body of systems and databases into discrete but coherent projects? Or is it even more fundamental — deciding what body of systems and databases you should even have?

➤ Check the assumption that most of your needs can be met by mainline database technology. The less valid it is, the less appropriate is classic SISP.

➤ Take a view of the problem of distribution of data and processing in your case. Does it raise real strategy issues (interaction between supply and demand factors, important psychological effects, impact on flexibility) or is it essentially a matter of supply-side problem-solving. Structure your planning accordingly.

➤ Encourage interaction and iteration in debates about distribution matters. Use intermediate drafts — part logical, part physical — of possible distribution schemes.

➤ Always make it quite clear what are the terms of reference of any given design for distribution of data and processing. Avoid confusion about the physical or logical features that it is showing or hiding.

18. Database: Flexibility and Constraints

ISSUES

What do you think of the following argument? We started out thirty years ago, storing data as fields within records and records within files. Then the database approach allowed data to be stored in a much more integrated and flexible way. Later the database approach itself matured; a modern database organised on relational principles is not as tricky to set up as the first-generation database, and it offers a very flexible means of storing information. With the old file-based approach, or even with first-generation database, you often found after the event that some of the ways you needed to access information in the database were just not practical. But nowadays a competently designed database can be flexible enough to meet most future information demands, even those that are as yet undefined.

The view that modern database technology is flexible enough to meet hitherto undefined demands for information, is more than an opinion about a technical matter. It has far-reaching consequences for the whole nature of strategic decisions about IT. Taken to its logical conclusion, this view denies that there is any important tradeoff between commitment and flexibility; it implies that you can combine the advantages of a large-scale database approach, with the freedom to define your needs in an *ad hoc* way.

This line of thought redefines IT decisions quite drastically; it suggests that many of the issues raised in this book can be defused: People only really begin to discover what they want from a system when the wrong system has already been delivered. *That doesn't matter*: with a flexible database, the system can easily be changed to make it fit the user's second thoughts. Deciding whether to adopt a two-year or a four-year planning horizon is a big issue. *Why should it be?* — why not just set up the database and go step by flexible step from then on? It is often hard to decide between alternative policies. *No it isn't;* there is usually only ever one sensible policy. Your real demand factor is always the definition in non-technical terms of an integrated database and your supply factor is the technical arrangements to set it up so that it is flexible. After that you can implement whatever systems you like at low marginal cost.

Even if you don't normally go very deep into supply-side technologies, you need some understanding of the capabilities of a relational database. You need to know how valid all these claims for flexibility really are; otherwise you will be on uncertain ground in very many debates about IT strategy. This briefing cautiously unravels the issues clustered in this area.

ANALYSIS

Of course, there is some truth in the opening argument, but how much? To debate whether it is seriously possible for the database to be flexible enough to meet practically all as yet undefined requirements, it is useful to start out with a representative case and to examine the kinds of modifications and enhancements that may be required.

The Troubles of Forest Oak Energy

Forest Oak Energy is a utility company, responsible for the supply of gas, electricity and a variety of other things (e.g. water and cable television) to buildings in a certain geographical area. For years work has been going on to design and implement a massive, all-encompassing set of database systems. Somehow there is always one more problem to be solved before anything gets fully agreed. Forest Oak managers never get to the point of being certain that at least one portion is totally correct and can be implemented; there is always some extra complication, some hitherto unsuspected connection between one portion and another. So they never take the plunge and do anything.

Now if the flexibility of the modern database is really so great, Forest Oak's problems are over. It can start by setting up a database that seems approximately right; when the inevitable problems arise, modifications can easily be made, without having to throw away what has already been built, and before very long Forest Oak is bound to arrive at an acceptable set of systems. Indeed, in this view of the world, the ineptitude of Forest Oak Energy's management team scarcely matters; they are saved by the flexible database.

As a preliminary to the discussion of the flexibility of the database, one important factor needs to be disentangled: the quality of the information analysis work. In general, somebody who is good at breaking things down logically and neatly, and can visualise that certain ways of structuring data might n t be relevant today but could be tomorrow, will develop a more robust, more flexible database system than somebody who doesn't possess those qualities — whatever the technology used. But that has always been true and it is not really the issue here. The interesting issue is whether the factor of modern database technology really makes a crucial difference. Can an averagely competent information analyst, in partnership with relational database technology, now produce a database with sufficient flexibility to rescue an organisation such as Forest Oak?

Comparative Convenience

The big advantage of first-generation database technology over pre-database, file-based methods of organising information is that most data items need be stored once and only once. This makes things less complex from the points of view of system design and regular operation, because updating a certain piece of data once in one place is less complex than having to update it in five different places.

If you have to amend the design of a file-based information system after it is already set up and running, you have to be very careful to amend all the relevant details consistently. Change a certain detail in four places without noticing that the fifth place also has to be changed and the consequences can be dreadful. It is comparable to deciding to change the name of a character in the draft of a novel from Nancy Wise to Eva Good; you have to catch every single reference, otherwise the reader will suddenly encounter an unintended new character. Making the changes can be hazardous; if you come across a Nancy Brass in the text, you have to decide whether this is the married Nancy Wise or some different character altogether. There are analogous awkward points in amending a computer system too. But with sufficient patience it can be done.

A database management system, whether first-generation or relational, stores and updates information in a centralised, non-redundant way, so it is often easier and more convenient to make changes to its design. There are simply fewer places that have to be changed, and thus fewer opportunities for overlooked inconsistency. The database management system isn't necessarily always superior to more primitive technology from the standpoint of making optimal use of hardware resources, but that isn't directly relevant to a discussion of information flexibility.

It is important to see that the advantage just described is one of comparative convenience. Many modifications can be made *more conveniently*. This is not the same thing as saying that the database approach allows something that is *impossible* in the file-based approach.

Characteristic Database Structures

A big issue in any real database is the way the data items themselves (e.g. customer name, customer address and so on, in the database of Forest

Oak Energy) are connected or linked together (e.g. which name corresponds to which address).

The first-generation database typically arranges items of data in hierarchies or network-like patterns. A hierarchy-network-patterned database is one whole intellectual construction; alter anything at one point and you have to check carefully how that may affect any other points. It is as if the current draft of your novel already contains a complex web of family and plot relationships between many characters and you suddenly decide to make Eva Good into the half-sister of Ferdinand Humble. Before fully commiting to this change, you need to work through all the implications to see if the resulting version of the plot will contain things that are impossible or very odd. Of course, it is possible to do this, but it is laborious and error-prone.

Both with a novel and with a first-generation database, you could eventually reach the point where the whole thing was just so complicated that in practice nobody could make any significant change and still be reasonably sure that the result would be correct. If Forest Oak were very close to that point with its first-generation database, and a new requirement arose that involved setting up a new link between certain pieces of data far apart on the database structure diagrams, the database administrator might prefer not to jeopardise the whole database structure by making changes whose precise implications he couldn't completely visualise.

A database organised in the modern relational style consists of sets of information arranged in tabular form; the whole database consists of many discrete tables, each rather simple in format. If a suggested new system facility entails some new logical link between certain existing data items, it is often possible to define one more table embodying that link, leaving all the other tables untouched. It is undoubtedly easier for analysts to sketch out, discuss and verify the structure of a database if it is organised in discrete relational tables than if it is structured in monolithic, network-like patterns.

So, in this respect, the network database has finite flexibility, whereas the relational database has infinite flexibility? Not really; the database administrator and the information analysts still need to possess some overview in their minds of the way the parts of the whole relational database form a coherent whole. Every time a new table is added, the database gets a little more complex and a saturation point will eventually come where it becomes too demanding for anyone to grasp the coherence of the whole thing. The big advantage of the relational database over earlier database technology is that you can get *further along the way* before reaching that saturation point.

It is more convenient and less error-prone to do multiplication sums with arabic numericals than with Roman numerals, and, if you have to work by hand, using logarithms is more convenient than doing a massive multiplication sum. But these are differences of degree; there is no one multiplication sum that is impossible to solve using roman numerals, but possible with arabic. It has always been very tricky modifying computer systems that are already up and running. Relational database doesn't change that in any definitive sense; but it does make modification more convenient and therefore less error-prone.

Flexibility Through Separate Views

Suppose that long after the database is set up, Forest Oak need to add new links between existing data items, without adding any new data as such. It seems a good idea to have a special weekly analysis of bills for embassies and consulates. This ought to be possible because there is already a 'usage code' in the database for each building, and one of its possible values indicates 'embassy/consulate'. At the same time, Forest Oak decides to to use this code as one of the parameters affecting the automatic calculations for some types of energy contracts.

With the relational database, it is much more convenient to define the extra links necessary to achieve this weekly analysis and the automatic calculations than it is with file-based or first-generation database technology. The reason for this illustrates an important concept.

With the first-generation database, the diagram showing the intricate network of links between data items is also a rough approximation of the way things are actually organised on disk. That isn't true of the relational approach; in the definitions of the database tables you only see the *logical structure* of the data required; you don't need to see all the *inner workings* of the data organisation on disk. In effect the supply factor (physical organisation of information on disk) is uncoupled from the demand factor (logical structure of the data required). That is why the relational approach is so much more convenient for the non-technical information analyst to work with.

This uncoupling also provides some flexibility for the technical expert responsible for ensuring that the system's performance is adequate. The inner workings of the database can be altered to improve performance (e.g. altering the way internal indexes are used, allocating disk areas differently and so on), without affecting the logical structure of the information at all.

The attractive idea of keeping the analyst's view of the logic of the database separate from the technician's view of its inner workings is often taken further. With many database systems, edited, partial views of the database are maintained for different groups of users; the full complexity of the database is hidden, so that people need only be aware of those elements that concern them. As well as being untroubled by things they don't need to know about, users can remain insulated from any changes that are made to any parts of their database lying outside their own view.

These facilities for providing different views of the database to different types of people are sometimes described by the grandiose name of *schema independence*. If one program is modified to use some additional data already in the database, the program's *external schema* (i.e. the view of the database that the program has) can be modified to include the new data, without affecting the *conceptual schema* (i.e. the total non-technical view of the whole database), or the *internal schema* (i.e. the total technical view of the whole database), or any other program's external schema. If the people responsible for the technicalities of the system want to change the internal schema, that should be possible without changing the conceptual schema or external schemas.

These concepts have only become really prominent with the rise of the relational DBMS. Nevertheless, the ideas were about during the 'seventies and it is feasible, though perhaps more awkward, for a non-relational DBMS to provide similar schema facilities. Not every DBMS, relational or otherwise, does provide the ideal schema independence sketched out above; it is more pragmatic to assess the degree to which any given DBMS approaches this model than to consider perfect schema independence as a *sine qua non*, which must be achieved before a DBMS product is even worth considering.

The Downside of Flexibility Through Views

But *definition* of links required between information items isn't the whole story. It may be easy enough for a general to define objectives on the map; it may still cost heavy losses to reach them. The abstract logic of the map is divorced from the physical reality of the battlefield. Similarly, Forest Oak may get the new weekly analysis, but at the price of tying up the computer for half an hour; the automatic contract calculation may now include the embassy/consulate code, but it may now take two minutes per contract instead of twenty seconds.

When a large-scale relational database is set up, all kinds of technical options have to be evaluated to ensure that the database as currently defined, with volumes of information and usage as currently projected, performs as effectively as possible from a technical point of view (the hardware resources it needs, its speed of response, etc.). It is quite possible that if a few more links between certain data items are added later on, this technical design may be thrown off balance. The resulting system may not produce wrong results, but its *performance* may be drastically affected for the worse. The analyst doing the work of defining such changes from a logical point of view can't be expected to foresee this; after all, the whole approach is to shield the analyst from awareness of such issues.

There is another price to be paid for the attractive concepts of keeping the inherent logic separate from the inner workings of the database, and having a variety of selective, non-technical user views. These things generate an overhead during the use of the database. Although a user may express a request to access information simply in terms of a personal non-technical view, ultimately the software retrieves the information from where it is physically stored on the disk. Therefore it has to perform a kind of translation of the request from non-technical terms to the technical terms necessary to find the information. The translation work is an overhead to be incurred whenever information is accessed, and this overhead may well incur a cost in more powerful hardware requirements or a slower response time.

Other Flexibility Demands

As a different kind of flexibility demand, suppose the database system needs to be changed to include some information that isn't actually there. Forest Oak already stores twenty pieces of information about each customer (address, type of customer, etc.). Now, for some reason, the new data item 'customer's bloodgroup' has to be added. If that item isn't in the system, then no technology, however advanced, can save you having to collect it, modify the design of the database and input the data. Adding simple new data items like this is far less taxing than adding new links. There is far less scope for disturbing an intricate structure, so the advance of database technology over the decades hasn't really made much of a difference to this kind of flexibility.

But another kind of flexibility case is much more interesting. Suppose Forest Oak wants to add links between certain data items that are in principle linkable, but in practice turn out not to be. For example, if one person already has several different energy supply contracts, the database already links them together; but now Forest Oak wants to be able to link contracts from the same family — husbands, wives, children and any businesses they run. Surnames may differ between members of a family and so may addresses — so the problem can't be solved merely by defining obvious new linkages between existing data items. There may be no alternative to a massive data collection exercise combined with some restructuring of important parts of the database. The march of database technology hasn't really made it much easier to solve this kind of flexibility problem. This is an important point because experience shows that many of the most important changes demanded of a database system do take this form.

It is clear that claims for the flexibility of the modern relational database can easily go too far, but in one important area flexibility has increased very significantly: one-off queries.

Suppose somebody wants to ask an *ad hoc* query about some information that is definitely in the database, but based on some linkage that has not been previously defined; e.g. 'How many units of electricity have we supplied this year to embassies or consulates, that don't have cable television?' With a relational database this type of request can often be handled by defining a *temporary* new table, or by joining together parts of two existing tables, that have not hitherto been processed together, to make them into one *temporary* larger table. The existing tables in the main database remain unmodified and the temporary tables go out of existence once the query has been dealt with.

This is a definite advance on anything offered by previous technologies. The downside is performance: it may be very easy to define some query nobody had ever thought of before, and to extract the information without much trouble — but crunching all the data together into the required pattern may still be expensive in its use of computer resources.

Other Genres of Information

For the reasons given above, modern relational technology can't quite live up to the most extreme claims for its flexibility. So far another complication has been left out of the discussion.

All the examples discussed have concerned data that can be readily structured into atomic elements (name, date of birth, sex, etc.), which can then be grouped and linked in various ways. The mainstream of modern database technology is directed at problems definable in this way. But what about completely different genres of information — a photograph of a customer's house, say? Though a few relational DBMS products may have an optional facility for storing such a photograph, it is only a sort of appendage to the underlying structure of the database. You can't carry out an *ad hoc* query to select (say) all customers whose houses seem to have at least three stories, at least one chimney and no television aerial, but whose account records show a monthly bill of less than $200. So if you have a relational database and your changes of requirement involve moving on to store a different genre of information altogether, you are still likely to have a lot to do.

This is not a far fetched point. More and more innovative uses of IT entail the *combination* of mainstream database technology with other technologies; for example: storing texts and/or graphics in the form of highly structured documents; storing colour photos, possibly with some form of image enhancement or pattern recognition to interpret them; storing maps or complex diagrams so that shapes can be manipulated in ways governed by the conventional data in the main database; storing images of documents, perhaps with optical character recognition to interpret the content; storing the rules of expert systems; and so on.

The textbook on databases by Elmasri and Navathe[1] identifies four broad categories of information storage applications that pose significant challenges to current database technology: engineering design and manufacturing; office systems and decision support systems; statistical and scientific database management; and spatial and temporal database management. Running through the textbook's summary of all the challenges associated with such applications, it is easy to form the impression that building a system of any sophistication that will actually work on the day it goes live is quite innovative enough; expecting that it will also be highly flexible for the years ahead is being rather ambitious.

Strategy Implications

Most of the briefings in this book discuss strategy decisions in terms of complex interactions between supply factors (such as database technology) and demand factors (such as information to be accessed in the database), or tradeoffs between commitment (such as up-front investment in one approach rather than another) and flexibility (such as combating uncertainty by postponing decisions). IT strategy is a fascinating field to work in primarily because these problems are so challenging.

If it were true that modern database technology was a supply factor that allowed all kinds of changes to demand factors (information required) at very little penalty, then IT strategy would be a lot easier. Choosing a certain combination of supply and demand in your IT strategy would not be a big commitment, because you would always retain the flexibility to change your demand, at negligible cost, whenever you liked.

In reality, generalisations about the flexibility of database technology are nowhere near that simple. Strategy decisions in this area need to be supported by awareness of the present state of database and related technologies. Otherwise, it is not possible to make sound judgements about the scope for flexibility that is left open by any particular decision, or to recognise those areas where a decision entails a major commitment, closing off certain avenues for a long time ahead.

PRACTICAL ADVICE

➤ Expect a database using modern relational DBMS technology to be generally easier to alter and hence more flexible than one based on earlier technology.

➤ Recognise that this is a difference of degree, not a quantum jump, which significantly reduces the need to plan ahead. In other words, the tradeoff between commitment and flexibility is not abolished.

➤ Remember that, within this general principle, some types of flexibility (e.g. *ad hoc* queries) are made considerably easier, and others (e.g. bringing out fundamental linkages that were hitherto latent) hardly at all.

➤ Don't forget that increased flexibility may be bought at the price of reduced technological performance: both as an ongoing overhead and as a falling-off in performance caused by incremental changes.

➤ Notice that some of the more advanced types of data don't belong in a relational database and for them it is early days yet for flexibility to be a major issue.

➤ In making a strategy, you usually have to take some view on the degree of flexibility that should be or can be expected. Make use of these points to form realistic judgements on that issue.

Part IV:

Level-
Based
Approaches

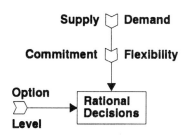

BRIEFINGS AND MODEL

This book begins by summarising a set of Reference Cases. Then comes an essay asserting that the level-based approaches often applied to IT strategy are inadequate for many cases. A Reference Model containing an interaction, a tradeoff and a blend is sketched out. In this model the two main sources of tension defining the problems are the Supply–Demand Interaction and the Commitment–Flexibility Tradeoff. In addressing these problems, the important thing is to find the right Option–Level Blend.

Parts I and III respectively are concerned with Supply–Demand and Commitment–Flexibility. Part II deals with options, one important element in the Option–Level Blend. This part of the book now deals with many other issues and concepts associated with level-based approaches.

Level-based Work and Decision-making

The product of the work done at a certain level of planning is often a 'model' — a carefully structured description of a present or future state of affairs. Modelling work is often so detailed that it can't really be called decision-making, let alone strategic decision-making. But decision-making may be entangled with modelling or other detailed level-based activities.

For example, a bad decision to set up a database system that doesn't meet the organisation's most important needs may perhaps be traced back to an earlier judgement that the situation called for detailed data modelling rather than process modelling. Or a decision to change the priorities of certain projects at a late stage in planning may force retrospective changes to the models and plans made at earlier levels and have chaotic consequences for rational decision-making.

Contrary to the impression often given by those marketing their own standard methodologies, the right choice of level-based activities and the right structure for them can vary considerably from case to case. Sometimes it may be sensible to develop a business model of the organisation before doing anything else; sometimes not. Sometimes it may be appropriate to define information structures in four successive steps with different degrees of abstraction; sometimes two steps would be adequate. Sometimes it may be important to encourage iteration between certain levels; sometimes discipline is more important. And so on.

The decision-maker need not be directly concerned with how modelling and other level-based activities are actually carried out. As the examples already given suggest, there are two main matters for concern, that can make a difference between good and bad decisions about the use of IT: deciding which particular types of level-based activity to undertake, and organising the relations between the levels effectively.

As the Overview table shows, the first three briefings in this part of the book tackle three of the most important choices that arise in finding the right form of level-based work for the particular case. The other four briefings discuss issues in the organisation of levels; three of them cover problems in relating specific levels together; the last examines the general principles of organising a level-based, decision-making process.

The Nature of Specific Levels

A decision to research consumer spending trends is not a decision on the same plane as one to do something specific, such as opening a shop. Similarly, the decision to build (say) an entity–relationship model is not a strategic decision in the same sense as one to set up a new telecommunications infrastructure to link up all the company's branches. Nevertheless, undertaking the market research is a big step towards opening the shop, and building an entity–relationship model has implications too. Though a 200-page data model is not a document full of decisions, it may well start out from certain strategic assumptions and implicitly reinforce them or alter their emphasis; also it will provide the detailed information that will be the basis on which later decisions are made.

There are many different types of model; a choice of one or more of them must be at the expense of others that are not chosen. An entity–relationship model will reveal certain aspects of the organisation that process modelling (say) will not, and vice versa. Since there will never be

Overview of Part IV Briefings

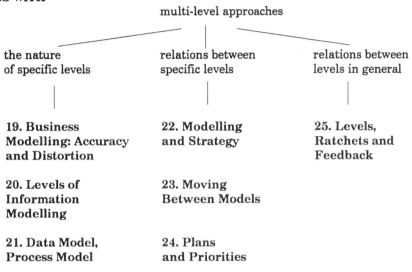

ISSUES WITH

multi-level approaches

the nature
of specific levels

relations between
specific levels

relations between
levels in general

**19. Business
Modelling: Accuracy
and Distortion**

**22. Modelling
and Strategy**

**25. Levels,
Ratchets and
Feedback**

**20. Levels of
Information
Modelling**

**23. Moving
Between Models**

**21. Data Model,
Process Model**

**24. Plans
and Priorities**

time to model every possible aspect, deciding how to model inevitably involves deciding which aspects are more important than others. Deciding that is closely related to making strategic decisions.

On a map of the earth, whichever cartographic projection it uses, some features are represented accurately and others are distorted. Exactly the same applies to modelling techniques. The important thing is to be aware that there are many different approaches available and to choose that which forms the most suitable basis for decision-making in the specific case you are dealing with. This principle applies to all forms of modelling, but the field of business modelling provides some good examples. **(19. Business Modelling: Accuracy and Distortion)**

Sometimes the problem is less in deciding which style of modelling to use for your specific case than in deciding the most suitable combination of styles of modelling. A completely non-technical description of information structures within an organisation is a very different thing from the technical database design. Normally models are needed at several levels, describing the body of information with greater or less emphasis on the technology practicalities, in order to clarify demand and optimise supply.

The issue arises: What combination of models of information at different levels is appropriate, to do justice to the issues of the case, without overwheming decision-makers with paper models? **(20. Levels of Information Modelling)**

A model of an organisation's data is a different thing from a model of its procedures. Do you need both types of model? Should you choose one or the other according to the case? Or model in a way that takes some account of both? Or have both models but emphasise one of them? Is there really a clear difference anyway? The last of this trio of briefings discusses such questions and shows why they matter to the decision-maker. **(21. Data Model, Process Model)**

Relations between Specific Levels

One of the main problem areas in any level-based approach is the relation between levels. In translating the words of a text from one language to another, there is usually an approximate one-to-one correspondence at the level of words, or at least sentences. But that doesn't apply so obviously in moving between, say, a model at the level of present information architecture and a model at the level of future database technical design. One great danger is that assumptions creep in almost unnoticed at the transition between levels. Another danger is that the findings at one level may invalidate much detailed work done at an earlier level. Conversely, insistence that work done at a certain level be consistent with the products of earlier levels may close off many promising options that should really be considered.

Any modelling has to be based on some terms of reference, some outline strategy or some rough perception of the nature of the problem to be tackled. But there may be an awkward friction between the modelling and the assumptions it rests on. Should you lay down an overall IT strategy first and then, at a lower level, carry out data modelling work? Or should you make a data model and then use it to determine your strategy? There is no short answer, except that iteration and interaction between the levels of decision-making and modelling are often needed. **(22. Modelling and Strategy)**

Since several models are often developed as successive stages, one interesting question is how to start out from one type of model and, through doing new work, arrive at a different type of model. If this is more than a pure translation process, how can you ensure that important matters for decision are explicitly decided, rather than accepted as unspoken assumptions? There are other questions too. In proceeding from the purely logical data model to the entirely technical, should you expand all detail at the same rate as you move between levels? How you should decide which detail to ignore and which to explore in great detail? **(23. Moving Between Models)**

The third briefing in this group distinguishes 'blueprints' — which are essentially descriptions of what is desired — from 'recipes' — schedules of actions to achieve what is desired. Some interesting issues arise from fitting the two types of document together in a coherent planning system that can be continuously updated. For example, how do you process the results of feasibility studies for new systems that may result in a reassessment of priorities, that may in turn affect five-year hardware plans already made? **(24. Plans and Priorities)**

Relations between Levels in General

A multi-level structure for forming and documenting decisions and plans, may embrace designs for a family of computer systems, plans for achieving them, explanations of overall business policy, data models and other components besides. The structure needs to be clear, coherent and elegant and it must also do justice to the issues involved. These desiderata are fairly uncontroversial, but achieving them all together is not so easy. Some organisations make plans that preserve clarity at the expense of doing justice to the issues. Others may do justice to the issues, though the sacrifice of elegance makes it hard to be sure.

There is much scope for confusion in designing a multi-level decision-making structure. For example: 'top-down' seems a naturally attractive concept to employ, but so does 'feedback'; isn't that a contradiction? And is 'step-wise refinement' the same thing as 'top-down'; or is it something different? Should the structure of decision-making be the same as the structure of the documentation describing the decisions? And so on. The last briefing tackles issues of this sort, which apply to the logic of any multi-level decision-making structure whatever the content of individual levels. **(25. Levels, Ratchets and Feedback)**

19. Business Modelling: Accuracy and Distortion

ISSUES

'Business model' is one of those terms whose seductive calls for rigorous definition are best disregarded. There is no need to enter a quicksand of abstractions, because the matter is really quite straightforward. A chart summarising the main things that go on in the organisation is a useful support for discussions at an early stage in IT decision-making; business model is a reasonable name for such a chart. The model can clarify the IT-independent contours of the business and it may be a useful reference work from which to carry out more detailed investigations. Thus it has much in common with a map.

Ironbark Insurance, for example, needs a new IT strategy and as a first step towards getting to grips with the issues and possibilities, it seems useful to make a model of the Ironbark business, showing the main things that go on there. Business modelling can be just as relevant when individual systems for specific parts within an organisation are under discussion. For example, Yellow Carbeen, the manufacturers of vending machines, are considering a project to introduce new JIT (just-in-time) inventory techniques; a model of the way the flow of goods is controlled at the moment is a necessary basis for any discussions. The same applies to Buloke in its planning of a new distribution system.

An organisation chart is useful but, as everyone knows, the theoretical lines of reporting are at best a fragment, at worst a distortion, of the way things really work. An overview of the different computer systems is also useful, but you don't usually want to assume that the structure of the computer systems is already the most appropriate there can be for that organisation.

The right business model for Ironbark is the one that will provide the clearest possible insight. The business model generally needs to be reconciled with the organisation structure and the computer systems overview in order to check that nothing important has been left out or misunderstood, but the prime basis for discussion will be the business model itself.

Some styles of business model consist of diagrams with boxes and other shapes, mostly containing no more than a word or two. Other styles are also mainly diagrams, but many of the boxes, shapes and lines have whole sentences of narrative attached to them. More wordy styles of model have hardly any boxes, shapes or lines, but consist of sentences and phrases carefully structured, for example indented in hierarchies.

Questions of model format are less vital than certain issues of principle. Any model will tend to emphasise certain aspects of an organisation at the expense of other aspects. Moreover a certain style of model based on certain principles will give a view of the organisation that is different from that produced by another style of model based on different principles. But does this really matter? That is the main discussion-area of this briefing.

ANALYSIS

A good start is to examine the notion that there may be a variety of different, valid approaches towards making a business model of an organisation.

Ironbark Insurance is a small company but it underwrites all the main classes of insurance. Its managers are prepared to replace all their administrative systems, if this is necessary to make better use of the opportunities of modern IT. They soon decide that it would be useful to have a business model, as a basis for structuring their discussions and a help in seeing the opportunities. How can there be different approaches to the building of this model?

Two Different Modelling Principles

Two analysts independently make a business model of Ironbark Insurance. In one model a whole chunk is devoted to Fire insurance and another chunk to Motor, Liability and Accident insurance together. This breakdown corresponds to the areas covered by two separate departments, each with profit responsibility, each carrying out its own fairly self-contained piece of work, each functioning independently of the other.

But the other analyst has modelled things differently. In this business model of Ironbark there is a chunk called Personal Underwriting and another called Commercial Underwriting. Within Personal Underwriting come all insurance for private individuals — Fire and Motor and other risks besides; Commercial Underwriting includes all insurance, of whatever type, for companies and other organisations. The justification is that if you look carefully at the way Fire and Motor insurance are handled for private individuals' policies, you find that the goings-on are all rather similar. Fairly junior people follow fairly predetermined rules; you don't conduct elaborate site inspections and throw a big lunch to get the business. This is quite different from Commercial Underwriting where most of the policies are big commitments treated as individual cases. Here quite different types of people follow quite different routines. So, the argument goes, if you want to understand what really goes on in this company, you need to seize on this distinction between Personal Underwriting and Commercial Underwriting. Neither analyst's approach is right *per se*. They have simply chosen to emphasise different principles in their modelling. Attaching convenient labels, the first analyst might be said to make *Organisation Unit* the primary principle, while the second concentrates on *Functional Genre*. Which is better depends a great deal on the circumstances of the particular case and the problems being tackled.

An intelligent model based on the *Organisation Unit* principle won't normally be a mere reproduction of the formal organisation chart. It will probably collapse a number of hierarchical levels, but identify separately some chunks that really exist as quite autonomous fiefs without being clearly differentiated on the organisation chart. A rigorous model where *Functional Genre* is the supreme principle may be extremely difficult to reconcile with the formal organisation scheme, but may be just the thing if you want to consider an radical reorganisation.

More Possible Modelling Principles

There are quite a few more principles that people sometimes use in business modelling. Take *Control Level*. Using this principle, many of the functions performed by the board of Ironbark Insurance would be modelled as the top level: ultra-strategic. At the bottom level might be the most trivial, initiative-free tasks of administering insurance policies and claims. In between would come the work of different levels of management, supervisors and so on. Some methods of modelling based on the Control Level principle assume that your model of any organisation will always divide everything up into three and only three levels. Another approach is to define whatever number of levels you happen to need in order to gain insight into the particular case. If you stress the Control Level principle your model may be significantly different from the models produced by the other two approaches mentioned so far. You are stressing a different aspect of the organisation that is being modelled.

Another approach is to build a model on the *Disassembly* principle. Just as a car can be broken down into chunks such as gearbox and engine, and these can in turn be broken into their constituents, so you can break down the functions of an organisation, proceeding through hierarchical levels that become steadily less general and more detailed. Thus, 'administer policies' might break down into 'write new policy', 'renew policy', 'amend policy' and these could be broken down further. The logic of breaking down the general into the more specific is the guiding criterion here; the result is practically certain to be a different model from any of the others seen so far. Models based on the Disassembly principle are quite popular. For instance a book by James Martin advocates a model organised in the following levels: Division (e.g. Manufacturing), Business Functional Area (e.g. Materials), Function (e.g. Purchasing), Sub-function (e.g. Supplier Information), Activity (e.g. Record Supplier Performance Data).[1]

Then there is *Sequence*: for example, the work of creating a new policy is broken down into ten steps. This usually differs from Disassembly, because in real life one doesn't sweep sequentially through a logical hierarchy from top left to bottom right; some things at a low level of detail from a purely logical point of view might be done first if they have a long lead time and aren't dependent on other things. Unlike a Disassembly-based model, a decent Sequence-based model will need to show how some things are dependent on other things, and how other things can happen in parallel.

Yet More Possible Modelling Principles

Another candidate modelling principle is *Interaction*. You might want to stress the way different activities in the organisation interact with each other. You would probably avoid making much breakdown, if any, of the work down by one clerk to administer a routine insurance policy. But you would show, say, how the premiums of all the routine policies were added together each year and compared to the claims received, and as a result new premium rates were set, affecting new policies thereafter. This kind of thing probably wouldn't be shown very clearly on any of the other models discussed so far.

(Existing) *Computer Systems* is yet another possible principle. The business model could be structured so that its pieces corresponded neatly to the existing computer systems. Those functions that weren't automated at all would be included wherever it seemed most natural in the structure. This is not a very common approach; it doesn't help very much if you are trying to ask radical questions about the structure of the existing computer systems. Nevertheless, it does make it easy to see what is automated and by which systems and what isn't automated at all. It may be the best approach if the organisation's systems are in crisis and the real issue is how to fight the most serious fires with the limited resources available.

Finally there is a miscellaneous class of *Other* principles, motivated by the circumstances of the case. With a company in a state of great potential change, trying out all kinds of new methods and products (Antarctic Beech Corporation, for example), you might use *Degree of Reality* as your main organising principle. The primary breakdown in the model might be between categories such as: traditional operational, innovative operational, innovative being experimented with, innovative under discussion, innovative possibility currently not explored.

Then again, you might decide that for one particular case the thing to do above all else was to model the way different parts of the business interacted with the outside world; the modelling conventions would expose which things were related to the *Outside World*, and what parts of it (e.g. holding company head office, government, customers, suppliers etc.).

What Models Really Show

Counting 'Other' as one, this gives eight alternative organising principles for a business model (*Organisation Unit, Functional Genre, Control Level, Disassembly, Sequence, Interaction, Computer Systems, Other*). If you take any one of these as the main feature of reality that you aim to expose in your model, you will very likely get a result different from the model that arises from concentrating on any one of the others. This doesn't mean that a model has to be based on one and only one of these principles, ignoring all the others entirely. What normally happens in a business model is that one or two of these principles are dominant, maybe one or two more are partially represented and the rest don't make any impact.

For example (to take one out of dozens of plausible possibilities), your business model of Ironbark Insurance might consist of one diagram for each of the main *Organisation Units*; each diagram might be structured to show four *Control Levels*; within each Control Level of each Organisational Unit, functions might be shown grouped together by *Functional Genre*. In this style of business model, no insight based on the principles of Disassembly, Interaction, Sequence, Computer Systems and Other is supplied at all.

Since Functional Genre is subordinate to two other principles in this example, it can't be modelled in the most elegant, most convenient way. Thus Personal Underwriting is distinguished from Commercial Underwriting on the basis of functional genre. But Personal Underwriting for Motor, Liability and Accident policies has to be recorded as one item in the part of the model for one organisational unit, while the same distinction is duplicated elsewhere within other organisational units.

Ironbark Insurance: Part of One Possible Business Model

		Motor/Liability/Accident Department	
	Marine/Aviation Departm	:GY	Strategic Direction
		Fire Department	th other insurers
STRATEGY	STRATEGY	Strategic Direction	g Rate Setting
		Treaties with other insurers	ison
		etc.	
TACTICS	TACTICS	Underwriting Rate Setting	
		Agency Liaison	nderwriting
		etc.	I Underwriting
		etc.	
CONTROL	CONTROL	Personal Underwriting	
		Commercial Underwriting	
		Statistics	
		etc.	
		etc.	nderwriting
		etc.	I Underwriting
		etc.	Processing
ROUTINE	ROUTINE	Personal Underwriting	counting
		Commercial Underwriting	
		Renewals Processing	
		Agency Accounting	
		etc.	
		etc.	
		etc.	
		etc.	

Outline

Logic

Approach of the

The Analogy with Cartographic Projection

There is nothing surprising about the conclusion that any method of drawing a business model will fail to do represent all aspects of reality equally neatly. A commercial business or any comparable organisation is complex; there is just too much in it to reduce to one set of diagrams on paper.

A good analogy is the problem of projecting the globe of the earth as a two-dimensional map. Any method of cartographic projection has to make compromises. Mercator's projection, for example, gives the true direction of one point in relation to another, so it is useful for navigation purposes, but the price paid for this is that comparative land areas are grossly distorted. Places a long way from the Equator such as Scandinavia and Greenland look much larger than they really are.

Mollweide's Homolographic projection achieves the opposite balance of advantage and disadvantage: relative areas accurate, but relative positions distorted. Bartholomew's Nordic projection deliberately represents the northern hemisphere as accurately as possible, but at the price of making the southern hemisphere come out very distorted indeed. Lambert's Azimuthal Projection is fine for whatever landmass you place in the middle of the map, but all the areas around the edges are distorted. Bartholomew's Re-centred Sinusoidal Projection gets the continental land masses quite accurate at the expense of the oceans. And so on.

The most important thing is to be aware that both terrestrial projection and business modelling are unavoidably like this. Only a very naive student of geography would think that only one projection of the globe was possible or sensible. The same applies to an IT strategist who acts as if there is only one good way to make a business model.

Since different projections have different tradeoffs of accurate and distorted information, you need to be aware of the particular tradeoffs of the projection you use. If you are using Mercator you remember that Scandinavia is not really as large as it looks in relation to other pieces of land. Similarly, if a business model has been built dominated by (say) the *Functional Genre* principle, that choice should be made clear and nobody should assume that it necessarily gives any clear insight into (say) *Interaction* or *Organisation Unit*.

Only a very odd geographer would draw a map projecting one continent in a way that showed relative area and another continent in a way that showed relative position. Similarly, if you're modelling a business, you should normally be consistent in the principles you follow. If you do decide to make a model of one department of a company on the *Functional Genre* principle and to model another department in *Disassembly* style, then at least be explicit about it, and explain the justification for the approach.

You would choose a map based on the most appropriate projection for whatever it was you wanted to do: Mercator rather than Bartholomew's Re-centred Sinusoidal for an ocean voyage; Lambert's Azimuthal Projection rather than Bartholomew's Nordic for settling boundary disputes in Antarctica. Similarly, it is seems sensible to choose the method of business modelling according to the nature of the strategic issues at stake. The most useful kind of model for Ironbark Insurance may be a different kind of model, stressing different principles, from that for Stringybark Assurance. At another time, when Ironbark's situation has changed, the most appropriate model to help decision-making may be based on entirely different principles from the present model. The right model for Forest Oak Energy may well stress different principles again.

Implications of the Cartography Analogy

Since different modelling principles are appropriate for different kinds of problems, it follows that anybody who always uses one particular way of modelling a business, irrespective of the circumstances, or even anybody who chooses one out of two possible methods each time, is probably not aware of the gross assumptions involved. The shrewd business-modeller chooses the principles to emphasise in a particular case, by deciding which kind of model will provide the most insight into the real issues.

A good way of evaluating the business modelling somebody else has done is to work out what principles the model emphasises. If it uses a miscellany of principles in different parts of the model for no apparent reason, then it is very probably a bad model. If the main principles are clear and are consistently used, the next test is whether these are the most appropriate principles that could have been chosen, for this particular case.

Now for some differences between business modelling and geographical projection. At the beginning of a typical household atlas, you can usually find at least a dozen of the established projection methods briefly described, with their pros and cons indicated. But business modelling is a different story. People who advocate their own special method of business modelling rarely spend much time describing those aspects where it falls short, those problems that it is not suitable for. You need to work these things out for yourself

Cartography is a mature field of knowledge and there is little opportunity for inventing original new projections, but this isn't so in business modelling. If you decide that in a certain case, the two big features worth bringing out are (say) Degree of Reality (one of the Other examples above)

and Organisational Unit, you may not find any such ready-made model-ling system in the books in the library; but you will probably find it easy enough to devise some conventions of your own as the basis for such a model.

Mutability of the Business Model

So far this briefing has practically ignored one key question. If the purpose of the business model is to help in taking decisions and making plans, couldn't some of those decisions and plans cause changes in the model itself?

Currently Ironbark Insurance only writes marine insurance as a junior partner with certain other companies who have the expertise to assess the risks and to handle the administration. This is understandable because marine insurance is more generally complex than most other classes of insurance. But Ironbark could decide to invest in new IT systems that enabled it to take a much higher profile in marine insurance business; the Ironbark staff would assess marine risks and handle marine administration. Assume that happens; what are the implications for business modelling?

Some business modellers would say that of course a business model built after that change in business practice is bound to look different from a business model built before it. But others would say that, as a matter of principle, a business model should be impervious to all but the most sweeping of changes; it should survive reorganisations and be inde-pendent of any use of technology. Martin's book advances a version of that position, and outlines a detailed model for a manufacturing company. It is debatable whether this model published in 1982 would help a manufac-turing company today that was interested in taking advantage of modern technologies such as EDI (electronic data interchange), CAD (computer-aided design), CIM (computer-integrated manufacturing) and robotics.

This raises a closely allied issue: to what degree is the business model meant to stimulate ideas for change? If the model is drawn in a very general way to maintain its immutable character, then it may not be any great stimulant of fruitful ideas for innovation. But even those styles of model that make few claims to permanence may have different effects. One style of modelling Ironbark might force the issue of what to do about marine insurance business on the board's attention; with other styles of model nobody might ever notice that marine insurance was an issue. But perhaps the model in a style which exposed the marine insurance issue would obscure other issues that were even more pressing.

Once again, the general truth about IT decision-making emerges. There is no standard answer; you need to be aware of the issues and their tradeoffs and tradeoffs; armed with that awareness, you then have to make your own judgement of what is best in the specific case.

PRACTICAL ADVICE

➤ Avoid the false assumption that there is one true business model of an organisation. There are only models that illuminate different aspects.

➤ Understand the differences between the main different angles that can be used as the basis for business modelling: Organisation Unit, Functional Genre, Control Level, Disassembly, Sequence, Interaction and Computer Systems.

➤ But check to see whether some other angle may produce an even more useful model for the particular case.

➤ Decide explicitly which of all the possible approaches your business model should be based on, by making a judgement on which aspects of the organisation need to be clarified and which you can afford to leave distorted or blurred.

➤ Don't be afraid to define your own conventions for the business model you make.

➤ Explain to everyone involved which particular form of modelling you adopt and what its pros and cons are.

➤ Get it clear whether (or better, to what extent) the business model you build should be regarded as impervious to change. Is it intended to stimulate ideas for innovation and improvement or to be a solid foundation block for more detailed work?

➤ Don't accept that there is any one generally applicable style of business modelling or set of modelling principles that is best in nearly all cases. Use your judgement to decide the right approach in each case.

➤ As far as possible, apply the above principles to all types of modelling, not just business modelling.

20. Levels of Information Modelling

ISSUES

The information that an organisation uses in its IT systems can be described from several different angles. In particular, the concept is widely accepted that a 'physical' (i.e. technical) view of the information should be distinct from a 'logical' (i.e. non-technical) view.

At the Lilli-Pilli Library of Recorded Music (the LP Library) there is a document of over a hundred pages called 'Comprehensive Data Model'. This detailed non-technical description of information structures is a very different thing from the library's 'Database Internal Schema', the technical design, that has been carefully tuned to optimise response time, reliability, security and so on. This document for specialists records how certain items of information are stored using the 'compressed heap' storage structure, while other information uses 'compressed B-tree' or 'compressed B-tree with unique keys'.

This distinction between the logical and the physical is valid and important, but in practice is not as clear-cut as it may at first appear. For example, data modelling lore recognises more than just two classic forms of detailed model. But, you may reasonably ask, what does all this matter to the decision-maker?

The main purpose of this briefing is to show that there is no self-evident pattern of levels of information modelling that is generally applicable to all or nearly all cases. Therefore the choice of the *kind of models* you decide to build is itself an important decision. In fact, it is closely associated with the challenge of resolving the interaction between supply and demand.

ANALYSIS

The *empirical formula* of a certain molecule, such as methyl alcohol (CH_4O) tells you what atoms make up the molecule, but says nothing about the way they fit together. You need to look at the *structural formula* to see, for example, that only three of the four hydrogen atoms are connected to the carbon atom. But in order to convey this more complex information, the structural formula has to be a two-dimensional diagram rather than a concise expression. The empirical and structural formulae of a molecule are two different views of the same thing. Neither is more real or more true than the other. If the information conveyed by the structural formula is relevant to your purpose, you use that. Otherwise, the empirical formula is easier to work with and avoids the distractions of details of no current interest.

In chemistry there are more than just these two ways of viewing a substance. Sometimes chemists find it most convenient to use another view midway between the empirical and structural formulae. Butane, for example, has the empirical formula C_4H_{10}; to write $CH_3CH_2CH_2CH_3$ instead requires little more effort, and has the advantage of conveying some useful structural indications (CH_3 and CH_2 are common building blocks in organic chemistry). Other types of chemists, physicists and biologists find it most convenient for their work to view molecules in other ways again. Science textbooks explain the different established ways of viewing matter (empirical formula, structural formula, etc.) and make it clear which is appropriate under which circumstances.

In IT, too, an organisation's data may be modelled in different ways that are convenient in different situations. If you choose an inappropriate form of modelling at some stage this can lead to bad decisions. This briefing falls into two main parts. First there is an account of some varieties of data model; after this essential preparation there is a discussion of how choices between these varieties can affect decision-making.

Entity–Relationship Modelling

It is best to start by looking briefly at certain classic modelling approaches that textbooks about databases often describe — data modelling's established equivalents of chemistry's empirical formula and structural formula.

Most data modelling currently done is some version of entity–relationship (E–R) modelling. This type of work is based on the idea of identifying the *entities* relevant to an organisation and the *relationships* between entities and thirdly, (although you wouldn't think so from the name) the *attributes* of the entities.

For example, in the case of the LP Library, Customer and CD are obvious entities. Provided the scope of the modelling covers the music contained on the library's disks, then Composer and Work and Performer are entities too.

The relationship between the two entities Composer and Work is 'one-to-many'; in other words, there can be many different works by one composer, but a work is generally by one and only one composer. The relation between the entities CD and Performer is 'many-to-many'; one performer can have made one CD or several; any CD may contain performances by one performer or by several. An entity–relationship

Typical Entity-Relationship Modelling Conventions

LP Library of Recorded Music

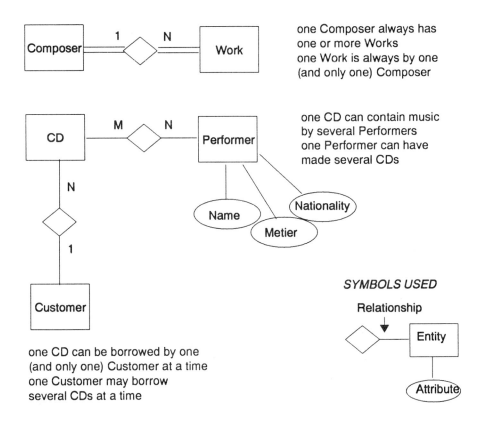

one Composer always has
one or more Works
one Work is always by one
(and only one) Composer

one CD can contain music
by several Performers
one Performer can have
made several CDs

SYMBOLS USED

Relationship

Entity

Attribute

one CD can be borrowed by one
(and only one) Customer at a time
one Customer may borrow
several CDs at a time

This simple model avoids many complexities.

For example:
. *suppose the library possesses several copies of a certain CD*
. *suppose the same performance appears on both CD and LP*
. *what is the relationship between Work and CD?*
   (remember some Works take less, some more than one CD)

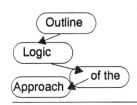

model (E–R model) goes further than this, into subtleties such as the distinction between 'optional one-to-many' and 'mandatory one-to-many' relationships, for example. The other component of this modelling approach is the attribute. An attribute is a data element associated with an entity; for example, among the attributes of Performer in the model may be Nationality or Metier (e.g. pianist, harpist, etc.).

This type of model describes information relevant to an organisation as logically and clearly as possible, without taking account of any constraints or stimulus arising from the technology that may be used to store the information.

The name of the modelling technique may vary from case to case; the superficial conventions for drawing lines between boxes may vary; some of the fine detail for handling special cases may vary.[1] There are purists who insist that an E–R model should meet the stringent requirements of the Fifth Normal Form of mathematical logic, but they are the exception.

Conceptual, Internal and External Schemas, and Other Terminology

A distinction is classically made between an E–R model and a database conceptual schema. A *database conceptual schema* is a real border-line document. It describes information primarily in non-technical, logical terms, as the E–R model does — but, unlike the E–R model, in a way that is deliberately well suited to the constraints and opportunities of one specific DBMS software product.

The true description of the database from the technical point of view is a different document, usually called the *database internal schema*. This fills in the numerous technical parameters required so that the description is not merely logically valid, but also technically complete and efficient.

In the classic setup, there is one more type of schema, associated with the conceptual and internal schemas. The term *external schema* is more or less equivalent to the term 'user view', that was once common, but has dropped away lately. Each application system or sub-system has its own external schema and each of these schemas is actually a subset of the whole conceptual schema. This means that users of the database only need to deal with the data relevant to their own application. Other data, which may be physically or logically adjacent in the database, can be kept out of the way to avoid distraction.

Thus, the term external schema is not symmetrical to the term internal schema. A database can have only one internal schema and only one conceptual schema, but it will probably have numerous external schemas. This schema structure is well recognised in the industry, even

The Classic Data Models and Schemas

Entity–Relationship Model *or simply* **Data Model**	represents the logic of data structures; no concern for the practicalities of implementation.
Database Conceptual Schema	represents the logic of data structures; but ensures structures are feasible for a certain (or a certain type of) DBMS software product.
Internal Schema	represents the way the content of the database is actually structured, for a certain DBMS software product.
External Schemas	are selectively edited versions of the Database Conceptual Schema; they allow you to view only those parts of the database that concern you.

though terminology varies. Schemas are sometimes called views; 'global' is sometimes used instead of 'conceptual', 'physical' instead of 'internal' and 'user' or 'local' instead of 'external'.

Some authorities make a distinction between 'infological' and 'datalogical' models: this boils down to the familiar contrast between the model that is natural and technology-independent (like the E–R model), and the model that provides a design for implementation within the constraints of technology (like the database conceptual schema).

The general term 'data model' is often used without qualification. Sometimes it stands for a non-technical model in E–R style; sometimes it embraces an organisation's whole set of models and schemas: E–R, conceptual and so on.

Semantic Modelling

This doesn't exhaust the variations by any means. There is growing interest in a form of higher level modelling often called semantic modelling or Enhanced–ER modelling. This approach aims to capture subtleties that straightforward E–R modelling excludes.

The concept of *classes* is a good representative example of semantic modelling ideas. In the LP Library you could model Album as a generic name or *superclass* which covered CD, LP or cassette; an album is always one of those three, but one particular album can't be both a CD and a cassette at the same time. This approach enables you to model more naturally and elegantly all those things that CD, LP and cassette have in common (as opposed to other entities, such as customers). At the same time, differences between members of the superclass can also be shown (e.g. the content of a CD isn't divided between two sides).

Analogously, Person could be at a higher level than Composer, Performer and Customer. But that illustrates a minor subtlety; this would be a different type of superclass structure because, although every Person would be at least one of those three things, somebody could conceivably be more than one of them; the violinist whose performance was on a CD might also be a member of the library.

This only gives a flavour of the approach. Models can be developed with very complex patterns of subclasses, superclasses, specialisations, categories, subtypes, composite objects and so on.[2]

E–R Model as well as Conceptual Schema?

After this overview of the main varieties of data modelling, it is time to examine the issues of principle they raise. In chemistry and other sciences it is relatively easy to decide whether the empirical formula or some other convention for describing the structure of matter is most suitable for your purpose. But modelling the structure of information in an organisation is rather different. Here considerable judgement is required to decide which levels of information description are most appropriate to the situation.

To develop database systems effectively at least two descriptive documents are usually needed: one describing the database in non-technical terms and one in technical terms (the internal schema). Putting everything together in one description is just too confusing. But you don't always need the *three* main levels — E–R model, conceptual schema, internal schema — exactly as described above. The classic approach isn't always appropriate. Often there is a question whether you really need a detailed, logical-not-technical, *E–R model*, independent of any DBMS software product, as well as a detailed, logical-not-technical, DBMS-specific *database conceptual schema*.

Suppose that the organisation has already standardised on one particular DBMS software product as part of its infrastructure. Suppose further that you judge that the data to be modelled can be handled well by that DBMS; then it could make sense to avoid producing a classic, detailed, DBMS-independent *E–R model*. Your early, highly summarised sketches, roughly depicting the main continents of your information world, will no doubt be DBMS-independent, but then any detailed modelling can be done in conceptual schema (that is, DBMS-related) terms.

The potential advantage is clear: if your judgement is correct, you may save a lot of effort. Also, modelling within the constraints of the capabilities of a familiar DBMS makes it much easier to get a grip on the details and spot complex areas where idealised aspirations should be cut back. When demands do have to be restrained in this way, it is generally best to take the decision early, before momentum has built up and arguments *ad misericordiam* can be deployed ('But five people spent a whole four-hour workshop making the data model subtle enough to handle the situation when the borrower of a CD is also the composer and a performer of the music on the CD, and now, three months later, you say it is a pointless complication. . .').

The potential disadvantage of allowing the supply factor, the DBMS software, to enter early to affect demands is that your judgement may be wrong or premature. Suppose the management of the LP-Library has a preference for the IMS software product because other institutions in the town have adopted it as standard. An early judgement is made that the library's database needs can be met by IMS. Therefore the detailed modelling is organised to produce data structures that fit comfortably within an IMS conceptual schema. But suppose that, in fact, some other DBMS would have been a far better choice. Had a DBMS-independent E–R model been made first, the library management would then have been better placed to choose the most appropriate DBMS. Moreover, the information analysts might have developed some deft and imaginative demands for IT systems that would never occur to someone whose modelling was constrained by an early decision in favour of one particular supply choice.

The discussion so far has been over-simplified because there are other important possibilities too. Many current DBMS software products share a family resemblance because they are based on *relational* principles. This means that a conceptual schema appropriate for one relational DBMS may be appropriate for several others too. This raises a new possibility: the 'conceptual schema' that could be used for any relational DBMS (but not other types of DBMS). Relational database technology generates another idea for variation: use relational principles of data modelling from the very start and progress through several stages by applying a number of successively more rigorous modelling principles. In this way, E–R model, conceptual schema and internal schema gradually merge into each other, rather than being sharply distinct documents.

Plainly these possibilities can suggest many further options for organising the levels of information modelling. The important point is that *there are* many options and much the same pros and cons apply as in the relatively simple choice just discussed.

Semantic Modelling: Pros and Cons

In semantic modelling the identification of superclasses and similar rather abstract analysis can be very illuminating in a data model as a means of gauging the scope and implications of possible demands. Unfortunately most of the currently well known DBMSes were developed long before semantic modelling became popular, and it may be difficult to carry forward all the subtleties of a semantic model into a DBMS's conceptual schema. In other words, it may be asking too much to supply the demands expressed in a semantic model.

Since this is quite a disadvantage the question arises: Why are so many people enthusiastic about this complex form of modelling? First, traditional data modelling is regarded as inadequate for handling certain demanding types of application (engineering design or cartography, for example). Second, even with more conventional applications, the semantic modelling helps in defining many of the constraints and business rules associated with the data, that will need to be programmed in the application systems. Third, there are expectations that the database software products of the future will be capable of handling the structures of semantic models.

Semantic modelling belongs outside the canon of classic styles of information modelling. In some circumstances, you may decide to make a semantic model as an initial step before embarking on the usual levels of data modelling. Or you may start with E–R modelling and break off to make a semantic model of one particularly crucial area. Or you may bank on semantic modelling and restrict your choice of DBMS software to that which is best able to handle its structures. Whatever you do, the choice should be based on a judgement of pros and cons, and these are likely to be further variations on those already discussed.

Other Modelling Variations

Only scientists at the forefront of research invent new conventions for describing matter or even dabble with little known alternative styles of formula. But in deciding just which styles of data modelling are most appropriate for the particular case there is considerable scope for inventing new varieties of model or taking up relatively obscure ideas. Here is one representative example.

Clearly, separate data models can be developed for the different *departments* of an organisation; there is nothing special about that concept. A more radical approach is to have separate data models for different *genres of information* within the organisation. For example, in one suggested method, each item of data is classed as either operational or administrative data, internal or external data, and inter- or intra-institutional data.[3] (How these labels are defined doesn't matter here; it is the concept of separation by genre that counts.) Thus eight data models can be built, ranging from the relatively exciting operational-external-interinstitutional to the dull administrative-internal-intra-institutional.

Keeping such models separate may well provide a convenient basis for discussing strategic decisions about the organisation's use of IT. In certain circumstances, it may be the most effective way of provoking debate about priorities or stimulating ideas for innovation. On the other hand, the modelling could be a failure if people found it too hard to classify many of the data items, or if the task of integrating some or all of the models later into one conceptual schema proved too awkward.

Summary

The issues discussed in this briefing illustrate how decisions about modelling and other level-based work can operate on two planes. Good decisions about which form of modelling to undertake are important in the same way as decisions about the right tools for the job in many other contexts. But, unlike the products of tools in most other situations, the models themselves will influence subsequent decisions, by reinforcing assumptions, building up momentum, exposing new topics for decision and so on.

There is no universally appropriate choice of levels and styles for modelling information. The purist who preaches that as a matter of principle, you must always make a classic (that is, detailed, logical-not-technical, DBMS-independent) data model, before you even think about the conceptual schema, is making an unwarranted generalisation. So is the consultant who enthuses: 'In our methodology, we always go through several stages, none of which corresponds exactly to any of the classic forms of data modelling; we find this method is invariably the most effective way of doing things.'

To deal with the issues effectively, the right approach is to judge what is best for the specific situation. That means avoiding dogma.

PRACTICAL ADVICE

➤ Before approaching the work of information modelling at any one particular level, tackle a more fundamental issue. Work out the most appropriate structuring into levels to handle the issues of the whole decision-making process.

➤ Be aware of certain classic styles of information model that are widely established and used — E–R data model, conceptual schema and internal schema. But don't feel bound to follow the textbooks.

➤ Consider semantic modelling. Be clear how it differs from other modelling styles.

➤ Make sure everyone is clear about exactly what is going on at any given level. For example, to what extent is pure non-technical logic being defined? To what extent are technological considerations taken account of? To what extent is the information description at a certain level to be regarded as the product of rigorous application of certain rules? To what extent is it impressionistic or judgemental?

➤ Confront the tradeoff: the more different levels of detailed description you adopt, the more thoroughly the ground is covered, but the more cumbersome the whole process.

➤ Remember that the more open and supply-independent data modelling is done, the more evidence on which to base a choice of supply and the more opportunity for stimulating creative ideas. On the other hand the more chance there is, too, of wasting time and producing ultimate frustration through the creation of pointlessly elaborate models.

➤ Consider variations of modelling styles that are not in the textbooks, but may suit the issues of the case.

21.   Data Model, Process Model

ISSUES

Primers on system development methods often contrast two types of modelling: data modelling and process modelling.

The data model of an organisation is concerned with entities and the relationships between them. For example, the data model of a library of recorded music shows how there are entities called Customers, any of whom may be borrowing CDs; a CD entity is related to one or more Musical Work entities, and so on. This kind of modelling can give a very detailed view of certain aspects of the organisation.

When somebody joins the library of recorded music, certain procedures are followed; they may include complications such as the issue of a temporary ticket to permit immediate borrowing and perhaps possible feedback — if somebody else recorded as living at your address was expelled from the library, you may have to pay all the outstanding fines before being allowed to join. A pure data model can't readily show this kind of detail about the organisation; a process model can.

How do these two types of modelling fit into an approach to IT decision-making? Should you always build a complete detailed model of each type? That seems a lot to ask, but then how should you decide what to do in any given case? This briefing helps to tackle that issue by looking at some points of principle raised by data and process modelling.

ANALYSIS

A firm distinction is commonly made between the data model (which may itself be divided into several parts describing data from different angles) and the process model, depicting the various processes within the organisation.[1] This distinction is a good starting point for discussion, but the interesting issues arise as the distinction runs into difficulties. Data modelling and process modellingmodelling;data-process distinction are not actually as different as chalk and cheese. Process models mention data, and data models often provide some indication of processes.

Data Models Also Describe Processes

At the LP Library information analysts have concentrated on building a data model, not a process model. The data model shows, for example, that the relationship between the entities CD and Performer is 'many-to-many'; one Performer can have made one CD or several; any CD may contain performances by one Performer or by several. Can this type of model give any indication at all of the way the library is organised, what happens there and the way information flows from one place or person in the library to another? Are customers of the library allowed to browse through the collection or must they ask for the CD they want to be fetched? Do the librarians check to see if the CDs are damaged when they are returned? The data model doesn't pronounce on these things explicitly; it is not that kind of model.

But the matter is not that simple. Very few data models can avoid using the *transaction entity*. An information analyst sets out to organise the model into entities and their attributes. Customer and CD are entities and so is Loan. This is a convenient method of analysis because certain pieces of information are obviously *attributes* of the Loan entity (e.g. date of original loan, number of reminders sent, fine outstanding). If they can't be attached to a separate entity called Loan, where else in the model can they be placed? (Some modelling conventions do avoid setting up a Loan entity; they allow a relationship between two entities to be given a name, e.g. Loan, and allow attributes to be attached to the *relationship*. However, this doesn't affect the argument here.)

A transaction entity doesn't stand for an actual thing you can see or touch, such as a Customer or a CD. Moreover it has a transitory nature, by comparison with the other more-or-less permanent entities in the model. Some conventions for data modelling acknowledge this by giving the transaction entity a special status, perhaps representing it on the diagram with a special shape. By their very nature, these transaction entities do convey information about processes, albeit somewhat indirectly. For example, by looking at the attributes of the entity Loan you can work out that the procedures of the library include sending out reminder letters if a loan is overdue, charging fines and so on.

So, although the data model doesn't provide a clear definition of the library's organisational procedures, it does provide numerous hints — perhaps even enough hints for purposes of strategic decision-making. In cases where the procedures of an organisation are relatively straightforward, or of relatively little importance to the matters at hand, it may be quite sufficient to work from a data model alone, because its transaction entities provide sufficient indication of the main procedures.

The Time Dimension

There is one important drawback to a classic data model: it lacks a time dimension. In some ways, the data model is like a snapshot and for some subjects a snapshot is the wrong medium. Though a snapshot can give a fairly accurate representation of a statue, it is less satisfactory for a 100 metres sprint. With a long exposure the runners will be too blurred for identification, but with a very short exposure the runners and spectators will be so sharp that there is no impression of movement; either way there is some kind of distortion. To get an accurate representation, an entirely different medium — motion video — is better.

The data model is a snapshot made with the exposure of one instant, as it were, and it will show that one CD is borrowed by one and only one Customer. Only common sense, not the model itself, tells us that over (say) a year, the same CD may be borrowed by many Customers in succession. On the other hand, a data model with an exposure time of, say, a year would cause other forms of confusion. In some cases, arguably even in the case of the LP Library, reliance on common-sense to make up for the data model's missing time dimension may still be a better approach than embarking on some other form of modelling to show such things explicitly. Nevertheless, if there are many such instances within one data model, common sense may be asked to bear an unreasonable load.

If most of the items in the data model's picture are fairly stationary, then you get a fine clear picture of their structure. If the picture is full of things in motion, with many transaction entities, the result may be a blurred and misleading picture. Moreover a photo giving a clear picture of a large statue, around which a blur of traffic is moving may be perfectly acceptable. Similarly, if the aspects of an organisation most important to strategy decisions are relatively statuesque, it may not matter that many of the peripheral details are blurred.

Process Models Also Describe Data

If a data model says something about processes, does a process model perhaps provide some understanding of an organisation's data too?

Process modelling methods (SA/SD or Isac, for example) tend to document explicitly a mixture of two kinds of things — events that happen and information associated with these events. Different methods employ different notational conventions but in most cases the central feature is a diagram, showing data used by and flowing between procedural steps. Usually high-level charts show the main sections of the whole model in a summarised form, such that one innocuous box in this chart may represent a page of seething procedural complexity on a diagram one level of detail lower down.[2]

In a library of recorded music, one simple diagram can summarise the normal procedure when a customer asks to reserve a CD, that is

Example of Process Modelling

LP Library: Reservation Procedure

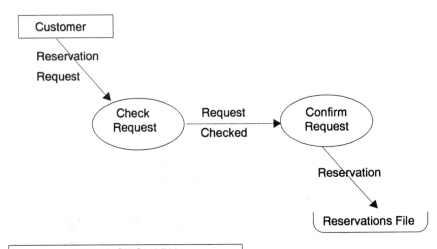

```
DATA DICTIONARY

Listing of all the data items contained in
Data Flows such as:
      Reservation Request
      Request Checked
      Reservation
and in
Data Stores such as:
      Reservations File
```

currently borrowed by someone else. This can be underpinned by more detailed diagrams, expanding the content of individual process circles. 'Check Request' can be broken down further on a second-level diagram, that could be quite complex; for example, suppose the CD requested isn't recorded as being out on loan at all, or suppose the customer requesting the reservation turns out not to be up to date with the library subscription. 'Confirm Request' can be a simple process or can itself be complex; perhaps it includes making a forecast of when the CD is likely to be available, bearing in mind that there are other reservations already outstanding.

The diagrams can't stand by themselves. Each of the 'data flow' arrows and 'data store' containers is broken down into data items, listed in a separate non-diagrammatic 'data dictionary'. Once all the items of data flowing between the hundreds of procedure steps in the library have been listed in detail, a very extensive 'data dictionary' will result.

At first glance, this dictionary to the data in the diagrams may seem to be merely a reproduction in a different format of the classic data model. But there is a crucial weakness inherent in data analysis which *hangs off* process diagrams in this way. The process model's diagrams and dictionary give a reasonable impression of the relationship between Customer and CD, because the borrowing and reserving of CDs are events which actually happen, for which procedures exist. But the data model also shows a relationship between the Performer (a conductor or singer, say) and the CDs on which the performances are to be found. This doesn't correspond to any specific event or process that occurs within the library; therefore it doesn't necessarily show up anywhere in the process model.

A pure data model can expose a great variety of different relationships between entities; the data dictionary which hangs off a process model exposes a certain subset of these relationships — only those corresponding to actual events or procedures. Therefore, if there are many important relationships that do not correspond very clearly to actual procedures, then data modelling is the natural approach. Conversely, there may be no such need; the data analysis that hangs off a process model may be perfectly adequate. In that case a separate data model may be an unnecessary luxury.

The Relative Mutability of Procedures

If the process model describes procedures and organisation, the question arises: Which procedures and organisation should it describe? Exactly the way things are now? How they obviously ought to be? One possible proposal for the way they might be? And so on. If process modelling is being used to help in coming to strategic decisions, these questions have to be asked.

Plainly the modeller ought to define the assumptions the model is based on. Has it already been decided to take the present organisation and procedures as fixed and use IT to automate things? Or to keep basically the same organisation but make changes wherever a new computer system makes it advantageous? Or is the organisation going to be changed in any case in some way that is already defined? Or is the process model to be used as the starting point for discussions of possible new procedures? Most organisations are in a state of flux to some degree or at least have the opportunity of being so. Unless there is some clear and coherent position on these issues, the model may be worthless.

The same considerations apply to the data model too — but generally to a lesser degree. A large part of a data model deals with things that seem immutable; for example, no matter how the library's procedures for lending out CDs may change, the CDs will still contain works by several composers and many works will still exist in several different recordings. A much greater proportion of the content of process models describes things that are within the power of the organisation itself to alter.

This line of thinking is taken a good deal further by some theorists who argue that, since a data model is inherently less mutable than a process model, it is a superior model on which to base strategic decisions. In fact, some go on to argue that the creation of a process-independent data model is an indispensable step in helping an organisation define its IT strategy. This is quite an influential view that needs to be examined carefully.

Data Modelling — Basis for Strategy?

The LP Library has a procedure allowing a library customer to reserve a certain CD that is already out on loan. The data model may possibly contain some hints about whether such a procedure exists, but it won't provide reliable answers to such questions as: Can an assistant query a database to see when the CD is due back? Can a reservation can be keyed in directly by a customer without bothering the assistant? Does the customer receive any hardcopy receipt after making a reservation? Is a fee payable, and if so, how is it calculated? Suppose the album is overdue; is the original lender pursued more vigorously than normal because the album has been reserved by somebody else? The data model isn't designed to reveal these things.

You might think that such questions show up the limitations of the data model but some data modellers argue that, on the contrary, they illustrate its advantages. The library's data model, so the argument goes, represents the essential framework of the organisation, within which its possible procedures can be fitted. The model probably makes it clear that the reservation procedures described could easily exist; perhaps they don't exist today, but, given the structure of the data they would require, they could exist tomorrow and a different variant could exist the day after. The data model also suggests fairly clearly that other conceivable procedures — e.g. to analyse the chemical composition of CDs and LPs — don't and probably won't ever exist.

This independence of the way the specific procedures happen to be at any particular time, is seen as making the data model the appropriate basis for serious decision-making. According to this line of reasoning, you may very well need process modelling at some stage, but only when you are working out the detail necessary to develop new systems already decided on. This view makes data modelling an important tool for long-term strategic decisions, and relegates process modelling to the role of documenting second-order detail.

Sometimes, an additional requirement is attached: as well as being procedure-independent, the data model should be independent of the form of the organisation at any given time. If, for example, the roles of the people managing and running the library were altered, the data model would remain unaltered, because none of the entities and relationships it describes would be affected. The addition of this requirement, though important, doesn't affect the main arguments germane to this discussion.

This is one of those arguments that, in its crude form, is quite easily attacked. For one thing, cases vary. Some cases, such as the LP Library, probably need data modelling badly because many of the important relationships are not procedural. Other cases, a steel mill perhaps, are probably unintelligible without a process model and have little need of extra data modelling. Since cases vary so much, any broad generalisations about the relative value of data and process modelling must be suspect.

There is another line of attack against data modelling extremism. The view that a procedure-independent data model should be used as a foundation for strategic decision-making implies certain things about the data model. For example, it means that the data model must not contain data items such as 'special indicator to show album has been reserved and is overdue', because that data item is obviously dependent on current procedures for handling reservations, and detail about current procedures is to be excluded. But if that kind of item has to be eliminated from the model, surely 'date due back' has to go too. That is also dependent on current procedures; the library could easily change its procedures so that an album could be borrowed indefinitely. But if that argument is valid, perhaps the data model should refer to 'borrowables' rather than LPs and CDs; one day the library might easily change its procedures to lend out other things too — books, fancy dress, crockery, say. But then it might change its procedures to do things other than lending out objects; it might start manufacturing aircraft, say.

If the data model is to be so resilient to changes of procedures that it will be just as valid when the library switches over to manufacturing aeroplanes then it will surely be so bland as to be worthless. This *reductio ad absurdum* suggests that there is no obvious boundary separating the data that is procedurE–Related from that which isn't. The procedure-independent data model is a chimera.

What does this prove? First, simple generalisations suggesting that data models are inherently more important than process models can't be trusted because there is no simple way of deciding what counts as procedure-independent data. Second, since that is so, you can draw the line between procedure-dependent data and procedure-independent data wherever you like — or better, wherever it best suits the particular case you are dealing with.

Model Choice is Related to Strategy

Most examples given in textbooks on modelling or system development are of cases where both data and procedures are fairly important, but where neither is really dominant: for example, Benyon's book on modelling contains a lengthy working out of a case of the administration of a shop.[3] This tends to disguise the great variety of applications in real life. Some are rich in information complexity: data modelling is very important and complicated, while process modelling is relatively trivial. Other applications are the reverse. Some applications have a different mix. Therefore the ability to make the right judgement on how to apply data modelling and process modelling to the specific case can be far more valuable than expertise in the finer points of any particular type of modelling.

Simplification based on unwarranted assumptions is all too easy. It may seem plausible to generalise that a library of recorded music is probably information-rich while a steel works is process-rich and a shop is somewhere in between. In fact a great deal depends on the organisation's policy for using IT.

For example, if the policy of the LP Library is to concentrate on developing systems providing information to customers and staff about which works by which composers by which performers are on which CDs, that would certainly be an information-rich application. To answer a query such as 'What recordings have we of any eighteenth-century piano concertos that are not by Mozart or Beethoven?' entails handling information items interrelated in quite complex ways. In this kind of case, it may be enough to concentrate on the data modelling side and rely on any relevant procedural aspects being more or less obvious.

But if the intention is to automate complex procedures, the opposite may apply. The LP Library's IT strategy might plausibly ignore the actual content of any CD and just store a unique reference number. Much stress might be placed on the sophisticated arrangements for chasing up late loans, scheduling visits by debt collectors to customers' homes and sending off messages about debtors to the city's town hall. With this strategy process modelling would be far more relevant.

Or, thirdly, if the systems envisaged were between those two extremes, then the case would fit the examples given in the textbooks that require both data and process modelling. Lastly, there is the important case where it doesn't matter greatly what modelling is done, because the most challenging, innovative and potentially most valuable part of the library's IT policy is in an area where modelling is of limited relevance. For example, the library may be pioneering new forms of 'user interface' for both information enquiry and processing of transactions. Tablets, mice and touchscreens may be used to interact with the system. Much effort may be devoted to producing attractive, easy to understand, screen designs incorporating colour graphics. Success in this endeavour doesn't depend on either data or process modelling.

Few real-life situations are so neat that these examples will suggest exactly what to do. They merely illustrate the kind of factors to be weighed up in deciding what degree of data modelling and process modelling, with what terms of reference, to apply at which points, in which order, to make decisions most effectively.

PRACTICAL ADVICE

➤ Get practised in distinguishing between those situations where the most useful method of description is data-oriented and those where process modelling will give a better insight.

➤ Don't forget that the two main forms of modelling overlap: a data model inevitably gives some insight into procedures, but it is unlikely to tell the whole story. Similarly, a process model can provide some insight into data structures.

➤ Don't assume that any one method of modelling is invariably better than any other; nor that any one case is inherently a data case or a process case.

➤ Be sceptical of those who advocate a data-driven, also known as procedure-independent, model as a matter of principle. These things are relative, not absolute.

➤ On the other hand, watch out for awkward implicit assumptions in procedure-driven models: are these today's procedures, tomorrow's procedures or what?

➤ Use your own judgement to decide which modelling approach is, on balance, most relevant to the issues raised by the strategy case.

22. Modelling and Strategy

ISSUES

If you asked someone to appraise the itinerary you had made for visiting the battlefields of the American Civil War, you would expect suggestions about places missed out or better ways of getting from one place to another, but probably not comments such as: 'This is all very well, but it rests on the unstated premise that visiting battlefields is a worthwhile thing to do'. Yet sometimes questioning the premise can be more valuable than appraising the detail.

The Library of Recorded Music in the town of Lilli-Pilli (hereafter known as the LP Library) hires out LP records, cassettes and CDs. The director of the library intends to develop new plans for using IT in the library. As a start he has commissioned a data modelling exercise. Now he wants to form a judgement of the model's value.

One approach is to appraise the sophistication of the modelling. The data model shows, for example, that the Library may have *several CDs* of music by *one Performer*; it also shows that among the data of interest *about* a Performer is *Metier* (conductor, soprano, etc.). But, you may ask, does that provide an adequate model of reality? A performer who normally plays the piano may occasionally make a recording as a conductor; can the data model represent that possibility adequately? Suppose a violinist who normally submerges his identity within a string quartet makes a recording as a soloist; what then? But to debate these nuances is to accept the unspoken premises of the data modelling exercise without demur. It avoids addressing the more fundamental issue of how valuable such a model really is in helping the director of the library make rational decisions about using IT.

A data model may be conceptually sophisticated and logically perfect and factually accurate, and yet, this briefing suggests, it may be practically worthless — if the modeller hasn't thought clearly about certain very basic issues.

ANALYSIS

In many ways it would certainly be convenient to begin with a pure, dispassionate data model, and only then proceed to take hard decisions involving commitments to systems and budgets and timescales. But in practice the simple approach of 'first-model, then-decide' is rarely tenable. Working out why this should be is the surest way of understanding the interactions between modelling and decision-making.

The Model, Reality and Selection

If this is a model, what is it a model of? Is it a model of the information in the computer database you plan to build or is it a representation of the way things really are — the objectively real description of the library that would still be valid, even if there were no question of using computers at all? The natural first reaction of many information analysts is to say that the model represents objective reality, independent of any particular automated systems. Understandably, they are attracted by the idea of having a model unsullied by practical complications, in order to offer the clearest possible view of the way things really are. That seems to offer a sound basis for decision-making; if necessary, the objective model can be used later by a database technologist as the starting point for a separate technically oriented version, tempered by whatever practical factors are relevant.

But the concept of model-as-objective-reality soon runs into trouble. Plainly any model must include certain data items and not others; otherwise it would be a complete representation of the entire universe. So on what basis does this model of the LP Library include some things and not others? Why is the address of each customer of the library mentioned in the data model, for example, but not the colour of customers' eyes? Why not the place of birth of each composer? Why is the date of recording of each piece of music contained on a CD not regarded as a relevant data item for inclusion in the model?

Even if there are no convincing answers to these questions because the choice of detail in the model is arbitrary and capricious, it may be argued that the model still represents objective reality — in the sense that the details it contains are true rather than false or imaginary. But this is a weak argument. You might as well say that a newspaper devoted entirely to news about royalty and film stars, or television highlights of a football match showing only the goals scored by one of the teams gave a picture of objective reality.

The information analyst may concede that argument as valid in theory, but contend that sheer common sense enables you to draw the boundary between the relevant and the irrelevant; sheer common sense should tell you that the colour of customers' eyes is not relevant. In practice though, there is usually an ample quantity of border-line cases where the selection is not self-evident. Suppose the model shows quite complex relations between entities such as musical works and CDs, but it doesn't analyse the relations between customer addresses? Two library customers might live in adjoining streets, but the data model isn't interested in geographical proximity; it has no data entity called 'district of the town of Lilli-Pilli'; and there is no data item to distinguish the local tax-payers from library customers who live in the hinterland. Who is to say by sheer common sense whether this choice of detail is right or wrong?

Entity–Attribute, Arbitrary Analysis

There is another important argument against the idea that a data model can be independent of decisions about systems. Even if the *scope* of the model is not an issue, its *internal detail* may have to rest on some rough assumptions.

Most methods of data modelling distinguish between *entities* (things that are of interest) and their *attributes* (what is worth knowing about them). At the LP Library, it seems natural to identify Performer as a thing and items such as Metier (e.g. soprano, cellist, conductor, etc.), Date of birth, Place of birth and Nationality as items worth knowing about a Performer. This entity–attribute distinction is fundamental in imposing order on the hundreds of different items contained in a detailed data model. If everything were described as an entity then you would soon have a model far too complicated to be intelligible. But although the distinction sounds natural enough, it doesn't rest on a very secure logical foundation.

Suppose a sceptic argues that a Date is the really interesting thing and the names of performers born on that day are among the items worth knowing *about* it. An entity–attribute analysis done on this basis seems odd, but there may be no way of showing that the sceptic is factually or logically incorrect. In *Data and Reality*, Kent discusses the differences between entities and attributes at length and finds it impossible to avoid this conclusion.[1]

In practice, one particular way of analysing an organisation's entities and attributes may seem *more natural* or *more helpful* than another — because of the assumption (which may be unconscious) that it is more likely to be relevant to any useful computer system. For example, it seems improbable that anybody would want to query the database: 'Have we any CDs of a symphony performed by a conductor with the same birthday as the composer?' But if the primary purpose of an intended system were to enable exactly that kind of question to be put, then the sceptic's analysis of Date as an *entity* could be very useful. However, if you judge that, in the computer systems you are likely to build, people will be interested in Date of Birth information only with a specific Composer or

Performer already in mind, then Date of Birth seems a very natural *attribute* of the entities Composer and Performer.

In other words, in order to decide between many theoretically valid ways of modelling some aspect of the organisation, you may need to take a view on which functions will be contained in a future computer system and which will not — even though you are still involved in the non-technical data modelling.

Some data modellers and some textbooks about databases do give the impression that the correct analysis into entities and attributes is in some sense *there* waiting to be found, like the solution to a chess problem. On that view any team of competent modellers, carefully using proven techniques, would be bound to come up with practically the same correct analysis. This is a false doctrine; competent people can produce any number of different models, if they make different assumptions about the purpose of the model.

Model and Purpose

The pure objective reality position isn't really tenable, and once the concession is made that any data model is necessarily selective, the discussion must shift to the basis for selection. If selection is necessary, it follows that the practical purpose of the model needs to be defined; otherwise there is no way of deciding the criteria for selection.

Some modellers take up a position at the opposite extreme to the objectivity argument and assume that the whole modelling exercise has one very clear purpose — to develop a comprehensive new computer system for the library, storing everything in a database that is relevant to its services and administration in any way and excluding what is not.

But this can be an awkward position to defend. For example, who says that developing a comprehensive system that automates everything is a good policy? If that strategy was already decided before the modelling started, how was the decision made? After all, there must have been other less comprehensive options available. How were these options evaluated? The data model itself can't have played a part in deciding the strategy since the modelling activity's terms of reference assume that the strategy of the comprehensive system is already settled.

Thus the data modelling is reduced to a mere activity for the implementation of a strategy — not an instrument for helping to make a strategy. You may find that perfectly acceptable. It can sometimes be quite sensible to use means other than data modelling to determine a strategy and then treat any data modelling as an implementation task rather than a strategy-forming activity. Nevertheless, many people in the world of IT are keen to believe that data modelling can indeed be relevant to making strategy decisions, not just to implementing them. The question arises: Is there any way at all of defending such an idea?

Data Modelling and Strategy-making

The most important argument available runs as follows. A data model based on a comprehensive approach to automation need not imply that a strategy of complete automation will in fact be adopted. It is intended as a basis for discussion: after discussing the whole model, you might quite well decide on a strategy of implementing only a part of it.

This sounds quite rational, but is probably just not realistic. In the case of the library, you may well spot, after a fairly limited investigation, without any detailed data modelling at all, that there are two virtually separate systems available for automation. One system is concerned with the pure administration of the library. (Who borrows which CD? What is the value of outstanding fines? etc.) The other system is concerned with providing non-administrative musical information. (How many CDs are there with Otto Klemperer as the conductor? Any piano concertos by Ravel? etc.) The administration system can work quite well if the only data item held about a CD is its number; it has no great need of information about the music contained on the CD. The musical information system on the other hand is almost exclusively concerned with the content of the CDs, irrespective of their loan status. Indeed, almost all of this musical information could equally well document the record collection of a private individual.

With this insight into the situation, a range of possible strategy options come to mind straight away. For example: do either one of the systems and not the other; do both in full; do both, but only the most important part of each; make an overall plan to do everything, give priority to the administration side and implement in stages with the option to halt after the first stage if money is tight; and so on.

You don't need to do all the work of producing a detailed data model, based on the assumption of complete automation, in order to get that insight into the various different strategies. Moreover, a complete data model is a very awkward document to use as a basis for discussing options of this kind. Its form is intended to describe one coherent system in detail, not to expose the implications of a range of alternatives. It may not even be possible to fence off neat subsets of the total data model cleanly. A many-to-many relationship between information entities in the complete data model could easily be a one-to-many relationship in a partial system; 'mandatory one-to-many' relations can become 'optional one-to-many' relations, and so on.

Also a choice between policy options has to be influenced to some degree by quantitative factors (volumes of data, costs, etc.). A data model normally shows logical relations without quantification. It shows that one CD may contain more than musical work, but it doesn't attempt to show, for example, whether the vast majority of CDs contain many different works or whether this just applies to a small minority of recital CDs. Experience shows that you can't turn a detailed data model into a manageable document for a discussion of strategy, just by writing a few figures against the lines and boxes of the diagrams.

So it is hard to believe that an information analyst seriously interested in genuine strategy discussions, about radically different alternatives, would really undertake the labour of drawing up the detailed model of a whole complete system first.

Handling the Model–Strategy Dilemma

There is a dilemma. You shouldn't set up your detailed data model until you have already formed your strategy, determining the scope of what needs to be modelled. But in deciding your strategy, it seems, you are denied the help of a data model in surveying the landscape of possibilities.

One pragmatic approach could be to start off with a highly summarised overview of the principal types of data that a total system might embrace. Use this as a basis for brainstorming through alternative, radically different strategies. Only after you have settled on the main outline of your strategy, you carry out the detailed work of modelling all the data items and relations that seem relevant.

But this crude outline makes it all seem too easy. For one thing, it may be necessary to go through several iterations of working documents of different degrees of detail, before deciding that the strategy is clear enough to justify detailed data modelling. For another, the shrewd IT strategist needs to spot that certain areas should have their data modelled in much more detail than the rest at an early stage — because of their far-reaching implications for the complexity of strategy options.

Also, it may sometimes be necessary to delve into matters of pure database technology during strategy discussions, well before any comprehensive data modelling is done. For example, certain possibilities under discussion may entail exceptionally high volumes of information or exceptional response time requirements or exceptional reliability demands — and these matters could be relevant to the appraisal of the strategy options.

Data Modelling and Key Factors

The logic of the discussion so far can be summarised roughly as follows.

It may seem initially to be a sensible thing to build a data model in order to obtain a view of the organisation, so that strategy decisions can be made. But in practice the model and the strategy can't be segregated so neatly, because the model can only be built by making *implicit assumptions* about the strategy. Therefore a much more subtle interaction between modelling and decision-making is called for.

But even this formulation still assumes that — providing things are organised in a sufficiently subtle way — the data model will provide important input to strategy decisions. Of course in many cases it does, but this is not necessarily so; a data model will not always expose the most important factors affecting strategy decisions.

Suppose, for example, that somebody who examines the state of the LP Library without any preconceived ideas comes up with two main factors. First, the acquisition policy of the library is lopsided because the person who orders new CDs is an opera buff; for example, there are five copies of Rossini's rarely performed *Elisabetta Regina d'Inghilterra* but only one copy of Tchaikovsky's *Violin Concerto*. Surely a better acquisition policy would make the library more attractive to customers. Second, the security situation is bad; practical tests have shown that the theoretical checks against theft of CDs can easily be circumvented by simple ploys and ruses. This seems a serious problem — quite how serious, nobody can say.

Building a data model out of entities and relationships and attributes won't expose these two key factors, but they may be just the factors that should determine the library's policy. Once the two factors are exposed, it becomes clearer what the real IT strategy decisions are. One option is to judge that both must be dealt with by new IT systems. A complicated system should be developed to collect statistics about the music that customers actually borrow and feed the figures back into ordering algorithms, so that the more Tchaikovsky is borrowed, the more new Tchaikovsky is ordered for the library. And, to improve security, all the borrowing procedures should be overhauled and supported by new systems containing far more controls. But a different option altogether is to judge that both the two key factors can be dealt with by means other than IT: put somebody else in charge of acquisitions and attach bleeping devices to CDs. With this second option, it would make sense to put these measures into effect, meanwhile avoid any commitment to new IT investment, and review the situation in six months. A third option might be somewhere between these two extremes . . .

Whatever the options are exactly in this case, data modelling is rather irrelevant. It doesn't help in identifying the key factors, doesn't help in defining the strategy options and doesn't help in deciding between them.

Data Modelling and Technology Possibilities

Suppose, as a different example, that the management of the Library has examined its situation very carefully and found that there are in fact none of these key factors that must be or can be dealt with by means other than IT. Assume that everyone agrees that new IT-based systems are desirable. Is it fair to assume that — providing things are organised with subtlety — data modelling will be a big help in developing strategy? A few years ago that *was* a fair pragmatic assumption, but no longer.

If many of the strategy issues are related to the structuring of information in such a way that it can be stored and accessed in databases, then data modelling is very likely relevant. But nowadays the main strategy issues may be dominated by technology possibilities other than database.

For example, suppose that the most interesting strategy possibility for the LP Library concerns on-line links with various library branches in the suburbs, and with large libraries in other towns and universities, and with the warehouses of CD manufacturers. In that case, it may be quite sensible to leave current internal systems as they are, keep data structures as crude as possible and concentrate most of the attention on the communications technology. Or artificial intelligence may be the dominant possibility. Perhaps it is felt that the way to get a competitive edge over rival libraries is to provide a facility for customers to pose queries, such as: 'Which work is the best introduction to the music of Schönberg?' or 'Can you recommend any relatively unknown romantic symphony?' (and of course to get sensible answers). Appraising that strategic possibility certainly requires some information analysis — but of quite a different kind from classic data modelling.

Summing Up

For the demand-side extremist — who holds that the managers of the library should just define their complete demands and then hand them over to the technologists, who will supply them — the arguments in this briefing may seem irritating and irrelevant.

The issue of the relation between strategy and data model, like many others in IT strategy, is associated with the principle that good IT strategy decisions may at times have to temper demand with the practicalities of supply. In other words, there is at least a possibility that the right strategy may not always be to automate everything conceivable.

A predefined step-by-step approach — however useful it may be for actually doing the data modelling — is far less appropriate for deciding the *premises* on which the modelling should be based. As this briefing suggests, making use of data modelling in the development of strategy is an enterprise fraught with dangers of unwarranted assumptions. It requires sound judgement of the issues that are relevant to the specific situation.

PRACTICAL ADVICE

➤ Don't do or say anything that rests on the assumption that a data model depicts objective reality.

➤ Avoid the trap of reasoning as if there were one correct analysis into entities, relationships and attributes for a given situation.

➤ Don't just make a model; decide what the purpose of the model is first.

➤ Ensure that the purpose of the model is sufficiently well-defined to serve as the criterion for including and excluding detail.

➤ Don't go too far with modelling detail before you have an explicit strategy that sets the boundaries of the model.

➤ Consider going through iterations of outline models and discussions of possible strategies.

➤ Be prepared to delve into quantification and technology implications at an early stage of data modelling.

➤ Watch out for key factors about an organisation that its data model can't possibly reveal.

➤ In situations when technologies such as telecommunications or artificial intelligence are more important than database, downgrade the relevance of classic data modelling.

➤ Apply the above principles to all types of modelling, not just data modelling.

23. Moving Between Models

ISSUES

A water colour sketch of a proposed new shopping mall and the architect's ground-plan should probably be *consistent* with each other, but, given either one by itself, you would not expect to be able to derive all the detail of the other. Studying an organisation — its business structure, its data or its procedures — generally leads to several models, representing the organisation from different angles, very likely with differing degrees of detail. Clearly, they should not contradict each other, but what else can be said about their relationships?

The models are normally developed as successive stages in a planning process. For example, a logical, technology-independent data model is in *some sense translated* into the physical model of a database taking full account of all the technical issues. If progress from model to model is no more than a translation process then relatively few important decisions arise. But, in practice, the translation is usually complicated by quandaries and compromises and feedback; and where these things exist there are issues of principle to be considered.

Then there are questions about the way progress is made through the modelling levels. Should you expand all detail in all areas, level by level, at the same rate? Should you deliberately cut off modelling at certain points, slurring over certain details? If so, how do you decide what to slur over? How can these matters affect the quality of decisions ultimately made?

This briefing explores the transitions between different styles of data model. The interest is not in how exactly the practitioner carries out the modelling task, but in the management issues arising from the fact that the task may be more than a steady process of translation on a broad front.

ANALYSIS

This briefing falls into three clear parts. You can't form realistic judgements about the way to organise detailed modelling activities unless you have a good idea of the kind of work this is: the first part of the briefing gives an impression of the demanding, laborious, vulnerable nature of entity–relationship modelling.

The second and most substantial part of the briefing discusses the most important form of movement between model levels: the translation of the non-technical, entity–relationship model into the technical design for a database. The stress, of course, is on the decision-making that may arise, rather than on the exact details of carrying out the work.

The third part of the briefing discusses a more general issue: should you carry out the modelling level by level on a broad front, or should you press ahead, bypassing certain details temporarily or even perhaps permanently?

Detailed Modelling is a Substantial Investment

An exercise to produce a detailed *entity–relationship model (E–R model)* is often an ambitious and uncertain investment. The data modeller sets out to record many subtle relationships between different aspects of the organisation, and generally depends on input from people who are not accustomed to approaching their normal work with the kind of thought processes that the data modeller demands. Nevertheless, the final version of the precisely constructed data model has to be very close to error-free. Subtle logical flaws can easily lurk unnoticed in the detail, but if they are not rooted out, the model may generate more confusion than insight.

Here is a brief taste of typical challenges confronting the data modeller. First, there is the problem of *homonyms* — the same term used in different parts of the organisation for different things; this often occurs with terms like product, part, account, order and region. Then, *synonyms* — two or more terms referring to the same thing; for example, sometimes terms like customer and client and account. Then, *unmentionables* — an entity existing in the real world, but not hitherto identified as such; for example, 'household', the group of related clients all living at the same address. Then, *false entities* — terms that are too vague to apply to any clearly definable thing; sales or inventory, perhaps.

It can be a tough task for the data modeller at (say) Ironbark Insurance to recognise imprecision in discussions with branch managers and business development managers and accounts clerks and board members, to spell out the nuances to them, explain why they matter, and get things properly thrashed out.

There are more difficulties too in discussing and verifying the *relationships* between entities and recording them in diagram form. As the example in the diagram shows, even for just two entities, such as Policy and Claim, there can be quite a variety of theoretically possible relations, each requiring a slightly different diagram. Ideally, the responsible people in the organisation should check out the diagrams that the data modeller draws and come back with comments such as: 'You've put

Detailed Distinctions in Data Modelling

Using modelling conventions to describe the logical relationships between policies and claims in an insurance company.

Which description is correct?

DESCRIPTION 1.
Every Claim must apply to (only) one Policy;

Every Policy must have (at least) one Claim.

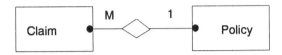

DESCRIPTION 2.

Every Claim must apply to either one Policy or none at all;
Every Policy must have (at least) one Claim.

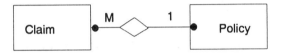

DESCRIPTION 3.

Every Claim must apply to either one Policy or none at all;
A Policy may have zero, one or more Claims.

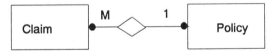

DESCRIPTION 4.
Every Claim must apply to (only) one Policy;

A Policy may have zero, one or more Claims.

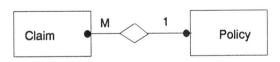

These four possible descriptions are mutually exclusive.
Probably DESCRIPTION 4 is correct for most insurance companies.

But if it is possible for one Claim to apply to more than one Policy,
then none is correct, and the modelling conventions must
be used to describe a fifth possibility.

a dot inside the line here in this box, indicating, according to your modelling conventions, that every policy *must have* at least one claim. That is wrong, but when you correct it, remember to preserve the right combination of dots and lines and boxes to show that one policy *may have* several claims.'

And that is not the worst of it. Suppose there are three entities involved: each *policy* is associated with one *reinsurance treaty*; and each reinsurance treaty covers many policies; and each *claim payment* applies to one particular reinsurance treaty; and each reinsurance treaty has many claim payments. Even an experienced data modeller can easily draw a model diagram whose dots and lines make unwarranted, perhaps false, assumptions. For example, you would be unjustified in assuming from the above facts that each claim payment applies to one and only one policy. That is an example of falling into a 'fan trap', in the jargon of the data modeller. There is also something called a 'chasm gap'.[1]

Models often extend into hundreds of pages of diagrams covered with shapes and lines and dots, all potentially capable of expressing such fine logical distinctions. Such models can easily become, as they say, unreadable at any speed. How much detailed modelling is truly necessary depends on the case, but plainly it is attractive to find ways of organising this work as elegantly and economically as possible.

This would be so even if the data model, once finalised, would stand by itself. But this kind of model is a means to an end. Before any new computer systems can result, all the detail of the model has to be translated and transformed in various ways. In the following discussions about transitions between models, ways of bypassing detail and so on, the models being discussed are elaborate, finely wrought, intellectual constructions of which the example diagram gives the merest taste.

From Entity–relationship Model to Conceptual Schema

With this preparation, it is time to discuss the most important form of movement between model levels: the translation of the non-technical, E–R model into an equally elaborate and intricate document, the technical design for a database.

One classic approach is to begin by translating the E–R model a *database conceptual schema*, which, though non-technical, calls for information to be structured according to some very precise conventions. Part of this work is mere transcription: e.g. ensuring all data items have unique names up to, say, ten characters long, with no spaces or punctuation marks. But there may be some more demanding work too.

Some parts of the E–R model may have to be recast to ensure that the conceptual schema suits the characteristics of the chosen DBMS software. For example, some types of DBMS are particularly good at handling information in the form of a hierarchy of one-to-many relationships. For example, at the LP Library of recorded music each person has many CD loans; each loan in turn has many events: borrow, first reminder, return etc. But a hierarchy-based DBMS can't represent many-to-many relationships so neatly. For example, one performer makes many recordings, but also one recording may be made by several performers. With a relational-style DBMS, many-to-many relationships can be handled quite neatly, but hierarchies of one-to-many relationships don't fit quite so well.

Clearly any such recasting of information structures has to be done with great care, because you don't want to introduce inaccuracies or gloss over important distinctions. On the other hand, it may well be sensible to drop or simplify certain details that seemed interesting in the data model but turn out to complicate the conceptual schema to little useful effect. Thus, supply considerations can interact with demand here. If so, the interaction should be handled rationally. Nuances shouldn't be lost by accident and neither should they be preserved at all costs.

Some theoretical principles exist for arriving at the optimum conceptual schema for a database that uses relational principles: for example, one textbook gives 'four measures of quality' for relational schema design (semantics of the attributes; reducing the redundant values in tuples; and a couple of others) and 'six inference rules for functional dependencies' (reflexive rule, augmentation rule and four others).[2] A certain Henry James character was said to care as much for the rights of women as she did for the Panama Canal; most people who design databases for a living have a similar attitude to this type of abstract theory.

From Conceptual Schema to Internal Schema

A database conceptual schema describes information primarily in non-technical, logical terms — albeit subject to various constraints. The *database internal schema* contains numerous technical design decisions.

The database designer has to take account of factors such as response time (the time an operator sits waiting while the computer accesses the database to respond to the input), transaction throughput (e.g. how many typical transactions can be handled per hour) and space utilisation (amount of storage required on disk). For many systems these factors have to be juggled with others such as the need to meet certain security requirements or ensure that the system can recover from certain technical failures within a certain maximum downtime. Considerations of ease of future programming to access the information can also be relevant.

The designer has many options for organising the data on disk, such as the esoteric-sounding 'compressed heap', 'compressed B-tree' or 'compressed B-tree with unique keys'. His task is to make the supply choices (compressed heap, etc.) that best meet the demands (response time, etc.).

His options are enlarged by the possibility of deliberate tampering with the logical structure that has been handed down. For example, the logic of the conceptual schema may imply that the database of the LP Library should store one body of information about composers and another body about musical works, and another about performers. The technical designer may judge that accessing information about *operas* is inherently more demanding than accessing information about other works (operas have many performers, they can extend over several CDs, etc.). Moreover most composers of opera wrote only opera and most performers of opera perform only opera. Therefore, to improve system performance, information about opera works, composers and performers may be held all together in a certain part of the disk. This is a purely pragmatic decision, which deliberately distorts the pure logic of the information structures.

Of course it is tempting to hand over the conceptual schema to the expert and leave him to cogitate on his compressed heaps. But, as the account just given suggests, even the database internal schema is the product of tradeoffs between the various technical and non-technical factors. The design which produces the swiftest average response time may not be the most effective in recovering from hardware failure. Improvement in accessing opera information may be bought at the expense of chamber music.

An expert on a certain DBMS may well be the only person in the organisation capable of optimising a system's response time, but issues such as how important response time is to the system's success and whether access security is a consideration that should, under some circumstances, take precedence over response time are management, not technical, issues. It is not really sufficient for non-technical managers to define some simple priorities on these matters as a diktat to be implemented by the technologists. Sensible decisions can only be made if the available options and tradeoffs are articulated first by those with the technical knowledge. There should be interaction and feedback between those who express non-technical demand and those concerned with technology supply.

Variants of the Transitions between Models

Some enthusiasts of relational database principles believe that all detailed modelling should be based on stringent relational logic, from the beginning, so that there are no great changes in character as one form of model is translated into another. Since relational principles are based on the logic of mathematical set theory, and since the early stages of data modelling normally involve people in the organisation who aren't accustomed to thinking in rigorous abstractions, this approach may be rather impractical.

Other plausible approaches tackle the issues of transition between models by taking very many steps, each a little more rigorous and more detailed than the last. This avoids the awkwardness of converting one massive model, with its own conventions and purposes, into another massive model, with different conventions and purposes. One proprietary modelling approach, ERA, arrives at a technology-independent data model in three steps, each containing four sub-steps.[3] Another variant is the Barbara von Halle thirteen-step approach to a data model, followed by a thirteen-step approach to database design — all intended to flow as easily as possible from the beginning through to the internal schema of a relational database.[4]

The potential problem with most multi-step processes is that you may discover at step 11 that you didn't make the best possible choice back at step 2. Do you then proceed anyway, knowing that your model isn't completely accurate, or do you backtrack, perhaps to get entangled in one feedback loop after another?

These and other approaches avoid an abrupt break between one model and another, but this isn't indisputably a good thing. If interaction between supply and demand is an unavoidable fact of life, it seems advisable to document issues, options, tradeoffs, interactions and decisions about compromises explicitly, rather than allow them to creep up and pass by unnoticed. For this purpose, an approach that moves between a small number of radically different levels of modelling may be better than one where models grow organically and almost imperceptibly through many tiny stages.

Racing Ahead on Detail

The discussion so far has left out one complication. When modelling an insurance company or a library, it is not compulsory to expand detail gradually, moving methodically through a number of levels, at the same pace all along a broad front with no exposed flanks and vulnerable salients, as it were. A bold general may employ armoured penetrations and airborne assaults that a more methodical colleague may regard as reckless; of course, the risks taken by a bold general can also bring disaster. Similarly there can be both advantages and risks attached to the idea of racing ahead with the detailed modelling of certain crucial areas of an organisation, leaving the rest several levels behind.

In the early stages of discussing Ironbark Insurance's demands for a whole range of improved IT systems a number of themes become apparent. Ironbark managers want: to introduce a number of innovative types of insurance policies *(theme a)*; to introduce more made-to-measure combinations of different types of insurance together in one policy *(theme b)*; to encourage commercial customers (companies rather than private individuals) to do all their business with Ironbark, instead of spreading it among several insurance companies *(theme c)*; and to assign a special 'account manager' to each commercial customer, to coordinate that customer's business *(theme d)*. Clearly, these four themes are interconnected and they are certainly very relevant to Ironbark's new IT systems.

It sounds as if this complex of relations between customers, different types of policies and account managers could be a very strong influence on the *complexity* of future Ironbark systems. The themes may appear simple enough in summary (one customer may have one or more policies; one policy may cover one or more different types of risk, and so on), but there may be some very awkward complications when you look carefully. Suppose one commercial customer is a partly-owned subsidiary of another; do they count as two separate customers for the purposes of theme d? Does theme b imply that any conceivable permutation of risks is possible in made-to-measure combinations within one policy or only certain defined combinations? Do theme a's 'innovative' policies merely insure innovative risks at innovative prices or will their whole structure be innovative (e.g. premium and claims calculated by reference to the status of other policies held by the same customer)? And so on.

Probably, detailed data modelling in those particular areas affected by themes a, b, c and d will be far more crucial to Ironbark's decision-making than modelling in most other areas. Therefore, why not race ahead modelling the detail in the key areas well before the rest of the organisation? It could be quite appropriate for Ironbark to analyse this complex of customers and policies through to say, Level 4 of their five-level modelling system, even while most of the rest of the detail remained sketched out with the precision appropriate to Level 2.

Racing Ahead — Pros and Cons

Racing ahead can help give you an early view of the interactions between demand on supply; in other words, it can make you aware of the constraints and the possibilities, and thus encourage more realistic decisions. It focuses scarce resources on those parts of the model that really matter, accelerates decision-making on the issues that count and may reduce the burden of detailed data modelling in other areas — or at least render it non-critical. Moreover it can minimise some of the stultifying aspects about detailed modelling.

One danger of plodding methodically forward, gradually defining all the detail of the whole organisation in different areas in parallel, is that you may only realise after many laborious months that you have drifted into plans for over-elaborate, idealised systems, that cost far more than necessary. Another disadvantage is that the heavy burden of keeping such large bodies of detail in order and the inconvenience of making sweeping amendments may sap the will and creativity needed to find elegant, ingenious new ways of using IT.

Of course, the approach of pouring analytical resources into a few key areas at an early stage at the expense of the whole front has its dangers too. If you defy methodical progress and race ahead in the areas that seem most important, then you are backing your judgement of what is most relevant to possible strategic decisions. Your judgement may be premature or wrong: perhaps some other area that hasn't been given priority turns out to be just as important; or perhaps the area chosen for special attention turns out a poor choice for study in isolation because it is too vulnerable to influences and decisions arising much later in other areas.

Where to Stop with Detail

One problem associated with 'racing ahead' is 'knowing where to stop'. At first, it may seem self-evident that if the organisation is to be modelled, then, however the process is organised, the ultimate result must be a fully detailed model. In practice though, any model, no matter how detailed, has to simplify by smoothing out certain complications, and decisions on where to simplify can be very important.

A model of a 40-metre long galleon is not normally produced by scaling down every single feature of the real ship by a factor of, say, 80. Certain detail is not reduced, it is completely eliminated. For example, theoretically there ought to be a tiny bottle of rum in the captain's cabin of the model (a few millimetres high and about one millimetre in diameter), corresponding to a real bottle in the real ship. Probably the modeller of the ship simply won't reproduce the bottle at all.

A data model is like a model galleon, in the sense that certain potential complexities are deliberately omitted. At the LP Library the data model shows, among much else, that a Composer (e.g. Mozart) is one thing and a Work (e.g. *Symphony No 41*) is another; any given Work was written by a certain composer. This part of the data analysis seems straightforward. But there is one famous exception to the rule that one work is written by one composer: *Pictures at an Exhibition*, a work written for piano by Mussorgsky and orchestrated by another composer, Ravel.

This poses an unpleasant dilemma: either you just lose that nuance from your data model (like the rum bottle in the model galleon) or you include it and thereby make all the normal cases unnecessarily awkward (e.g. for every piece of music, you say, there are potentially two composers: one who wrote the notes and one who made the orchestration).

Before you decide on that point, you have to be aware of other awkward, but exceptional, cases; e.g. Beethoven's *Second Symphony* in an arrangement for piano; the two sonatas by Brahms for clarinet and piano, which are exactly the same music as the sonatas for viola and piano, apart from the change of instrument.

Is it really worth making certain parts of the data model significantly more complicated just to cater for a miscellany of very exceptional cases? In a computer system based on a comparatively coarse data model, people can usually find a way of handling the tricky cases: for example, treat 'Mussorgsky–Ravel' as a completely different composer from either Mussorgsky or Ravel. Very often this kind of kludge is preferable to going into all the possible complications.

On the other hand, sometimes an apparently arcane nuance really will matter. *Pictures at an Exhibition* is only one work, but a popular one. It would be rather mortifying if you found that within six months of the system going live, every terminal had a yellow label stuck to it saying: 'Reminder! Most customers want the orchestral version of *Pictures at an Exhibition*. The computer will only find it for you if you search under Mussorgsky–Ravel. But for the piano solo version, you must search under Mussorgsky.'

Judgement on Where to Stop

Judging where to stop detailed modelling can be very difficult. It may be feasible and desirable to take a broad brush approach in some areas, because any detail lost won't be very important and any kludges required won't be particularly messy. In other cases, some rarely occurring details that are very awkward to model may still need to be included, if the consequences of slurring over them are considered unacceptable.

The trouble is that you may have to do considerable work to reach the position to be able to make the judgement. For example, as well as assessing the complexity of increased detail in the non-technical data model, you may also have to gauge the effect on the technical design of the database.

Two constantly recurring themes are illustrated again. First, there can be no firm, star lardised rules for deciding which details should be edited out and which left in. Second, to decide the scope and complexity of the demands you decide to meet you need to take a view of their supply implications.

PRACTICAL ADVICE

➤ Bear in mind that data modelling is often a cumbersome, hazardous process. Use it as elegantly as possible, where you really have to.

➤ Recognise that translating a model at one level into a model at another often requires considerable judgement rather than just the application of a standard method.

➤ Make the nature of the translation between the two levels, and the judgements employed, explicit. Be constantly on guard against unwarranted unassumptions that creep in when moving between any two levels.

➤ Be alert to the fact that there will very likely be some coarsening of the data analysis in the transition from E–R Model to Conceptual Schema. Make sure it has no important implications; or if it does, don't allow it just to happen; ensure that a decision is consciously taken and its consequences are well understood.

➤ Pay particular attention to the transition between the demand-oriented conceptual schema level and the supply-oriented internal schema level. Have some feeling for the kind of design criteria that arise. Respect the expertise of the database specialist, but make it clear that some design criteria raise management rather than purely technical issues. Don't hand down a diktat; set up opportunities for interaction and feedback.

➤ Be aware of approaches that involve a large number of levels with small gradations between them.

➤ Don't model everything with equal detail, at least not at the same time. Forge ahead examining the detailed data structures of areas that can have a significant impact on the shape of IT strategy as a whole.

➤ Confront the difficult judgements that are unavoidable in resolving what is important enough to warrant intricate modelling and what is not.

➤ Apply the above principles to all types of modelling, not just data modelling.

24.   Plans and Priorities

ISSUES

Compare a data model or business model with a schedule of the data centre's personnel requirements over the next five years or with the critical path analysis that shows the main activities within a certain large project that is structured in three phases. There are many interesting issues associated with the models, but in one important respect the other two documents are more complex.

A model is normally like a photograph; it describes one state of affairs at one time. The state of affairs may be very complex, but at least there is just one coherent thing to describe. Schedules of personnel levels or project activities are more like a motion film because they show numerous states of affairs — how the data centre's personnel profile will look next month, how it will be slightly different the month after, and the month after that and so on. This characteristic raises a number of issues.

For example, the extra time dimension makes it more complicated to ensure that the different elements all fit together properly. Then there is the question whether the degree of detail in plans should vary according to its distance into the future. The problem of ongoing plan updates is also a tricky one, because it raises the issue of assessing the relative importance of new ideas that come up — in other words, setting priorities. Priorities themselves hold some hidden snares. They are all the more awkward when the priority attached to a project appraised this month may be affected by the priority that will be attached to a project whose feasibility study is due for completion next month.

Models describing actual or desirable states of affairs eventually have to be brought together in one coherent body of plans together with schedules of activities intended to achieve objectives the models describe. This briefing explores the issues that arise.

ANALYSIS

First, some clear distinctions are needed between several different types of planning material. With that foundation, you can begin to unravel the complexities of multi-tier approaches, that distinguish, for example, the long-term from the medium-term plans. This kind of planning system is incomplete unless it has a mechanism for updating the plans with details of newly approved projects in a continuous way; consideration of that problem leads to a discussion of the issues around the concept of priorities.

Blueprints, Recipes, Plans and Reasoning

People sometimes use the terms 'information plan' or 'information planning', perhaps with 'strategic' in the phrase too. The precise titles documents have is rather a trivial issue. The important thing is to maintain distinctions between the different genres of planning material.

In *The Blind Watchmaker* the ethologist Richard Dawkins describes the difference between a blueprint and a recipe very clearly.[1] Although his real concern is theories of embryology, he contrasts the simple examples of a *blueprint* of a building with a *recipe* for cooking a cake. The blueprint is in essence a scaled-down model of a building, whereas a recipe is a set of instructions which, if obeyed in the right order, will result in the cake. The difference is shown if you ask which part of a document (blueprint or recipe) corresponds to a certain part of the real physical object. A certain floor of a building is described by a certain part of the blueprint, but an individual slice or crumb of a cake can't be matched against any specific word or sentence in the set of instructions in a recipe.

A comprehensive recipe contains all the instructions necessary to make a cake; a comprehensive blueprint describes a building well enough to enable someone to do the work of planning how it can be built. If one document mixes up recipe-style instructions with blueprint-style descriptions it will probably generate confusion. Similarly, when you document decisions, objectives, activity schedules and similar planning material for the application of IT, enforcing a clear separation between blueprint-like information (e.g. descriptions of the way certain systems will work) and recipe-like information (e.g. activities to be carried out in order to develop the systems) helps maintain clarity.

The word 'plan' in English can be used in various contexts; for example, a plan of a mansion (plan in the sense of blueprint) or a plan for supplying the Stalingrad garrison by air (plan in the sense of recipe). Therefore 'plan' is a handy broad term to cover both blueprint and recipe documents, while 'planning' is a good term to cover the main subject of this briefing — the process of bringing blueprints and recipes together into one coherent structure.

Generally, a plan document describes *one objective* (blueprint) or *one way* of doing things (recipe) rather than exposing and reasoning about *several possible* objectives or ways of doing things. It describes the way a mansion is intended to be; it doesn't justify the choice of imported brick rather than the available options of local stone. It lists the detailed schedules for aircraft missions; it doesn't weigh up the reasons that the garrison have decided to stay, rather than take the option of trying to fight their way out.

A document which mixes up detailed description of one objective or course of action with explanation and justification and discussion of options can be very confusing; but that is no excuse for not seriously discussing and documenting possible options *in some other document*.

Thus, at any given time, an organisation may well possess a set of documents, defining its IT strategy — blueprint-style plans, recipe-style plans and the reasoning behind those plans. But this is to over-simplify: the whole set of material will be affected by the passage of time and naturally the plans and intentions for the near future will be more detailed than those for the distant future. Many complications can arise.

Issues with Multi-tier Planning Systems

The managers at Corkwood Bank are attracted by the idea of introducing an IT planning system based on three tiers: a five-year long-range strategy, a three-year medium-term plan and a one-year short-term schedule. This proposal raises far more difficulties than at first appears.

First of all, the distinctions between the two genres of plan — blueprint and recipe — need to be maintained, if the planning is to be clear. There can be blueprint-style data models, for example, with different degrees of detail, according to how close they are to being implemented in systems; and recipe-style development schedules, where the closer activities are planned in more detail than the more distant. Also the distinction between the plan documents and the reasoning explaining the content of the plans needs to be maintained, if the plans are to carry conviction. Keeping all these distinctions clear in a multi-tier planning structure can be quite complex.

Against this background, several fundamental questions need to be raised. For example, is it an inherent part of the planning system that the tiers cover the periods five-year, three-year and one-year? Or do they just happen to be that way at the moment? Could they perhaps be six-three-two at some time in the future? Probably the main advantage of the *fixed term* approach is that the fixed periods for IT planning can be integrated with the standard periods used in planning other aspects of the business. On the other hand, a *variable term* approach allows the periods covered by the three tiers to vary to suit the content of the plans themselves. After all, if a building takes six years to build, it seems odd to make plans for the first five years and not the sixth, on the grounds that your company's standard planning period is only five years.

Next, how are the plans contained in the five-three-one compartments revised? Is this done on a *rolling* or a *replacement* basis? With a rolling approach, the five- and three-year plans are modified every year: the content of the four (or two) years remaining in the plan is revised, and one more year is added at the end. With a replacement approach each tier's plan runs its course (at least in theory) and is then replaced by a new, full-length plan.

In practice, all these issues intersect. For example, if plans are updated on a rolling basis, but the terms of each tier are also variable, then the range of possible modifications that can occur each year becomes rather complex. Therefore 'fixed term' tends naturally to be associated with 'rolling revision'. Again, if you like the idea of introducing radical new multi-year replacement sets of plans from time to time, then it may seem an unwelcome constraint to insist that each new replacement plan must have a term of exactly five years or three years or whatever the standard is. In other words, variable term belongs naturally with replacement.

Planning systems with fixed term tiers (five-three-one, say) seem to have one obvious drawback. If you agree with the general principle that an organisation's planning horizon should be determined according to the circumstances, it follows that the horizons in the planning system should vary from time to time, or at least be variable in principle. Moreover, the rolling approach that goes naturally with fixed term means that you never extend your horizon by more than one year at a time; this makes it awkward to tackle some of the essential tradeoffs between commitment and flexibility.

A variable term, replacement approach therefore seems to offer a better framework for weighing up horizon tradeoffs. However, generalising about multi-tier approaches is dangerous, because a lot still depends on what kind of matters are planned with what degree of detail in which tier. At any rate, the important thing is to at least be aware of the issues in multi-tier planning and work out a coherent position on them.

Priority-setting: Need and Confusions

Most large organisations need to maintain some form of multi-tier plan, although its logic and degree of detail vary considerably. This means that they have to contend with another troublesome problem.

New ideas for systems or extensions to systems or other types of IT investment will crop up from day to day and be evaluated. Presumably if a feasibility study shows that some new idea has exceptionally high merit, then the existing plans have to be updated to accommodate it. But it may not be easy to assess whether any given idea has *sufficient* merit to justify this — especially since an adequate assessment of merit may involve comparison with the results of other feasibility studies about projects that are rivals for investment capital. In other words, some system of priority-setting for possible projects is needed; otherwise there is no way of deciding which should be incorporated into the overall plan.

If some parts of Corkwood Bank's planning documentation simply say 'here are the priorities we have set', without saying or even implying what that means, that can lead to what might be called the *First Confusion*.

The word 'priority' has a surprising number of different implications. Suppose somebody says: 'In our system planning this year, our priorities are: 1. new cash dispenser system, 2. expert system for assessing new loans, 3. new treasury management system'. This could mean: 'Here is our order of preference for the things we'd like to do — other things being equal, if we could choose only one.' But it might mean something very different: 'We've already decided to do all three; we've ranked them here in order of the expected impact on our organisation.' Or, to take a third possible meaning: 'We shall definitely be doing all three, but we've listed them in order of the sequence of their implementation.' Or, as a fourth option, different again: 'We'll devote most of our budget to item 1, rather less to item 2 and even less to item 3.' Or a fifth interpretation might be: 'The order of the list isn't very important. What's crucial is that we've excluded the proposals for office automation and new branch accounting systems.'

If you never quite decide just what the list of priorities signifies, you may end up with hazy plans whose parts don't fit together convincingly. So the first test of a good list of priorities is that the meaning of 'priority' should be crystal clear.

The *Second Confusion* arises when the list of items prioritised doesn't contain similar items. Suppose the agreed list of priorities is: '1. customer service, 2. efficient database queries, 3. return on capital'. They are different kind of things that overlap each other very awkwardly. Isn't the end purpose of improving customer service to improve the return on shareholders' capital? If so, what does it mean for customer service to stand higher up on the priority list than return on capital? With this kind of uncertainty, nobody can be quite sure what conclusions to draw from the priority list.

The *Third Confusion* can arise if there is more than one list and the relation between the lists is not carefully defined. For example, suppose one list of priorities is: '1. new cash dispenser system, 2. expert system for assessing new loans, 3. new treasury management system', while the other is: '1. customer service, 2. efficient database queries, 3. return on capital'. Perhaps this should be interpreted as: 'Customer service is our top priority in general terms; as a natural consequence of that, a new cash dispenser system must be our top priority in system development.' But it could mean, instead or as well: 'When making any awkward decision about the details within any new system — whether it be system 1 or system 99 on the priority list — remember to choose the option that gives most weight to customer service.' Or a third possibility: perhaps these are two independent lists that still have to be merged by brainstorming before any credible policy can be defined; perhaps the rankings on the two lists are incompatible and some hard decisions are called for.

Plainly, if there are several priority lists, everyone involved needs to understand how they relate to each other; otherwise some very confused discussion can result.

BSP Priority Planning

IBM's BSP methodology includes a method of priority-setting, but it applies after the whole body of projects to be undertaken has already been decided. Sequence, not choice of projects, is the issue addressed by this method.[2]

Each project is assessed on sixteen criteria, which are arranged in four groups. The *Potential benefits* group is made up of the Tangibles, Intangibles and Return on Investment criteria. The *Organisational impact* group is made up of Number of organisations and people affected, Qualitative effect and Effect on accomplishing objectives. The Likely success group is made up of Degree of business acceptance, Probability of complete implementation, Prerequisites, Length of implementation, Risk and Resources available. The *Demand* group is made up of Value of existing systems, Relationship with existing systems, Political overtones and Need. The method is to award each project a score on each of the sixteen criteria and arrive at a total score per project to determine priority and therefore sequence.

Since this method only deals with sequence, rather than the more fundamental matter of choice or rejection, it is all the more interesting that it is so complex. You could argue that the more complex the criteria are, the more advisable it is to apply judgement rather than a predefined method. The contrary argument is that a very intricate but definable problem is best approached by defining procedures, assigning numbers and abiding by the results of formulae.

The BSP priority-setting method can be applied well or badly. Its starting point is that all projects will be implemented and the only issue is sequence. Somebody who forgot this and gave a project a low score on the grounds that it might never be needed would be falling into the First Confusion enunciated above.

Some of the criteria seem to be separate but overlapping. Rating a project high for Return on Investment and low for Effect on accomplishing objectives, or very high for Intangibles and very low for Qualitative effect, seems so odd that it suggests a case of the Second Confusion.

Again, if each of the sixteen criteria is regarded as a variable independent of the others, there are in effect sixteen parallel lists, each implying a different priority order for the body of projects. Some understanding of the way the sixteen criteria relate to each other is called for. Simply adding together sixteen scores-out-of-ten is probably an example of the Third Confusion.

Continuous Studies and Priorities

Corkwood Bank has a problem common to many large organisations. Feasibility studies for new projects or other types of investment are constantly going on. After each, a decision has to be made whether to undertake the project or not. The decisions are unavoidably interrelated; since the organisation's resources are finite, the more money is spent on one project, the less is available for others. Plainly this is a greater problem than merely deciding the sequence within a plan of projects that have already been approved.

If it were possible to synchronise decision-making (for example, make all the decisions together in one process in the first week of January every year), the problem would be more manageable. But that synchronisation is not practical for many reasons. Thus, for example, in July, decisions have already been taken on some of the feasibility studies already completed this year, but on others the decision is pending; some other studies are currently in progress and some other studies are due to start next month or the month after. How can the organisation make reasonably timely decisions and also ensure that over any given period it achieves the best mix of choices?

In Corkwood's planning system every candidate new project is assigned to a certain category; e.g. compulsory projects (amending a system to handle new tax regulations) are distinguished from voluntary (generating some new reports from the database); new systems are distinguished from system enhancements; activities of a mainly technical nature (e.g. convert a system to run under a new operating system) are distinguished from those of a business character (e.g. automate a new area of the company); new technology is distinguished from familiar technology. For each candidate project, a financial payback value is also calculated.

At any given time, there is a queue of candidate projects arranged in priority order. In this case, priority order doesn't simply mean sequence of implementation. When a new candidate project joins the queue its category is one big factor. For example, if something is truly compulsory, it must go near the front of the queue. Also a certain quota of capacity is set aside each year for new technology. Then there are guidelines to ensure that not too much and not too little is spent on maintaining and enhancing existing systems. Therefore one big factor affecting a new project's place in the queue is the competition from other projects in the same category. Of course, financial payback value is also a relevant factor in determining a project's place in the queue.

The exact procedures used to place a new project in the queue aren't relevant here. The important thing is that this priority list is a queue of possible projects waiting for resources — but the kind of queue where newcomers can push in if they deserve to. Although any given project may take some time to reach the head of the queue, the relatively competitive projects soon become apparent. Some weak projects will never get to the head of the queue, being elbowed aside by new joiners, and once this becomes obvious, they are formally dropped. Thus this use of priorities is in effect a decision-making selection mechanism as much as a scheduling one.

PRACTICAL ADVICE

➤ Be crystal-clear whether any document is a blueprint or a recipe in character (use 'plan' when a generic term is required).

➤ Support the content of blueprint and recipe plans by explanatory reasoning and evaluation of options in separate documents.

➤ Be very cautious about the logic of multi-tier planning approaches that assign different degrees of definition to plans in different years in the future; it can be very tricky to work out what they actually entail.

➤ Distinguish fixed term from variable term planning systems.

➤ Distinguish planning systems that work mainly by updating plans on a rolling basis from those that update by replacement of complete plans.

➤ Don't talk about priorities without making it clear what you mean by the concept.

➤ Ensure that any lists of priorities contain items similar in kind that don't overlap.

➤ If you have several priority lists, clarify their terms of reference so that the relation between them is sensible and well understood.

➤ Consider the idea of developing a planning method that automatically assigns competing projects a place in a priority queue according to predefined factors.

25. Levels, Ratchets and Feedback

ISSUES

Whatever the problem-area — transport policy, military strategy or a morning's shopping — it is generally a sensible thing to take certain fundamental decisions before coming on to other matters that are more detailed — in other words, to structure decisions into levels. Much IT planning and decision-making falls naturally into a structure of several levels, too. But as the range of decisions, models and plans extends across several levels, the logic of the level-based structure itself begins to raise issues.

This area can turn out far more bewildering than may at first seem likely. For example, a 'top-down' approach seems a naturally attractive concept, but then so does 'feedback'. Should you have feedback in a top-down approach? Is 'stepwise refinement' the same thing as 'top-down' or is it a different concept altogether? And where do 'bottom-up' and 'middle-out' fit in? And so on. Very often the causes of bad decisions or chaotic changes of decisions can be traced back to confusions such as these about the essential logic of multi-level decision-making.

This briefing is concerned with the logic of any level-based structure for IT decision-making, rather than with issues applying mainly to particular levels and models. It shows how some of the questions arising here are both complex and important.

ANALYSIS

People at Candlebark Insurance are considering a certain standard approach to IT strategy, that proceeds through eight levels. The underlying logic of the approach is simple: the decisions and plans made at each level expand those at previous levels, translating them into more detailed, practical or technical terms. The logic of the level-based structure seems to be straightforward. You work on Level 1 until you are satisfied with it; then you move on to Level 2; when that is complete you move on to Level 3. . . and so on.

The best introduction to the real issues of level-based logic is an analysis of the typical inadequacies of decisions resulting when this *straightforward model* is followed blindly.

Premature Decisions and Unsupported Decisions

The first snag with the straightforward model that the sharp people at Candlebark notice is that you may not be in any position to take the decisions that are called for at a certain level — at least not in any definitive way that can form a reliable basis for later levels.

Level 1, for example, is about defining the organisation's strategic aims. Suppose that at a certain point in the discussions the chairman of Candlebark identifies the following three key objectives: to cut administration costs as a percentage of premiums by 10% within five years; to ensure that most growth in premium income comes from developing new markets; and to become more customer-oriented generally. But the managing director of Candlebark wishes to argue for a different set of objectives: to cut administration costs by 15%; to concentrate on new types of insurance policy rather than new markets; to reduce the ratio of claims to premiums from 88% to 86%; and to become more customer-oriented generally. Suppose somebody else proposes a third set of aims with other emphases and somebody else a fourth. How can anybody decide between these different options? How can any informed debate take place?

To demonstrate that one particular bundle of aims is a better basis for strategy than another bundle may be impossible, except by using data about the feasibility and implications of the different options. But such detailed data can't be collected at Level 1; it is the kind of material that only arises at later levels. But, according to the straightforward model, you can't progress to the lower levels before you have made the decisions required at Level 1.

In other words, a straightforward level-based structure may lead you into premature and therefore arbitrary decisions. If that happens, then there is no particular reason to believe that the more detailed decision-making about the use of IT, that comes later, will be the best available for the organisation.

Suppose now that everyone does agree on clear policies at Level 1. At Level 2 the intention is to expand these relatively broad aims into more specific measures. The aim of being more customer-oriented has to be expanded into specific measures. But which measures in particular?

There may be a lavish smorgasbord of ways of making Candlebark more customer-oriented. Surely the Level 1 policy of becoming more customer-oriented can't literally mean: 'Do every conceivable thing that might in any way make us more customer-oriented'. Surely you must serve yourself with some of the smorgasbord items and leave some of the others untouched. But how do you decide which?

One facet of the problem is that up at Level 2 the information on which

Candlebark Insurance
A Smorgasbord of Ideas for Becoming More Customer-oriented

Design policy documents that are much easier for the ordinary person to understand — in content and layout

Keep branches open on Saturdays

Give a discount to loyal customers

Provide a new service (perhaps based on expert system technology) to help a customer decide more easily the insurance cover he really needs

Offer easier payment methods, through improved links with customers' banks

Speed up payments on small claims by an average of two days

Install an ombudsman to resolve disputes with policy-holders

Introduce more streamlined, less forbidding procedures for reporting claims (perhaps allowing access through videotex)

Open more branches, especially in department stores

Redesign the layout of customer reception areas in branch offices

Reduce the amount of data that holders of complicated policies (such as employer's liability) have to provide the insurance company

Store policy conditions in a textual database so that staff can answer customers' questions more readily

Set up a telephone advice service accessible to customers at evenings and weekends

Make details of any policy accessible from any branch in the country

Reduce the role of the agents

Build electronic mail links, including voice annotations, with the insurance departments of commercial clients

Start a Global Clients Service

---

to base an informed choice may not be available (the problem of premature decisions already noted). The other difficulty is that Level 2 is supposed to be guided by the decisions made at Level 1; it is meant to generate decisions that follow on naturally from the previous level. But the pronouncements at Level 1 may well contain no guidance at all to help choose certain ways of becoming more customer-oriented and reject others.

It seems natural to go back to Level 1 to ask for more clarity and precision in its decisions. This can be a delicate matter; it may involve asking just how much effort should be put into measures to achieve the aim of being more customer-oriented, say, as opposed to other aims such as cutting administration costs.

But the straightforward model rules out any backtracking of this kind. It may provide the illusion that the decisions at each level follow plausibly on from decisions at previous levels, while in fact it forces you to make decisions that are not really supported in that way at all.

Chaotic Decisions and Drifting Decisions

Another drawback with simple level-based decision-making may reveal itself after Candlebark has struggled through quite a number of levels.

At Level 6, say, it becomes apparent, for the first time, that the features demanded by the Global Clients system (conceived in Level 2 and expanded in levels thereafter) pose the most extraordinary technology demands. If the technical people actually manage to set up a distributed database to meet those demands, visitors will come from far and wide to see their breakthrough achievement. But nobody has ever taken a conscious decision to accept all the risks of attempting technology breakthroughs. Back at Levels 2 and 3 people simply described the facilities they demanded in non-technical terms, without making judgements on how simple or how arduous the supply might be.

To make things worse, it turns out that over at the rival Stringybark Assurance, where the idea of a global clients department also came up, they steered clear of the ambitious aims that Candlebark set in Levels 2 and 3. Stringybark is now developing a more modest Global Clients system, that meets 90% of Candlebark's demands with one quarter the time and cost.

Suppose somebody at Candlebark down in Level 6 wants to speak up in favour of this kind of modesty: to argue that the demands expressed are just too ambitious and to suggest that a better buy might be a system that met only 90% of the demands. That will mean persuading the people who did the Level 5 work to change their plans, too; but then the Level 5 plans will be inconsistent with Level 4's, so they have to be changed too; and so on all the way back.

The straightforward model doesn't allow such backtracking in theory, though it may have to happen in practice, in order to avoid absolutely preposterous results. In effect, a choice may arise: you can take a decision that may have a chaotic effect on the whole set of decisions arranged in levels, or you can simply accept the uncomfortable fact that the strategy has developed into a form far from the optimum, but changing it is just too painful.

Suppose now that back at Level 1 Candlebark specified three main aims — cutting administration costs, achieving growth in premium income through developing new markets and becoming more customer-oriented. In theory, the decisions at each of the subsequent levels should elaborate these aims, spell out their practical implications and so on.

Suppose that the detailed plans eventually produced at Level 6 manifestly are motivated by *two* of these three aims, but they contain nothing of much relevance to the aim of developing new markets. Moreover, some parts of these Level 6 plans are clearly directed towards a different, desirable aim, reducing the ratio of claims to premiums — even though, as the minutes of Level 1 show, this was considered as a formal aim and judged to be less important than the three aims adopted. Plainly, somewhere in the passage through the levels one aim has dropped out and another has crept in. In other words, *drift* has caused a decision that was taken at a higher level to be altered.

To say that drift occurred during a level-based planning process is not necessarily to make a criticism. The things that really count are surely the quality of the resulting decisions and the economy of effort with which they were reached. But in practice, drift that develops imperceptibly or drift that is virtually forced because decisions at earlier levels were unrealistic, are rarely associated with good decisions, economically reached.

On the other hand, a straightforward level-based approach that strictly censors ideas that might possibly cause drift has its drawbacks too. It may well fail to do justice to essential issues and stimulating possibilities.

The Essential Dilemma and Essential Criteria

Four genres of potential difficulties with level-based structures have been identified: premature, unsupported, chaotic and drifting decisions. They undermine the assumption of the straightforward model that each level of work can be completed before the next level starts, and once completed, will not normally be amended later.

Such difficulties are not unique to IT; they are characteristic of level-based approaches in decisions about any technology or indeed about any field at all. However, in most other applications of a technology, decision-making, use of the technology and enjoyment of the benefit all belong within one unit of an organisation. With IT investments there is often an awkward split. Much of the decision-making and most of the technical application of technology is in the hands of IT specialists; but the IT specialists can't be aware of all the relevant non-technical aspects, and the return on the investment is dependent on the departments of the organisation whose work is affected by the systems. Hence the attraction and also the danger of level-based logic.

There seems to be a dilemma. On the one hand, the issues are often so complex and heterogeneous and affect such different people that there is no alternative to organising IT decision-making in levels. On the other hand, the straightforward approach seems to be vulnerable to many problems likely to produce inadequate decisions. One natural approach seems to be to allow some degree of backtracking to revise decisions made at earlier levels when necessary. But once this point is conceded, how can anarchy be avoided?

Plainly it is possible to divide up a certain body of subject matter over levels in various ways. One way can be judged superior to another, if it seems less vulnerable to the four types of problem described above: for example, if it calls for relatively few decisions to be taken that are likely to be called into question by decisions arising at a lower level. Also, the role of backtracking can be defined in a level-based structure in various ways. One structure can be judged superior to another, for a given case, if it allows and encourages just enough backtracking to do justice to the complexities of the subject-matter; that is, it is neither too rigid nor too casual.

The problem then is to find the level-based structure that best meets these essential criteria for the particular case. There are no simple rules to follow; judgement is required. The purpose of the material in the rest of the briefing is to outline some general concepts and distinctions that can help in considering possible approaches, and in fighting some of the confusions that can arise.

Tests of Serious Solutions

Some proponents of level-based approaches respond to the difficulties that have been outlined with a shrug of the shoulders: 'But our methodology *is* more subtle than the straightforward model. If you need to, you are allowed to go back from one level to revise the product of the previous level.' Some even suggest that you can go back from any level to any other at any time and they provide diagrams with suitable arrows to prove it. This is often no more than a false solution, that entirely fails to address the real issues of level-based logic.

There are several tests of the seriousness of claims about the possibilities for backtracking. First of all, the time actually budgeted for going through the levels and completing the whole exercise needs examination. If the total budget for some planning exercise is the sum of the budgets required to carry out each level just once, then this really means: 'You are allowed to go back from one level to revise the product of the previous level, *but only if you've done the work so badly that you absolutely have to put it right, despite going over budget.*' This is no solution at all to the problems traced out so far; it is merely a hope that they won't occur.

There may be a substantial budget allocation for non-sequential activities, but now the question arises: Is it *generalised* (simply, say, a 20% safety margin to be used as needed) or *directed* (for example, a budget for carrying out Levels 3 and 4 twice because, it is thought, that is the area where the most crucial interactions between decisions will occur)? Clearly, the latter approach is the more encouraging, because it shows that the potential problems have been recognised and considered.

Thirdly, if plans have been made for carrying out specifically named levels more than once, then the question arises: Is this reflected in the proposed method of carrying them through? For example, if you fully intend to carry out Level 3 twice, it may well be sensible to produce a rather provisional outline the first time. It could be wasteful to perfect every detail, knowing that it will probably have to be revised anyway.

Tests like these help show how seriously to take the arrows on the diagrams of any proposed level-based structure.

Elaboration, Feedback, Ratchets

There are many pitfalls in designing a level-based approach that does make a serious attempt to handle the specific features of any particular case. A useful start is to get a clear view of certain basic concepts.

The underlying mode of progress through any level-based structure is *elaboration*. The work at each level elaborates on the products of previous levels, by making things more detailed or more concrete and practical.

Sometimes, through the exploration of detail, it proves necessary to backtrack and modify the products of previous levels. This is *feedback*.

Thus, a good level-based structure should guide effective elaboration at successive levels, in a way that does justice to the issues and is economical of the effort of decision-makers. It also has to allow the possibility of feedback, since it is vain to assume that all decisions at each level will always survive the detailed workings at other levels. But it should not abdicate control by simply allowing any feedback at all to occur at any time between any levels.

A ratchet is a bar which allows a wheel to turn only in one direction, because it engages teeth on the rim of the wheel to stop it ever turning back. In the logic of decision-making, a *ratchet* can be regarded as an agreement that what has been decided at a certain point will stand; it may be elaborated at later levels but not changed by feedback. An economical planning process has to use ratchets to some degree; otherwise it cannot be controlled.

There is a tradeoff between discipline and freedom. If too much *feedback* between levels of a structure is allowed, the result may be anarchy, or at least perfectionism in the bad sense. But if everyone of many levels of decision-making is closed by a *ratchet*, with no opportunity for feedback, then relatively slight inaccuracies may be magnified during the progress from level to level and decision-making may drift out of touch with reality.

These three concepts of elaboration, feedback and ratchet are useful tools to expose the essential logic of a level-based approach to any particular case, and to show where it stands on the tradeoff between discipline and freedom.

Varieties of 'Top-Down' and 'Stepwise Refinement'

The appropriate balance between discipline and freedom varies from case to case, but it is useful to be aware of several different classic approaches to level-based structure. They are best illustrated by unpacking 'top-down' — a term used with so many contradictory meanings that it is best avoided altogether. Here is a comparison of three different approaches to an artificial planning problem.

If you were planning to emigrate, you might decide that the right approach to this large project was to deal with the following three topics in order: first, find a job in the other country; second, buy a house there; third, arrange the children's education. With this approach, you would begin working on the first topic; only after finishing it, would you begin working on the second; only after that was complete, would you begin on the third. The rationale might be that it was simply pointless to plan the house until the job was resolved or the education until the house was resolved. This approach can be called *logical priority*: there is no elaboration of one topic by another (house-hunting adds no detail to job plans), though work within each separate topic can be divided up into levels of elaboration. A ratchet closes after the decisions are taken on each topic (in the example difficulties with education would not be expected to cause feedback to alter job plans).

But you might approach emigration planning quite differently. You might open a file on each of the three topics from the start and pursue them all simultaneously. With this approach, rough plans on all the main topics would probably exist at a fairly early stage, although none would be in a finished state; and right up to near the end there would always be the possibility that work on one topic might lead to minor changes on some other topic. In this approach, there are no ratchets at all and many elaboration and feedback possibilities exist.

A third classic approach falls between these extremes. You might divide the planning exercise into a number of clearly demarcated levels, each in greater detail than the last, with the intention that, once any given level was completed, its product would not be changed (thus introducing ratchets — as with the first approach and not the second). But the content of each step might be heterogeneous (job, house and education); the levels might differ in their degree of detail because each elaborated the product of the previous level. Thus, at the end of level 1, you would have summary plans on the job, house and education topics; in level 2, you would add detail on all these fronts, without actually changing anything that was decided in level 1; and so on.

The second and third of these classic approaches can each be called by the term 'stepwise refinement', which is generally taken to mean a gradual process of refining the understanding of different parts of a problem and adding more and more detail to different parts of a solution. But there is a dangerous ambiguity in the word 'step'; the concept of the ratchet makes it easy to expose the important distinction. For the second approach, which is ratchet-less, the term *footstepwise refinement* can be used, because it contains many small steps towards a goal, rather like the footsteps of a hunter stalking a prey. The third approach, with its ratchets, can be called *staircasewise refinement* because each 'step' in this process is clearly and formally demarcated as a stage along the way, like the steps of a grand staircase. This ambiguity of 'step' makes it advisable to avoid the term 'stepwise refinement'.

Bottom-up, Middle-out, etc.

Bottom-up is another good term to avoid, because it is often used in a rather paltry sense, to denote any approach that isn't 'top-down' — which is itself an unclear term. When bottom-up does have a more precise sense, it usually means the same as *middle-out*, which is a preferable term. *Inside-out* is yet another term for the same thing.

With a *middle-out* approach you might tackle the emigration problem by first deciding in which district of which town to live. With that decision firmed up, you would begin to consider apparently more fundamental matters such as finding a job in the new country and others such as arranging children's education. Here the decision in the middle would be elaborated fully before a ratchet turned to protect it from feedback. At least that would be the intention. One trouble with a middle-out approach is that it may not be robust. For example, finding a job sufficiently near your chosen district might be impossible and you might have to go back and un-ratchet your original decisions. This unwanted feedback might mean that the initial middle-out planning was wasted.

Middle-out is a preferable name to bottom-up for this approach, because in practice, the details you start with are always 'in the middle'. It is never really sensible to start at the bottom with the most low-level possible details: ordering the taxi for the airport, arranging milk deliveries, deciding which weekly magazine to take for TV programmes, say — before you even know whether emigration will be possible.

Implications and Practical Examples

Here is a summary of the reasoning of this briefing so far. A level-based approach to a complex IT decision-making process is a practical necessity. But there are certain pitfalls: decisions can be premature, unsupported, chaotic or drifting. Therefore in each case, the challenge is to design the level-based approach that best does justice to the issues and avoids the typical difficulties. How is that to be done? A useful start is to clarify the basic concepts of elaboration, feedback and ratchet and then to recognise how they open up many varieties of level-based structures. There are at least four classic varieties: logical priority, footstepwise refinement, staircasewise refinement and middle-out. Of course combinations are possible too. Armed with that awareness you are well placed to find the right structure for your own particular case. Here are example cases, applying each of the four classic forms of level-based logic.

Smoothbark Assurance provides an example of the principle of *logical priority*. The company's investments in new computer systems over the previous three years have been so disastrous that the whole business is in jeopardy. Its managers begin by making a one-year *Rescue Plan*; among the key measures here are savage pruning of the scope of the systems and recruitment of some new IT specialists. Once this plan has been agreed and work has begun to carry it out, they move on to planning a two-year, so-called *Competence Phase*; this contains measures to rectify a number of shortcomings, which, they feel, should not be found in any competently run company. Once the main details of the Competence Phase have been agreed, they go on to plan a subsequent two-year *Innovation Strategy*, in which at last there is scope for innovative measures rather than salvaging disasters or eliminating obvious inefficiencies. In the logic of this case, Smoothbark closes the decisions of the Rescue Plan with a ratchet before moving on to anything else, because in the desperate circumstances that has priority. Similarly, the Competence Phase is closed with a ratchet because the minimum standards it aims for have to be achieved before Smoothbark can plausibly think of becoming an innovating company.

Ironbark Insurance takes an approach that owes most to the logic of *footstepwise refinement*. Early on, its managers identify some broad aims — introduce new types of insurance policies, improve coordination of the policies of commercial customers, and so on. Rather than develop these themes level by level on a broad front, they concentrate on exploring the detail of certain key organisational and technical aspects of certain aims that seem to be particularly crucial. At any given time in their planning process, the plans are rather like an unfinished oil painting; the whole design is roughly sketched out, with some parts elaborated much more than others. There is always the possibility of feedback from the work on one part of the design affecting another.

For its new Global Clients service, Candlebark uses *staircasewise refinement*. First, a five-page document outlines the features of the new service, the organisation of the new department and the scope of the IT systems envisaged; a ratchet closes. A level lower comes a document of twenty-five pages with correspondingly more detail and quantitative data on these same things; another ratchet closes. A level lower, service features, department organisation and IT systems are described and quantified in a document of a hundred pages; and so on.

Stringybark Assurance follows a *middle-out* approach. Very early on, a detailed data model is built of that very taxing business area that is concerned with combined insurance policies — bundling together fire and burglary and liability and other types of insurance, all in one policy with one premium. Having got that data model clear the planners then develop their ideas further in several directions simultaneously — 'upwards' to the more abstract definition of the place of combined insurance policies in the company's business strategy, 'sideways' to the modelling of other parts of the business in similar detail, and 'downwards' to the particular technical problems posed by these combined policies.

As suggested above, there can be no plausible example of a genuine *bottom-up* approach. An insurance company would produce some bizarre IT applications if its people started by writing the system error messages manual or designing the slides for the data preparation staff training course or negotiating quantity discounts for diskettes, before they took any other decisions whatsoever.

Deciding or Documenting?

Despite the analysis in this briefing, some may still feel that a straightforward, ratchet-rich approach, based on the idea of demand preceding supply, is a very natural approach to IT strategy definition. But there is another distinction still.

The term 'strategy definition' is actually ambiguous. Does it mean the work of *arriving at* your strategy or does it mean the *documenting and publicising* of the strategy that you have arrived at? There is not much wrong with documenting your strategy in a way which makes it look as if it was arrived at in a neat, logical demand-driven way. That is usually the best method of helping people get a clear view of what the logic of the strategy is. But that doesn't mean to say that you actually have to arrive at that strategy in that same way.

Michael Jackson, a guru on methods of system development, has pointed out that, although some simple variety of 'top-down' may be a convenient way of describing things when they are already well understood, it may not be a good way of developing, designing or discovering anything. If this seems a rather obscure intellectual point, Jackson provides a convincing analogy. A maths textbook presents theorems in a logical order; a theorem once proved may be used later on in the book to help prove other theorems. This is the obvious, natural way of presenting that body of knowledge to anybody who wants to study it. But nobody pretends that all the theorems were actually discovered in this way or in this order. The order of description is not necessarily the order of development.[1]

In other words, when you have already made your decisions, a simple level-based structure, with technology entering at a lowish level, can be a very convenient means of describing the decisions and implications to someone else. In fact, the more carefully structured into natural levels it is, probably the clearer things will be. But the best means of actually arriving at those decisions and assessing their implications may be a far more subtle interplay of levels, ratchets and feedback.

PRACTICAL ADVICE

➤ In working through a level-based planning approach watch out for the dangers of premature, unsupported, chaotic and drifting decisions.

➤ Even better, design the level-based planning approach from the start by judging the most likely sources of interactions between decisions at different levels and hence the areas most vulnerable to these problems. The more complex interactions there are, the more backtracking between levels is probably needed.

➤ Distinguish elaboration (adding detail to decisions made at previous levels) from feedback (backtracking to change decisions made at previous levels). Restrain feedback when necessary to avoid anarchy. Encourage feedback when necessary to do justice to the issues of the case.

➤ Recognise the need for ratchets in the level-based structure. Decide where to build them in. Ensure people understand what they are and why they are there.

➤ Break down misleading terms such as 'top-down' and 'stepwise refinement' into clearer concepts. Be aware of the differences between three classic structures: logical priority, footstepwise refinement and staircasewise refinement. Decide which you should be using in which parts of your decision-making. Ensure other people understand.

➤ Consider also the logic of 'middle-out' structure. Discard 'bottom-up' as needlessly confusing.

➤ Reserve the option of arriving at your decisions by a variety of subtle procedures, while yet documenting the results in neat, simple levels.

➤ Remember to take account of all the above distinctions when managing the specific level-based activities: data modelling, business modelling and so on.

Part V:

Special
Approaches

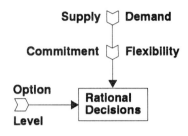

Supply ▽ Demand

Commitment ▽ Flexibility

Option ▷ → Rational
Level   Decisions

BRIEFINGS AND MODEL

So far, successive briefings have added more and more detail within the framework proposed in the Reference Model of IT decision-making. Parts I and III explore the problems raised by the Supply–Demand Interaction and the Commitment–Flexibility Tradeoff. Parts II and IV discuss the most common approaches to handling these problems and arriving at decisions. The briefings in this part of the book discuss certain other, more specialised approaches.

Varying the Assumptions about Decision-making

The approaches discussed in Parts II and IV, though varied, refrain from challenging certain assumptions.

For example, whether the discipline of the approach is rigid or supple, IT decisions are usually regarded as resulting from investigations, discussions, reports and presentations. There is a presumption towards the verbal and the judgemental. The first two briefings in this part of the book examine the idea of adopting a more quantified or more rigorous approach to decision-making.

Most discussion of the logic of decision-making assumes that there is one process to be examined, albeit often structured in levels. How could things be otherwise? Suppose the board of a company decrees that in future any investment proposal related to IT will only be approved if three department heads agree to share the costs equally. This stipulation is bound to establish a certain environment, where ideas for certain types of projects will flourish while others wither and die. Setting up this particular environment is itself a decision which may be good or bad in its influence on later decisions about specific projects. In effect, the decision-making process is split over two tiers. The third and fourth briefings examine approaches to IT decision-making that decide separately on some organisational or accounting environment that will have a strong effect on more specific decisions.

Even the first four briefings in this part of the book share the tacit assumption that taking a decision is a different thing from carrying it out. But the logic of building prototypes and undertaking experimental projects is to try out different supply and demand possibilities before major decisions are taken. The last pair of briefings shows how such approaches blur the distinction between deciding and doing.

None of the ideas in these briefings is likely to remove the need to organise a complex decision-making process in levels, nor do they undermine the desirability of seeking out and comparing options. They simply offer fresh ingredients to the variety of concepts available for mixing into the Option–Level Blend.

Approaches that Quantify Supply and Demand Factors

Suppose it were possible to define and quantify all the supply and demand factors, present and future, relevant to a situation. Then IT strategy decisions could be plausibly regarded as the solutions to problems that, however complex they might be, had well defined inputs. The first briefing looks at the issues that arise from the idea of measuring IT supply and demand factors, and using the measurements to drive decision-making. In particular, how is it possible to measure the quantity of demand as yet unmet? (**26. Metrics: Pitfalls and Shortcomings**)

The next briefing discusses a narrower but more powerful approach. Sometimes detailed decisions need to be resolved at one time in one planning process, even though the interaction between the supply and demand factors may be very awkward to study, and there may be many sources of uncertainties ahead. Why not apply general-purpose techniques from the field of operations research — linear programming or decision theory, for example — to such problems? These techniques can only be applied if there is a credible way of quantifying most of the relevant factors and defining their interactions. That is feasible in some cases, but not in others. (**27. Applying OR Techniques**)

Overview of Part V Briefings

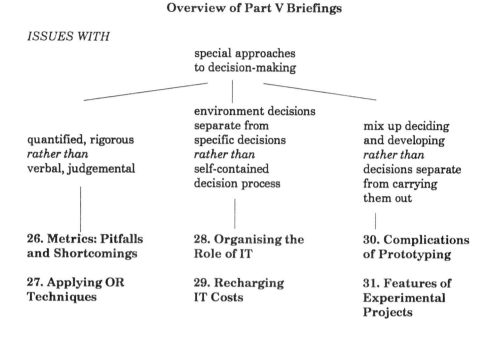

ISSUES WITH

special approaches
to decision-making

| quantified, rigorous *rather than* verbal, judgemental | environment decisions separate from specific decisions *rather than* self-contained decision process | mix up deciding and developing *rather than* decisions separate from carrying them out |

26. Metrics: Pitfalls and Shortcomings

27. Applying OR Techniques

28. Organising the Role of IT

29. Recharging IT Costs

30. Complications of Prototyping

31. Features of Experimental Projects

Approaches that Establish a Certain Environment for Decision-making

Since the Supply–Demand Interaction and Commitment–Flexibility Tradeoff are often so hard to resolve in one planning process, why not diffuse decision-making? Begin by deciding on an organisational or accounting environment that is designed to guide more specific decisions in desirable directions. This is rather like a finance ministry or central bank endeavouring to establish the right conditions in a national economy, so that individual entrepreneurs are encouraged and steered towards effective investments.

How should IT people and units — typical supply factors — interact with other business units and their broader policy — demand factors? Naturally the basic principles of good organisation (clear lines of responsibility, good communications and so on) are important, but it is an interesting idea to go further and deliberately design organisational arrangements in some particular form, that has a clear influence on future decisions. For example, to decide to organise the IT department like a commercial bureau is to opt for a certain mechanism for processing the supply and demand possibilities open to the organisation. Different possibilities may be identified and different choices made if the IT department is organised in some different way. Therefore the decisions that set up such organisational arrangements can themselves be regarded as strategic decisions. **(28. Organising the Role of IT)**

Many organisations have a system of charging the costs of IT systems to the departments that use the systems — simply because it seems a sensible thing to do, as a matter of good practice. But if you are really concerned to ensure that the supply and demand factors of IT interact to the full benefit of the organisation, why not set up a sophisticated method of charging the costs of supply to those parts of the organisation that generate the demand, and let the economics of this market dominate decision-making? After all, that is how money helps organise the complexity of the real economy. A continuous internal market in IT services can be a mechanism to reduce the need for elaborate, dirigiste planning procedures. **(29. Charging IT Costs)**

Mixing Deciding and Doing

The other pair of briefings in this part of the book describes a third line of approach. Decisions are often difficult — especially when the Supply–Demand Interaction is intertwined with the Commitment–Flexibility Tradeoff. So why not blur the distinction between taking a decision and carrying it out?

The notion of building scaled-down 'prototypes' of new computer systems is attractive. It aims to ensure that people understand what they are agreeing to before huge investments are made in complete new systems. In other words, prototyping offers a new approach to finding the appropriate mix of supply and demand factors for a system, while gaining the advantages of flexibility, without apparent penalty. But surely a well managed system development project should proceed in a controlled, methodical step-by-step fashion. Since prototyping involves darting backwards and forwards between levels, trying out ideas, scrapping them, investigating other possibilities and so on, there may be a conflict in objectives here. The next briefing looks into the logic of prototyping and related approaches to system development. **(30. Complications of Prototyping)**

Most new systems are intended to be operational for at least a few years. But suppose the main objective of a certain project is to gain experience and knowledge by experiment rather than to build an operational system. Suppose that the system built is certain to be thrown away after a short time and it may well be modified drastically during its short life. Then the Commitment–Flexibility Tradeoff takes a very different form. Moreover, if the immediate motivation for the system is not cost-savings or increased profits, but experience and insight gained, then the experimental project can be seen as one more special way of approaching the Supply–Demand Interaction. It helps in finding the right balance of factors for building a full-scale system that can be justified later. The last briefing looks into the logic of projects and portfolios of projects, whose justification is experiment. **(31. Features of Experimental Projects)**

26.   Metrics: Pitfalls and Shortcomings

ISSUES

The Chief Information Officer of Candlebark Insurance is debating IT policy with the MIS Director:

'We're spending too much on maintaining existing systems and not enough on new development.'

'Oh no, we're not.'

'Oh yes, we are.'

'Oh no, we're not — and to prove it, here are the statistics showing that the percentage split of software costs between new development and maintenance was 57–43 five years ago, there has been a steady trend leading to the current figure of 68–32, and the breakdown for our industry as a whole is 63–37.'

The debate seems to have suddenly moved to a far more rational plane. It must surely be a good thing to base decisions on facts rather than intuitions. There can still be disputes about the conclusions to be drawn from facts, but, on the whole, the chance of reaching sensible decisions seems to be improved.

If you have a fever, then a doctor who uses a thermometer to take your temperature, is probably more competent to decide whether you have 'flu or malaria than one who just puts a hand to your brow.

Other things being equal, it seems desirable to use clear, quantified facts as a basis for reasoning about the way an organisation uses IT. But the interesting issue is *how far* to go in measuring quantities and drawing conclusions from them. Is it merely sound practice conducive to clear thinking to quantify factors that are readily quantifiable — just as writing grammatical sentences in reports and ensuring that the key people turn up for important meetings are sound practice? Or is there much more to it than that: can a measurements-based approach be an important means of shaping the decision-making process?

ANALYSIS

To benefit from the use of IT metrics, you need to be well aware of some characteristic problems associated with them. This briefing charts the main pitfalls surrounding the desirable objective of useful, quantified measurements. The trick is to produce credible measurements by avoiding the pitfalls.

Rhetoric — For and Against

There is a moderate *prima facie* case in favour of quantification, but some enthusiasts oversell their ideas.

'If you can't measure it, you can't manage it. And if you can measure it, you can manage it.' As a slogan to prod managers who are too lazy even to want to know how much their organisation spends on IT, this is fine rhetoric. But as a piece of reasoning, it is quite bogus. You may not keep a thermometer in your study to *measure* the temperature, but whenever it feels too warm or too cold, you can still *manage* the temperature by opening a window or switching on a fire. On the other hand, you could be in the Sahara Desert with an expensive thermometer; you could *measure* the temperature with great precision, but that doesn't mean you could *manage* it.

Pro-metrics hype of this sort needs to be defused. Deciding what a certain measurement actually signifies can be quite hard, and the less you are influenced by invalid logic or a hyped bias towards metrics the better. Otherwise you may end up feeling that any argument based on measurements, no matter how tenuous and question-begging, must be superior to any other form of reasoning.

There is also a counter-slogan: 'If you can count it, it doesn't count.' This one is presumably not intended as a serious piece of logic. It seems to contain two different points. Firstly, trivial things like the annual costs for diskettes are easy to quantify, whereas important things like the opportunities in the organisation for using expert system technology are difficult or impossible to quantify. Secondly, when you measure things such as the time a clerk takes to fill in a certain form, you often get an untypical result, because the people whose activities are being measured act untypically.

Both these points are surely valid. But they don't destroy the case for measurements; they simply stress the importance of using them sensibly, rather than being carried away by uncritical enthusiasm.

Practicality and Cutoff Problems

The most obvious problem is *Practicality*. It may be impossible or just too awkward to collect the measurements you would like to have. For example, it would be good to know how much time was spent by technical support staff looking after the database over the last five years, but records breaking down the work of these staff just haven't been kept. Or it would be good to have accurate figures splitting the utilisation of mainframe hardware over all the different application systems, but it would take too long to set up all the technical arrangements to monitor the hardware to make those measurements accurately.

There is no great logical problem here; the problem is a practical one and the solution is often to make assumptions and to use estimates that are definitely not exact. However, sound judgement is needed to decide where assumptions can reasonably be used instead of actual measurements, and to judge how accurate the estimates really need to be.

Practicality problems sometimes merge into *Cutoff* problems. Measurements such as the ratio between expenditure on software development and expenditure on software maintenance, or the ratio between end-user computing and mainframe computing, or the calculation of a certain average IT spend per employee all seem to be attractive tools to clarify what is really going on. Leaving aside the question of the feasibility of collecting the raw information for these measurements, there can be a different problem: How do you make the cutoffs demarcating the categories and defining the formulae that the analysis rests on?

For example, if two man-years are spent developing a new reporting facility that extracts data from a large operational system (original investment sixty man-years), is that work development or maintenance? Suppose it was two man-weeks; suppose it was an essential project forced by a change in government regulations; would these things make a difference?

Where is the cutoff between the categories of end-user computing and mainframe computing? Do all PCs count as end-user computing? What about PCs that are mainly used as terminals to mainframes? Or occasionally used as terminals to mainframes? Or PCs that serve networks?

The 'IT total spend' from which your 'IT spend per head' is calculated must surely include some people costs. Presumably it includes the costs of employing the full-time database administrator and presumably not the entire costs of the secretary who uses WordPerfect for an hour per day to produce letters. But where do you make the cutoff?

None of the examples given is insoluble but they show how tricky it can be to set boundaries. As in many other areas of IT strategy, the challenge is to be clear, consistent and sensible. Wherever you cut off between categories, you need to make it clear where you are making the cut. You need to apply cutoff rules that are consistent between different systems or different installations or different parts of the organisation. And you need to find the method of cutoff that will generate the most useful insight.

Definition Problems

The next problem is very important because it is so insidious. Suppose somebody produces a measurement that (say) 45% of the work of a certain department is automated. What does it mean to say that a certain percentage of a certain department is automated?

There are two approaches to meeting this kind of difficulty. One approach is to give an exact definition: for example, to say that 45% of the work of a department is automated is the same thing as saying that 45% of all the processing steps are automated or, alternatively perhaps, that 45% represents the money savings compared to the hypothetical case where there was no form of automation whatsoever. This approach is often unsatisfactory; the definition itself raises further awkward questions and there may be no plausible definition that can be applied usefully across a variety of different cases.

The other approach to defining the wellnigh indefinable is to say that the figure is of course subject to the Practicality and the Cutoff Problems and so it should be regarded as impressionistic rather than defined precisely. This is often an unacceptable piece of logical legerdemain. Somebody may say that a bottle is about 45% full of wine, while willingly conceding some margin of error, on account of the Practicality and Cutoff Problems. Maybe, examined more closely and having defined more precisely the way surface tension should be accounted for, it would be measured as 49.7% full.

But suppose somebody says that a bottle is 45% full of *optimism*. Then all the talk in the world about Practicality and Cutoff Problems, and how the number might really be 49.7%, and how a measurement within 5% or 10% is accurate enough, won't satisfy somebody who wants to know what it really means to say that a bottle is $N\%$ full of optimism. The very concept begs definition. Similarly, in IT metrics, measurements such as '$N\%$ of the department is automated' call for definition, quite apart from any issues of Practicality or Cutoff.

This poses an unpleasant dilemma. Either you define the meaning of certain measurements precisely and unsatisfactorily or you hope your colleagues or clients don't notice that they haven't been defined at all.

Quality and Subjectivity Problems

Many measurements that are vulnerable to the Definition Problem also suffer from the Quality and Subjectivity Problems. Some desirable items of evidence are unlike money or time or percentages in that they don't even look as if they lend themselves to measurements. For example, it isn't obvious how you can quantify the innovative talent of an organisation's business analysts or the IT knowledge of its secretaries or the effectiveness of its training procedures or the efficiency of its job scheduling procedures in the event of emergencies.

Of course you can devise questionnaires and checklists and scoring schemes covering such subjects, just as you could devise checklists and scoring schemes to determine who was the world's greatest human being or what was the most original work of art — if you really had to. Some companies in the computer services industry offer techniques to attempt this task.

The best chance of giving some meaning to such quality measurements is to devise a measurement system and then to apply it very widely. For example, if the quality of the procedures for mainframe job scheduling in an organisation's data centre is scored at 6 out of 10, that may not mean very much in itself. But if the average score from hundreds of other organisations is 8.5, then it may perhaps have some indicative value.

Of course there are still some questions begged, among them the matter of subjectivity. If the score is assessed by an outside observer (a consultant, say), then somehow all outside observers have to be made to score on consistent criteria. If the score is derived from the opinions of people actually involved (those who create demands and provide supply), then the measurement is potentially affected by human motivations and attitudes — pride, modesty, fear, dissatisfaction, rivalry, flattery and so on.

Convenience Problems

In the range of problems mentioned so far there has been a gradual movement away from what might loosely be called objective problems (e.g. Practicality) to more subjective problems (e.g. Quality). The next one to be mentioned is primarily subjective in this sense.

During the Vietnam War, people in the Department of Defense gave metrics a bad name. They fell into many of the errors already covered in this briefing, and also provided some neat examples of another genre of error: collecting the information that is convenient to collect and assuming that it is the only information that counts. For example, counting the number of bombing raids is convenient, but measuring their effect on the enemy is relatively difficult; therefore (in quotes, as it were) just count the raids and assume damage to the enemy's capacity is in proportion. Counting up dead bodies in a village is convenient, while quantifying the degree of sympathy for the government among the inhabitants is difficult. Therefore (in quotes) the more dead bodies in a village, the fewer the Viet

Cong left and the greater the proportion of villagers supporting the government.

Similarly, it is hard to quantify the quality of the management of a data centre, but convenient to measure the quantity of documented procedures possessed by the management. Thus, the assumption can easily creep up that the more procedures there are, the better managed the data centre must be.

It is hard to measure the quality of each application system in any objective sense, but relatively convenient to send out questionnaires to users asking them to score each system out of ten. Never mind that a system may score high, because people are ignorant of all the extra things that might be done if modern technology were used properly. Or the system may be highly valued because it prodigally offers lavish facilities that can't be justified on any rational comparison of costs and benefits. Never mind the fact that a certain system may score low because of teething troubles that, on any impartial view, are the inevitable price to be paid for introducing such an advanced system. Or people are dissatisfied with developments that offer little obvious benefit, ignoring the fact that these are investments in a foundation intended to allow many demands to be met far quicker and more cost-effectively in the future.

As these examples suggest, forming a qualitative judgement of the management of the interaction between supply factors and demand factors is a delicate task. It is easy to fall into the trap of regarding crude, incomplete figures that happen to be convenient to collect as accurate information about a complex matter.

Interpretation Problems

Clearly, very soft measurement data, such as scores judging quality of procedures, have very little value unless placed in the context of many other measurements from other situations. But quite hard financial data are also of limited value unless there is some basis for comparison. If the managers of Candlebark Insurance know that its IT cost per head is $15,000 per year, they may have difficulty in drawing any immediate conclusion. But if they know the equivalent figure for all the main companies in the insurance industry, then their own figure becomes very interesting. Seeing Candlebark's own trend in the split between maintenance and development is moderately interesting, but to draw conclusions, it would be very useful to know the trend in the industry as a whole. If these industry-wide figures could be supplemented by the figures for arch-rival Stringybark Assurance that would be even better.

Unfortunately, useful comparison material is very hard to come by. A few companies in the computer services industry maintain and sell this kind of information, but you have to take a lot on trust. They are unlikely to let you dig deep into their figures, if you want to satisfy yourself (for example) that their information about the insurance industry is based on a sufficiently large and balanced sample, or if you want to check how recently all their raw data were collected. Before spending much time on activities to produce IT metrics in your organisation, it is worth looking ahead to judge how feasible it will be to use comparison data for interpretation of the results. Otherwise you could be wasting your time.

There is another, opposite problem, even if comparison data are available. Bodies of detailed measurements offer many opportunities for selecting data to fit preconceived conclusions. Suppose the MIS manager of Candlebark wants to show that the organisation is not spending enough on computer systems. He makes a comparison with an industry norm for IT spending as a percentage of premium income; then he makes a comparison with an industry norm for IT spending per person employed; then he makes a comparison with an industry norm for annual growth rate in IT spending. He can show the board whichever of these three comparisons suits his case and keep quiet about the other two. A good PC spreadsheet makes it easy for him to try out endless combinations of data in charts of different formats until hitting on the chart that gerrymanders the data most convincingly.

Is this a problem, exactly? If, for some well founded reason, from some other source, the judgement has already been formed, perhaps not. But if you want to use the figures to help work out what the answer should be, then metrics comparisons have to be used with extreme care.

Practical Use

You can't use a sextant to navigate when the stars are covered by fog, use rifle bullets to stop tanks or use a scythe to cut your fingernails. These are plain neutral facts; they don't prove that nobody should ever use sextants, rifles or scythes for any purpose. With a good understanding of the pitfalls of IT metrics techniques, you can use them in so far as they are appropriate to the specific situation. But if you are not aware of their shortcomings, you may end up trying to cut your fingernails with a scythe, as it were.

Assume that Candlebark Insurance does generate some measurements about its IT activities and the people involved are shrewd enough to trek around the pitfalls and still arrive at some respectable numbers. How are these numbers likely to help Candlebark in making its IT strategy decisions?

Much of this book is concerned with the idea that IT strategy is concerned with the interaction of supply and demand factors; where can metrics fit into this way of looking at things? The most promising part of the equation for metrics is the supply-side; it is usually feasible to avoid most of the pitfalls and collect measurements of costs and quantities of PCs and network capacity and technical support staff and so on. Possessing figures of this sort must surely be of some value in debating decisions.

Measuring the way different types of demand factor have been met or are being met by the supply factors is more tricky but still possible. For example, 32% of the costs of supply (hardware, software, specialist staff, etc.) went on meeting demands for system maintenance; or 42% went on demands for IT from the Fire department (which only has 23% of the premium income); or 89% went on systems classified as 'routine administration' (as opposed to 'speculative innovation' or 'mission-critical'). There can be formidable Cutoff problems, but still, with a really intelligent approach, it may well be possible to generate some useful information.

The Problem of Quantifying Demand

The real point of discussing IT strategy at all is to decide what to do next. A large part of that debate involves taking a view of what currently unmet demands might be supplied in the future. This is the area that reveals the shortcomings of metrics techniques. It is practically impossible to find any credible way of quantifying what unmet demand exists or could exist or ought to exist.

Attempts to do this often founder on the Convenience problem. Plausible statistics may appear to provide definite information: for example, that there are most opportunities for new systems in Candlebark's re-insurance department or that Candlebark's main system for Policy Renewals ought to be redeveloped to meet new demands. But on a closer examination such findings often prove to be based on data that were convenient to collect, which in fact only justify their apparent conclusions, if you are prepared to gloss over some tenuous assumptions along the way.

The problem of Definition is also very awkward here. What does it really mean to say that a certain percentage of a certain department is automated? This question is hard to answer, because it raises a certain rather fundamental issue. Does it make sense to assume that at any given time there is a certain discoverable, measurable total quantity of IT demands within an organisation that are waiting to be supplied?

Certainly there is a specific number of symphonies by Beethoven that are available to be performed; in a certain sunken galleon there may actually be a specific number of gold coins waiting to be found. But many other things can't be thought of in this way. To say that Beethoven only wrote a certain percentage of all the symphonies that were available for him to write seems absurd; no economist believes that there is a certain specific volume of world trade that is available for the world to achieve.

IT demands are like those cases in the second group. Many of the other briefings show how an organisation's decisions on the use of IT result from a complex interaction where demands are both constrained by supply practicalities and stimulated by the availability of supply resources. In other words, as with world economic activity, demand for IT isn't something that is just 'there' to be surveyed and measured, quite independently of any considerations of the cost and practicalities of supplying it.

For the demand-side extremist there is, as a matter of principle, one complete set of system demands just waiting to be defined and handed over to the technologists who will do whatever it takes to supply them. If such a complete set of demands did, in some sense, exist, then statistics might be able to show the proportions currently met and unmet. But, in the great majority of cases, IT strategy is more subtle than simply the automation of a firm set of plausibly automatable things. Therefore, while metrics can be regarded as a useful tool for understanding the way things are at the moment, it is best to be very cautious in drawing conclusions about what might be done in the future.

PRACTICAL ADVICE

➤ Look for ways to quantify factors that are relevant to the present state of supply and demand. That should raise the quality of the IT strategy debate.

➤ Be wary of the many traps in collecting measurements. The Practicality problem and the Cutoff problem mean that measurements of current supply and demand can only be approximate. The Definition and the Quality/Subjectivity problems mean that you have to attach quantities to factors that really have no clear definition. The Convenience problem means that your data may be biased towards what is convenient to measure rather than what really matters. The Interpretation problem means that it may be very debatable what conclusions can be drawn from the measurements.

➤ Employ this analysis of the potential problems to look critically at the measurements anybody else offers.

➤ Don't accept quantifications whose logic is based on the notion that there is in any given organisation a certain fixed quantity of demand just waiting there to be identified and measured.

➤ Don't endeavour to generate measurements of the future demand or of future supply. That is a matter for you to decide. IT metrics can tell you where you are, but they can't tell you where you ought to be going.

27.　Applying OR Techniques

ISSUES

Operations research (OR) techniques have long been the Cinderellas of IT decision-making. While other less compelling methods flourish, OR techniques languish unconsidered.

Many IT strategy problems arise from quite complex interactions between supply and demand factors. Unravelling interdependencies, examining possibilities and making choices can be a tedious, uncertain business, if the work is done at the committee table. But OR offers a range of powerful, general-purpose techniques for tackling very complex problems. Why not use OR techniques to process the factors in IT decisions?

One drawback is that OR techniques require you to quantify the elements of the problem and that is often a stumbling-block with IT strategy decisions. On the other hand, there need be no suggestion that you should rely on OR to approach every single problem. OR can be kept for those cases where the problem can be plausibly described in terms of the interplay of factors expressible in quantitative terms.

This briefing explores the possibilities for applying decision theory and linear programming techniques to IT strategy decisions.

ANALYSIS

To tackle most strategic decisions effectively you need to identify the main options available, compare them and evaluate them. Formal OR techniques are most relevant in cases where the identification of the options is relatively easy, where choice between them is difficult, and where quantitative values can be attached to the main factors affecting each option.

The techniques really come into their own in two main types of case: where the problem contains complicated patterns of uncertainty and where very many interdependencies between different options exist. For example, you can't choose between options a, b and c for system 1 in isolation; you have to take account of decisions on system 2, but they, in turn are affected by decisions on system 3 . . .

The account of the Mulga Group's use of OR begins with decisions where uncertainty is the main difficulty, and moves on to decisions that are dominated by complex interdependencies.

The Mulga Group's Conversion Problem

The Mulga Group is a famous 'high street' retailer of electrical goods. The company has just taken over the country's largest distributor of video-cassettes, compact discs and similar consumer products. The takeover is intended to bring synergy of operations and this will require integration of computer systems.

Mulga now possesses two data centres with totally incompatible systems: one in Birmingham and one in Plymouth. This is obviously not a sensible arrangement: as a way of supplying current demand for systems it is less efficient than having one data centre. Worse, major new developments are stifled. Mulga managers dream of having a distributed but integrated set of systems and databases linking retail outlets, warehouses, branch offices, regional offices, head office and so on. This idea raises many issues, but the double data centre arrangement is plainly an undesirable complication. Until that boil is lanced, as it were, Mulga can't make serious plans for substantial new developments.

The decision is quickly taken that the Plymouth data centre will close and its systems will be converted to run at Birmingham. This will be no small task, since the two data centres have incompatible hardware, programming languages and system development methods. Thus Mulga presents quite a good example of a case where a real supply-side issue — data centre arrangements — dominates strategy decisions.

The simplest approach would be to *convert* all the Plymouth systems to run at Birmingham, doing the work as quickly as possible, consistent with producing robust, stable new versions of all the systems. The snag is that this would generate so much work that there would be hardly any capacity available to do anything else for at least two years. Then after the two years, when Mulga can at last contemplate major new investments, some of the systems that have cost most effort to convert will probably be candidates for immediate replacement by totally new systems.

Mulga could use the circumstances of the conversion to implement many *enhancements* to each system, so that the new Birmingham version not only ran in a different technological environment, but incorporated many attractive new features. For some systems, there is a temptation to go further and completely scrap an old Plymouth system, *redeveloping* a brand new Birmingham version. The trouble with taking this approach to every single system is that Mulga would enter a period lasting perhaps five to seven years of painful, protracted relocation from Plymouth to Birmingham. That seems very unattractive.

In summary, part of the problem is this. For each system in the

Plymouth application portfolio, there are three main options: a, convert technically without any functional enhancement; b, convert technically with functional enhancements; c, redevelop. For each system, the pros and cons are different and a choice has to be made.

But another big difficulty exists: uncertainty. In one way, the people in the best position to estimate the effort required for options a, b and c for each of the Plymouth systems are the analysts and programmers in Plymouth. But all their experience is in using the SA/SD analysis and design techniques and the Dibol programming language for systems using an Rdb/VMS database on Digital hardware. At Birmingham, most systems use the Cobol programming language, and access an IDMS/R database on an IBM mainframe; also all the design and documentation activities are done using the Knowledgeware CASE (computer-aided software engineering) tools. Thus any estimate that the Plymouth people make of the work needed at the Birmingham data centre will be subject to a wide margin of error. That uncertainty is the most worrying part of the whole problem.

Applying Decision Theory

For each of the systems concerned there are *three options*: a, convert technically without any functional enhancement; b, convert technically with functional enhancements; c, redevelop with functional enhancements. Since the main source of worry is the uncertainty over the costs of these options, *three cost estimates* are made (in the first table of figures): a best guess, an optimistic guess and a pessimistic guess.

The decision has already been made to move to the other data centre, so the financial *benefit* of option a can be set at zero and the benefits for options b and c can be assessed as marginal benefits over a. They are projected over five years and expressed as a net present value (NPV) to provide a figure for comparison with the costs of carrying out the work required by the option (in the right-hand column of the first table).

By subtracting the benefits from all three costs guesses in turn, a set of *net cost* figures is produced for the three options on optimistic, best guess and pessimistic bases (second table).

The *maximin principle* of decision theory can now be applied to the figures in the second table. To decide between the three options a, b and c, look only at the pessimistic column of each and choose that option which has the most favourable outcome in the pessimistic column. The way this particular table of values has been set up, the most favourable outcome is the one with the *lowest net cost*; therefore in the case of System 1, a is the option to choose.

This maximin principle is a way of playing safe; it is appropriate for

Data for Decision Theory Reasoning

SYSTEM 1	COST			BENEFIT
	optimistic	best guess	pessimistic	NPV
a pure conversion	60	80	100	0
b conversion + enhancement	140	180	220	100
c redevelopment	150	210	270	150

SYSTEM 1	NET COST (COST less BENEFIT)		
	optimistic	best guess	pessimistic
a pure conversion	60	80	100
b conversion + enhancement	40	80	120
c redevelopment	0	60	120

SYSTEM 2 (based on above Net Cost figures)	MINIMAX REGRET		
	optimistic	best guess	pessimistic
a pure conversion	60	20	0
b conversion + enhancement	40	20	10
c redevelopment	0	0	10

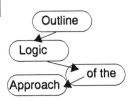

one-off, unique decisions, with potentially profound consequences, where caution is desirable. Since System 1 happens to be the backbone system of Mulga's business, which keeps track of distribution, maximin seems the right approach.

But Systems 2–11, though important, are not quite as special as System 1. If you have a set of decisions to take of roughly similar type, it seems odd to be cautious about all of them. Will not bad fortune on one be compensated by good fortune on another? Why not take some account of the best guess and optimistic estimates as well? Suppose it did turn out that the optimistic forecasts came true; by choosing a, you would have incurred a cost of 60, when by choosing c, the net cost could have been zero.

For this situation, the *minimax regret principle* is appropriate. Here is the way it would work with System 2, which just happens to have the same pattern of estimates as System 1. For each column (optimistic, best guess and pessimistic) call the best of the three outcomes 0 and calculate the difference between it and the other figures in the column. The meaning of this is, for example, that if you choose option b and the best guess estimates turn out right, then you will regret losing the opportunity of saving 20 that was offered by c. The rule then is to choose the option that minimises the maximum amount of regret you could experience. As the third table shows, choosing a, the worst outcome is regret to the value of 60. Choosing b, the worst outcome is regret to the value of 40. Choosing c, the worst outcome is regret to the value of 10. On this basis, the right choice is option c.

Decision Theory Variations

The techniques discussed so far are appropriate if there is one major source of uncertainty, for example the amount of work required at the Birmingham data centre. That doesn't mean that estimates for every other relevant factor have to be perfect; it does imply that they are much less variable than the main source of uncertainty. Mulga is fairly happy with the benefits estimates used for systems 1–11 so far; but with projects 12–16, the benefits are much more uncertain. Estimates can be made, but they seem just as uncertain as the estimates for the costs of the work at Birmingham. In other words for each system there are three options, and for each option there are six figures: optimistic, best guess and pessimistic for costs and the same for benefits.

In this kind of situation logic based on the minimax regret principle becomes rather complicated; a *Bayesian* approach is more appropriate. You attach a percentage probability to all the figures. If, for example, it is assumed that the best guess of the costs is 60% likely to be correct and the other two costs forecasts are each 20% likely, then these weightings can be used to calculate an average costs figure. In a similar way average benefits can be calculated. From these an average net costs figure can be calculated. The option with the best average net costs figure is then the winner.

System 17 poses a rather special uncertainty problem. As with the others, there are three options: a, pure technical conversion; b, conversion with enhancements; c, redevelop with enhancements. A general election is due within two years' time and if there is a change of government, there is a strong possibility that consumer credit law will be altered in a certain area of retailing. If that happens, System 17 will certainly have to be either drastically altered or completely redeveloped, depending on the content of the new legislation.

In other words, there is a combination of choices open to Mulga and there are also *stages of uncertainties* in the future that are not under Mulga's control. This logic can be shown in a network diagram, which suggests a way to solve the problem. For each action open to Mulga at each stage (e.g. *conversion*), make a cost estimate. (The cost of the second tier *amend* actions will vary, depending whether a converted, enhanced or redeveloped system is being amended.) For each of the uncontrollable uncertainties (e.g. CHANGE IN LAW?), estimate a probability (e.g. 60%). For each of the nine possible outcomes, estimate any associated financial benefits.

With that information, all that remains is a laborious calculation to work out which of the three options currently available will lead to the most favourable result *on average*.

Linear Programming

The decision theory techniques help in choosing between options a, b and c at the level of individual systems, but they don't help in finding *the best mix* of a, b and c choices for Mulga in total. For example, since the c options generally entail more work than the a or b choices, the more systems for which c options are chosen, the longer the whole conversion period will last. But suppose the result is a four-year conversion period; that might be just too long for Mulga to accept.

Mulga can formulate the whole strategy problem quite differently: decide between the a, b and c options for each of the seventeen systems, in such a way that the balance of benefits over costs is maximised, but subject to the constraint that the total work required is no greater than 1440 man-months (forty people working for three years). Put this way, the problem is to find the best mix of options for the systems within the constraints.

Network of Uncertainties

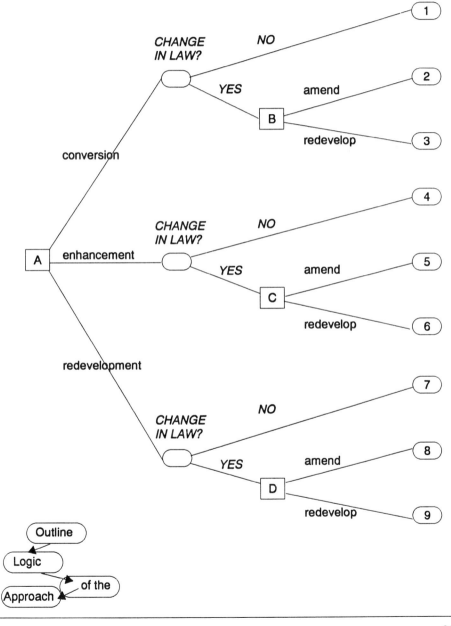

This is the type of problem that linear programming (LP) handles well. The mathematics of linear programming is quite complex, but that doesn't matter, because computer software products are available to solve LP problems once they are expressed in the appropriate form.

In this case, the problem is defined by the following data. Activity 1a (option a for System 1) has a certain net cost (say, 80) and requires a certain number of man-months (70, say); 1b is net cost 80 and man-months 140; and so on through to 17c. Out of 1a, 1b and 1c, one, but only one, must be chosen; out of 2a, 2b and 2c, one, but only one, must be chosen; and so on. The task is to choose the combination of activities out of 1a to 17c, subject to the constraints just given, in such a way that the total man-months work required by the chosen activities, is no greater than 1440, but the total net cost is as low as possible.

Given that problem definition, an integer linear programming package can work out the appropriate answer. Why an *integer* linear programming package? Classic linear programming may return answers to industrial problems such as make 1,367.28 kg of chocolates and 294.7 kg of caramels. In Mulga's problem it would clearly be absurd to do activity 1b 3.7 times or 0.61 times. So any valid solution has to involve doing the activity either 0 or 1 times. Restricting acceptable solutions to whole numbers makes the mathematics more complicated, but this doesn't matter because the calculations are all handled in the software package.

Linear Programming Refinements

You may think that the problem described could be done on paper without resorting to a software package that implements an advanced mathematical technique. But once you've developed the habit of defining problems in LP form, you can build in extra conditions that could never be handled reasonably in any other way.

For example, you can define that there is a maximum of 800 man-months of programmer work available and 640 man-months of systems analyst work. Instead of specifying a total workload for each activity, you then specify how much programmer time it requires and how much systems analyst time. That would be a much more refined version of the problem to be solved.

You can go further by allowing for the use of temporary staff; e.g. a maximum of 200 man-months of extra programmer work and 120 man-months of systems analyst work is acceptable. A price can be attached to these staff resources, so that the more they are used, the more their costs increase the costs of the work done. The LP software works out all these tradeoffs and comes back with the optimum answer to the problem as a whole.

If required, you can take account of links between systems. For example, maybe for system 12, it is only sensible to redevelop the whole system (option c), if you also redevelop (rather than convert or enhance) system 18 too. A constraint can be added into the definition of the problem to say that 12c without 18c is an invalid combination. The package would take this into account too, while doing all the calculations necessary to arrive at the optimum tradeoff.

Relevance of OR to IT Decision-making

Plainly you wouldn't use OR techniques to make a data model of an organisation or to document which information is used by which function of the business. OR techniques help you make clear-cut decisions, that can set the agenda for more detailed work to be done.

IT strategy decisions invariably offer options and alternatives to be compared and evaluated. There may be complex, awkward uncertainties. The problem may be to find the right mix of choices, rather than merely make a number of separate choices. You might think then that formal OR techniques would be part of the armoury of every professional advisor on IT strategy. And yet they are used quite rarely. Why?

Admittedly, OR techniques can only be applied when the main factors in the strategy problem can be quantified. This may be very awkward to do or may entail a gross over-simplification. But there is nothing to stop you using decision theory or linear programming to examine an approximation of the problem and taking the results for guidance, in order to direct less formal investigation; you don't have to accept the proposed solutions as the definitive answers.

Decision theory and linear programming are not the only possible techniques; some problems are better handled in other ways. For problems with labyrinthine complexes of uncertainty factors, Monte Carlo simulation can be useful. A computer program goes through the labyrinth perhaps several thousand times — in a way that is random, and yet guided by estimated probabilities; then it averages out all the results. Some research has been done to apply the logic of valuing options traded in a stock market to general management problems, where an investment today brings *flexibility* tomorrow, rather than a direct cash return. Many investments in IT infrastructure have this characteristic.[1] Other possible techniques are queuing theory (for problems where agents can only access scarce resources after waiting in queues to be served) and game theory (for studying situations where several agents interact with each other, each pursuing its own strategy).

One reason for the lack of attention to OR techniques in recent years is that many of the neatest examples of OR in use — such as those in this briefing — occur in the environment of mainframes and minis. Most of the exciting developments and so most of the challenging strategic decisions during the 'eighties were associated with personal computers. But now that personal computers are well established in organisations, many of the most innovative ideas involve linking them up in architectures that support distributed databases and distributed processing. The complexities of these developments will surely generate problems for which OR techniques are appropriate.

Another aspect of IT decision-making during the 'eighties was the trend towards demand-driven planning. Of course, if you believe in first defining the demand-side and leaving the supply-side to take care of itself, then you have far fewer problems. To do that is to abandon any attempt to find an optimum balance between supply and demand factors. But once you look at problems in terms of the *interaction* between supply and demand factors, then OR techniques come into their own. Use of OR techniques is in fact a special case of progress through the evaluation of different supply–demand options. They can be a useful supplement to the usual, relatively informal way of comparing options.

PRACTICAL ADVICE

➤ When problems are complex and the problem content can be expressed in quantitative terms, look seriously at the possibility of applying OR techniques.

➤ If the essence of the problem is a complex pattern of uncertainty, then choose decision theory as the natural technique.

➤ If it is right to be cautious about one major decision, use the maximin principle of decision theory.

➤ If there are several different, roughly comparable decisions to be taken, use the minimax regret principle.

➤ For problems where uncertainties arise in several stages, use Bayesian decision theory.

➤ If the essence of the problem is interdependency between many different choices, then choose linear programming as the natural technique.

➤ Once you are accustomed to expressing problems in linear programming format, go ahead and build in the extra refinements that would be impossible in a problem-solving exercise on paper.

➤ Use OR techniques sometimes to produce approximations of solutions before going on to take decisions by less formal methods.

➤ Be ready to use other OR techniques besides decision theory and linear programming, when the problem demands it.

➤ Remember that OR techniques are actually a special approach to the evaluation of different supply–demand options. Therefore they should generate decisions that set the agenda for more detailed work such as modelling.

28. Organising the Role of IT

ISSUES

Organisational issues are generally rather awkward to regulate in tightly ordered patterns, but one distinction is well worth the effort of capturing. The organisational issues raised by IT are most commonly considered to be matters such as changes to work content, needs for different reporting structures, feelings of alienation among workers and the like. These are indeed important, but certain other issues, that can also be called organisational, have an extra twist to them. These are the issues concerned with the way the management of IT and the work of developing IT systems are arranged, controlled and regulated, in the context of the organisation as a whole.

This abstract formulation needs to be unpacked with an example. The decision is taken at Candlebark Insurance to develop a new system that will calculate premiums in certain complicated cases where previously intricate manual calculation was necessary; this has consequences for the content of the work done by certain clerks in the underwriting departments. Also, the decision is taken that from now on the policy information and the claims information will be tightly integrated in a new database; this has repercussions on the way the claims department interacts with the underwriting departments.

Work content and departmental interaction are two *classic organisational issues*. But what about the *organisational interaction* between Candlebark departments and IT management — which produced these decisions about the systems for recalculating premiums and the new integrated database? At some point somebody must have decided that ideas about new IT developments should be raised and discussed and decided on within some particular organisational framework rather than some other.

Decisions about the way IT people and people in other departments should interact in order to make decisions about IT are themselves strategy decisions of an organisational character. They set up an environment for decision-making that may foster either good or bad decisions subsequently. This briefing explores this line of thought.

ANALYSIS

In practically any organisation, decisions about new systems and databases and so on are reached by a certain form of organisational interaction between the managers who control IT resources and managers of other departments of the business. From now on this will be called the *IT–business interaction*. To demonstrate that genuine issues are at stake here, it is worthwhile to see how different organisations can decide to set up quite different forms of *organisational environment* for the IT–business interaction.

Alternative Organisational Principles

For a business as large as Candlebark Insurance, a whole procedural paraphernalia is associated with the process of taking decisions about the use of IT. For example, there are defined procedures for generating proposals for new projects and defined criteria for evaluating them; there are job descriptions for the people involved in such things, IT professionals and departmental managers, and so on.

Candlebark's procedures are quite detailed, but they all fit into a very clear, underlying philosophy. The whole body of Candlebark's IT activities is divided up into five large segments (actually they have a more grandiose, though rather confusing, title), roughly but not exactly corresponding to actual divisions of the company. For each segment there is an important manager, an IT specialist, who is a kind of 'champion'. In effect, the segment champions contend with each other for IT resources: programming manpower, money to invest in those systems with a border-line justification, priority to be given to a certain on-line system on the mainframe, etc. They are rather like cabinet ministers trying to get as much of the government's budget as possible for their own department. The segment managers' first priority is to keep the customer departments in their segments happy.

At Stringybark Assurance, a comparable insurance company, the procedures for taking decisions, evaluating projects and so on are based on quite a different principle. The data centre is run on very strict commercial lines, with published pricelists for resources: computer time, programming work, support for PC software and so on. The prices fluctuate in line with availability and demand. The commercially aware people in the data centre will sometimes haggle over terms, before making binding contracts with departments for systems. If you bargain hard, you can even get penalty clauses for late delivery included in the deal. The managers of the data centre are judged primarily by one thing: the data centre's profit. In this setup, there is no need for Candlebark's segment champions. Any manager with any financial responsibility within any part of the Stringybark structure is allowed to make deals to buy IT resources.

Interface Arrangements Viewed as Coherent Environment

Of course, various detailed questions spring to mind. Who adjudicates between segment champions at Candlebark? How large is the permanent staff attached to each champion? How do the non-IT people in the Candlebark departments interact with their champion? Are Stringybark departments allowed to go to an outside computer bureau if its charges are lower? Can the Stringybark data centre ever go bankrupt? Can it borrow funds for investment? These issues are interesting, but they don't undermine the logic of either approach. Appropriate answers can be filled in without doing violence to the essential features of the environment that each of the companies has chosen for its IT–business interaction.

As described, Candlebark and Stringybark have adopted two rather extreme approaches, but in each case the company's IT activities unfold within a certain environment, that is coherent. Each detail of the organisational arrangements fits together naturally with the others to form one consistent whole. For example, Stringybark's idea of judging the managers of the data centre by their profit performance can't work effectively unless Stringybark also give many individual 'consumers' the right to spend money, thus forming a genuine market environment. Such details only make sense in combination together.

These environments have an organic, evolutionary character. Champions at Candlebark are motivated to generate sensible ideas for their segments of the company to use IT, by the combination of pressure from the non-technical managers they serve and scorn from rival segment champions if they make preposterous claims on resources. There are built-in regulating features, to provide correction of any shortfall in performance. If Stringybark has an inefficient data centre, it makes a loss; eventually its manager is fired and replaced by a better manager who can make a profit; the result, at least in theory, is a more efficient data centre.

Whether Candlebark or Stringybark has the more appropriate environment isn't the point here. Many other styles of environment are available. An article in *Computerworld* in July 1989, sketched out five possibilities: it called them the Service, the Partnership, the Vendor, the

Expansion and the Strategic models.[1] There is no need to go into them here; the important thing is that a variety of significantly different environments is possible, and the best one for any given case depends on the specific details of that case.

The Literal Approach

Suppose that, for good or bad reasons, a firm's managers are not in the least interested in this talk of organisational environments. You could simply identify quite a large number of possible procedures, management tasks, control functions and so on, covering matters such as *how* a new project is approved, *how* the technical support of PC users is organised, *how* departments are made financially responsible for data centre costs, *how* definitions of different players' responsibilities are drawn up and so on. Quite a long, standard checklist can be drawn up, with items structured in natural groups — all items concerned with procedures at project level in one place, items concerned with human resources somewhere else, and so on. The checklist can be used to drive discussions about the appropriate procedures for each item in the particular circumstances of a given organisation.

There is a big disadvantage with this literal approach. It is like trying to design a steam locomotive (or understand an existing design for one) by taking each detail separately. Despite all the painstaking effort, you may still fail to get the essential features to work together, or you may suggest changes to one part that turn out to do violence unexpectedly to other parts.

Some companies in the computer services industry do offer a service to clients based on this literal approach. It may be of value under some circumstances, but as a study of the IT–business interaction *as a strategic issue*, it is extremely weak. Deciding whether a particular organisation should adopt the same principles as Candlebark or Stringybark, say, is a genuine strategic issue — or actually a meta-strategic issue, since the decision on that issue will shape the context for strategic decisions taken later on.

The Murray Pine Case

The case of Murray Pine illuminates some more aspects of the IT–business interaction. Murray Pine is a large publishing organisation, with seven large-scale *companies*, each with 200 to 400 staff; one publishes a national newspaper; one is a leading publisher of academic textbooks; one publishes all kinds of books — dictionary, coffee table, travel, novels; another publishes magazines; and so on. There is a substantial but strictly organised head office. The 200 people there are organised into eight *departments*, each with its own identity. The departments cover affairs such as legal, PR, personnel, finance, innovation and so on.

Each of the seven companies and the eight departments has its own IT arrangements, ranging from mainframe through minicomputer to PCs. There is also a Murray Pine data centre which develops and runs systems; some parts of the group use it a great deal, others hardly at all. There is a large typesetting bureau, based on a substantial computer installation; again, some parts of the group use this a great deal, others hardly at all. The organisation as a whole has several thousand PCs. Support for users of PCs is decentralised; in some parts of the organisation, there is no formal support; in some parts, there is an 'information centre' containing enthusiastic, knowledgeable PC support staff.

The whole of the group's IT strategy is up for discussion, and the IT–business interaction is one important area. There is no shortage of issues; here are some of them. How should expert data centre staff interact with other parts of the group — like a commercial bureau or as unpaid consultants? How should the head office departments interact with each other — should concepts like cooperation, common policies, collaboration, etc. apply? How can a department (e.g. personnel) control the data centre, running systems (e.g. payroll) mainly for the benefit of the companies? How should the innovation department be concerned with innovative ventures in the companies — should it stimulate, subsidise, evaluate, lead, be informed on a quarterly basis? Should there be a common approach to PC support throughout the group or is liberty a higher value? Should the typesetting bureau be treated as if it were an independent entity? If not, should it be integrated with the organisation's whole IT policy or protected (e.g. perhaps the bureau should be used by the other units of the organisation for their typesetting unless an outside competitor is at least 10% cheaper)? Should there be any organisation-wide IT policy (other than platitudes of course); in other words, should people sometimes be overruled, against their own interests for the greater good of the whole group?

Probably the only reliable way to arrive at coherent decisions on such matters, is to examine the implications of a few possible 'environments', each based on certain simple principles, and then to decide which is the best buy, given all the circumstances. A plausible environment needs to provide reasonably coherent answers on all the main issues. For example, with an environment whose essential principle *is extreme decentralisation,* the answers on most of the issues are fairly obvious: no coordination or common policies; the costs of any shared activities to be recharged at commercial rates; and so on.

Murray Pine actually decides on a marginally more subtle environment. It gives a high priority to generating and controlling innovation on an organisation-wide basis. The innovation department has a very large budget that its manager is meant to use to subsidise innovative projects throughout the organisation. However, apart from that considerable point and all its ramifications, all the other arrangements are left as decentralised (that is, formally uncoordinated) as possible. All the answers on the more specific issues reflect that principle.

Forest Oak and Database Responsibilities

The case of Forest Oak Energy illustrates how more detailed aspects of the IT–business interaction can sometimes have strategic implications. Managers of the energy authority in Forest Oak have expansive plans for developing database systems. They have heard that in a well run database environment, an important distinction should be kept between the *data* administration (DA) and the *database* administration (DBA) functions; one is more technically oriented than the other. But, they ask themselves, what is the difference? Who does what exactly? How are areas of potential overlap resolved? Does it really matter very much?

For this kind of issue, too, there is a contrast between the literal approach and the 'environment' approach. The answer, under the literal approach, would be a list of responsibilities for each function.[2] For example, the DA might be responsible for ensuring that any given department at Forest Oak always knew any given item in the database by the same name; if two departments wished to refer to the same item by different names, that would be recorded in a kind of thesaurus. Then, the DA might be the only one person in all Forest Oak authorised to change the official description of a data element, as published throughout the organisation. The DA would be responsible for providing PC-based tools for project teams to use in data modelling, and also be a member of the working group on system development methodologies. And so on. The DBA's responsibilities might include: naming conventions within the database (e.g. names of tables and columns); database design standards (e.g. use of indexes, maintenance of referential integrity); guidelines to be followed by others for recovery logic in application programs; instructions to the operations department for backup and recovery of operational databases; database performance modelling. And so on.

But under the environment approach, the whole matter can be described quite differently. There are two distinct issues. *Issue 1* arises from the fact that as a database becomes more and more closely defined, there is a progress in its definition from the 'logical' (non-technical) to the 'physical' (technical). This raises the problem of handover points from person to person — potentially problematical because the handover is just the place in a relay where runners tend to drop batons. *Issue 2* arises from the fact that a database crosses system and organisation boundaries; one part may be used by two or more different departments and/or by two or more different systems. Plainly there is a potential dispute over who is responsible for what.

Forest Oak decides to handle this state of affairs by recognising *four main organisational elements*: one, the people who design business needs for individual systems and departments, without worrying about technology at all; two, the DA, who operates throughout Forest Oak with a mild technology bias; three, the DBA, who operates throughout Forest Oak and is exclusively interested in technology; and four, technologists who work in project teams to develop and maintain individual systems.

Within this setup, each element interfaces only with the one next to it. Thus, Issue 1 (logical-to-physical) is approached by having three and only three forms of handover between elements: one-to-two, two-to-three and three-to-four. Issue 2 (sharing) is tackled by defining quite clearly that elements one and four operate department- or system-specifically, while elements two and three operate organisation-wide. From these principles the more detailed definition of individual tasks and responsibilities can readily be worked out.

This may or may not be a good solution in Forest Oak's circumstances. It may or may not be compatible with the organisation's policy on prototyping, for example. Possibly it is incompatible with a general policy to make even complete technologists aware of the organisation's business objectives. However that may be, at least things are expressed in a format that permits rational discussion to arrive at some better arrangement, if there is one to be found.

Implications for Decision-making

The issues discussed in this briefing have been primarily concerned with the structure that allows non-IT, demand-producing people to interact with IT, supply-producing people in an environment with generating and self-regulating properties. This organisational environment is, as it were, the ecology in which the interaction of demand and supply factors produces ideas for new projects and approaches; some will survive and be carried through and others will not survive.

If an organisation has an effective approach to the problem of IT–business interaction, it will usually be possible to summarise its essential principles or underlying philosophy relatively briefly and show how its more detailed features follow on naturally. If this isn't possible, if the set of organisational procedures can't be derived from any underlying premises, they very likely form an incoherent whole, with many arbitrary and contradictory features.

In some cases, the essential features of the environment where IT–business interaction occurs may be very powerful in determining the decisions actually taken at a micro-level. They may sharply reduce the need for macro-level strategic decisions. For example, at Stringybark, with its stress on treating the data centre like a commercial bureau, there is relatively little scope for multi-lateral collaboration between departments and data centres to define frameworks and infrastructures to support families of systems; that kind of activity would conflict with the chosen entrepreneurial ethos.

From this it follows that the appropriate organisational arrangements depend on the subject matter they have to contend with, the needs and possibilities actually facing the organisation. Is intense collaboration between different units a necessity in the present situation at Murray Pine or Stringybark or Forest Oak? The answer will have far-reaching implications for the underlying organisational principles adopted.

PRACTICAL ADVICE

➤ Regard the relationship between the IT resources and the rest of the organisation as the environment, that will influence the shape and content of specific decisions. Therefore, treat the matter of getting that environment right as a question for strategic decision in itself.

➤ Visualise this environment as a whole entity, based on certain underlying principles and forces. Don't deal with dozens and dozens of organisational procedures on a piecemeal basis.

➤ Determine the appropriate underlying principles and forces for the organisational environment as a matter of strategy. From these broad principles, all the detailed procedures and steering committees and job descriptions can follow naturally.

➤ Consider two classic organising principles as candidates. One is close identification between individual segments of the whole organisation and specific portions of the IT resources that serve them. The other is the pseudo-commercial internal market in IT services.

➤ Whatever principles you adopt for the organisational environment, decide them for yourself. Don't simply let them develop in an incoherent, arbitrary, inconsistent way.

➤ Make sure your IT environment is consistent with all the other aspects of your IT strategy: experimental innovation, database infrastructure and data modelling procedures, to name only a few.

29.   Charging IT Costs

ISSUES

It seems a sound idea to have a procedure for recharging the costs of IT to the departments that use the systems. Very often this is done as a matter of principle, following from the view that an organisation's expenses ought to be analysed as far as possible, so that different departments are aware of the costs they incur. If pencils and central heating and window-cleaning are charged back, why not IT?

But when it comes to making strategic decisions about IT, the recharging procedure may have little or no impact on the decisions that are taken. This is not necessarily a criticism. If the whole of a very substantial capital investment can be considered as part of *one project* — a project to launch an innovative new product, say — then the interesting comparison is between the total cost of the project and the benefits expected to accrue to the organisation. Debates about the way the money may in due course be split up and recharged in various ways around the organisation need not have much, if any, effect on the investment decision.

The situation changes when the investment considered can't be considered as part of one coherent project; for example, if the suggestion is to acquire a high-resolution, colour laser printer that will be shared among four departments. Then the only way of taking a rational decision may be to work out how the cost ought to be apportioned between the different departments, and for each to see whether its portion of the costs can be justified.

In practice, a great many IT decisions are about resources that have to be shared between different departments or different systems, just as much of the management of a national economy is concerned with determining how the wealth and resources of the whole community should be shared out. In a national economy with stringent, dirigiste planning procedures, bureaucrats hand down decisions about the allocation of resources. In an open, market economy, by contrast, money plays the main role in allocating goods according to needs. A similar approach can be applied to an organisation's management of IT. A charging procedure offers the prospect of reducing the need for detailed organisation-wide planning procedures that may be based on unrealistic assumptions or require unknowable information. It provides a mechanism for matching supply and demand on a more piecemeal but perhaps more efficient basis.

Even in an extremely free market economy, a finance ministry can influence the transactions that occur between individuals, by its decisions on money supply, exchange rates, taxation and so on. Similarly, the decisions that occur within an organisation's internal market for IT can be affected by the details of the charging method; for example, the method can be specifically designed to encourage certain types of IT investments rather than others. Moreover most people accept that not all decisions about the allocation of resources in society should be left to blind market forces; perhaps some decisions about IT resources in an organisation require the equivalent of interventionism too. This briefing looks into the way such ideas about charging IT costs can work out.

ANALYSIS

The *costing* and the *charging* of IT services can be treated as two different things, requiring different calculations. However, to go into reasons why this may be necessary and how it might be done would be a distraction. This briefing will concentrate on *charging* as a means of apportioning the costs of shared resources and thereby influencing decisions about IT.

Charging can influence decisions in two main ways. First, if a new venture is under consideration, each person due to pay a share can compare the *expected charges* with the expected advantage or utility of the venture, and decide on that basis whether to be involved or not. Second, a person who is already incurring *actual charges* for some existing service, can decide whether to continue using the service or to switch to some other service whose charges are more favourable. The detailed analysis in this briefing takes it for granted that the charging methods discussed exert influence on decisions in both these ways.

Three Aspects of Charging

One of the shared IT resources at Candlebark Insurance is an 'information centre' (IC) of experts who advise and train users of PCs in departments throughout the organisation. The work done by these experts is charged to the departments by applying an hourly rate to the time actually spent.

This very simple example serves as a basis to distinguish certain aspects of any charging procedure. First, the charging method described rests on certain *charging principles*. In this case, the two main principles are: all charges should be based on actual services rendered to the customer, and this should be done in such a way that the total costs of the IC are recovered. Thus the rate per hour charged is set high enough to finance those information centre activities that can't be recharged as actual services; e.g. sending experts on courses or holding strategy discussions with Candlebark's board.

Second, *the constituents of the charging formula* are chosen and arranged in such a way as to implement the chosen charging principles. This is a different aspect. You could implement the same principles but use a different charging formula with different constituents; for example, part of the charge could be a fixed sum per visit.

The third aspect is *the collection of data* in order to fill in the values for the constituents in the charging formula that, in turn, implements the charging principles. Probably the information centre staff fill in regular timesheets, but the data could be collected in other ways: for example, each expert could sign a logbook or key a password into a computer system, when entering or leaving a customer department.

In this example, collecting charging data should not be a great problem. On the other hand, charging for use of a mainframe computer in a large-scale, multi-processing environment might require hardware and software monitors and considerable technical expertise in order to collect all the data about resource usage required by the charging formula. But however onerous it may be, collecting the data needed is essentially a practical problem. The interesting issues that affect strategic decisions are associated mainly with the charging principles, rather than with the constituents of the charging formula or with the data collection.

Classic Charging Principles

There are three classic principles of IT charging. The *Straight Recovery* principle is to recover actual costs through the charges, while apportioning them as fairly as possible between the various users of any shared resource. The *Economic Cost* principle is to recover actual costs through the charges, but to ignore the criterion of fairness, by setting prices that guide behaviour in ways regarded as economically sensible. *Market Discipline* entails setting charges for IT services to customers as a commercial business would; whether income is greater or less than actual costs depends on how the market develops.

The difference between Straight Recovery and Market Discipline is fairly clear. Applying Straight Recovery, the manager of the IC uses arithmetic to work out the charge per hour he needs to set; he totals up his expenses for the year and the number of hours of support and divides one by the other. With Market Discipline, he sets the rate per hour as an entrepreneur would; he takes account of the rates charged by outside competitors; he also recognises that if the rate is too high people will try and get by without any support at all; then he sets the highest rate he thinks the market will bear.

Economic Cost shares with Straight Recovery the objective of recovering total costs but has an extra subtlety. Suppose Candlebark's IC manager has invested in developing his staff's expertise in statistical software packages and associated mathematical co-processor hardware, primarily in order to support the insistent requirements of the actuaries in the Life Assurance department. He can recover his investment by charging the department, but having made the investment, the marginal costs of providing similar services to any other departments are relatively low. If the Economic Cost principle is in operation, the IC manager can offer these services at bargain rates to stimulate the interest of other departments.

This seems unfair to the Life department, but may be beneficial to the company as whole. The Life department is apparently able to justify expert time spent on this subject at, say, $130 per hour, but for the Claims department, the opportunities for using statistical software packages are less exciting and $80 per hour is the ceiling above which the idea isn't viable. With a Straight Recovery approach to charging, the price would never be as low as that and the Claims department could never afford to explore the possibility — but with Economic Cost principles in operation it can. In a way, Life is unfairly treated; on the other hand, the department is still no worse off and the company as a whole may be better off.

Economic Cost really comes into its own when an organisation makes substantial investment in extra hardware capacity. For example, suppose the volume of work forces investment in a larger mainframe, but the next step up the upgrade path is a much more powerful configuration that is then only 70% utilised. It could then make sense to 'dump' spare capacity to anyone who can use it at bargain prices.

Similar logic could apply if the organisation made a big investment in a system that stored images of documents in bit-mapped form on optical disk, with the ability to reassemble the image of any document and display it on a screen or print it out. If the Claims department could afford to meet the entire cost of a configuration of this expensive technology in any event, then it could be sensible to let other departments use any spare capacity at a special low rate.

Variations of the Classic Principles

Very few organisations actually operate systems based on a pure form of one of these principles. For example, one sub-approach is to be basically

Straight Recovery but allow some use of Economic Cost, subject to special authorisation. Another sub-approach is to operate Straight Recovery or Economic Cost, but raise the cost by a so-called profit margin of perhaps 10%. Another sub-approach is to be basically Market Discipline, but to erect formal and informal barriers against outside competition.

Some organisations remove major items of capital expenditure from the charging process altogether and then apply one of the three principles to the remaining costs. Thus, for example, the charge for using part of the mainframe capacity might reflect the running costs but not the depreciation of the hardware, which would not be charged back. Another approach is to give each department a predetermined free allowance for use of certain resources and to levy charges for usage above those levels.

What about Candlebark's principle that all charges should be based on actual services visible to the customer? This example shows the point that, although a charging procedure generally has to rest on one of the three main principles already mentioned, other important principles, albeit of a less fundamental character, are often involved, too.

The basic principle at Candlebark is straight cost recovery — but done in such a way as to be based on actual services visible to the customer. At Ironbark, straight cost recovery is also used and the customer also pays for services received, but defined differently. For example: upgrading one release of WordPerfect to the latest release is one service with a standard price, whether it takes five minutes or five hours. At Stringybark straight cost recovery is also used, but in conjunction with a quite different principle. There IC support is like a compulsory insurance policy: you pay a fixed amount per PC whether you need it or not.

Examples of these secondary principles are easily found with other IT resources. For example, the contrast between charging for support of expert staff by the hour and charging by the service is analogous to that between charging for a mainframe system according to usage of resources, such as I/O operations or disk accesses, and charging by business measures such as the number of transactions processed. Although an insurance-cum-maintenance contract isn't quite a relevant model for charging for usage of mainframe systems, there is a choice between charging on the basis of a fixed price quotation made at the beginning of the year and working out the charges afterwards when all the figures are available.

Straight Recovery Becomes Economic Cost

One problem with the notion of recovering costs in the fairest possible manner is that it can be very hard to determine what is fair.

Apportioning the costs of, say, a printer may be straightforward: 17%

of the pages printed this month were for the Life department; therefore this department is charged 17% of the monthly printer rental. But suppose two systems have their own on-line terminals simultaneously accessing a large mainframe and both accessing the same large database. Apportioning charges for usage of mainframe hardware and database resources can be a formidable job because computer system architecture forces all transactions and enquiries to wait in queues to pass through bottlenecks in the system. For example, transaction A from one system spends one second occupying resources within the mainframe configuration, but transaction B from another system spends two seconds; should B be charged twice as much? Surely not, since transaction B would never take two seconds if transaction A weren't already there forcing B to wait in queues to enter some of the bottlenecks. In fact transaction A goes through quicker because a special switch is set in the operating system giving that kind of transaction priority. Maybe it should be charged more for the privilege? But then what would be a fair charge for the priority?

Before long you end up in some very complicated simulation modelling of the workings of computer architecture. Hardly anybody will be expert enough to judge whether the solution you produce is really fair or not, so is it really worth the effort? Moreover, as you approach the conclusion that the fair apportionment required by Straight Recovery is really a chimera, you may well find that the alternative, Economic Cost principle has some attractive, positive aspects of its own.

Economic Cost charging allows you to go a very long way from the model of simply recharging the costs of the printer in proportion to the pages printed. The intention is to set charges for all resources in such a way as to optimise usage for the benefit of the organisation. Therefore you could raise all print costs well above their true level — make them double for example. Gaining that money would allow you to charge for database usage at below its real cost. The purpose of this price manipulation might be to discourage excessive printing and encourage database queries instead, and thereby (you may feel) to encourage application systems designed in the style of the 'nineties rather than the 'seventies.

There are many other variations of Economic Cost charging: different charges for large and small users; quantity discounts; quantity penalties and so on. Some organisations have adopted a more formal version of Economic Cost charging. Each application system purchases 'resource packages'. Each package consists of, say, 1% of the data centre's CPU power, 1% of the disk storage, 1% of the memory. The charge per package is 1% of the total data centre costs. The effect of this scheme is to encourage an efficient spread of resources; for example, a system that needed 1% of the CPU power, 2% of the disk storage and 7% of the memory would be charged for seven packages.

Practical Effects

How can a charging procedure really affect an organisation's important decisions — as opposed to merely adding to its internal book-keeping?

How do the three main principles compare? First of all, *a Straight Recovery* system tends to collapse into an *Economic Cost* system, if applied carefully in any circumstances that are at all complex. It turns out so awkward to devise a truly fair approach to dividing up the costs of a big data centre, with its database and teleprocessing arrangements, that value judgements inevitably creep into the charging mechanism. On the other hand, a really extreme *Economic Cost* system, with weekly special offers, tempting quantity discounts, auctions of convertible warrants and a market in three-month imaging workstation futures may or may not be a good thing; but if you are inclined to go that far, you may as well go the whole way and have a fully entrepreneurial *Market Discipline* system. The real choice then is between a moderate *Economic Cost* and a fairly realistic *Market Discipline* system.

Which of the two is more likely to stimulate rational decisions for the good of the organisation? Before considering that, there is a side-issue to be cleared away. At first glance, there may seem to be something wrong with any organisation operating a charging procedure based on either principle, if the main IT resources (data centre, IC, etc.) do not *in fact* at least recover their costs in charges. But the important objective of a charging procedure isn't to balance books; good decisions are what really matter. Suppose an organisation operates a Market Discipline procedure, and the data centre makes a notional loss year after year, but the organisation as a whole makes shrewd, well-informed decisions about using IT to assist the business. That organisation is surely better off than one whose data centre is theoretically profitable, but which makes timid, sub-optimal decisions about using IT.

The typical situation where a good charging procedure can lead to good decisions occurs at project level. There are, say, four significantly different options for doing the project and a fifth of not doing it. If the boundaries of the project and the discrete cost and benefit elements of its activities can all be identified reasonably well, and if there are no awkward interdependencies with other projects, then what you need is the best available estimate of the true costs to the whole organisation of each of the options being considered. A moderate Economic Cost system is likely to be the most convenient way of generating that knowledge.

Suppose that the main activities of a project can be identified reasonably well, but unfortunately there are some awkward interdependencies with other projects. For example, the new Global Clients system is under consideration, and some of the resources it needs (e.g. specialist staff) may not be available if the Expert Agent system goes ahead. But that system may not go ahead because . . . In this situation, it could be an arduous task to cost out options on a truly realistic Economic Cost basis. Here things are much easier if Market Discipline is in operation. You go to the entrepreneurial data centre manager, whose personal income is related to the notional profit of his department, and ask him to provide firm quotes. He then bears the risk of juggling conflicting demands.

Since it is not really feasible for an organisation to operate Economic Cost and Market Discipline procedures simultaneously, the decision between them should probably depend on the profiles of the actual projects that are likely to come up. If most projects can be assessed in reasonable isolation, then Economic Cost; if decisions about most projects are tangled up with those on other projects, then Market Discipline. However, these are just glib generalisations on quite a deep subject.

The Infrastructure-driven Approach

There is an important special case. An organisation might decide to invest in an infrastructure of technologies such as telecommunications networks, distributed database arrangements, free text database expertise and so on. Then the policy might be to encourage departments to develop new systems within that infrastructure. The costs attached to individual projects would then be related to the marginal costs of using the infrastructure, ignoring the original investment. Low costs should make it easier to justify projects. This could be a fine strategy for giving the organisation a flying start into new technology. Or, of course, an opportunity for disaster if the infrastructure turns out to have been set up badly, or if the wrong technologies have been selected for promotion by infrastructure.

In this setup, the charging method can play no part at all in the original infrastructure investment; but it must play a vital role in appraising new projects. Probably it should be a specially designed system on the border between Economic Cost and Market Discipline. It needs to be very cleverly skewed away from simple cost recovery in the direction of encouraging people to do the right things, but not so entrepreneurial that a drive to maximise margin goes against the main objective of the strategy of encouraging imaginative use of new technology.

PRACTICAL ADVICE

➤ Make up your mind whether you want to charge back IT costs just because it is a sound general management principle — or whether charging is to be used as a powerful mechanism for influencing strategic decisions.

➤ If charging is meant to influence IT strategic decisions, reduce the amount of upfront planning of demand factors that goes on. If you can't do that, you may be simply adding extra layers of bureaucracy.

➤ Distinguish between three things: the principles on which a charging procedure is based; the constituents of the charging formula that implements the principles; and the collection of the data needed by the charging formula.

➤ Consider three main classic principles of charging: Straight Recovery, Economic Cost and Market Discipline. As a first step to defining the charging arrangements you set up, choose between these three.

➤ Devise the charging algorithm according to the strategic issues faced by the organisation. Don't be afraid to adopt a modified version of one of the classic principles, but be conscious that you are doing so, and have good reasons for it.

➤ If there are many relatively discrete alternative projects and project options to be compared, Economic Cost has theoretical advantages. If most possibilities are linked up with many others in complex ways, Market Discipline may well be better.

➤ If you are adopting a relatively supply-heavy policy with up-front investment in technology infrastructure, carefully tune the charging arrangements to fit in with that policy.

30.   Complications of Prototyping

Aeronautics engineers don't move straight from a blueprint on paper to the full-size metal aeroplane; they build cheaper prototypes in between. It is well known that one of the main problems in developing computer systems is the difficulty of making a reliable definition beforehand of what people require from the system. Even projects that are methodically carried out in a step-by-step fashion by competent people run into this problem. Surely then it should be good practice to develop prototypes of computer systems too.

The idea of prototyping is to avoid the normal step-by-step development procedure: instead, a simplified version of a system is set up, tried out and revised in an iterative way. This should ensure that people understand what they are agreeing to, before huge commitments are made in the detailed work of building the new system properly.

But there is a potential conflict. Prototyping generally involves darting backwards and forwards between levels of detail, trying out ideas, scrapping them, thinking of other possibilities and so on. If it goes well, the result should be systems that are more reliably defined and take better advantage of IT opportunities. The downside risk is that abandoning a methodical discipline can lead to an ill controlled project drifting through endless iterations, without taking a clear route to the most appropriate system.

When a prototyping exercise drifts off course or otherwise turns out badly, it often turns out that the broad term 'prototyping' has been used to embrace several different concepts that may at times be in opposition to each other. This briefing examines the way prototyping can affect the decision-making process and thereby uncovers some useful distinctions within prototyping itself.

ANALYSIS

In the classic, methodical approach to developing computer systems, each stage in the process builds on the work of the previous stage. Gradually the system is defined in more and more detail until the complete system comes into being. That structure is fine for many parts of many projects; projects in many fields other than IT are also done in that way. But sometimes a different approach can be much more appropriate. To see why, start by looking carefully at the assumptions built into the stage-by-stage approach.

The Stage-by-stage Approach

A construction project — a large new hotel, say — may well start with a sketch on one sheet of paper, but soon an architect will have drawn up detailed plans. Soon after that, ribbons will be stretched across the site, ditches will be dug, foundations laid, and gradually, stage by predefined stage, the building will rise, until it is complete. Often the only sensible way to build a new computer system is to follow an analogous procedure. Early on, the scope of the whole project is well defined, like the plans of an architect. The work of the succeeding stages (that is, most of the project) translates these plans into reality as efficiently as possible.

With this approach, there is no intention that far-reaching new problems should be *discovered* during the process of building a hotel or a computer system. If it does turn out later that the restaurant is far too small for the number of guests, or that the ground is too soft to support a building of the intended size — in other words, if the architect has to go back and make substantial changes to the plans, and the builders have to knock down or modify construction work already done — then everyone agrees that this is a black mark against the architect or the project managers.

If, two-thirds of the way through development of a computer system, it turns out that the proposed method of inventory reordering is impractical, or that the planned configuration where users access data through the crude but inexpensive terminals just can't support the workload, or that the intended method of sales analysis doesn't provide the information the marketing department really needs, then it is very likely that some work already done will have to be discarded or modified and the people responsible for the project deserve criticism. The stage-by-stage approach has been applied incompetently.

There is an important nuance here. Even in stage-by-stage hotel construction, there is always scope for adding in *more detail* to the design at later stages; the detail isn't all implicit in the original blueprints. For example, the style of the chandeliers in the restaurant probably won't be decided until a relatively late stage. The important point is that, when the time comes to decide on the chandeliers, it will be possible to make a reasonable choice, without encountering any far-reaching problems. But you shouldn't find that, in order to have adequate chandeliers in the dining room, the ceiling has to be strengthened and the whole building rewired. That would be more like patching up embarrassing mistakes than filling in detail.

Similarly, there needn't be anything wrong with deciding the exact format of a certain stock control report at a late stage of system building. But if it turns out that, in order to produce an adequate stock control report, the logical structure of the database has to be altered and a different type of printer installed, then somebody can be said to have blundered.

Defying the Stage-by-stage Approach

In some cases, you may judge that there are so many uncertain factors relevant to a particular system development, that, even after a lengthy process of holding meetings and exchanging documents, it is still doubtful whether the right decisions have been made as the basis for building the system. In other words, you may judge that, if you start building now, the chances are high that you will discover later that something embarrassingly equivalent to rewiring the building to accommodate the chandeliers is needed.

One rational solution is to prototype — to set up a computer system project, in the full expectation of discovering new complicating factors *en route* and of backtracking to alter work already done. In this approach, you deliberately make project plans to construct provisional versions of parts of the system, try them out and tear them down again — perhaps going backwards and forwards through certain stages many times, before each matter is resolved. These retrospective revisions are regarded as inherent in the project structure, not as unfortunate mishaps that deserve criticism. There is no close parallel to this in hotel construction projects.

But this line of approach seems to carry the quaint implication that a prototyping project can never be badly managed or out of control. In fact, there is still plenty of scope for bad management of a prototyping project. For one thing, to spend, say, three times longer on a project than forecast must be a bad thing — prototyping or not. Also, since the point of the prototyping arrangements is normally to ensure that the right system demands are defined, tests of success or failure do exist. Does the full system that finally emerges in fact cover the most appropriate demands, cause less disappointment and confusion among its users than usual? Does it cause fewer demands than usual for modifications in its first two years? And so on.

There is quite a big management challenge to be faced. If you don't start out with a clear idea of what you want to build, if the scope of the system is highly flexible, how can you ever have a well controlled project?

But if it is not well controlled, how can you expect to get value for the effort that goes into the prototyping?

Hill Banksia's Personnel Modelling

Hill Banksia is a very large firm of accountants. In recent years, the firm has expanded and it now offers a wide range of complementary professional services, such as management consultancy, recruitment services, relocation planning, market research and so on. Hill Banksia managers want to set up a personnel modelling system, to help ensure that they have the right mix of people and skills in the organisation. They find it so difficult to decide on the shape of this system, that they opt for an iterative, prototyping approach to its development.

The broad outlines of the personnel modelling system are fairly clear. It should store information about individual members of staff and about all the individual job-slots in the organisation. As well as showing which person is in which job at any time, it will show what qualities a person possesses and what qualities any given job demands. To take a simple example: some persons speak French and some don't, some jobs require a French speaker, some don't. For many jobs, the qualities defined may include logic such as: 'the holder of this job needs to have worked for at least two years in some other specified job; after three years in this job, anyone should be ready for a certain other specified job'. The model will be able to make projections; for example, to see the situation in five years time — making assumptions about retirement, deaths, leavers, business growth etc.

The advocates of the system point out five main benefits. 'First, every year dozens of graduates are taken on; the model can tell us how many graduates and of what type we need each year. Second, we have to be careful when recruiting experienced people aged over 40, because they can block the paths of those people who've been with the company all their career; the model can help us set quotas for the over-40s. Third, if and when the Board decides to adopt any form of positive discrimination policy towards any group in society, the model will help organise that policy. Fourth, we can measure the success of our overall personnel policy by generating statistics to show how many people are over- or under-qualified for the jobs they do. Fifth, if any radical organisational change is ever considered, the model can help us see the implications and form the personnel policy necessary to handle the change.'

Uncertainties about System Features

The description just given may sound fairly definite, but in fact, the people at Hill Banksia are unsure on a number of points that could make a very big difference to the scope of the system. Here are some examples of uncertain points.

Which staff should the model cover? Should it be a generalised model to cover everyone who does any kind of work within Hill Banksia or should it only cover people above a certain cutoff point in seniority; and if so, where should the cutoff be?

The model is an instrument for forming macro policy (e.g. 'we need to recruit fifty-three graduates this year'), but perhaps it should also be used in micro decision-making (e.g. 'a vacancy has arisen and here is a list of the three best qualified candidates for promotion').

Probably the hardest question of all is how to get the computer system to describe the qualities of people and jobs. Being able to speak French or not is a relatively easy thing to code in a computer system — in fact, untypically easy. How do you code for sales ability? For expertise in inflation accounting? For resilience in tense, crisis situations? Should you code for alternatives: for example, 'strong sales ability and moderate French is acceptable; so is moderate sales ability and strong French; but moderate sales ability combined with moderate French is not'?

Should the model concentrate on projecting scenarios (e.g. 'given these assumptions, here is the scenario that will result in five years time') or should it also tackle the demanding task of working back from scenarios (e.g. 'given this desired scenario for five years ahead, work out a quarter by quarter recruitment plan to enable us to achieve it')?

Much of the model's logic will have to work by chance (e.g. in projecting five years ahead, it selects at random a certain number of people deemed to leave or die and chooses at random between equally qualified candidates deemed to occupy vacant slots). Can this randomness lead to unreliable results? Should the model be run a number of times and the results averaged to iron out randomness?

To what extent will the personnel department need to tinker with the model once it is set up? No doubt there are certain parameters they will set (e.g. 'assume staff turnover is 2% higher in year 3 than in year 2'), but is it necessary and/or desirable for them to try out modifications of the essential logic of the model: for example, alter the logic of the way the model decides which is the most appropriate candidate to move into a new job-slot that becomes vacant?

Hill Banksia personnel managers conclude that it would be irresponsible to make a firm project plan now to build a system when there are so many uncertainties. It sounds attractive to have a very sophisticated, very powerful model, but extra features probably come at the price of making the model more complicated for people to use. The real trouble with trying to arrive at a 'best buy' choice of features is that everyone concerned finds it so difficult to gauge how complicated the possibilities on many of these issues actually are, and how beneficial they would be if implemented. You can't choose a best buy if you have no clear view of what is on offer.

The answer to the dilemma is to build a simplified prototype system that will help everyone to get a better view of the possibilities on these key demand issues.

Prototype Simplification

The whole logic of the prototyping approach rests on the assumption that you can develop and modify a simple prototype system far quicker and more cheaply than a real, operational system. This means there must be a whole set of substantial features that can reasonably be left out of the prototype, even though they are required in the real system. Unless that is so, you can't plausibly claim to be prototyping at all. Building a more or less full-scale system and then modifying it drastically from the very start shouldn't count as prototyping.

In Hill Banksia's case many simplifications are indeed possible. The prototype system can't be used by more than one person at a time. There are no security features, such as passwords, that would obviously be necessary in any real system of this sort. The prototype system is set up to work with not more than 200 staff and 50 jobs. If it had to process the likely full-scale volumes it might take all weekend.

The prototype has no facilities for inputting new data or for modifying data, and neither does it check for any errors in its data. A test file of imaginary data is set up at the beginning. The real purpose of the prototype exercise is to see what the computer model might *do with* the raw information in its database; how the information gets there is not a big issue.

The prototype system generates a fair number of printed reports and screens in response to queries. Very little effort is spent in tidying these up to improve the format; the content is what counts. There are, however, a few very important screens where considerable effort is taken, because they encapsulate some of the most crucial features of the model.

Every time the model has to be rerun with different parameters, a programmer goes away to study the program listing and decide how to make the change; this may take anywhere between five minutes and five hours. Plainly, a neater, more professional approach than this will be needed in any real system.

Supply Factors

The prototype work at Hill Banksia is done entirely on one PC. The Clipper database software is used to store and access the data. The programs are written partly in the Clipper language and partly in Basic. This combination of technology supply factors may not necessarily be used in the real system. The best technology for prototyping may not be the best for the actual system.

The people who set the prototyping strategy for this Hill Banksia system have to juggle with several factors. One objective is to sacrifice as many of the finer points of the likely final system as possible, while still providing something that is realistic and easy to work with. But that objective is associated with another: the technology supporting the prototype must make it as easy as possible to develop and modify the system. There can be a conflict here. The only way to get an adequately realistic prototype system might be to use technology that isn't ideal for quick modification. Or the judgement might be that the most important thing of all is to use technology which makes it very easy to change the system — even though this means the system won't do justice to certain key features.

There is another supply–demand complication. *One typical outcome* of a piece of prototype work is this: 'Now that we've clarified our view of what a personnel modelling system should be like, we can commit to a normal project for building the system. The technology involved will be quite different from the prototype: programs in Cobol accessing an IDMS/R database running on a departmental minicomputer.' The *other typical outcome* is this: 'Now we've clarified our view of what a personnel modelling system should be like. It will be an expanded version of the prototype system that we ended up with. There is no reason that the real system can't also run on a PC using Clipper, as the prototype does. Therefore we shall build the real system by grafting onto the prototype software all the additional software necessary to cover those things that we deliberately excluded from the prototype.'

Thus, in terms of the supply-side there is a distinction between the prototype system which is thrown away after it has served its purpose and the prototype system which is expanded to become the real system. When setting up a prototype project there is a three-way decision to be made: take the throwaway approach, take the expansion approach or, third (if there is some good reason), postpone the choice between throwaway and expansion. Which of the three is appropriate will depend on the circumstances of the case. The important thing is to confront and resolve this three-way choice, and to ensure that everybody involved is aware what the policy is.

Supply–Demand Problems

As formulated, the possibilities discussed so far disguise another potential problem. A prototype system programmed in Clipper on a PC can probably be reprogrammed fairly readily for a real operational system, using IDMS/R on a mini. The technology environments are different, but not so radically different that they are suitable for completely different types of application. But suppose it turns out that Hill Banksia's personnel modelling system isn't best suited by normal database technology at all — whether it be Clipper on PC or IDMS/R on a mini or any other similar products.

It may become apparent from the prototyping work that the system's most important demands are best met by some form of artificial intelligence technology such as expert system. Or perhaps they really need the special form of database that is good at storing texts. Perhaps the Hill Banksia personnel managers discover that structuring information about qualities in the form of predefined codes doesn't work at all well. Instead the idea of storing passages of text about people and jobs seems more promising; the texts can then be searched on individual words like 'French', 'sales', etc. If that were to happen, the logical thing would be to scrap the prototype project and start a new prototype with the technology that seemed more appropriate. Persisting in a prototype with the wrong kind of technology is likely to force the demands of the system into supply channels that aren't really suitable.

Another potential problem arises. The list of things excluded from a prototype very often includes such things as support for multiple users, elaborate security features, ability to recover smoothly from unexpected technical failures and ability to handle correctly unpredictable combinations of events. Very often to build in such features would make the system so elaborate that its value as an easily altered prototype disappeared. But for certain systems, just these features could be among the most important issues — systems to control planes landing at airports or to adjust proportions of chemicals in pipelines, for example. In such cases, prototyping probably can't help in making decisions.

Prototypes and Infeasible Demands

Even in cases where there is from the beginning little doubt that the real system will use normal main-stream database technology, there can also be a real problem. For example, the HyperCard software product is sometimes used for prototyping on a Mac, because it is a nimble, elegant development tool. A manager might say: 'I'd like a system that works exactly like this prototype we built with HyperCard, except — it must run on my department's IBM System/38 instead of the Mac, hold a database of a hundred megabytes instead of one megabyte and be accessible by twelve people at a time, instead of just one.' Unfortunately there is currently (mid-1991) no obvious, grown-up equivalent of HyperCard available on System/38 and most other minis and mainframes, so this demand could be very hard to meet.

This is a special case of a more general point. Prototyping can help system definition by filtering out aspirations that are excessively ambitious or so vague that they just can't be defined sensibly at all. But prototyping can be harmful with certain aspirations which can certainly be defined and tried out, yet are extremely expensive in technical effort or hardware resources to implement properly. What looks simple on a prototype system may be excessively costly on a real system. The prototype can give misleading signals about this aspect of the interaction between demand and technical supply.

It can be dangerous to sever the link between supply and demand factors in this way. At Corkwood Bank the strategy is to develop a whole family of new systems, to process the main body of the organisation's transactions; this entails a major investment in system developments over several years. One purpose of the new scheme is to bring together summarised management information. The idea of using HyperCard on a Macintosh to prototype requirements for management information alone, leaving aside all the complications of the rest of the processing, is an engaging one. This may be a sound approach to *clarifying demand-side wants*, but a HyperCard prototype can say nothing about the ease or difficulty of supplying the management information demands in the context of systems that process the transactions. Corkwood's real operational systems may be using two-phase commit distributed database processing on networked minis, processing thousands of transactions a minute. In this context it could be a formidable task to supply the management information exactly as defined by the HyperCard prototype. Or maybe not. The point is that prototyping doesn't raise or answer this kind of question.

Distinctions Between Prototyping and Other Things

Terms like prototyping, pilot project, experimental development and experimental project are used rather loosely by IT people. This tends to blur some important distinctions. Here is an analysis of a variety of different cases, that are united by the rejection of a classic stage-by-stage approach to developing an operational system.

In the Hill Banksia case described above, the organisation's management decide at an early stage that they would *commit to having* an operational personnel modelling system. The activities described in this briefing are part of a particular method of approaching that chosen goal.

This is a different case from an organisation which rejects classic stage-by-stage development by setting up a limited experimental project — whose primary purpose is *to help decide whether* there should be any commitment to any operational system at all. For example, a brief experiment might be set up in order to determine whether a certain IT-based product or service is both feasible and viable. As the table shows, there is a distinction between the *A cases* — development of operational systems, but without following a strict stage-by-stage approach — and the *B cases* — experiments with no prior commitment to an operational system.

The A cases break down into the following four: use a simplified system in order to help define requirements, throw it away, build the real system (AA); use a simplified system to help define requirements, then expand and extend it in order to build the real system (AB); set up a normal (not simplified) system by stage-by-stage methods, but, as soon as it is ready, start modifying it and expect to proceed in this way for some time before the system is in an acceptable state (AC); use technologies that permit fast development (which happen to be technologies commonly used for AA and AB cases), in order to bypass some stages in a methodical development process — not really to permit iterative definition, rather to get the operational system ready as quickly as possible (AD).

The B cases (experiments that may or may not be followed by operational systems) can be broken down into two categories. One is: develop and use an experimental system, throw it away, assess the results of the experiment, perhaps build the real operational system, perhaps not (BA). The other is: develop and use an experimental system, assess the results of the experiment, perhaps expand and extend the experimental system in order to build the real operational system, perhaps not (BB).

These six are all possible strategies that exist to be chosen before a project is started. Choosing one of these six at the start and sticking to it gives a better chance of a well controlled project. A project given the label 'prototype' which starts off in, say, an AA-ish vein and ends up as an AC probably hasn't been well-managed.

Though some people do apply the word 'prototyping' to all six cases, in this briefing the term is used only for the AA and AB cases. Cases AC and AD are rather dubious forms of development. Cases BA and BB raise special issues and are discussed in Briefing 31 as experimental projects.

Alternatives to Conventional Step-by-step System Development

A   *Ways of Developing Operational Systems*

        AA   use 'prototype' system to clarify requirements;
                  throw away;
                  build operational system

        AB   use 'prototype' system to clarify requirements;
                  expand into operational system

        AC   conventional step-by-step development;
                  but start modifying as soon as system live

        AD   use short-cut technology, but without
                  iterative clarification of requirements

B   *Ways of Running Experimental Projects*
    (no initial commitment to an operational system)

        BA   use experimental system to test uncertainties;
                  throw away;
                  maybe / maybe not go on to build operational system

        BB   use experimental system to test uncertainties;
                  maybe / maybe not expand into operational system

Demand-side and Supply-side Prototyping

The typical prototyping exercise is primarily intended to clarify *demands* for certain system features, treating the manner and economics of their *supply* as a secondary matter.

Within demand-side prototyping, at least two motives can be distinguished. There is prototyping work done in order to examine correctness of understanding; e.g. 'This part of the prototype system on the PC embodies my understanding of what we agreed yesterday on the essential logic of your over-40s policy; let's check it out'. This is distinct from work to establish the desirability or practicality of certain features; e.g. 'This screen design will help us decide whether it is really a good idea to put all the summary data about over- and under-qualified people on one crowded screen and if not, which fields can be left out'.

Hill Banksia's personnel model prototype is used for both types of demand-side definition. But a prototyping activity may also be intended for supply-side purposes too. Suppose, for example, that Hill Banksia wanted to store various sensitive documents as images on compact disc as part of the system. The prototype might be used to test out the viability of this particular supply factor; it might test whether the system could provide adequate response times in extracting a document from a compact disc and displaying it with adequate resolution on a screen.

Since prototyping tends to use technology that enables limited systems to be built quickly, people sometimes talk as if the purpose of prototyping were to save time. This is only true in a certain sense. Typically demand-side prototyping is worth doing because it results in a *better* definition of the demand factors of a system than a definition in the form of a requirements document that everyone has signed off. The definition is better because it is less likely to gloss over the niggling points that cause trouble later on, and less likely to be undermined by subsequent changes of mind. It may well be quicker to define requirements on paper than by prototyping, but since requirements defined unreliably only store up problems for the future, the demand-side prototyping approach may save effort *in the long run.*

There can be a variety of motives for *supply-side prototyping.* For example, the prototype version of a database system can help make many of the design decisions more reliable. It can help validate the correctness of the data structures; it can allow the collection of more accurate information to quantify the variables of a system — not necessarily in absolute terms, but very often in the comparative volumes of certain transactions and queries. Partly as a consequence of these things, it provides the opportunity to try out different technical designs to see which is most efficient.

Psychological Factors

There are also arguments for prototyping that go beyond its effectiveness at helping to firm up system demands. Many IT managers suggest that it is *inherently* good that the non-technical people out in the organisation, for whose use systems are finally built, should feel closely involved with the process of system development. Prototyping encourages this in a way that formally structured, paper-based approaches don't. Thus, the argument runs, even if it could be shown that prototyping didn't make system development any more efficient, even if it made development somewhat less efficient, it might still be justified by the atmosphere of togetherness it fosters.

But the psychological arguments are not all one way. There is the danger of the prototype that is never concluded, because of the perpetual drifting from one iteration to another. This can lead to extreme problems if different people develop the prototype in separate directions, and if confusion arises over which version has been updated to take account of which suggestions for improvement. A naturally associated problem is that, if changing the details of the prototype is so easy, some people feel little incentive to keep documentation of what they have done and why.

Then there is the problem of potential frustration. Suppose it takes three months to arrive at a prototype system, containing the essential required features but without those parts that are necessary, though less controversial. Then it is very discouraging for the people in the user department to hear that another year must go by before the full-scale, industrial-strength version of the system is ready, complete with proper data input validation and security of information accessed by multiple users and so on. Conversely problems can also arise if the computer people themselves are discouraged by this effort gap between prototype and full-scale versions. They may allow a patched up, simplified system to slip into existence as a supposedly reliable, production system.

PRACTICAL ADVICE

➤ If defining key demand factors on paper proves troublesome, consider a prototyping exercise.

➤ But recognise that prototyping shouldn't be an escape from taking decisions. Prototyping is expensive in time and money. Only resort to it when you judge it would be unsafe to go ahead without it, and then manage the definition of objectives and the use of resources very carefully.

➤ Be tough about excluding as much non-critical detail as possible from the prototype.

➤ Decide whether the prototype system is meant to be thrown away after it has served its purpose or to be expanded in due course to become the real system. Ensure that everybody involved is aware what the policy is.

➤ Distinguish classic prototyping projects from other kinds of projects that also deviate from the usual stage-by-stage approach: for example, experimental projects, or simply projects that take dubious shortcuts to develop operational systems.

➤ Regard prototyping mainly as a means to firm up the demand factors of a new operational system when the supply factors are not in doubt.

➤ Be clear what exactly your prototyping objectives are: for example, to confirm the correctness of understanding of demands or to stimulate and experiment with different demands or to try out different supply options or to collect information about supply factors.

➤ If there is an awkward interaction between supply and demand factors, watch out: it may be a very tricky task to organise a prototyping exercise effectively.

31. Features of Experimental Projects

The difference between prototyping and experimenting may seem a fine one, but it helps impose order on an area of sliding distinctions.

Most new systems that are developed to be operational for at least a few years. Most of the principles on which IT strategy and system development rest are associated with that reasonable assumption. Sometimes an operational system is developed through an iterative, prototyping process, but prototyping is a means to an end; the end remains an operational system, that needs to be stable and effective and, all being well, should run for years.

Sometimes the wisest judgement about a certain area of technology or business is that uncertainty is the most important factor. Perhaps an idea emerges of using IT in some new way to achieve some new business objective, but the commercial or technical viability is very uncertain. Although the uncertainties may be too great for commitment to a full-scale system, the idea may be too attractive to leave in a 'pending' tray. The way to make further progress may be to run a small-scale system under artificial conditions for a brief period to explore the uncertainties.

With the *classic prototype*, the reasoning might be: 'We definitely need a personnel modelling system and we shall develop one. We have difficulty visualising its shape in several important areas. We'll adopt an iterative, prototyping approach to its development'. But the logic of the *classic experiment* often runs: 'We have five adventurous ideas for IT-based changes to our business and they all have potential. Though the chance of any one being viable is probably well under 50%, there's an excellent chance of at least one being successful. We'll set up some experimental projects to help us pick the real winners.'

With an experimental project, the payoff is the relevant experience and knowledge gained, rather than cost-savings, increased profits or any of the benefits than underlie the logic of normal projects and strategies. This briefing examines how these differences can affect the whole strategy problem.

ANALYSIS

When it was launched in 1843, Brunel's *Great Britain* was the largest ship ever built and it combined the new features of the iron hull and screw propulsion. One night the ship went aground on a sandbank, because nobody had foreseen that the huge amount of iron in the ship would affect the captain's compass. The simple solution adopted in iron ships thereafter was to mount the compass at the top of a mast and view it through a periscope.

This example illustrates a couple of points. First, if you are not prepared to make mistakes and learn by experience, you will never make any progress. Second, to minimise the embarrassing equivalent of a huge iron ship on a sandbank, try to do most of the learning in relative privacy on small-scale projects.

Characteristics of Experimental Projects

Part of the purpose of an experimental project is to filter out unforeseen problems such as the iron hull affecting the ship's compass, but the truly unforeseen problems are, of course, so unpredictable that the experimental project can't be guaranteed to expose them. Nevertheless the main issues or potential problem areas where uncertainty exists can usually be identified; the project can be structured to investigate those matters as efficiently as possible. The definition of such a project should not be simply a description of the system to be implemented; it will also make explicit certain underlying assumptions that the project will test or certain awkward areas that the project will explore.

This kind of project doesn't only produce a working computer system; the report analysing the experience of the project and documenting what was learned is just as important. It will record surprises, confirmed expectations and solid statistical data, and perhaps give an assessment of the viability of building a full-scale system, based on an analysis of the outstanding risks.

The control structure needed for a normal 'system build' project can be essentially simple, even if the project contains thousands of activities. The project is divided and sub-divided into sensible, natural segments and there is a procedure for checking actual performance against plans and budgets. Thus, if there are no major variances between planned and actual progress, there is no need for major management decisions during the project.

With an innovative, experimental project, things are more complex. There may well be two structures: the normal structure containing all the activities for building the system and, superimposed, a review structure that is far more than just checking progress against plan. For example, this kind of review involves comparing the new information generated by the project against initial assumptions and making choices between alternative paths for varying the scope of the experiment. In other words, the organisation of the project will combine the logic of the construction plan for a building with the structure of a programme of laboratory experiments.

Sometimes experimental projects are confused with projects that use prototyping as a means of developing an operational system, but there are some important differences. The typical prototype is for internal use, in order to help people within an organisation firm up their definition of the real demands of the system they intend to build. The quality of the system's information and its processing don't matter too much; the data in the prototype system may be quite imaginary, the format of its printouts may be extremely ugly and so on. But with an experimental system intended, say, to allow a small number of volunteers to test out a possible new information service, quality may well be an important issue. It may be acceptable to operate with a small percentage of the total data and to leave out certain facilities entirely, but whatever is provided may well have to be of high quality. Otherwise, there may be no meaningful responses from the test market on questions such as 'How keen would you be to pay for this service, if it were offered commercially?'

The Balanced Portfolio of Experiments

Usually, if an organisation sees one opportunity for innovation that requires experiment, it sees a fair number. Different people in the organisation may champion different IT-based opportunities, each with different pros and cons.

If there are numerous opportunities it is unlikely to be sensible to carry out every conceivable experiment, so how do you decide which experiments to undertake and what shape to give them? The natural approach is to adopt the principle of the balanced portfolio of experiments. In other words, an important justification for any experimental project is that it tests out some important feature or concept not already covered by another project in the portfolio. A project that, deep down behind the superficial detail, is exploring possibilities already being tested by another project, doesn't have strong claims to enter the portfolio.

This justification of a project by showing how distinct it is from its fellows is quite a bit different from the normal approach of justifying a project by showing how it will contribute directly to the health of the organisation.

Red Box Data Services (RBDS) and its Portfolio

Red Box Data Services (RBDS) is a computer services bureau, forming a minor part of a multi-national conglomerate. The parent company has plans to make RBDS the spearhead of a new drive into the 'electronic publishing' market. RBDS will develop a range of information services based on the pattern of a customer using a terminal (typically a personal computer) to access information stored at the main RBDS installation. RBDS will offer a range of different databases of information, suiting different needs and tastes.

This is an ambitious venture. There are already some other well-established companies in the field and substantial capital is required to set up such services properly. But RBDS's parent has the capital available and RBDS has brought together a bunch of bright people; they hope to devise more original ways of accessing more imaginative collections of information than any competitors already in this market.

The people at RBDS identify their essential strategy problem — one characteristic of situations like this, where an organisation tries to make innovative use of IT to change its products and markets radically. It would be possible to make a list of hundreds of different, plausible on-line database services that RBDS might offer. For example, there are many alternative subject areas as candidates, from heraldry through to geology. Within any subject area, there are many different genres of information, from news snippets through to astronomical reference works. There are many types of target customer, ranging from the general public through knowledge-based professionals (e.g. lawyers) to scientific researchers. These are only some of the variables defining each possible service.

RBDS managers can map out the range of possibilities, covering choice of subject, type of information, type of customer and perhaps ten other main variables. But it is very hard to choose from such a menu and be convinced that the combination chosen has a better chance of being a winner than any other conceivable service based on a different combination of variables. There just isn't enough information available to be able to make that kind of judgement.

RBDS forms a policy based on a portfolio of experimental projects whose primary aim is to generate knowledge. Each project will offer an information service for a short time, to a limited audience, with limited volumes of information, cutting as many corners as possible. Once they have learnt from several of these experiments, RBDS managers hope to have enough information to make shrewd plans for large investments in cleverly devised, operational, built-to-last, money-making on-line information systems.

The first four projects in the RBDS portfolio provide information in four different subject areas. Red Mahogany deals with anthropology and matters on its boundary in disciplines such as linguistics, archaeology, palaeontology and sociology. Red Pine deals with all topics in the humanities (literature, philosophy, history, etc.), Red Rivergum with ecology and Red Sallee with Italian culture.

The projects divide neatly into two pairs. Red Mahogany and Red Pine both provide on-line 'current awareness' information; if you are interested in the field it covers, then one of these services can keep you up to date with new discoveries, results of new research and so on. Red Rivergum and Red Sallee are each concerned with providing a database you can refer to; there is no particular bias towards information acquired last month as opposed to last year or last decade.

Supply- and Demand-driven Experiments

Red Mahogany and Red Pine, the two 'current awareness' services, both concentrate on storing information *about* new journal articles recently published or soon to be published in their fields. They don't store the complete texts of articles; they store abstracts of articles, together with publication details. The idea of each service is to make it easy for anybody to know which articles in which journals to chase up, in order to keep up to date with the subject.

Besides subject area, there are some very important differences between Red Mahogany and Red Pine as experimental projects. There have to be; otherwise it wouldn't be sensible to include them both in the portfolio. The best way to see the difference is to listen to the arguments put forward by each project's 'champion' within the RBDS organisation.

The champion of *Red Mahogany* argues that his project is special because it offers a very special *physical interface*. Instead of laboriously keying in instructions to search the database, the user will be able to use a mouse or a touchscreen to initiate searches. Also, the *logical interface* will be exceptionally comprehensive. He means by this that, although many services allow you to search the database on individual words (for example, find all articles whose title contains the word 'phoneme'), Red Mahogany contains dictionary and thesaurus facilities, to help you choose the words to search on. There you can see, for example, that 'allophone' is a term related to 'phoneme', though not exactly a synonym, while 'phone' is a rather broader term than 'phoneme'. The other main distinctive feature of Red Mahogany is its 'document delivery' facility; the user can place an order for any of the articles contained in the database, and within a few days a photocopy will be faxed or delivered by post.

The champion of *Red Pine* doesn't deny Red Mahogany's claims, but he has a different justification for his project. He argues that Red Pine, unlike Red Mahogany, tackles certain organisational and technological issues of great importance. In the long run, any operational on-line information system will be far more cost-effective and flexible if it is integrated with other computer systems that typesetters use to produce the text in its normal printed form in books and magazines. Red Mahogany ignores this issue and just keys in text that has already been published. The great interest of Red Pine is that it aims for one-time keying of text. Manuscripts will be captured in computer form for the database and then passed on a tape to the computer systems of the typesetters and printers. Alternatively, the data can be received on tape from typesetters and passed into the Red Pine database without rekeying. There are many tricky technological and organisational problems associated with these aspirations. Not surprisingly then, Red Pine has less energy than Red Mahogany to devote to the more superficial features of the service.

What the two champions have actually said is that most of the justification for Red Mahogany is the experience it will generate of *demand* factors — the nature of possible services and markets — whereas Red Pine's main justification is the experience it will generate of *supply* factors — the organisational and technological practicalities of providing services to the market. This is a very big difference between the two projects.

Aeronautics engineers have a rule of thumb that you should never try out a new engine and a new airframe at the same time. An IT experiment is best designed to be innovative in *either* demand *or* supply, but not both. Otherwise, if you experiment on too many fronts at once, it may be hard to draw any useful conclusions from the results.

Two Very Different On-line Database Services

The other two projects, Red Rivergum and Red Sallee, are both designed to experiment mainly with demand factors. The big difference between them lies in the nature of the information stored in their databases. The *Red Rivergum* service is based on the idea of storing a great variety of information about its subject of ecology; for example, the complete texts of some very learned articles, other articles that explain things in the language of the layman, polemical articles, book reviews, news items, notices of coming conferences, statistical information for reference, bibliographic references to all kinds of articles and publications, and so on. For Red Rivergum's champions, this variety within one database is the project's main justification.

By contrast, *Red Sallee's* database is essentially the content of just one large reference book, a cultural guide to Italy. This is a rather upmarket work; it doesn't just tell you that Perugino's *Virgin and Saints* is in the Vatican Museum; it also discusses that work in the context of Perugino's whole *oeuvre* and compares Perugino to other Umbrian painters of the period. The Red Sallee enthusiasts divide up this whole Italian guidebook into many chunks of about a hundred words each; and these chunks are fitted together into a hierarchy. Thus the chunk describing the Virgin and Saints painting nestles within the chunk Perugino, which is within Vatican Museum, within Vatican City, within Rome, within Italy. The idea is that database users should navigate up and down this tightly organised hierarchy, as well as jumping across levels, e.g. to find any Perugino paintings that are in the Florence part of the structure.

These differences in the databases lead to differences in technology: Red Sallee uses relational database, while for Red Rivergum free text database software is appropriate. Thus they have quite different supply factors. However, RBDS already has some experience of these technologies, so gaining experience in them is not an important aim of either project. Of course, if this were the very first time that the company had come into contact with the technology of storing large quantities of text in a database, then Red Rivergum would be classified as a project experimenting in both supply- and demand-side factors. That might be a reason for criticising it as excessively experimental.

Four Project Structures

All four projects are intended to develop and for a brief period use *throwaway systems*. If one of the projects is so successful that the decision is taken to build a similar real-life, operational, industrial-strength system then the experimental version of the system will still be thrown away, just as if it were the balsa-wood model of an aircraft due to be built in a factory.

This is a vital feature of the logic of all four, but for Red Pine alone, there is a special qualification. Its software may never be used again, but if a solution is found to the challenging integration problem it addresses, then much of the analysis and design work will be extremely valuable. These intellectual products may be reused in building a real system, just as left over Roman bricks were sometimes reused in the building of medieval churches.

Red Mahogany has the simplest project structure. First the system is built. Then it is used for a fixed experimental period of two months. After that, work is done to evaluate the experience and draw conclusions.

Red Pine's structure is rather more complex. First the system is built. Second, it is used for an experimental period of up to three months. During that time, any problems that mar its ambitious integration aims are dealt with in 'fire-fighting' mode. Whatever happens, a guillotine will drop after three months. Then, work is done to evaluate the whole experience and draw conclusions.

A Portfolio of Experimental On-line Database Projects

	Red Mahogany	Red Pine	Red Rivergum	Red Sallee
Subject	anthropology, etc.	humanities	ecology	Italian culture
Service	current awareness	current awareness	reference	reference
Main Drive	demand	supply	demand	demand
Distinctive Features	special interface (physical and logical)	integration with print production	many types of information; loosely structured	one book; strongly structured
Project Structure	single experiment	experiment, including fire-fighting	experiment 1; open-ended review; then experiment 2	experiment 1; review of one issue; then experiment 2

Red Rivergum's structure gets more complex. First a system is built. Second, it is used for an experimental period. For this, there is a fixed budget which the project manager may spend as he thinks best; for example, he can have many users working intensively or fewer using the service over a longer period. Third comes a mid-project review. There is already a 'wish-list' of possible desirable features that are left out of the starting system; at the mid-project review, decisions are to be taken on which of these should now be added in (there isn't sufficient budget to include them all). Fourth, those chosen features are built in, to produce an enhanced version of the service. Fifth, analogously to the second stage, the enhanced system is tried out as usefully as possible within a fixed budget. Sixth, work is done to evaluate the whole experience and draw conclusions.

Red Sallee's structure also has its own special features. First a system is built. Second, analogously to Red Rivergum, it is used for an experimental period. Third, there is a mid-project review. With Red Rivergum, many items are on the agenda for the mid-project review, but here with Red Sallee things are different. Almost certainly the big issue for review will be the ease and utility found in navigating around the structures of information. Even before the project starts, three main possible decisions seem likely to be available at this review point: either stop, because the project has already served its purpose; or make some fine tuning of the facilities for navigating through the structures of information; or else decide that the use of relational DBMS was misguided and build the system all over again — using some other technology (hypertext or expert system, perhaps). In the latter two cases, the fourth, fifth and sixth stages are analogous to Red Rivergum's.

Thus all four of these experimental projects have different structures. One of the characteristics they all share, however, is that there is very little scope for spontaneous iteration. For example, during the experimental period of two months, people will doubtless be making suggestions for minor improvements to the Red Mahogany system; but they will not cause the system to be continually altered on a day to day basis.

There *can be* sensible experimental projects that do allow frequent *ad hoc* changes in response to feedback, but they are tricky to control — bearing in mind that experiments must yield clear results within a small budget. Remember that the objective is not to build a desirable system, nor even to define the detail of a desirable system; it is to collect sufficient experience to judge whether to make a commitment to the detailed work of defining and developing a system.

General Implications

For the majority of large organisations, the main IT strategy will be built around operational systems that must be built to last. There are relatively few cases like RBDS where a large part of the projects are experimental.

However, as technology develops, proliferates and offers new opportunities for imaginative innovation, very many organisations are likely to need to have *some* experimental projects that are subject to the principles described in this briefing. Then the degree of experimentation, its place within the logic of IT planning and decision-making as a whole and the way it should be organised to generate and spread knowledge most effectively all become strategic issues for the organisation.

PRACTICAL ADVICE

➤ Always keep in mind the possibility of setting up experimental projects — projects not necessarily intended to develop operational systems.

➤ Preserve a clear distinction too between the genuine experimental projects — generating knowledge, that may or may not lead to operational systems — and operational systems developed through prototyping or in a similar flexible, iterative style.

➤ Make certain that everybody recognises an experimental project for what it is — not as a low cost, low commitment way of developing an operational system. Explain that different principles apply to planning and carrying out such a project.

➤ Design an experimental project by deciding what the subject matter of the experiment actually is — demand factors such as market response or the right shape for a new service or supply factors such as the effectiveness of certain technology or the repercussions of certain organisational problems. The more clearly you define the subject matter of the experiment, the better.

➤ If the overall IT strategy calls for a variety of experimental projects, coordinate their design and the ground they cover, in order to achieve a balanced portfolio.

➤ Work hard to find the right control structure for each experimental project. This will usually be more complex and call for more management decisions than that of a normal development project.

References

Introduction
1   Shamelessly selective, edited extracts from the voluminous documentation about IBM's BSP methodology.

Reference Model
1   Shakespeare, *King Henry IV, Part 1*, III, i.
2   Frederick P. Brooks Jr, *The Mythical Man-Month* (Addison-Wesley, 1975).

2. The Trend to Demand-driven Planning
1   Richard Dawkins, *The Extended Phenotype* (Oxford University Press, 1982).

4. Problems with Demand-then-supply
1   Ted Nelson, *Computer Lib/Dream Machines* (Tempus Books of Microsoft Press, 1987), p. 54.

5. Classifying IT Role-players
1   William W. Cotterman, Kuldeep Kumar, 'User Cube: A Taxonomy of End Users', *Communications of the ACM*, November 1989, pp. 1313–20.

6. Coping with Technology Uncertainty
1   *Byte*, December 1990, pp. 418–19; quoting from Raymond Kurzweil, *The Age of Intelligent Machines* (MIT Press, 1990).
2   *PC Magazine*, Volume 9, Number 6, p. 64; Volume 10, Number 2, p. 67.
3   *PC Magazine*, Volume 6, Number 5, pp. 10–11; Volume 10, Number 5, backcover.
4   *The Economist*, December 22, 1990, p. 124.
5   Sam Fedida, Rex Malik, *The Viewdata Revolution* (Associated Business Press, 1979), p. 1.

7. Supply–Demand: Links and Snags
1   for example: *DBMS*, January 1991, p. 40.

12. Dealing with Unquantifiable Benefits
1   for some examples: Walter M. Carlson, Barbara C. McNurlin, 'Measuring the Value of Information Systems', *I/S Analyzer*, Special Report, 1990.

13. Setting a Planning Horizon
1   *MacUser*, October 1990, Buyer's Guide, p. 32.

17. Strategic Information Systems Planning
1   James Martin, *Strategic Data-Planning Methodologies* (Prentice Hall, 1982).
2   S. Holloway (ed.), *Proceedings of BCS Database Conference 1985* (BCS Publication, 1985).

18. Database: Flexibility and Constraints
1   Ramez Elmasri, Shamkant B. Navathe, *Fundamentals of Database Systems* (Benjamin/Cummings, 1989), pp. 641–50.

19. Business Modelling: Accuracy and Distortion

1   James Martin, *Strategic Data-Planning Methodologies* (Prentice Hall, 1982), chapter 2.

20. Levels of Information Modelling

1   The example diagram is based on conventions suggested in Ramez Elmasri, Shamkant B. Navathe, *Fundamentals of Database Systems* (Benjamin/Cummings, 1989), chapter 3; for another example of the many possible conventions, see briefing 23 below.

2   see Elmasri and Navathe, chapter 15 for detail.

3   William H. Inmon, 'Divide and Conquer', *Database Programming & Design*, October 1990, pp. 71–73.

21. Data Model, Process Model

1   David Benyon, *Information and Data Modelling* (Blackwell Scientific, 1990), pp. 53–63.

2   The example diagram is loosely based on conventions suggested by T. DeMarco.

3   Benyon, pp. 181–230.

22. Modelling and Strategy

1   W. Kent, *Data and Reality* (North-Holland, 1980).

23. Moving Between Models

1   Diagram conventions are a simplified version of those used in David Benyon, *Information and Data Modelling* (Blackwell Scientific, 1990), chapter 7.

2   see Ramez Elmasri, Shamkant B. Navathe, *Fundamentals of Database Systems* (Benjamin/Cummings, 1989), pp. 355–83 for detail.

3   Al Foster, 'A New Era for Data Modeling', *DBMS*, November 1990, pp. 42–52; December 1990, pp. 68–72.

4   Barbara von Halle, *Database Programming & Design*, October 1990, pp. 11–15; November 1990, pp. 13–16.

24. Plans and Priorities

1   Richard Dawkins, *The Blind Watchmaker* (Longman, 1986), pp. 294–8.

2   James Martin, *Strategic Data-Planning Methodologies* (Prentice Hall, 1982), chapter 6.

25. Levels, Ratchets and Feedback

1   Michael Jackson, *System Development* (Prentice Hall, 1983), p. 370.

27. Applying OR Techniques

1   *The Economist*, August 12, 1989, p. 58.

28. Organising the Role of IT

1   Michael Sullivan-Trainor, 'Changing the fixtures in the house that IS built', *Computerworld*, July 24, 1989, pp. 51–60.

2   for example: David P. Croft, Barbara von Halle, *Database Programming & Design*, July 1990, pp. 13–16; Deborah L. Brooks, Barbara von Halle, ibid., August 1990, pp. 13–15.

Case Index

General Index